Antisocial Behavior
in Children and Adolescents

Antisocial Behavior
in Children and Adolescents

A Developmental Analysis and
Model for Intervention

John B. Reid, Gerald R. Patterson, and
James Snyder

American Psychological Association
Washington, DC

Published by
American Psychological Association
750 First Street, NE
Washington, DC 20002
www.apa.org

To order
APA Order Department
P.O. Box 92984
Washington, DC 20090-2984
Tel: (800) 374-2721; Direct: (202) 336-5510
Fax: (202) 336-5502; TDD/TTY: (202) 336-6123
Online: www.apa.org/books/
Email: order@apa.org

In the U.K., Europe, Africa, and the Middle East, copies may be ordered from
American Psychological Association
3 Henrietta Street
Covent Garden, London
WC2E 8LU England

Typeset in New Century Schoolbook by City Desktop Productions.

Printer: Sheridan Books, Inc., Fredericksburg, VA
Cover Designer: Naylor Design, Washington, DC
Technical/Production Editor: City Desktop Publishing

The opinions and statements published are the responsibility of the authors, and such opinions and statements do not necessarily represent the policies of the American Psychological Association.

Library of Congress Cataloging-in-Publication Data

Antisocial behavior in children and adolescents : developmental analysis and the Oregon model for intervention / edited by John B. Reid, Gerald R. Patterson, and James J. Snyder.—1st ed.
      p.   cm.
   Includes bibliographical references and index.
   ISBN 1–55798–987–8
      1. Conduct disorders in children—Treatment. 2. Conduct disorders in adolescence—Treatment. 3. Antisocial personality disorders—Treatment. I. Reid, John B., 1940– II. Patterson, Gerald R. III. Synder, James J.

RJ506.C65 A55 2002
618.92'858—dc21   2002018257

British Library Cataloguing-in-Publication Data
A CIP record is available from the British Library.

Printed in the United States of America
First Edition

Contents

Contributors

Deborah Capaldi, Oregon Learning Center, Eugene.
Patricia Chamberlain, Oregon Learning Center, Eugene.
Betsy Davis, PhD, Oregon Research Institute.
David DeGarmo, Oregon Learning Center, Eugene.
Thomas J. Dishion, University of Oregon, Eugene.
J. Mark Eddy, Oregon Learning Center, Eugene.
Philip A. Fisher, Oregon Learning Center, Eugene.
Marion Forgatch, Oregon Learning Center, Eugene.
Hyman Hops, PhD, Oregon Research Institute
Kathryn Kavanagh, Oregon Learning Center, Eugene.
Leslie D. Leve, Oregon Learning Center, Eugene.
Kevin Moore, Oregon Learning Center, Eugene.
Gerald R. Patterson, Oregon Learning Center, Eugene.
Katherine C. Pears, Oregon Learning Center, Eugene.
John B. Reid, Oregon Learning Center, Eugene.
Lisa Sheeber, PhD, Oregon Research Institute.
James Snyder, PhD, Wichita State University
Mark Stoolmiller, Oregon Learning Center, Eugene.
Karen Yoerger, Oregon Learning Center, Eugene.

Preface

Beginning in the 1960s with clinical case studies, members of our group have worked programmatically to develop effective techniques to treat and prevent serious conduct problems in children and adolescents. Like other clinicians at that time, we experienced consistent failure using individual psychotherapy techniques. These treatment failures led us to begin a parallel program of basic research to better understand the development of antisocial behavior that we hoped would lead in turn to the development of effective clinical and preventive interventions.

Forty years later, we have learned a great deal about the life course development of serious behavior problems from early childhood through late adolescence and early adulthood. Importantly, we have learned that developmental trajectories leading to serious delinquency, drug use, and school failure often begin early in childhood and are continuously shaped through social interactions with family members, teachers, and peers. We have developed, refined, and extended a life-course model of conduct problems, and then used this model to inform the development and improvement of clinical and preventive interventions. This has been an intense process in which developmental findings led to and were subsequently influenced by intervention trials in an iterative process.

This volume is an attempt to document the integrated development of a developmental model of conduct problems and a set of linked evidence-based intervention strategies. At this point, we are gratified that our basic research has led to significant increases in the understanding of delinquency, and that several of our interventions have been found to have positive long-term effects on children and families within the context of a randomized trial. This volume also begins to describe our more recent and continuing efforts to extend our models to impact other clinical problems and to shape our intervention strategies to fit within larger service systems.

Because of the complexity of the topics addressed, our research program has been multidisciplinary, building on substantive and methodological literatures in many fields, including developmental, clinical, and community psychology; criminology and sociology; epidemiology; biostatistics; and genetics. The work has been published in over 100 scholarly journals and in over 200 edited volumes. Although the hub of the research activity has been at the Oregon Social Learning Center (OSLC) in Eugene, Oregon, we have collaborated with researchers and services providers across North America and Europe.

Our goal in writing this book was to organize in one place our research and thinking about the development of antisocial behavior, from toddlerhood through adolescence. The organizing framework has been labeled *Coercion Theory* (Patterson, 1982). It is presented along with supporting data in part two of the book (chapters 2 through 8). The central theme is that the development of antisocial behavior is a developmental series of social interactional processes, glued together by negative reinforcement contingencies, that progress from dysfunctional and acrimonious parent–toddler interactions to similar interactions with teachers, peers, and others in the child's environment. The early coercive family processes lead to oppositional and aversive child behavior on the one hand, and to ineffective parenting on the other. Taken together these early child and parenting problems lay the ground work for subsequent conflict and failure with peers and teachers during the elementary school years, and to the development of severe antisocial behavior during middle and high school, a lack of supervision by parents or custodians, and a strong affiliation with other antisocial individuals. In addition to increasing risk for delinquency, the theoretical formulations and supporting longitudinal studies attempt to explicate the role of this ongoing set of processes to other serious problems and disorders that are close relatives of delinquency during adolescence such as school failure and dropp ing out, substance use, health-risking sexual behaviors, and depression.

In part three of the book (chapters 9 through 14), the interventions that have been developed by the Oregon group are described, along with data supporting their usefulness. Our strategy has been to develop interventions that are carefully targeted at antecedent social interactional processes that have been shown in our longitudinal research to be implicated in the development of antisocial behaviors. Therefore, although the interventions are all organized around coercive processes involving the children and those with whom they interact, they differ significantly depending on the developmental level of the children and the nature of their social contexts. We focus on both preventive "universal" strategies and intensive "selected" and "indicated" interventions, as well as interventions designed for various family structures and situations.

Most of the developmental and intervention research has been conducted in Oregon by over 700 researchers and staff members who collaborated with us at the OSLC, the Oregon Research Institute, or the University of Oregon. Although most of the researchers have moved to other universities, institutes, and clinics, this work can probably be best described as an *Oregon Model*. We have attempted to describe our developmental models and interventions for the reader who has had at least undergraduate training in delinquency and child development. We have also attempted to provide sufficient empirical evidence to make this volume useful and interesting to researchers, clinicians, and other professionals working in this area.

Acknowledgments

Support for this project was provided by Grant No. RO1 MH 50259, Antisocial and Other Personality Disorders Program, Prevention, Early Intervention, and Epidemiology Branch, NIMH, U.S. PHS; Grant No. RO1 MH 59780, Child and Adolescent Treatment and Preventive Intervention Research Branch, NIMH, U.S. PHS; a grant from the Edna McConnell Clark Foundation, 250 Park Avenue, NY, NY; Grant No. RO1 MH 54257, Antisocial and Other Personality Disorders Program, Prevention, Early Intervention, and Epidemiology Branch, NIMH, U.S. PHS; Grant No. RO1 DA 12231, Prevention Research Branch, Division of Epidemiology and Prevention Research, NIDA, U.S. PHS; Grant No. RO1 HD 34511, Center for Research for Mothers and Children, NICHD, U.S. PHS; Grant No. RO1 MH 54248, Prevention and Behavioral Medicine Research, Division of Epidemiology and Services Research, NIMH, U.S. PHS; Grant No. R37 MH 37940, Antisocial and Other Personality Disorders Program, NIMH, U.S. PHS; Grant No. R21 DA 14617, National Institute on Drug Abuse, NIH, U.S. PHS; Grant No. RO1 MH 54703, Child and Adolescent Treatment and Preventive Intervention Research Branch, DSIR, NIMH, U.S. PHS; Grant No. RO1 MH 59127, Child and Adolescent Treatment and Preventive Intervention Research Branch, DSIR, NIMH, U.S. PHS; Grant No. RO1 MH 38318, Child and Adolescent Treatment and Preventive Intervention Research Branch, DSIR, NIMH, U.S. PHS; Grant No. RO1 MH 37911, Behavioral Sciences Research Branch, Division of Neuroscience and Behavioral Science, NIMH, U.S. PHS; Grant No. RO1 MH 58337, Sociocultural Processes and Health Disparities Program, Developmental Psychopathology and Prevention Research Branch, NIMH, U.S. PHS; Grant No. P30 MH 46690, Prevention and Behavioral Medicine Research Branch, Division of Epidemiology and Services Research, NIMH & ORMH, U.S. PHS; Grant No. RO1 MH 60195, Child and Adolescent Treatment and Preventive Intervention Research Branch, DSIR, NIMH, U.S. PHS; Grant No. RO1 MH 50714, Child and Adolescent Treatment and Preventive Intervention Research Branch, DSIR, NIMH, U.S. PHS; Grant No. AO109623, DHHS, U.S. PHS; Grant No. 6403-075-LO-B, NIH, U.S. PHS; and Grant No. RO1 DA 07031, National Institute on Drug Abuse, NIH, U.S. PHS.

The work reported here could not have been completed without the long-term and intensive collaboration of the staffs of the Eugene 4J, Springfield, and Bethel School Districts; the Oregon Youth Authority; the Oregon Department of Corrections; the Oregon Services to Children and Families; and the Lane County Department of Youth Services and Department of Mental Health. Over the last 40 years our research has received consistent support from the National Institute of Mental Health, the National Institute of Drug Abuse, and the National Institute of Child Health and Development; specific gratitude is acknowledged to Saleem Shaw, James Breiling, Doreen Spilton-Koretz, Della Hann, and Elizabeth Robertson. Finally, and most importantly, we thank the several thousand families who have participated in our intervention and developmental studies.

Part I

Introduction

1

A Brief History of the Oregon Model

Gerald R. Patterson, John B. Reid, and J. Mark Eddy

There is an old saying attributed to many writers: "If you want to understand something, try to change it." In a very real sense, that could be the core message contained in the present volume. Researchers began in the early 1960s by trying to change a variety of problem child behaviors including aggression. We and our colleagues at Tennessee found that we could train parents in such a way that problem behaviors were reduced. The initial success encouraged us to move to the more complex question concerning how it was that children developed problems in the first place. The twin focus on intervention and theory fit with very nicely with a society that was becoming increasing concerned with rising crime rates and juvenile violence. This, in turn, led to four decades of relatively continuous support from the National Institute of Mental Health and from private foundations. The present volume summarizes the outcomes of the four decades of research that ensued for both intervention and theory.

This first chapter is a brief account of the journey. It will become apparent from the overview that the studies did not move in the linear and inexorable fashion portrayed in some histories of science. In our own case, the many setbacks, twists and turns, and many cul de sacs define a journey unlikely to appear in any journal article. In the discussion that follows, the focus moves alternately from intervention to measurement to theory more or less in the sequence that we encountered these problems.

Beginnings

Intervention Problems and the Academy

In the early 1960s a small group of investigators (including Patterson, Willliam Bricker, and Jim Straughan) at the University of Oregon Psychology Department decided that existing treatments for aggressive children were not effective. Several of us shared the task of running a small outpatient child-guidance clinic, a core component in the newly created clinical training program. The psychodynamic play-therapy treatment techniques that Patterson had been trained to use at one of the nation's best child-guidance clinics (Wilder Clinic, St. Paul, Minnesota) were considered state of the art. As a young assistant professor, it was his task to train graduate students, such as John Reid, to apply these procedures to children referred for treatment.

During treatment, we routinely asked the parents (almost always mothers) how the treated child was doing. About two thirds of the time, we received reports that were mildly supportive of our efforts to treat. We learned later that mothers' reports showed little correlation with objective measures of treatment outcomes (Patterson & Narret, 1990; Patterson, Chamberlain, & Dishion, 1993). We seldom asked teachers or used objective measures to assess outcomes. However, the review of traditional therapies by Levitt (1957, 1971) showed that the traditional treatments were not effective for children with hyperactivity, oppositional behavior, and aggression. The fact that these problems constituted about two thirds of the children referred for treatment posed a major problem. As young professors, we felt challenged to design interventions that would be successful and to accompany them with more objective measures of treatment outcome.

We began by applying some operant procedures to very simple problem. However, the only cases made available to us consisted of hyperactive and autistic children. It turned out, of course, that neither of these types of problems have simple solutions. With autistic children, our applications of simple contingency procedures were dramatically unsuccessful. At that time, we had no idea of the density of reinforcing contingencies required to bring about the stunning changes that has been achieved with these cases by I. Lovaas and his colleagues (Lovaas, 1978, 1987).

In contrast, the work with hyperactive children in the classroom setting was immediately successful. Using simple reinforcement contingencies to strengthen behaviors that would compete with hyperactivity (e.g., sit still, attend), we produced very rapid and seemingly dramatic improvements in classroom behavior (Patterson, 1965). In the studies that followed in rapid succession, the effects were replicated; and the procedures developed further (e.g., Nixon, 1966; Patterson, Jones, Whittier, & Wright, 1965; Anderson, 1964). These findings led to the more practical approach of training the teacher to use positive and negative contingencies with children in the classroom setting (Hops et al., 1978). The Oregon studies were part of a network of researchers across the country that has resulted in carefully research technology for effective classroom management. Walker (1995) summarized the findings from this line of productive work. Our own group moved on to focus upon families and aggressive children.

Measurement: The Centrality of Observation Data

In the 1960s, young child clinical psychologists participated in a dubious charade. As graduate students, we were wedded to the idea of objective measures. In keeping with our belief, we recited daily canticles from the book of statistics. However, when it came to the real business of assessing and treating children in the clinical setting, we abruptly ceased to be scientists. We turned instead to projective tests and to untested treatments based on psychoanalytic ideas. At no time did the science or the facts of psychology influence our efforts to assess and treat aggressive children and their families. This created several problems. One Achilles heel was that the majority of mothers seemed to report improvement regardless of what treatment was provided (Patterson & Narret, 1990; Patterson, Dishion & Chamberlain, 1993). Using this criterion, everything worked, and nothing worked any better than anything else. We needed to find some more objective means for assessing treatment outcomes.

One of the strengths of the operant behavioral position lies in its insistence that claims for behavior change be based upon observation data. Thus, as we began to experiment with operant procedures, we also began to develop observation codes. We drew upon our early training as psychologists and addressed the usual psychometric issues concerning reliability, validity, event sampling, and convergence. We spent over 3 years completing the pilot methodological studies for the Family Interaction Code system (Reid, 1978). Our colleague Phil Schoggin introduced us to R. Barker's programmatic studies of children in natural settings (Barker, 1963; Barker & Wright, 1951). Their narrative accounts provided sequences of events occurring in real time, a notion that was quite appealing.

Observation presented us with a host of new concerns. One of our first was with the best means of training observers to be reliable (Reid, 1967; 1970). There was also a long and complex series of studies trying to define what the impact of observer presence had on classroom or family interactions (reviewed in Jones, 1973; Jones, Reid, & Patterson, 1975; Patterson, 1982). For example, in one series of studies we found that observers provided similar estimates of parent and child negativity to that obtained via tape recorders placed in the home and turned on at random intervals. Studies were also carried out to examine the possibility that families could fake good or fake bad during home observation sessions (Johnson & Lobitz, 1974). The findings showed that although both normal and distressed families could fake bad, distressed families had difficulty faking good. Studies reviewed in Patterson (1983) showed similar findings for observations of married couples and for teachers in classroom settings.

The accurate feedback that observation data provided enabled us to identify the intervention components that worked and those that did not work. Observation procedures were used to evaluate the operant procedures applied to hyperactive children in the classroom. The contingencies were designed to strengthen behaviors that would compete with the presenting problem behaviors. The initial results were encouraging. It was a beginning. We now understood a tiny bit about changing behavior, and more importantly we were beginning to understand how to measure behavior changes occurring in natural settings.

Our First Theory and Our First Cul de Sac

Our efforts to build a theory about problem children also began in the early 1960s. In this formulation, responsiveness or lack of responsiveness to social stimuli was thought of as a trait that could lead to a wide spectrum of problem behaviors (Franks, 1965; Patterson, 1960; Patterson & Anderson, 1964). There were a number of studies that suggested this was a promising approach. For example, Lykken (1957) had found that "psychopaths" were significantly less responsive in avoiding aversive contingencies (punishments) than were "non-psychopaths." In a similar vein, Levin and Simmons (1962) found that clinical samples of boys were relatively nonresponsive to positive reinforcers from adults.

To test some of these hypotheses, a series of laboratory studies were carried out using a Gewirtz (1967) type instrumental conditioning procedure. The results, summarized in Patterson (1965), showed that boys rated out of control by teachers were less responsive to parental disapproval and were more responsive to positive reinforcers delivered by peers. The peer findings were replicated in the study by

Patterson and Fagot (1967): Boys most responsive to peer reinforcement tended to be more out of control in the classroom.

As in the observational work in the laboratory studies, considerable time was spent on examining such methodological concerns as reliability, stability, and response preference biases (Patterson, 1965; Patterson & Fagot, 1967; Patterson & Hinsey, 1964; Patterson, Jones, Whittier, & Wright, 1965). To test for generalizability, we constructed alternative procedures for measuring responsiveness (Fagot, 1966). A mobile laboratory was built to facilitate collecting data when parents and peers served as reinforcing agents. Several contemporaries, such as Harold Stevenson and Robert Cairns, also succumbed to the allure of these procedures as a means for the scientific study of responsiveness to social reinforcers.

However, after a decade of work, the procedures and findings stood as empty as the Mayan ruins at Chitzen Itza. We decided to abandon the paradigm, as did our contemporaries. What produced the mass exodus was a set of findings showing that most of the variance in the change scores was attributable to method. Preference change measures were primarily accounted for by patterns of alternation identifiable at baseline (Patterson & Hinsey, 1964). The coup de grace came with Parton and Ross's (1965) report demonstrating that measures of changes in rate were produced by a variety of variables other than reinforcement per se. By the late 1960s, we had shifted our emphasis almost entirely away from laboratory studies of aggression reinforcement responsiveness to observation in natural settings.

Now, 30 years later, we are again interested in measures of responsiveness to social contingencies. In a recent proposal, we hypothesized that responsiveness might be a mechanism that varies as a function of genetic contributions. In retrospect, the question was a good one; it was just that our technology was not up to the task. For example, Snyder and Patterson (1986) described an alternative procedure for measuring responsiveness based on interactional sequences occurring in natural settings. We fully expect that in some future study the variable of responsiveness will arise phoenix-like from the ashes.

Finding a Focus: Parent Training Therapy

As we worked in the homes of families with aggressive children, we were surprised to find how little connection there was between mother-reported improvements and what we actually saw in the home and the classroom. The lack of correspondence between parent and observer data had been noted by others, but at the time we were unaware of these systematic studies (Fontana, 1966). Now we know that a poor correspondence between parent and observer reports of behavior change is ubiquitous (Atkeson & Forehand, 1978; Patterson et al., 1993).

Observation data also quickly identified a basic flaw in Skinner's early position on the ineffectiveness of punishment. Based on his position, we instructed parents of problem children to focus entirely on the of use positive reinforcement for competing prosocial child behaviors. In spite of parent reports of progress, observation data for the first few cases showed no significant reduction in child aversive behavior. It was only when we added punishment-type procedures, such as time out or point loss, for deviant behavior that the observation data showed clear changes. This phenomenon is now well understood. For example, Wells (1995) recently reviewed a set of six carefully controlled laboratory studies that demonstrate the same conclusion.

Ideas about the centrality of parental contingencies and the need for observation data to assess the efficacy of intervention with aggressive children were part of the Zeitgeist at Oregon and at other centers around the country. During this period there were frequent informal contacts with Connie Hanf at the Oregon Medical School and Bob Wahler at Tennessee. In retrospect, it is difficult to say where each specific idea came from that eventually became parent-training therapy. However, at each center the ubiquitous single-subject graphs were posted on the walls for all to see. The observation data showed that family changes actually occurred and that they persisted.

It looked like science, but it also felt like good clinical process. We were (and are) convinced that we were really helping people. The clinical and observation procedures were published in reports by Patterson, Cobb, and Ray (1972 & 1973); Patterson, Reid, Jones, & Conger (1975); and Reid (1978). By 1968, we had standardized the assessment procedures and, to some extent, the treatment procedures as well. Each family was observed during baseline, treatment, and follow-up. The findings for the cases treated from 1968 through 1977 were summarized in Patterson (1979b).

In the early 1970s we began a series of randomized studies based on group rather than single subject designs (Patterson, Chamberlain, & Reid, 1982; Walter & Gilmore, 1973; Wiltz & Patterson, 1974). Do the procedures produce reliable changes in a significant proportion of the cases treated? Do the procedures produce results that persist (Patterson & Fleischman, 1979)? The data showed the answer to both questions was an emphatic "Yes!" Finally, do the parent-training procedures work when applied to chronic offending adolescent delinquents? Reports by Bank, Marlowe, Reid, Patterson, and Weinrott (1991) and Reid, Eddy, Fetrow, and Stoolmiller (1999) showed a significant reduction in police arrests and long-term reductions in costs due to institutionalization for the experimental group.

The Winds of Change

However gratifying these early successes, they carried with them strong winds of change. It led us eventually to find a new setting for our work and to design our own work environment. It also led to modification of how outside groups perceived what we were doing. For example, emphasizing the key role of punishment in weakening aggressive or antisocial behavior, the use of group rather than single subject designs, and extensive use of statistical analyses offended some of our radical behaviorist colleagues. As a result, we were gently dropped from their list of so-called good scientists. We were often cited at national conferences sponsored by behaviorists to highlight parent-training research, but we were not asked to be among the presenters.

At the same time, the flurry of findings from our approach to treatment and theory caused a storm of protest from some members of the psychology department at the University of Oregon. The psychoanalytic component in the department was offended that we had ignored all of their variables. There were angry confrontations with Gestaltists and attacks on the behavioral position in brilliant lectures by the new revolutionaries from the cognitive sciences. The mission for the psychology department was to build the new cognitive science. Similar paradigm confrontations were going on across the country. In our own battles we lost half of our collaborating colleagues. For psychology, it marked the advent of a new paradigm, probably a long overdue vitalizing event.

For our developing social learning group, the long-range effect of the palace revolt was very positive. A small group of us retreated to the sanctuary of a nonprofit research corporation, the Oregon Research Institute (ORI). ORI had begun several years earlier on the crest of a new wave of federal funding for psychological research. The ORI administration gave us space and encouraged us to apply for research funds at National Institute of Mental Health (NIMH) and the National Science Foundation (NSF). The intellectual climate at the institute was both benign and intense. An exciting and multi-disciplinary group of investigators worked on problems of personality, measurement, cognition, and prediction (including G. Bechtel, L. Goldberg, P. Hoffman, L. Rorer). Summer meant marvelous congeries of visitors and consultants with world-class skills in a variety of areas (e.g., W. Edwards, W. Norman, D. Peabody, A. Tversky). As a group, we began to develop a working environment that we felt maximized our scientific productivity.

Performance Theory

In the early 1970s, based upon our analyses of observation data, we were being encouraged by others to develop a theoretical statement about children's aggression. For example, there were invitations to present at the Minnesota Fifth Symposium on Child Psychology (Patterson & Cobb, 1971) and at the University of Iowa conference on the control of aggression (Patterson & Cobb, 1973).

We decided that, eventually, a theory of aggression would have to account for individual differences in aggression. From this perspective, it would be necessary to demonstrate that variables thought to produce aggression must be shown to account for significant variance in whatever variables were used to assess the criterion. Based upon our understanding of Paul Meehl's position, the restricting assumption was that the same agent-method measures used for the model could not also be used to assess outcome (e.g., we would not use mother ratings to measure both family variables and child adjustment).

Our acceptance of the idea of a performance model led to an immediate reminder of our limitations. It had been known for some time that reinforcement variables could not account for individual differences in aggression or in any other response. As demonstrated in the laboratory studies by Herrnstein (1961) and many others, there simply was not a linear relation between response strength and reinforcement density. For each individual, the slope tended to become asymptotic at the upper levels of reinforcement. In keeping with this idea, our observation data from nursery schools showed no correlation between density of reinforcement and frequency of child aggressive behavior (Patterson, Littman, & Bricker, 1967). It is probably no coincidence that Skinnerians had long ago decreed that the study of individual differences was an exemplar of bad science.

We focused instead upon questions about reinforcement that could be answered with available technology. For example, why does one kind of coercive behavior, such as arguing, occur at much higher rates than does hitting? Additionally, why is that coercive behaviors occur at higher rates on some days or in some settings as compared to others? These questions led us to what we call the stimulus control studies.

The Stimulus Control Studies

Our first entree into the homes of clinical cases suggested that much of the conflict behavior was reflexive and not under direct cognitive processing. The conflict bouts between family members had all of the overlearned qualities one finds in observing someone drive their car. As we examined the sequential family interactions we could begin to see why this might be so. It became apparent that there was a surprising similarity across problem children in the networks of stimuli that controlled their coercive (e.g., noncompliance, temper tantrums, hitting) behavior (Patterson & Cobb, 1971; 1973). These overlearned patterns of action and reaction were run off repeatedly. We determined empirically what the controlling stimuli were by carrying out endless lag one analyses that described the immediate impact of one person's behavior on that of another (Patterson, 1977a; Patterson & Cobb, 1971; 1973).

When observing in the home, it was apparent that the moment-by-moment changes in rates of deviant behavior were determined directly by the controlling stimuli and only indirectly by changes in reinforcement. Is the sibling there and is the sibling teasing? Presumably, intraindividual fluctuations in rates of deviant behavior over time were determined by variations in the density of controlling stimuli (Hops, 1971; Patterson, 1977). Calculating fluctuations in density of controlling stimuli and the concomitant fluctuations in density of deviant behaviors was an onerous task. But the findings provided immediate support for the hypothesis. For example, Hops (1971) showed that across days the density of controlling stimuli correlated significantly with the density of social behavior. The correlation was .50 for one boy and .59 for another. Comparable data for a single problem child with over 50 observation sessions produced a multiple correlation of .61 (Patterson, 1973).

We also examined the question of why some coercive behaviors occurred at higher rates than others. The hypothesis was that behaviors with the highest relative rates of negative reinforcement would also have the highest rates of occurrence. For example, Patterson (1982) showed that the likelihood of negative reinforcement (summing across subjects and time) correlated .59 with likelihood of occurrence for seven coercive responses in one sample and .93 in another sample. The greater the relative payoffs (in negative reinforcement) were, the greater was the relative rate of occurrence.

The findings were greeted with indifference. It seemed clear that it is a tactical error to provide answers to questions that no one has bothered to raise. Nevertheless, as authors of this forgotten prophecy, we still find it intrinsically interesting to know that the more extreme forms of coercion occur less often than the less extreme forms and that frequency covaries with density of negative reinforcement.

The stimulus control studies assisted us in making sense of our parent-training efforts. For example, knowing that many of the coercive conflict bouts were on "automatic pilot" suggested that one an important function of parent-training therapy is to get the various steps in family conflict under direct cognitive control.

Negative Reinforcement

We knew by the early 1970s that coercion was the key mechanism by which family members train each other to be aversive and aggressive. We also knew that negative reinforcement defined this process. In coercive, dyadic process, one or both members use aversive reactions to exert short-term control over the other. The theory details the means by which these short-term effects produce long-term increases in pathology. We could see that being coercive was often functional in terminating conflicts among family members. What was frustrating was that knowing was not the same as being able to prove that what we saw was actually a causal variable. We reacted by designing a series of experiments to test the relevance of parental negative reinforcement in altering prosocial and deviant behaviors (Devine, 1971; Patterson, 1982; Woo, 1978). The experiments offered strong support for the idea. However, the question remained as to whether that was the way the process actually operated in homes. How much of individual difference variance could negative reinforcement account for remained unanswered for another decade.

Building Macro and Micro Models

The theory building and interventions might have rested here forever but for pressure exerted by S. Shah in the NIMH section of crime and delinquency. In the late 1970s, it was strongly suggested that our future depended upon our ability to both intervene and explain delinquent behavior. We were encouraged to address directly the problem of treating delinquent behavior. It can safely be said that sociologists were less than delighted by our sudden appearance in their territory. However, we applied for and eventually were funded to design a treatment study appropriate for chronic offending adolescents. At the same time, we were funded to design a passive longitudinal study that would begin with fourth grade boys and their families living in high-risk sections of our small metropolitan center.

We knew that we did not have the intellectual capital required to build a microsocial performance theory of delinquency. As noted earlier, we could not measure the negative reinforcement occurring in families (Patterson, 1982). Also, we could not measure the reinforcement for aggression supplied by peers (Patterson et al., 1967). In lieu of our inability to solve these critical problems, we decided to move to the next level of variable. This level consisted of parenting variables, which we assumed would control the reinforcing contingencies supplied for prosocial and for deviant behavior. We decided that the key to this effort would rest on our ability to adequately measure parenting variables and child aggressive outcomes. We also decided to invent more powerful measures of such parenting skills as discipline, monitoring, family problem solving, involvement, and support. Prior efforts to measure parenting skills using monoagent and monomethod approaches had not been successful. The findings simply did not replicate (Schuck, 1974).

The NIMH under the leadership of Shah was extremely supportive and eventually funded a 2-year pilot study so that we could solve the problem of how to measure the complex parenting skills, child adjustment, and contextual variables. For each of the 13 key concepts in the coercion model, we planned to use indicators based on reports from multiple agents and methods. This strategy would make it possible to test models of delinquency based on modern structural equation modeling. The measures from the planning study were revised and tailored for use in the longitudinal Oregon Youth Study. The first wave of data was collected at the fourth grade level and used to test the parenting models as summarized in *Antisocial Boys* (Patterson, Reid, & Dishion, 1992). Multimethod and multiagent measures of discipline and monitoring accounted for from 30% to 50% of the variance in latent constructs measuring antisocial behavior. The outcomes of applying this measurement strategy to three different longitudinal samples provided one of the data base for much of the present volume (e.g., chapters 3, 4, 5, 6, and 7).

Context

In the early 1980s and through the 1990s, we worked on the impact of context, such as divorce, social disadvantage, parental stress and depression, and antisocial behavior, on child adjustment. How did context impact family processes? Was the contribution of context to deviancy direct or indirect? We assumed that context influenced child outcomes only to the extent that parent and child interactions were altered (Patterson, 1983). The studies strongly emphasized the mediational role of parenting practices. For example, it was assumed that boys in divorced families evidenced problems only if good parenting practices were disrupted (Forgatch, Patterson, & Ray, 1996). The mediational role for parenting practices seemed to work for both intact and for transitional families (intact to single parent, etc.; Bank, Forgatch, Patterson, & Fetrow, 1993). Many of the well-known contextual variables seemed to load on a single factor as shown by Capaldi and Patterson (1994). The studies of context are reviewed in chapter 6.

A Developmental Model of Delinquency

We discovered that an understanding of delinquency required that we study two very different trajectories (Patterson, DeBaryske, & Ramsey et al., 1989; Patterson, Capaldi, & Bank, 1991). One path would be characterized by preschool antisocial behavior, followed by early arrest, and then chronic and violent juvenile offending with the eventual outcome as a career adult offender (Patterson, Forgatch, Yoerger, & Stoolmiller, 1998). The longitudinal data showed that 71% of all the chronic juvenile offenders had moved through all the prior points in the trajectory (childhood antisocial, early arrest, and chronic offending). This implied a single path to adult career offending. Furthermore, the data also showed that each of the points in the juvenile trajectory was maintained by the same mechanisms. The shared mechanisms were disrupted parenting, socioeconomic status and transition frequency. The extent of movement in the progression was determined by the level of involvement with deviant peers. This implies a single theory will explain all of the points on the juvenile trajectory.

The second path began in late adolescence and had a set of determinants significantly different from those that held for early-onset arrest (Patterson & Yoerger, 1997a). The eventual outcome was transient juvenile offending and no greater risk for adult offending than one would find for juvenile nonoffenders. The details of the early- and late-onset models are presented in chapter 7.

Individual Differences in Reinforcement by Family and Peers

It was the mid-1990s before we were able solve the problem of applying reinforcing contingency variables to the individual differences problem. After working at OSLC as a postdoctoral fellow, Jim Snyder was a regular consultant at OYS during the early

1980s. Our discussions often had a tendency to drift back to the unsolved problem of individual differences and reinforcement theory. As a result, we did develop a better procedure for using sequential observation data to determine whether a consequence functioned as a reinforcer in a natural setting (Snyder & Patterson, 1986). We eventually struggled through some of the ideas in the matching law (Davison & McCarthy, 1988). The laboratory procedures were obviously much too constrained to serve directly as a metaphor for our problem. Rather than just two response levers, we were studying up to 27 different behaviors in our code system. Unlike the laboratory procedures, there was no fixed supply of reinforcers in the natural environment (e.g., if response A is reinforced, that does not reduce the supply available for response B). Nor are family interactions governed by a fixed variable interval schedule.

What did apply from the matching law studies was the idea that reinforcement must be examined at the intra-individual level. This would require that observation data be collected, not just for the coercive event and the reinforcement provided, but also on the payoffs accruing to the whole range of social behaviors that occur in that setting.

We believe now that the central reinforcement provided by families occurs during family-conflict episodes (Patterson, 1982). "How well does coercion work during family conflict?" is the *wrong* question. Reframing it from the intra-individual perspective, the question becomes "How well does coercion work during family conflict compared to everything else the child does during family conflict bouts?" What is the *relative* rate of reinforcement for child coercion during family conflict bouts?

This formulation led to the pivotal publication by Snyder and Patterson (1995). We showed that knowing the relative payoff for child coercion in terminating the conflict was correlated with the relative rates of occurrence for coercive behaviors associated with these bouts. The rates of coersion also predicted the child's rates of deviancy observed a week later. If we then added how frequent conflicts or training trials occurred, we could account for over 60% of the variance in individual differences in deviancy.

Snyder and his colleagues went on to replicate this effect by using an OSLC treatment sample of boys and girls (Snyder, Schrepferman, & St. Peter, 1997). The analyses of relative payoffs for coercion during family conflicts plus density of conflict accounted for significant variance in predicting police arrest 2 years later. The Snyder studies are summarized in chapters 4 and 5 of this volume, including their application to peer reinforcement for deviant behavior. The work has also been extended in the recent analyses of negative reinforcement to long-term outcomes in the randomized trial for the divorce study (see chapter 11).

Snyder and his colleagues showed how the process of selecting friends is related to the individual's disposition to maximize immediate payoffs. Deviant children select deviant peers. Deviant peers reinforce each other for deviancy (see also Dishion, Andrews, & Crosby et al., 1995; Dishion, Spracklen, Andrews, & Patterson, 1996b). Peers who maximize the child's immediate payoffs get selected as friends. The message is that the child is not just a passive recipient of what the environment offers. Rather, the child actively selects an environment and in the process actually shapes much of it to maximize the payoffs (e.g., the child is the center of a very dynamic system that he or she, in part, creates). The selection of deviant peers insures the maintenance of deviant behaviors as well as the development of new forms of deviancy.

Our studies show that the extremely antisocial 10-year-old is likely to be one of the first to be out on the streets, unsupervised by adults (Stoolmiller, 1994). The analyses of videotaped interaction for antisocial and nonantisocial dyads by Dishion and his colleagues generate interaction data that again fit a matching law analyses (Dishion, Andrews, & Crosby, 1995). The findings show that antisocial boys are mutually reinforcing for rule-breaking talk, and that this talk predicts both later delinquency and later substance use. The deviant peer metamorphosis takes place in a microsocial matrix. These findings are reviewed in chapters 5 and 7.

H. Hops and his colleagues have carried on a fascinating application of coercion theory to the study of depression (Hops, 1992). It can be seen from these studies that one function served by depressive symptoms is to have a powerful impact in actually altering the context in which the depressed individual exists. One implication of the studies reviewed by Hops in chapter 8 is that the relative rates of reinforcement for depression may account for significant variance in depressive outcomes.

Interventions: Change in Center in Clinical Policy

To this point, our research in understanding, measuring, and intervening with conduct problems was centered in middle childhood—a developmental period with which we had a good deal of experience. Our primary focus was to understand the processes that occurred within troubled families and how to change them. During the 1970s, the therapy components had been steadily changing to accommodate the omissions that characterized these problem families. It was true that the parents tended to be noncontingent, but they were also not involved; and they were very inadequate at tracking or monitoring the whereabouts of their child. Each new problem became a crisis; their family problem-solving skills were practically nonexistent. We also added a school-achievement component to the intervention (e.g., school card, homework site, and time in home).

During this time, we also tried to push our interventions as far as we could and began working with older and with more severe cases. This strategy worked fairly well until we basically hit the wall in two studies that we began in the late 1970s. In one, we conducted a randomized trial with a sample of chronic and serious adolescent offenders (averaging over six offenses at intake) referred by the juvenile courts (Bank et al., 1991). We compared our parent-training model to an individually focused therapy intervention conducted by juvenile department probation officers. The second project was an attempt to train child welfare caseworkers to use the parent training approach with families who had been referred for abuse and neglect Fleischman (1982). It was at this point, as we were trying to export our interventions into the community, when our theory-based interventions started to falter. It took us awhile to understand that we needed to expand our underlying models developmentally into adolescence and into settings outside the family.

In the adaptation of the parent-training model for working with adolescent delinquents and their families, we used the same sets of direct parent-training techniques, as before but included a stronger emphasis on parental monitoring. The intervention and follow-up presented many obstacles and took nearly a decade to complete. We found that the parent-training condition (PT) produced better outcomes in terms of rates of subsequent arrests than the individual therapy provided in the control intervention (Bank, Marlowe, et al., 1991). We felt that, clinically speaking, we felt the effects on the parent-adolescent relationships were extremely weak. Most of the youngsters in the PT group continued delinquent activity, though at lower cumulative rate than the controls. We were convinced that, by itself, parent training was not sufficient as a treatment for chronic delinquents. it remained for Chamberlain (2000) to add one of the missing pieces. Moreover, the intervention was extremely demoralizing to the therapists, and we concluded that though it produced superior results in terms of subsequent arrest rates, parents were presented with problems that were much more complex than parents of younger children; they were more apathetic and demoralized and were resistant to intervention. These families were less cohesive, and the parents had significant mental health and substance use problems of their own.

About this same time, we began another initiative where we trained caseworkers in three protective service branch offices to use and test our parent-training procedures (Fleischman, 1982). Only a two-week training was provided. No means were provided for close supervision within the staff. The intervention format fit with neither the administrative structure nor the professional styles of the social workers at the agency. We had simply failed to find a niche for parent training within the existing structure. These experiences convinced us that we needed to better understand community contexts before we could integrate our programs into existing community services, and more fundamentally, that we needed to rethink our overall research paradigm of doing basic research to identify intervention targets, and then hatch carefully controlled efficacy trials in our institute environment.

During these first 15 years, we had made substantial headway and encountered grave difficulties. We had developed a theory-based intervention that looked promising for working with latency-aged aggressive children and their families. We had developed an innovative measurement system and had begun to develop a research staff that was focusing on increasingly complex methodological issues. We were attracting talented young researchers who wanted to collaborate with us and be mentored at our center. During the next 10 years, we refocused on basic research on theory and methodological development. During that period, we made substantial progress on several problems that turned out to be central to our overall aim of developing effective interventions across the young life course.

Developing Interventions Across the Developmental Continuum (1980–1990)

Theoretical and Methodological Progress

During this period, we devoted most of our efforts to expanding our knowledge and models of the variables and processes involved in the development of conduct problems, serious delinquency, and drug use during childhood to adolescence. After some pilot work and careful reviews of the existing developmental studies of conduct problems and antisocial behavior (Loeber, 1982; Loeber & Dishion, 1983), we initiated two longitudinal studies in 1983: Fagot began with toddlers of both genders; Patterson began the OYS with fourth grade boys. Although these two studies were begun independently (Patterson's at OSLC, and Fagot's at the University of Oregon), Fagot moved her research to OSLC in the mid-1980s, thereby adding early developmental expertise and a valuable data set that would bear fruit for us in the 1990s when the subjects in her data sets approached the ages of Patterson's sample when he began. Fortunately, these two research groups had collaborated on the development of multimethod assessment batteries, a number of direct observational coding systems for home, school, and lab settings. During this period, our developmental models expanded dramatically in terms of age spans covered and types of variables and contexts in which they were studied.

Our central focus remained the further understanding of the relationship of problem child behavior to the moment-to-moment social interactions in which the developing child was involved, but other factors received attention as well. The social interactional processes of children with persons other than parents, such as teachers (Fagot, 1981; 1984), siblings (Patterson, 1984c), and peers (Dishion, 1990; Patterson & Dishion, 1985) were studied and incorporated into developmental models of conduct problems and depression (Patterson, 1990). We also studied parent characteristics as they related to parent-child interaction and antisocial outcomes (e.g., Forgatch, 1987; Patterson, 1980; 1982; 1986a), as well as social and economic disadvantage (Larzelere & Patterson, 1990), family stress (Patterson, 1983), divorce and separation (Forgatch, Patterson, & Skinner, 1988). We studied processes other than microsocial exchanges within the family, such as problem solving and negative emotion (Forgatch, 1989); social perception, attribution, and negative parental biases (Holleran, Littman, Freund, & Schmaling, 1982; Reid, Kavanagh, & Baldwin, 1987); attachment classification (Fagot & Kavanagh, 1990); and parental supervision (Stoolmiller, 1990). We also conducted studies of the consistency of child aggression across social settings (Dishion, 1990; Harris & Reid, 1981; Loeber & Dishion, 1984).

In addition to working on research of developmental processes in multiple contexts, we conducted studies on the relationship of key family processes and the development of conduct problems to skill deficits (Dishion, Loeber, Stouthamer-Loeber, & Patterson, 1984), drug use, (Dishion, Patterson, & Reid, 1988), school problems, (Ramsey, Patterson, & Walker, 1990), and depression (Patterson & Capaldi, 1990).

The study of these processes and context during the 1980s led to the testing of a new generation of more comprehensive and complex developmental models that began to provide insights on how our interventions needed to be changed and refocused if we were to be able to develop interventions across development and settings (Baldwin & Skinner, 1989; Patterson, 1982; 1986; Patterson & Bank, 1986; Patterson, Dishion, & Bank, 1984).

As the modeling studies in the late 1980s indicate, we were able to move from a total emphasis on naturalistic observation data in family settings to a more balanced multiagent, -method, and -setting assessment system. This involved increasing our reliance on standard report measures used in this area. We developed our own parent daily-report instruments (Chamberlain & Reid, 1987), global rating scales for use by independent observers and interviewers (Weinrott, Reid, Bauske, & Brummett, 1981), latent constructs that defined a large number of variables (Capaldi & Patterson, 1989), and more sophisticated observational systems for use in multiple natural and laboratory settings (Chamberlain, 1988; Dishion,

Crosby, Rusby, Shone, Patterson & Baker, 1989; Reid, 1982; Reid, Baldwin, Patterson, & Dishion, 1988). We were able to move to more complex biostatistical models during this period with the additions of Bank and Stoolmiller to our research teams.

Developing Intervention Capacity

We continued to work with families who were experiencing severe child behavior problems, family stress, and multiple personal and legal problems. In addition to the families of chronic delinquents described above, we worked with families of young children referred for serious physical abuse (Reid, Taplin, & Lorber, 1981) and families who were screened on the basis of extreme levels of child problems, parental resistance, and family stress (Patterson, 1985). Families in these groups were enmeshed with other agencies (and often in multiple service or treatment programs; or involved in litigation over termination of parental rights), and as a group, these families were extremely challenging. At the clinical level, we learned a great deal about making our parenting interventions relevant in a variety of contexts and constellations of problems, how to get parents to focus on improving their interactions, and how to increase their motivation to work on their parenting (Patterson, 1985; Reid, 1985). We used home-observation data to compare the patterns of microsocial interactions between the abusive parents and their children to those in our previous studies with less distressed families. We found more intense, but very similar, basic parenting processes in these more difficult families (Reid & Kavanagh, 1985). Observational methodology was developed to study the process of family resistance to parent training and to identify therapist and intervention characteristics that were associated with high and low resistance. To this end, we developed a coding system for quantifying key interactions between parents and interventionists, for examining the relationship between resistance and child outcomes, and for improving systems for measuring treatment fidelity during sessions (e.g., Chamberlain, 1988; Chamberlain & Baldwin, 1988; Chamberlain & Ray, 1988; Patterson & Forgatch, 1985).

Although we improved our intervention techniques during this period and, in retrospect, our interventions with these extremely difficult families were somewhat effective (Patterson & Forgatch, 1995), in the early and mid-1980s we were still operating without a comprehensive developmental model to guide us. Importantly, as was the case in our work with families of older, chronic delinquents, we were still not well integrated into the community service networks in which these families were embedded. We were still trying to work with other agencies without a base of mutual self-interest, understanding, respect, and cooperation.

Developing Interventions in the Community

At the same time that we were conducting our longitudinal research and our controlled interventions, we still pursued our interests in family-based approaches to delinquent teenagers. An opportunity arose in 1983–1984, because the state of Oregon decided to downsize the state training schools. The plan was to release all but the most dangerous delinquents into community-based programs. Chamberlain wrote a proposal to the state to offer specialized foster care as an alternative to incarceration. The proposal was developed not around the table at our weekly seminar, but with the relevant state agencies. The theoretical proposition was that skillful parenting might be effective in helping delinquents if the parenting was done by fresh families who were not demoralized by years of failure, not angry at the youngster, not socially stressed or economically disadvantaged, and who had a good family support system. The notion was to distinguish the acts of parenting from the person doing it. The plan was to recruit strong families and train the parents in noncoercive parenting, intensive supervision, and good problem-solving skills. The plan was also to develop a case management approach for each youngster in which parole officers, social and mental health workers, and educators collaborated with the foster parents to separate the youngster from the delinquent peer group and activities, and for the youngsters to begin succeeding in school and normative extracurricular activities. At the same time, the youngsters' own family was helped to deal with whatever situational or mental health problems they were having, and they were encouraged to use the time away from their youngster to learn better skills and strategies in preparation for his or her return home. Aside from the novel attempt to use the same family process model for a very different context and with different adults as providers, the new piece was the development of the intervention in collaboration with the community agencies that were intimately involved in providing services to the youngster. Data on reduced rates of aggressive behavior or better school attendance were not high on the priority lists of the community partners. Fundamental questions were: Could service be offered for less cost than institutionalization, could the community be protected, and would the intervention prevent reincarceration to the training schools? The intervention program was developed and revised continuously over the subsequent 10 years until it became an accepted and respected program in the state. It got consistently good marks on annual state audits of costs and recidivism. In addition to leading rather quickly to the development of a very promising alternative to incarceration (e.g., Chamberlain, 1990), it gave us an additional and compatible perspective and strategy for developing interventions.

Our previous work had been organized around a rather traditional model. First, do basic epidemiological and longitudinal research to build a developmental model of the disorder or problem. Second, use that model to design an experimental intervention that precisely targets the most powerful and malleable antecedents and mediators. Third, carry out a highly controlled randomized trial. Fourth, replicate it if possible. Fifth, disseminate the intervention via a community randomized trial. This fifth step is often the stumbling block. We have come to label this as an inside-out approach. That is, we develop an intervention inside the controlled environment of a research or university facility, and then take it out to the community for dissemination.

The approach used to develop the Treatment Foster Care (TFC) intervention might be termed an outside-in approach. That is, although it is informed by a continuing basic-research base, its actual development was conducted in the community context. In that way, it should be possible to deal with most of the obstacles that block the transfer of technology from research to applied settings. Rather than later having to decide continuously which parts of an experimental intervention can be adapted to the needs of a community and which cannot, one can begin to deal with those issues from the beginning. Even if the specific parameters of service structures vary from community to community, the variance within the class of communities is probably less than that between research and community settings. In addition, there is the issue of credibility. It has been useful to us to have prospective community collaborators check us out with parole officers, teachers, or protective services workers with whom we have worked in the past.

After the TFC program was well integrated into the community, and after it appeared to be a useful intervention in the overall context of community services, Chamberlain brought the intervention back into the research environment to develop an assessment strategy and a randomized intervention design. She then prepared a research grant to fund the research aspects of the project. This strategy of community collaboration and development was to become a continuing feature of much of our work in the next 10 years. Not only was it an effective strategy for developing a series of treatment foster care interventions, but the community-based building and partnerships developed would make it easier to take our center-based (inside out) interventions into the community.

Expansion of Scientific Methodology, Developmental Models, and Interventions (1990–1999)

By the late 1980s, we had developed a reasonably coherent and plausible model of the development of conduct problems from middle elementary school through mid high school (Patterson & Bank, 1989). We had made substantial progress addressing methodological problems that allowed us to define constructs with multiple indicators across agents, methods, and settings (Capaldi & Patterson, 1989; Patterson, 1986; Patterson & Bank, 1986, 1987) and use structural equation modeling techniques to frame tests of our theoretical and intervention models (Bank, Dishion, Skinner, & Patterson, 1990; Bank & Patterson, 1992; Patterson, Bank, & Stoolmiller, 1990). We were also beginning to support the assumption that the same family and contextual mediators involved in the development of conduct problems were involved in the development of substance use, school failure, and depressed mood. Beverly Fagot's research program was tracing the development of social behavior from toddlerhood into school entry, but the links between early social interaction within the family and child conduct problems were not yet established. Evidence was accumulating that the same sorts of parenting interventions that we were using with older youngsters were equally or more effective with preschool children (Webster-Stratton, 1985; 1990). This was not surprising to us because there were enough longitudinal data for us to make some guesses about the early development of coercive parent-child interaction, about its sequelae when the child entered school, and about the additional challenges of relating to the social and behavioral demands of the classroom and peer group. Indeed, on the intervention side, Dishion and Patterson (1992) found age effects in our early clinical data from the 1960s and 1970s that clearly indicated that parent training worked better for younger than older children.

In broad brush strokes, the 1990s at OSLC might be described as an explosion of intervention and theoretical work on a variety of levels, and this activity was fueled by the conception and funding of the Oregon Prevention Center in 1990.

Throughout the 1990s, we had a number of interventions being tested in the field, all driven by the same basic theoretical models, using similar multimeasure assessment strategies, assessing overlapping mediators and outcomes. We had refined our parent-training techniques and adapted them for children at different developmental levels and for families living in different situations and contexts. Parent training continued to be the centerpiece of our interventions, and we used our longitudinal work to target different aspects of parenting for youngsters of different ages.

By 1990, when we were writing our first Oregon Prevention Center proposal, we understood the importance of intervening early in the developmental cycle, though most of our intervention experience had been with children from middle childhood to middle adolescence. In fact, during the 1990s there has been an increasing portion of our intervention work focused on the preschool and school entry years (Fisher, Ellis, & Chamberlain, 1999; Forgatch & DeGarmo, 1999; Reid, 1993; Reid, Eddy, Fetrow, & Stoolmiller, 1999), while continuing to address intervention issues with older children and adolescents (Chamberlain & Moore, 1998; Chamberlain & Reid, 1998; Dishion & Andrews, 1995; Dishion, Andrews, Kavanagh, & Soberman, 1996; Dishion, Kavanagh, & Kiesner, in press). Our intervention strategies now address children's behavior problems from about age 3 to age 18, and across family contexts such as single mother, stepfather, and foster homes, as well as homes with antisocial siblings and antisocial girls.

As part of the variety of interventions we have been funded to develop, we have conceptualized intervention trials as experimental longitudinal studies and have carefully collected assessment data across all of these trials using our multiple-method and multiple-agent technology. Most of the assessment batteries for these interventions include observational data collected in one or more settings of home, classroom, playground, and laboratory. Furthermore, all interventions are manualized, which enhances fidelity; fidelity checks are also built into each intervention strategy.

Findings from our intervention and longitudinal studies were beginning to indicate that there is an orderly progression of potentially malleable and developmentally linked antecedents and mediators across accessible social domains. This suggested that there are many powerful and potentially malleable antecedents at many developmental points and in many domains over the early life course. This led us to seriously question our singular emphasis on clinical strategies to deal with full-blown conduct disorder and to consider the early life-course prevention strategy. That is, it might be feasible to use our emerging model to target antecedents and mediators of conduct problems as they became potent over the course of development. Rather than seeing early oppositional and later conduct and substance use disorders as clinical entities in the 1990 Prevention Center proposal, we conceptualized these clinical phenomena as parts of a developmental trajectory, in which poor outcomes at earlier points were antecedents for poor outcomes at later points in development.

For example, difficult infant temperament or maternal depression and family stress are antecedents for subsequent poor outcomes such as coercive parent-child interactions. These coercive interactions are, in turn, malleable antecedents for subsequent outcomes at school entry, such as poor peer and teacher relations in the first grade; these school factors become malleable antecedents for academic failure and truancy, which are, in turn, antecedents for association with delinquent peers, poor supervision, and so on. Both the developmental continuity of antisocial behavior and its antecedents and mediators across time and contexts and the fact that contextual factors (e.g., divorce, job loss) could introduce new and powerful risks for poor child adjustment at any time in development forced us to reconsider our clinical, relatively nondevelopmental approach and conceptualization of intervention. In the context of such long-term developmental trajectories, the traditional 1- or 2-year follow-up studies of interventions were appearing more and more inadequate. Thus, we have sought and been successful in securing funding to continue to collect long-term follow-up assessments for much of our intervention work, and we are continuing with that strategy. In addition to providing critical data on the malleability of specific behaviors and long-term sequalae of these interventions, these follow-up data will be incredibly helpful in understanding the cost effectiveness of particular interventions undertaken at various points along the developmental trajectory.

We have dealt with a number of very difficult issues during the 1990s, including both intervention and theoretical challenges. For example, Dishion's Adolescent Transitions Program (ATP) randomly assigned families to four groups: parent training, adolescent skills, both parenting and adolescent skills, and a biblio-video control. Much to our surprise, the teenagers in the adolescent skills groups enjoyed their weekly sessions but also showed significant increases in drug and alcohol use (Dishion, McCord, & Poulin, 1999; Poulin, Dishion, & Burraston, in press). Dishion and his colleagues concluded that putting youngsters with conduct and substance problems together in group-treatment settings provided regular weekly opportunities to establish relationships with other troubled youth, and the intervention did, in fact, produce an iatrogenic effect. Chamberlain and Reid (1998) found similar iatrogenic effects for delinquent adolescents randomly assigned to a group-home setting as compared to foster homes in the community. Boys subjected to the group-home intervention as compared to TFC were supervised less well, associated regularly with deviant peers (with no adult supervision), and were arrested more often. These results taught us that interventions with problem and delinquent teenagers should not be developed for group settings, including group sessions, camps, and other recreational, academic, or peer related activities. This result has now been replicated by Joan McCord using the Cambridge-Summerville data (Dishion, McCord, & Poulin, 1999).

Also on the theoretical level, we responded to work conducted by behavior geneticists suggesting that parenting interventions are unlikely to account for outcome variance in children's and adolescents' development (e.g., Plomin & Daniels, 1987; Rowe, 1994; Scarr, 1992). These reports and claims are serious and have motivated OSLC investigators to establish a twin sample in Oregon, to investigate assessments of observed versus reported twin behaviors, and to examine closely the methodology of the published twin and adoption studies. Results from observation data indicate that, there is far more variance accounted for by environmental variables in the prediction of children's maladaptive behaviors than previously suggested in the literature. It also seems that the estimates of variance accounted for by genetic factors are probably inflated (Leve, Winebarger, Fagot, Reid, & Goldsmith, 1998; Stoolmiller, in press).

At a practical level, we needed to develop the data management and biostatistical capability, expertise, and methodology to deal with large longitudinal data sets and to develop and test complex developmental models. During the 1990s, we have developed our capabilities with growth modeling, using visualization and latent growth modeling techniques in particular. Our associations with Hendricks Brown and Bengt Muthen and the Prevention Science Methodology Group have been pivotal and extraordinarily helpful in these endeavors. Also emerging from those associations has been our ability to adapt missing data technologies for use with our large longitudinal data sets (Duncan, Duncan, & Stoolmiller, 1994; Patterson, 1993; Stoolmiller, 1995; Stoolmiller, Duncan, Bank, & Patterson, 1993).

As our theoretical structures and biostatistical capabilities have matured, we have needed to continually upgrade and improve our data management and direct observation technologies. Currently and for the last several years, we have been in the process of moving to a completely digitalized video and video coding system. Our programming department has already created software to take advantage of the dramatically reduced processing times for locating specific images and codes. For example, finding each episode of a child's negative behavior followed by a parent's negative response over a series of home observations or laboratory tasks can be accomplished in minutes as compared to hours for locating the same segments on videotapes.

Our analysis strategies with observational data have also improved sharply with Stoolmiller's use of individual observation sessions or lab task segments as indicators for an observation latent construct (e.g., negative behavior chain). This technique has substantially increased reliability and validity of observation-based assessment (Stoolmiller, Eddy, & Reid, 2000).

Implications

Modern dynamic theories of child development say that to understand aggressive children, we must look for answers within the child (i.e., their attributions, their internal representations). The micro- and macrotheories plus the intervention strategies outlined in this volume all say otherwise. If we are to change aggressive childhood behavior, we must change the environment in which the child lives. If we are to understand and predict future aggression, our primary measures will be of the social environment that is teaching and maintaining these deviant behaviors. The problem lies in the social environment. If you wish to change the child, you must systematically alter the environment in which he or she lives.

This not the end of the journey; it is more like an early draft. But what is described in this volume is at the very least a workable theory about where child aggression comes from and how to change it. The fact that the same variables found in the theory also drive the intervention and prevention procedures should make the theory even more interesting. It is a theory of aggression that works.

Part II _____

Coercion Theory: The Development of Antisocial Behavior

2

The Early Development of Coercive Family Process

Gerald R. Patterson

A theory that purports to explain children's aggressive behavior must begin with an explanation of how it begins. It must also address both the Scylla of stability in expression of aggression while also explaining the Charybdis of developmental changes in the forms taken by aggression. This chapter is focused on both questions.

The general strategy is to think of infant and caregiver exchanges as reflecting complex contributions from the contextual matrix in which these interactions are embedded. Some processes may partially reflect long-standing biological processes (e.g., birth complications, genes), and others represent contextual intrusions, such as divorce, depression, and maternal stress. The key idea is that the impact of these contextual variables on child outcomes is mediated by the nature of the infant and caregiver exchanges.

Finally, the antisocial individual carries the dual burden of recognizable deviancy plus obvious social incompetence. Understanding how coercion begins requires that we also study the beginnings of social incompetence.

Mothers and Infants in the Coercion Process

Infants in an Uncertain World

The term *coercion* refers to the contingent use of aversive behaviors of another person. The idea of *contingency* lies at the core of coercion theory (Patterson, 1982; 1995; 1996b). The term implies a connection between one event and another. In the discussions that follow, we are particularly interested in the connection between the infant's behavior and the reaction of the caregiver. We are also interested in its inverse, that is, the reaction of the infant to the mother. We believe the mutual contingent reactions of the caregiver and infant represent a fundamental building block for the relationship that emerges during the preschool years. It rests upon the idea that behavior is, to some extent, governed by immediately impinging events. As we shall see, positive reinforcement, punishment, and negative reinforcement all play central roles in the coercion model. The definition of contingency will also require not just one, but two conditional probability values. More of this will be covered later.

Coercion theory takes the idea of contingency from its historic place in laboratory studies (Herrnstein, 1961) and places it in a dyadic context (Patterson, 1979, 1984a). This implies that although contingencies supplied by the environment control the infant, it is also the case that the contingencies supplied by the infant control the social environment, including the caregiver.

In effect, one of the early tasks confronting the infant toddler is to shape his or her own social environment. It is not dissimilar from that faced by the elementary school-aged child. How does one convert the social environment into a predictable place containing minimal uncertainty?

One might think that an infant has only the most limited array of tools for altering the social environment. But crying, fussing, and temper tantrums are readily available to almost all infants; and as most parents can attest, they provide a powerful set of contingent arrangements for altering parent behavior. I have seen an infant's smiles and vocalization shape the behavior of an entire roomful of adults. In the hands of an infant, even rudimentary language skills can serve as powerful reinforcers in shaping the behavior of most adults.

The attachment and the social interactional theorists are in surprising agreement about the centrality of contingencies in the socialization process (Patterson, 1982; van den Boom, 1995). The two groups even use the same language to discuss the nature of contingent interactions. For example, van den Boom's (1994) sensitive descriptions of the contingent and noncontingent mother sound very much like the behavioral definition with its matching of the mother's reactions to what the infant is doing (Martin, 1981). The infant cries, the mother appears. The events are correlated; an infant's cry produces a predictable outcome. One might, therefore, think of all contingencies as simply members of a more general class of events that increase predictability or reduce uncertainty.

However, the idea of contingency carries with it more than just the reduction of uncertainty. For example, we could cue the mother to walk over to the infant every 60 s and gently talk and caress him or her for 10 s. The world would become a predictable place; and, in that sense, there is a reduction of uncertainty. However, these predictable components in the environment are not examples of contingency. This is because the events are in no way tied to the behavior of the infant (i.e., it is not p[outcome/infant behavior]). It is not what the infant is doing that makes the world a more predictable place. Contingency carries with it the connotation that the infant's behavior somehow gives control over the mother's behavior (and she over the infant).

Knowing the infant's behavior reliably produces a certain caregiver reaction is not a sufficient base for predicting that this particular infant behavior will be selected more often in the future. We need more information. There are two conditionals to consider. The first is the likelihood that when the infant smiles (B), the mother will react (A) by smiling, giving us p(A/B) (e.g., the likelihood that the infant will be reinforced for a smile). Attachment theorists and social interactionalists both emphasize Watson's (1979) contribution to the definition of the term contingent. As he noted in his now classic essay, it requires not one but two conditional values to define what we mean by contingency. The second conditional describes the likelihood that the mother will smile at infant regardless of what the infant does, p(A/all non-B). One side effect of the contingencies embedded in caregiver-infant interactions is a reduction in uncertainty for the infant. If this were so, then sequences of mother-infant interaction should show that adjacent events on the time line tend to be correlated. Studies of primates (Altmann, 1965) and humans (Raush, 1965) are in surprisingly close agreement on this issue. These studies showed that the best predictor for the next event in a social interaction sequence is information about what happened at T-1 (the immediate antecedent). For a clinical sample of hyperactive boys, Raush found that the immediately prior social behavior accounted for about 30% of the variance in predicting the next event. Karpowitz (1972) studied families of out-of-control children and found that the immediate antecedent accounted for about 50% of the variance.

There is some reason to believe that being reared in an at least minimally contingent environment may be a condition that is necessary for survival. Mineka, Gunnar, and Champoux (1986) observed rhesus monkeys reared in contingent and noncontingent environments. Those reared in contingent environments produced increased exploratory activity and less fearfulness, two of the criterion measures for effective socialization. They also cited studies showing similar results in experiments with rats. Seymour Levine (personal communication, September 18, 2000) reviewed findings from studies of rodents and monkeys to show that being reared in noncontingent environments and environments with low levels of positive reinforcement were associated with atypical patterns of cortisol production. These findings strongly support the idea that living in a contingent environment may be a key component for normal development.

Intraindividual Level of Analyses

To the novice parent, infant crying becomes one of the most salient features of life with the newborn. When the desperate parent discovers the correct response, the infant selectively reinforces (e.g., the crying stops). The parent is presented with a very aversive stimulus (the crying). It persists until the parent presents the correct response. Then, and only then, the crying ceases. This is almost a textbook example of escape conditioning or, in operant terms, negative reinforcement. It is an odd fact that one of the first tasks presented to the infant is to use coercion to train his parents in parenting skills.

There is a paradox here, one that can only be resolved by thinking about the contingency concept from a very different perspective. If the caregiver's reaction is reinforcing to the infant, then why this is not followed by an increase in infant crying? Bell and Ainsworth (1972) collected data on both distressed and nondistressed rates of crying during the first year of life. Their data showed clear correlations between the frequency mothers ignored crying and the frequency of infant crying. Although no attempt was made to observe maternal contingent or noncontingent caretaking, they concluded that this was clear evidence for the fact that maternal caretaking did not function as a reinforcer. The fact that contingency must be defined by not one but two conditionals has often been overlooked by developmentalists, as pointed out by both Watson (1979) and Gewirtz and Boyd (1977). We need to know the likelihood that the caregiver reacts appropriately to crying ($p1$). We also need to know how often all other infant behaviors are followed by appropriate caregiver reactions. In other words, to understand reinforcing effects we need to proceed from an intraindividual basis. This means that if we are really only interested in studying the effect of a reinforcer on a particular aggressive response, we must still collect data on all of the other behaviors occurring in that setting together with a tabulation of the frequency with which they are reinforced. In may seem paradoxical, but it ultimately means that to understand differences between children we must examine all of the within-subject responses together with their relevant reinforcers.

As shown in Figure 2.1, understanding even the relatively simple exchanges between infant and caregiver requires that we proceed at an intraindividual level. Here, we need the following pieces of information: What proportion of infant crying ($p1$) is followed closely in time by mother attending? What proportion of all other infant behaviors ($p2$) is followed closely in time by mother attending? Gewirtz and Boyd (1977) conducted an elegant series of single-subject studies using an ABA design that showed clearly that brief intervals of maternal responding to nondistressed cries did, indeed, function as a reinforcer and reliably increased the frequency of infant crying. In the Gewirtz study, the mother reacted only when the infant was crying, so we might assume that the value for $p1$ was 1.00, and the value for $p2$ was 0.00. But, obviously, most mothers attend to the infant when he or she cries, but this accounts for only a small proportion of the total amount of mother's attending behaviors.

Answering the question raised by Bell and Ainsworth (1972), we need to proceed with an intraindividual level of analyses. For a given infant, does the caregiver attend only when the infant cries? Alternatively, does she react positively at very high rates to infant efforts to communicate, vocalize, make facial expressions, and smile? How often the infant cries varies as a function of the relative payoffs. If cry-

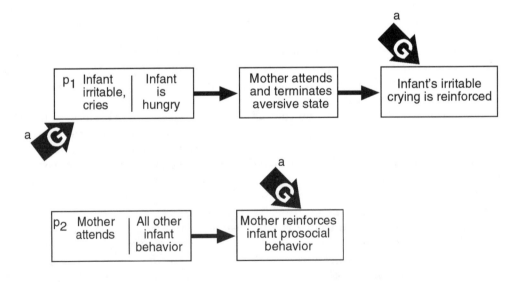

[a]G refers to mechanisms that may be sensitive to biological contributions.

Figure 2.1. Intraindividual levels of analysis: Two conditionals for a contingency model.

ing pays off relatively better than anything else he or she does, then you can bet on crying.

Figure 2.1 outlines the strategy for studying coercive process for infants and toddlers. Notice that understanding the coercive infant behavior requires that we also collect data on the contingencies provided for the infant's socially competent behaviors. We believe that the strategy should make provisions for the inclusions of biological variables, including pre- and postnatal complications and genes. In the present context, we hypothesized that infant irritability and infant responsiveness to reinforcers may reflect biological dispositions. At present there are no data from behavioral-genetic studies that relate to these hypotheses.

Context

Like Belsky, Rovine, and Fish (1989); Laub and Sampson (1988); Sampson and Laub (1993); Snyder (1991); and many others, we believe that the impact of contextual factors—such as divorce, parental depression, neighborhood, and socioeconomic status (SES)—play an important role in determining family process. However, in accord with these investigators, we also hypothesized that these variables make only indirect contributions to child outcomes. We hypothesized that the impact of contextual variables on child outcomes is mediated by the extent to which they alter the social interaction of caregiver and infant. The findings relevant to the mediational model are extensively reviewed in chapter 8. The present section is narrowly focused upon contextual variables thought to influence toddler and preschool family processes.

As shown in Figure 2.2 we assumed that the variable most likely to be associated with the initiation of the coercion process consists of an interaction (product) term based on two contextual variables: A difficult temperament infant confronted by a caregiver who is only marginally competent. The lack of competence may reflect the impact of the disrupting context in which the family lives. We examine the contribution of each of these contextual variables in the following sections.

Temperament

Most investigators believe that differences in child temperament play a central role in initiating a coercive process. Laboratory studies of infants now routinely include measures of infants' fussy, irritable, crying, and distancing behaviors (e.g., Shaw & Winslow, 1997; van den Boom, 1994). Because temperament variables seem to emerge so early in development, the conventional wisdom postulates that it has biologic roots. For example, Goldsmith and Campos (1986) review the evidence relating findings from twin and adoption studies to temperament. An even stronger support for a biologic base for temperament is found in the abundant literature on pre- and postbirth complications as they relate to temperament differences (e.g., studies showing the relation between birth weight, pregnancy complications, and premature birth; Hack, Klein, & Taylor, 1995; also the large-scale study by Kratzer & Hodgins, 1997, relating birth weight to later development of conduct disorders). Similarly, the extensive analyses of a Danish cohort by Brennan, Mednick, and Kandel (1991) demonstrated a significant relation between birth complications and

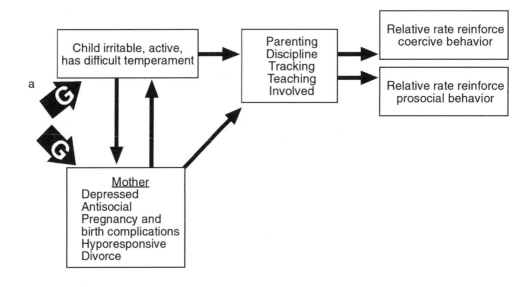

^aG refers to mechanisms that may be sensitive to genetic contributions.

Figure 2.2.   Content and the coercion dyad.

adolescent and adult violent behavior. It is interesting to note that there was no relation between birth complications and property crimes.

Shaw and Winslow (1997) provided a very thoughtful review of the issues and findings for infant assessment of temperament. As they pointed out, much of the support for a significant relation between infant temperament and later externalizing problems rests upon data for samples of preschool and school-aged children rather than infants. The strong connection found between temperament and older children's adjustment outcomes are typically based on mothers' ratings for both independent and dependent variables. When the shared-method and shared-rater bias is removed, most of the empirical connection vanishes (e.g., Bates, Bayles, Bennett, Ridge, & Brown, 1991). The Owens, Shaw, and McGuire (1993) longitudinal study of 293 infants used both observation data and maternal ratings of temperament collected at 12 and 18 months to predict behavior problems at 2 to 3 years of age. There was very little evidence for convergence across methods.

Perhaps these difficulties are to be expected. How does one obtain convergence across multiple measures on a process that is just in its initial stages? In our own studies of both normal and clinical samples, we were unable to obtain convergence across teacher, parent, and observer data for ages 3 through 6 years. However, interestingly enough, any one method was stable across time. Fisher and Fagot (1996) were able to show that when the child was in the second grade, there was a very modest convergence across parents, teachers, and observers. Given these findings, then it is not surprising that no one, including Bates and Shaw, finds convergence for toddlers and infants.

Presumably, such early measures of infant temperament will interact with caregiver skills to predict long-term outcomes in child adjustment. There is good reason to believe that for samples of older children, the mothers' perceptions of temperament correlate with their parenting practices. For example, Fagot and Gauvain (1997) showed that maternal ratings of child temperament at 18 months predicted mothers' observed problem-solving behaviors at 30 months. The longitudinal study by Guerin, Gottfried, and Thomas (1997) provided some of the strongest data supporting the claims for the significant correlations of temperament to negative child outcomes. Temperament ratings collected from parents when the child was 30 months predicted teacher ratings of child's attention and thought problems at 12 years of age. Hetherington (1991) also reported significant correlations between maternal ratings of temperament and parenting practices.

Pathological Caregivers

As shown in the review by Downey and Coyne (1990), caregivers who are either schizophrenic or depressed are about equally likely to produce a child who is maladjusted. Field (1995) cited several studies including her own showing that depressed mothers place their infants at significant risk for problem behaviors. The microsocial analyses showed that maternal depression was associated with mothers spending less time looking at the infant, touching, and talking; and mothers were more likely to have more negative and fewer positive facial expressions. The infants, in turn, have lower activity levels, vocalize less, look away, protest more often, and have more negative facial expressions. Infants of depressed mothers were more negative, even when the infants were interacting with mothers who were not depressed. These findings for infants are very reminiscent of findings showing that depressed mothers had reduced activity levels and were less positive and more distant in their interactions with older children (Breznitz & Sherman, 1987; Downey & Coyne, 1990; Forehand, McComb, & Brody, 1987).

Field (1995) concluded that maternal depression during pregnancy is associated with infants who are more fussy and difficult to soothe. As she notes, it is not clear whether the nonresponsivity of the infant is caused by the maternal depression or perhaps by infant hypoarousability.

Extreme Environments

There are now a number of longitudinal studies showing that divorce is a contextual variable associated with increased risk for both antisocial behavior and school failure (Forgatch, Patterson, & Skinner, 1988; Furstenberg, 1988; Hetherington, Cox, & Cox, 1979; Zil, 1988). Structural equation models (SEMs) from the Oregon Divorce Sample consistently showed that the effects of stressful events that accompany divorce on child adjustment are mediated through parental discipline and problem-solving practices (Forgatch, Patterson, & Ray, 1996; Forgatch et al., 1988). Single mothers whose parenting practices were not disrupted were at significantly less risk for negative child outcomes. The studies also showed that antisocial mothers were also at greater risk for repeated family transitions and for disruptions in parenting (Capaldi & Patterson, 1991; Patterson, 1999). In a sense, children involved in divorce are doubly at risk because of the disrupting effect of divorce-induced stress on parenting and the increased likelihood that the caregiver is antisocial and, therefore, at best, only marginally skilled in parenting (Bank, Forgatch, Patterson, & Fetrow, 1993; Capaldi & Patterson, 1991). There is growing evidence that mothers living in poverty and teenage mothers are both at grave risk for disrupted parenting (Ricciuti & Dorman, 1983; Wilson, 1974). We hypothesized that recently divorced mothers are at risk for disrupted parenting and indirectly for producing distressed-coercive infants. The single-mother studies are reviewed in detail in chapter 12.

Although one of the outcomes of stress is an increase in irritability (Forgatch et al., 1996), distancing is another path that may be of equal importance. The distant, uninvolved caregiver can have a profound impact on infant development. Hart and Risley (1995) carried out one of those tiny studies where the results have revolutionary implications. They observed 42 families in hour-long sessions in the home on a monthly basis for 2.5 years. Beginning when the children were about 7 months of age, each utterance by infant and parent was coded and tallied. They found an average of 178 utterances per hour for families on welfare as compared to 487 per hour for families of professionals and 301 for working-class families. It may well be that some of this is related to the child's evocative (genes) impact on the parents. Be that as it may, these are amazing differences in the sheer amount of training (environment) provided for language use. The exchanges were also coded for five qualitative dimensions of parenting, and these variables were used to predict child IQ at age 9 to 10 years. The parenting variables assessed prior to 3 years of age accounted for 61% of the variance in the IQ measure. It is important to note that even the impact of context in such extreme environments as poverty and neighborhood on child outcomes is malleable. Within the last decade, a new genre of prevention studies has shown that prevention trials can be tailored for mothers living in such contexts (Field, 1995; Olds et al., 1997; van de Boom; 1994). The results of these trials showed that strengthening parenting skills serves as an effective protective factor.

Biological Variables as Context

An impressive body of research reviewed by Quay (1987) showed a consistent correlation between measures of hypoarousability and measures of antisocial behavior. The findings suggest that, as infants, the yet-to-be antisocial individual might be less responsive to caregiver contingencies. The caregiver may also be less responsive to infant behaviors, as suggested in studies by van den Boom (1994) and Field (1995). Hyporesponsiveness on the part of either the caregiver or the infant could contribute significantly to risk for negative outcomes.

As noted in chapter 1, laboratory findings from the 1960s showed that antisocial children and adults were less responsive than normal children to either social reinforcers or to aversive consequences. Lykken (1957, 1995) suggests that hyporesponsiveness reflects heritable contributions. Although this may be so, it is also reasonable to hypothesize that living in a noncontingent environment would reduce responsiveness to contingencies when they are presented, as shown by Cairns (1979b).

We are convinced that biology will be shown to play an important role in explaining the early beginnings of the coercion process. We were, therefore, very disappointed when we turned to a half century of behavior genetics (B-G) research and found the data to be extremely limited. The vast bulk of the studies ignored the key question of how it is that heritability determines coercive or aggressive outcomes. The twin and adoption designs employed in the B-G studies have contributed little if anything to our understanding of how aggressive behavior in children comes about. We believe, however, that with some modification, adoption designs could be directed to this task. Because of the potential importance of this contribution, the next few pages briefly focus on the difficulties encountered in B-G studies to date.

The strategy adopted by behavioral geneticists generates estimates of variance accounted for by heritability (G) and by the environment (E). In their reviews of this extensive literature, Rowe (1994) and Harris (1998) offer little or no support for the idea that siblings share a common environment and find instead that most of the variance in phenotypes, such as aggression, reflect the contribution of G. In effect, parents contribute little if anything to long-term child outcomes. Their conclusions are consistent with their finding in that estimates of environments shared by siblings tend to be very close to zero. The findings reiterate the theme that biology is important but do not explain how G variables work. Before we can initiate genetically informed designs that will perform this function, there are some problems to consider. Although the problems are well known, it is seldom that they have been effectively addressed by B-G investigators.

The problems were reviewed in detail in *Behavioral and Brain Sciences, 13,* (1990) and then repeatedly emphasized by the developmental psychology community, such as Baumrind (1993), Bronfenbrenner and Ceci (1994), Collins, Maccoby, Steinberg, Hetherington, and Bornstein (2000), and Hoffman (1985); and methodologists, such as Stoolmiller (1998, 1999) and Turkheimer (1991). The three most salient methodological concerns are (a) restricted range, a problem for both adoption and twin designs; (b) failure to meet the equal environments assumption (EEA), an acute problem for twin designs; (c) and inadequate attention given to measurement problems for both designs. In each case, failure to correct the problems produces inflated estimates of heritability and leads to underestimates of shared environment.

By definition, children in adoption studies are not placed in homes that sample the lower half or lower third of our society. As Turkheimer (1991) and Stoolmiller (1999) pointed out, the effect of this restricted range is to reduce the correlation of the environment (E) with outcome variables. Most of the twin samples reflect a similar restricted distribution. For example, a recent analysis of large-scale twin studies in Sweden and the United Kingdom (Eley, Lichtenstein, & Stevenson, 1999; p. 158) was accompanied by the following remark, "As with all volunteer twin samples, there was a bias toward higher SES-level families." As pointed out by Lykken, McGue, and Tellegen (1987) and others, families volunteering for twin studies tend to be middle class. The implication is that in twin studies, the volunteer samples represent a variation on Stoolmiller's (1999) theme of truncated distributions and the consequent underestimates of E and overestimates for G.

For twin designs, the analyses of heritability require that the EEA be met (e.g., the environments shared by Mz twins does not account for the Mz similarity in phenotypes). There are now three large-scale studies that show this assumption is not tenable (Carey, 1992; Rose & Caprio, 1987; Tambs, Harris, & Magnus, 1995). Carefully measured studies would show clearly that twins' shared experiences significantly determine phenotypic similarities. This means that measures of heritiability based on 2(Mz-Dz) may be confounded.

There are repeated findings showing that estimates of G and estimates of shared environment vary widely as a function of type of measures employed. In general, it seems that estimates based on parent or child reports often produce high estimates for G and very low estimates for shared environment; however, just the reverse set of findings is generated in studies that employ observation measures. Emde et al. (1992) and Miles and Carey (1997) described meta-analyses of 24 studies using twin and adoption designs and concluded that the most salient findings were the dramatic contribution of method of measurement (e.g., lower heritabiltiy and higher estimates of shared environment when observation measures were used; Leve et al., 1998) collected both parent ratings and observation-based measures in a twin study. Based on parent ratings, the estimate of heritability based was .40 with the estimate for shared environment at .41. Heritability estimates based on observed child behavior was .24 and for shared environment .28. Deater-Deckard (2000) studied 120 preschool twins. Based on maternal reports, the estimate of heritability for conduct problem behaviors was .59 as compared to the estimate of 0.0 based on observation data.

Our general position is that even though some mechanisms in the coercion process will reflect biological underpinnings, the coercion process itself is eminently malleable. The evidence from prevention trials strongly supports the idea that the social environment can be altered in such a way as to reduce the risk for negative outcomes. This optimistic view is based in part on findings from laboratory studies that employ cross-breeding and cross-fostering designs and from the last decade of prevention studies that involve at-risk infants. For example, the beautifully designed cross-fostering studies of primates by Suomi (1995) and his colleagues showed that well-established heritable patterns could be disrupted by placement in homes with effective foster mothers. In the same vein, programmatic studies of mice by Cairns (1996) and his colleagues collected data from a cross-breeding design for aggressiveness over 30 generations. Their data showed that a few minutes of experimentally administered defeats in combat bouts radically altered the disposition to attack in future bouts (e.g., the contribution of genes is eminently malleable).

In her review of observation studies, van den Boom (1994) noted that heightened infant irritability is generally associated with a lack of maternal involvement. As she also pointed out, the lack of maternal involvement seems frequently found in low-SES families. Presumably, increasing maternal involvement could produce decreases in infant irritability. Low-SES mothers with irritable infants were trained to be sensitively responsive to infant cues. Data showed predicted reduction in infant irritability that held up in a 3-year follow-up study (van den Boom, 1995). Although the design is somewhat flawed because of significant differences in baseline measures for experimental and control group, results from other prevention studies support the general idea that infant-caregiver interactions are malleable. Olds et al. (1997) provided convincing data showing dramatic and long-term effects for home visitation with at-risk mothers. The intervention was much more intensive than the van den Boom procedures. There were 9 home visits during pregnancy and 23 from the child's birth to 2 years of age. The caregivers tended to be young, unmarried, and low SES. The visits focused on a wide range of problems from health care (e.g., to reduce smoking, alcohol use, and pregnancy complications) to promoting emotional and cognitive development, clarifying goals, and solving problems concerning work, communications, and education. The large-scale prevention trials have been replicated. The long-term effects ranged from reducing risk for child abuse and child neglect, fewer subsequent pregnancies, and fewer maternal arrests. The intervention-prevention studies reviewed in chapters 10–13 constantly reiterate the optimistic theme associated with the malleability of both parenting behaviors and child outcomes. The optimism is based on randomized trial designs and careful measurement.

Some Speculations About Gender Differences

There is a fascinating consistency in the literature about preschool children that merits both our comment and speculations as to its origins. In her most recent review of gender differences, Maccoby (1998) notes that reliable gender differences in aggression appear as early as 3 years of age. Similarly, Achenbach, Howell, Quay, and Conner's (1991) national survey of parents' ratings on the Child Behavior Checklist (CBC-L; Achenbach & Edelbrock, 1979) showed that by age 4 to 5 years, the difference between boys and girls on the aggressive behavior scale were already apparent (by about 2 items on a 25-item scale). The increased rate of aggression for boys was maintained till about midadolescence. Teacher ratings showed similar effects (Achenbach, 1991a). What causes these differences?

We assumed that the variables leading to gender differences in aggression by age 3 or 4 years reflect the interaction between biological and environment variables. In this section, we speculate about what these interactions might be. We take the position that there may be not one, but two, rather different paths to aggressive behaviors. The two paths may reflect fundamental differences in the manner in which biology contributes to aggressiveness in male and female toddlers.

Of the two, the coercion path is probably the most likely route to problem-child outcomes. It can be described as the outcome of a five-step dance: (a) infant is aversive, (b) caregiver is aversive, (c) infant escalates aversiveness, (d) caregiver responds positively, and (e) infant terminates aversive behavior. Obviously, the dance has many possible combinations and permutations (e.g., either the infant or the caregiver may initiate it). However, each of the five steps is thought to be likely candidates that covary with biological variables. Each, therefore, becomes of great interest and considering gender differences.

1. We hypothesized earlier that infant irritability might reflect heritable components. Having one or more biological parents who are antisocial not only speaks to a risk for heritable components but, in addition, also increases the risk that the infant will be raised in an aversive environment (Bank et al., 1993; Patterson et al., 1992). However, we do not think that the gender differences begin here. The reason is that we have found no studies that show male infants are more aversive than are female infants.

2. Given an aggressive caregiver, the likelihood increases that the infant will respond in kind. This is a variant of the well-known continuance variable from the coercion model p Infant Aversive/Caregiver Aversive (Patterson 1982). It is quite possible that one of the key gender differences occurs here. The hypothesis is that biological variables may significantly relate to gender differences in negative reciprocity (e.g., males are more likely than females to react negatively to an aversive stimulus).

Biological variables need to be broadly defined for these analyses. The study of extremely antisocial adolescent boys and their babies showed that 21% of the births required intensive care, and 37% were premature (Fagot, Pears, Capaldi, Crosby, & Leve, 1998). As noted earlier, there is now ample evidence for a correlation between birth complications and antisocial outcomes (Brennan & Mednick, 1997; Brown et al.; 1991; Pasamanick, Rogers, & Lilienfeld, 1956).

Biological contributions include information both about heritability and information from pre- and postbirth complications. Many B-G studies fail to take this into account; this constitutes attributing the total effect to G.

Evolutionary theory suggests that if mothers were disposed to react with anger to infant aversive behaviors the babies would be less likely to survive. Therefore, We suspect that females at risk for reciprocal aversive reactions have already been deleted from the gene pool. Specifically, we would hypothesize that girls would be less likely than boys to react aversively to caregiver or sibling aversive intrusions. During the interval from 12 to 24 months, for girls as compared to boys, the likelihood of continuance should be significantly lower.

3. We also hypothesized that during this early stage (12-24 months), boys are more responsive than are girls to negative reinforcement contingencies. Specifically, following a conflict bout, boys will more likely experience a win as a reinforcer. This, in turn, could be tested by demonstrating with observation data that on the next occasion boys are more likely than girls to employ the same or similar response. The strategy for testing a hypothesis of this kind is detailed in the study by Snyder and Patterson (1986).

It follows, then, that having biologic parents who are antisocial is likely to have a different effect for girls than for boys. In conflict bouts, boys with this biological history should be more likely than girls to find winning to be reinforcing. The reason why we think this might be true is based on laboratory studies of caregiver-infant interaction. Martin (1981) showed that parental-responsiveness measures correlated with infant coerciveness for boys but not for girls. The fact that this was replicated by Shaw and Winslow (1997) is noteworthy and suggests that the key may lie in the fact that boys may be biologically wired to be more responsive to negative reinforcement whereas girls are not.

As the hypotheses were presented, they described a situation where biology seems to conspire to increase the prevalence of coercive boys but decrease the prevalence of girls who become coercive as a result of processes related to negative reinforcement. However, the second path to problem-child outcomes may redress the seeming imbalance.

We suspect that there is one further safeguard against girls becoming extremely coercive and antisocial. In the past decade, careful microsocial analyses of exchanges with both preschool and adolescent peer groups showed that antisocial boys select peers who will reinforce them for being antisocial (Dishion, Andrews, & Crosby, 1995; Snyder, West, Stockemer, Gibbons, & Almquist-Parks, 1996). In effect, reactions of the peer group serve to supplement and even increase support for some forms of deviancy. However, there seems to be no such supplement for young antisocial girls. The study by Fagot and Hagan (1985) showed that by 18 to 23 months, there were higher mean observed aggression scores for boys than for girls. Male peers were significantly more likely to respond to aggression by males with both positive and negative consequences, whereas girls' aggression was most likely to be ignored. Boys aggressive behavior also tended to receive more negative feedback from teachers than did girls. This, in turn, was similar to the findings for parental reactions to male and female aggression (Fagot & Leinbach, 1987a, 1987b). Parents tended to react negatively to aggression by boys but less so for aggression by girls. It is as if aggression by toddler girls is nonfunctional (i.e., it has little or no impact on the environment).

Even if female toddlers learned to be coercive at home, the reaction of young male peers would be to reject her (because she is a girl; Maccoby, 1998) and to ignore her aggressive behavior. We speculate that the reaction of female peers to her attempts to be coercive or antisocial would be to reject her. Unlike aggressive boys who are rejected, there is no group of deviant peers standing at the door waiting to receive her. From this perspective, it would be expected that an extremely antisocial 6-year-old girl would be a low base-rate event.

One important injunction is that the Oregon infant and toddler longitudinal studies have typically sampled middle-class families. The effect is to produce a restricted range of values for measures of both parenting and child outcomes. As shown by Stoolmiller (1999), this, in turn, has major implications for one's effort to correlate parenting practices with child outcomes. Depending upon the degree of restriction in range, such correlations may be reduced by a factor of 2 or 3. Future studies of gender differences should involve a full range of families' SES levels, including those who are at extreme risk for producing problem children.

Summary

We assumed that the coercion process might be set in motion when the infant is 10 to 18 months of age (or perhaps earlier than that). Contextual variables characterizing either the infant, the caregiver, or both determine the onset of a process that leads to a distressed, irritable infant. Although future multivariate studies may show that these contextual variables conform to a simple additive model, our best guess is that the interaction of infant with caregiver-contextual variables will be the most effective predictor of these negative outcomes.

The core of the model concerns the focus upon observed microsocial exchanges between infant and caregiver that define a powerful negative reinforcement mechanism leading to coercive child outcomes. The bidirectional nature of the effects means that the dyad itself can change dramatically in relatively short periods of time; both the infant and the caregiver become increasingly coercive.

There is no doubt in our minds that biological variables will be shown to make important contributions to the contingency mechanisms that determine these outcomes. Nevertheless, the prevention studies reviewed above also strongly suggest that these mechanisms, however determined they may be, are eminently malleable.

Toddler and Preschool Progression to Antisocial Outcomes

One of the fundamental problems in developmental psychology concerns modeling the changes in form of social behaviors that occur over time. In the present context, there are major differences between the irritable-distressed behavior of the 10-month-old infant and the temper tantrum and physical attack of a toddler in the preschool group. What mechanism, or mechanisms, account for these changes in the topography of infant coerciveness? What is the commensurate progression for caregiver behaviors? We hypothesized that the changes in infant coercive behaviors form an orderly sequence, a kind of progression that moves from distressed infant to toddler noncompliance and from there to temper tantrums to attention getting, hitting, fighting, and stealing (Patterson, 1992; Patterson et al., 1992). Unfortunately, the requisite data that would enable us to construct a comparable progression for caregivers and for peers are not yet available.

The formulation draws heavily from the longitudinal studies carried out at Pittsburgh by Daniel Shaw and his colleagues (Shaw & Winslow, 1997). The progression begins with the process that lays down the essential coercive exchanges between infant and caregiver. The data for a group of normal preschool boys (Eddy & Fagot, 1991) are summarized in Figure 2.3. Of the 59 boys, 44 were described by the mother as being disobedient; of these, about half were also described as having frequent temper tantrums (Patterson, 1992). The progression seems to be transitive in that 23 of the temper tantrum boys were also described as disobedient; only 1 child arrived at temper tantrums by some other route. About two thirds of the boys with temper tantrums had moved on to engaging in physical attacks. What is of particular interest is the fact that this orderly progression, as reflected in mother's ratings, was clearly in evidence when the boys were 18 months of age and remained in place when they were 4 to 5 years old. Further follow-up studies showed that boys who had moved to temper tantrums and hitting in the progression were also at significant risk to be identified later as stealing and fighting by their second grade teachers (Patterson et al., 1992). A similar progression (noncompliance, coercion, externalizing) emerges in the programmatic studies by Shaw and Winslow (1997) and colleagues.

The progression toward increasingly severe forms of coercive behaviors would be paralleled by a relative slowing in the development of prosocial skills. Presum-

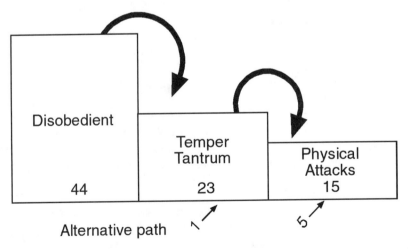

Figure 2.3. Basic coercion progression for boys, 24 to 36 months (Patterson, 1992).

ably, these two trajectories reflect the relative rates of reinforcement for coercive as compared to the relative rates of reinforcement for socially competent behaviors. Each child selects the set of behaviors that will maximize immediate payoffs. The implication for treatment is straightforward. The most rapid changes during intervention should occur when the focus is simultaneously on reducing relative rates of reinforcement for deviancy and increasing relative rates of reinforcement for prosocial behaviors.

Further Growth: Hyperactivity

The coercive behaviors continue to escalate in amplitude such that the toddlers' coercive behaviors are not only definitely noticeable to others but are a matter of some concern. Details of the escalation process are described in Patterson (1980) and Snyder, Edwards, McGraw, Kilgore, and Holton (1994). Presumably, this escalation provides one of the prime mechanisms producing changes in the form of coercive behavior. The findings from Snyder et al. (1994) showed that in conflict situations, members of distressed families are more likely than are members of normal families to escalate the amplitude of their coercive behavior. Members of distressed families are significantly more likely to reinforce escalation than are members of normal families (e.g., if one member escalates, the other is more likely to terminate the conflict). Escalating from yelling to hitting works. We also hypothesized that strong negative emotion works in a similar way. Anger seems to be one of the more powerful forms of escalation. In certain situations the use of anger would increase the likelihood of the other family member backing off. In this case, anger works. This implies that the expression of strong anger and rage is learned and is another byproduct of the coercion process. During intervention, as the child's coercive behavior become less functional, the accompanying anger also diminishes.

Rage and anger are some of the most salient features of the coercive children. As family despot, they control the family and all of its members. The angry frown and frequent explosions suggest that their reign is not a happy one.

The toddler is a predictable disruptor of family gatherings. Some of these attacks on other children inflict real injury. By the time the child is a preschooler, there has been an increase in new forms of problem behaviors. For example, the child is noticeably distractible, has difficulty in sitting still, interrupts, and talks incessantly without seeming to listen to what others are saying, breaks things, and may have one or more speech problems. Other family members begin to describe the child as a handful, and he or she might be labeled as immature or, perhaps, hyperactive. As shown in Figure 2.4, this process is well under way by 48 months. Not only is the child likely to be labeled as hyperactive, but also the parenting practices are clearly disrupted. This is most apparent during discipline confrontations where parental efforts to set limits are, by and large, ineffective.

The careful reviews of hyperactivity by Barkley and Biederman (1997) suggest that a large proportion of hyperactive problem children are identified as early as 2 to 4 years of age. Although Tryon's (1993) actigraph data showed higher levels of activity (even during sleep) for these children, one has the definite impression that the aversive quality of their interactions has more to do with the fact that their social behaviors simply do not fit very well. Their timing is off. They tend to be doing

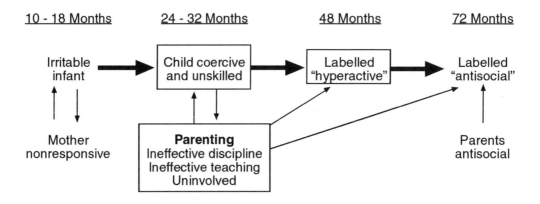

Figure 2.4. Progression to hyperactive and antisocial behaviors, of preschoolers.

the wrong things at the wrong point in time. Rather than hyperactive, the more appropriate label might be intrusive and or immature.

In passing, it is worth noting that hyperactivity has been shown to be significantly correlated with perinatal risk conditions and with lower SES (Barkley, 1990; Campbell, Breaux, Ewing, & Szumnowski, 1986; McGee, Williams, & Silva, 1984). Hyperactivity is also correlated with school failure and rejection by normal peers (Barkley, 1990; Hinshaw, 1992; Whalen, Henkker, Castro, & Granger, 1987). It is interesting to note that all of these risk variables also correlate with antisocial behavior.

Progression to Overt Antisocial

It is well known that measures of hyperactivity tend to be highly correlated with measures of antisocial behavior (Hinshaw, 1987). For example, at 10 years of age in the OYS, about 50% of the children scoring high on a composite score for hyperactivity also scored high on a composite score for antisocial behavior. We hypothesized that for preschool samples, hyperactivity and antisocial behavior are really two early points in the progression that lead to early-onset delinquency (Patterson, DeGarmo, & Knutson, 2000). The term comorbid implies different causal mechanisms. By way of contrast, we believe that the two sets of problem behaviors share a process in common. Presumably, they share disrupted parenting skills as a causal mechanism. To test these hypotheses, Patterson et al. (2000) studied 10-year-old boys and demonstrated, first, that there was a strong path from a latent construct for hyperactivity to a latent construct for antisocial. The path was .59 (p = .05). However, as noted in Figure 2.5, the path became nonsignificant when a latent construct for disrupted discipline was introduced (Patterson et al., in press). In keeping with the shared-maintenance hypothesis, the path from discipline to hyperactivity was .59 and from discipline to antisocial, it was .77. In effect, the relationship between hyperactivity and antisocial behavior is entirely mediated by parental discipline practices.

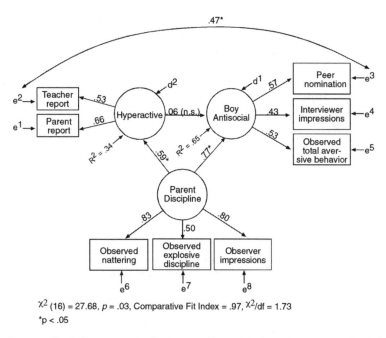

χ^2 (16) = 27.68, p = .03, Comparative Fit Index = .97, χ^2/df = 1.73

*p < .05

Figure 2.5. Parent discipline as a mediating mechanism (from Patterson, DeGarmo, & Knutsen, 2000).

However, some mechanism is required to explain why one individual moves forward in the progression and another does not. It would be expected that almost all antisocial boys would have also been identified as hyperactive; but only about half of the hyperactives moved on to become antisocial. We hypothesized that the key differentiating factor will be found in a special subset of parents who would not take antisocial behavior seriously enough to use effective discipline (i.e., parents who themselves were antisocial). In fact, several decades of studies showed that the presence of antisocial parents significantly differentiates hyperactive from antisocial children (Biederman et al., 1996; Hinshaw, 1987; Loney, Langehorne, Paternite, Whaley-Klahn, Blair-Broeker, & Hacker., 1980; Stewart, Cummings, Singer, & DeBlois, 1981). The study by Patterson et al. (2000) provides additional support for the hypothesis in that the path coefficient from the latent construct antisocial parent to antisocial child was .31 (p = .05). By contrast, the path coefficient from parent antisocial to hyperactivity was .19 (nonsignificant). In the same study, early-onset delinquency assessed at age 14 years by both official records and child self-report was significantly correlated both with the hyperactivity and the antisocial constructs assessed at age 10 years. However, in a SEM when the contribution of antisocial child behavior was partialled out, the contribution of hyperactivity became nonsignificant.

The Changing Context

The developmental changes in the topography of the child's behavior described here do not occur in splendid isolation. Rather, they are accompanied by profound changes in what the problem child and family members feel and in how they perceive each other. As noted earlier, there is a subtle but extremely important indirect contribution made to child outcomes made by contextual variables, such as stress, parental depression, divorce, poverty, and so forth. Presumably, changes in context may alter the parenting interactions and in so doing alter child outcomes. We now extend this model by noting that the quality of parent-child interactions and child outcomes may alter such contextual variables as emotions, attributions, and beliefs. Taken together, the two sets of feedback loops define a very dynamic system (Patterson & Granic, 2001).

The basic contextual model summarized in Figure 2.6 traces the contribution of culture to parental belief systems that, in turn, impact parenting practices. From this perspective, parental beliefs make only an indirect contribution to child outcomes as mediated by parenting practices. This is in keeping with conclusions reached by Darling and Steinberg's review (1993) showing that parental beliefs, values, standards, norms, and attitudes about childrearing were, by and large, correlated only at low levels with child outcomes. Rather, it seemed that what parents believed tended to impact what parents did, and in turn, it was the parenting practices that directly related to child outcomes. For example, different ethnic groups might have different beliefs about the function of family, what parenting might be, or the value of academic achievement. The extent to which these beliefs moderate and impact parenting behaviors directly determines child outcomes.

As noted earlier and now again in Figure 2.7, both parental and child anger are thought to be products of the process (e.g., much of the anger seen in these families is a product of escalation during conflict bouts). Anger and irritability are so much a part of daily life in these families that it is, therefore, not surprising to find many who believe that anger reduction should be the primary target for treatment of problem children. Although anger reduction by itself is not sufficient for producing change in child outcomes, Kendall, Ronan, and Epps (1991) showed that the addi-

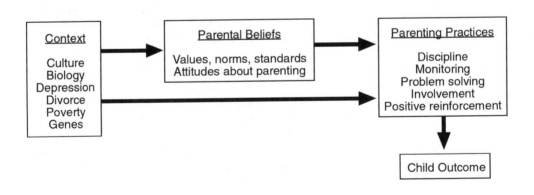

Note: The list of contextual variables is not intended to be exhaustive.

Figure 2.6. Parental beliefs, parenting behavior, and child outcomes.

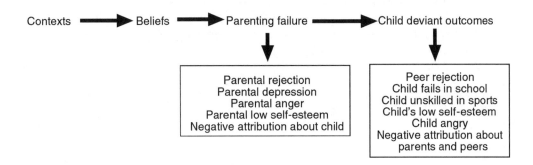

Figure 2.7.   Some predictable sequelae.

tion of anger control techniques to Parent Management Therapy significantly enhanced outcomes.

Rejection by the parent, and by the child for that matter, is another salient feature of these families. As was the case for anger, we hypothesized that parental rejection is a secondary product of the process rather than a primary cause. Correlational analyses of the OYS longitudinal data were consistent with the hypothesis. The data showed that frequent discipline confrontations and school failure both contributed significantly to parental rejection (Patterson, 1986). Again, probably because of its saliency, many therapists have traditionally focused on rebuilding the relationship of parent and child as the prime target for treatment. Although perhaps eminently sensible in terms of what can be seen in these families, relationship enhancement treatments have failed to survive in controlled studies; and this approach has instead is often employed as a comparison group in random assignment studies of treatment outcomes (Patterson, Dishion, & Chamberlain, 1993).

Angry siblings, peers, and parents are thought to be natural outcomes for the coercion process as is rejection by each of these social agents. These outcomes or products are thought, in turn, to disrupt future parenting practices (Patterson & Granic, 2001). The longitudinal data examined by Snyder and Schrepferman (2000) showed that the interaction between the maternal negative attribution about the child and the coercion variables significantly predicted future antisocial outcomes. However, maternal negative attributions alone did not predict long-term child outcomes. Negative emotion and negative attributions are thought to play important roles in that this more dynamic version of the coercion models by functioning as feedback loops that enhance future negative outcomes.

All of the variables listed in Figure 2.7 as sequelae have attracted theorists to give them primary status as direct causal agents and as focal points for treatment procedures. For example, low self-esteem and negative attributions are both viewed by some theorists as important causal mechanisms that directly determine child outcomes. Unfortunately, a good deal of the enthusiasm for causal status is based on simple correlational studies where it is shown that low self-esteem, anger, rejection, or negative attributions correlate positively antisocial behavior. In their enthusiasm to place emotional and social cognitive variables as causes, many researchers leap directly to the conclusion of direct causal status. In that each set of investigators restricts their vision to a resolute determination to reject the null hypothesis, none of these variables has been placed in serious competition with variables that involve contingencies of any kind or even compared negative emotion and social cognition in the same multivariate design.

We are currently funded for multivariate comparison studies of this kind and, shortly, should be able to provide a much more interesting discussion of the direct and indirect contributions made by each of these variables to antisocial outcomes (Patterson & Stoolmiller, 1999; Snyder & Schrepferman, 2000).

Summary

We have made a case for a coercive process that begins during the first year of life. Presumably, the initial process is the outcome of the interaction between two sets of variables. One set includes the biological dispositions (pre- and postbirth complications, genes) brought to the exchange by the infant. The other set concerns the dispositions brought by the caregiver to the exchange. The latter might include biological variables (perhaps irritability, depression, and hyporesponsiveness) or some aspects of the caregiver's history, such as social disadvantage, antisocial, or recent divorce. Although the process is thought to be eminently malleable, for some small group of infants, the process tends to move forward to increasing amplitude and more extreme expressions of coercion. During the toddler years, it also becomes apparent that the process is accompanied by a wide range of social incompetence (see chapter 3 this volume).

As the coercion process unfolds, it generates negative emotions and negative cognitions, not only for the problem child but for family members and peers alike. These by-products of the process are thought to function as feedback loops that increase the risk for increasingly disrupted interactions in the future with a commensurate increase in future negative child outcomes.

The remainder of this section of the volume traces the trajectory that leads to chronic juvenile and adult offending.

3

Competence in Early Development

Leslie D. Leve, Katherine C. Pears, and Philip A. Fisher

Research on coercion theory provides strong evidence that inadequate discipline and poor parental monitoring are key factors in the emergence and maintenance of antisocial behavior. However, psychosocial maladjustment is not the only outcome of interest—it is critical to society that children become competent and productive adults. In this chapter, we broaden the focus of the coercion model to examine the processes involved in the development of competency in early childhood, a less developed area of research at the Oregon Social Learning Center (OSLC). We consider the roles that coercion theory parenting constructs (positive reinforcement, effective discipline, and monitoring), in combination with the early contextual variables of social referencing, attachment, and scaffolding (i.e. parental instructional style), might play in the development of competence in young children. We draw on a variety of sources for the discussion in this chapter. Numerous OSLC studies have included such contextual variables. In some instances, the research tested the validity of direct versus parenting-mediated paths to child outcomes. More commonly, the research examined various sub-components of the model—for example, the relationship between attachment and parenting characteristics.

Child Competence as an Outcome Variable

There is an extensive literature on child competence spanning the past two decades. One strain of research in this area has focused on how children in adverse circumstances manage to thrive (Black, Hutcheson, Dubowitz, Starr, & Berenson-Howard, 1996; Brody & Flor, 1998; Brody, Stoneman, & McCoy, 1994; Diaz, Neal, & Vachio, 1991; McCord, 1991; O'Connor et al., 2000; Sameroff, Bartko, Baldwin, Baldwin, & Seifer, 1998; Sameroff & Seifer, 1983). Other work has examined child competence under typical developmental conditions (Keogh, Juvonen, & Bernheimer, 1989; Roberts & Strayer, 1987; Verschueren & Marcoen, 1999). Numerous researchers have found evidence that competence is a developmentally continuous construct, such that early competence is related to competence later in development (e.g., Black et al., 1996; Cairns, Cairns, Xie, Leung, & Hearne, 1998; Englund, Levy, Hyson, & Sroufe, 2000). In addition, positive associations of competence with prosocial interaction and emotion regulation (Connolly & Bruner, 1974; Roberts & Strayer, 1987; Sroufe, 1989) make competence a good proxy for overall psychosocial adjustment.

Roberts (1986) described two domains of competence. *Cognitive competence*, which involves goal-oriented behavior resulting from an underlying planning process

(Baumrind, 1971; Block & Block, 1980), and *social competence*, which involves behaviors facilitating the initiation and maintenance of positive interaction and the ability to regulate affect within such interactions (Baumrind, 1971; Lamb, Easterbrooks, & Holden, 1980; Sroufe, Schork, Motti, Lawroski, & LaFreniere, 1985). Although these two domains are conceptually separate, in most interactional contexts, both may operate simultaneously (Matas, Arend, & Sroufe, 1978; Roberts, 1986).

Some research has examined how competence develops (or fails to develop) within the context of parent-child interaction. For example, Olson, Bates, and Bayles (1984) examined the role of mother-infant interaction in the development of children's cognitive competence. Using data from a longitudinal study, Olson and colleagues conducted a path analysis and found that maternal warmth at 6 months, instructional interaction at 13 months, and verbal interaction at 24 months (in combination with socioeconomic status) were strong predictors of cognitive competence at 24 months.

Roberts (1986) examined child competence within the context of parental warmth, control, and responsiveness, considering the extent to which the relationship between child competence and parenting fit a linear model. The results suggested that nonlinear models are more appropriate. In a second study, Roberts and Strayer (1987) examined parental responses to children's emotional distress and how these responses related to child competence. The results suggested that responsiveness was an important predictor of competence, that it was distinct from the parenting dimension of "parental warmth," and that the responsiveness-competence relationship may have been nonlinear in nature.

Brody and Flor (1998) tested a model in which "no-nonsense" parenting, mother-child relationship quality, and maternal involvement in school were treated as proximal variables in the prediction of competence. In this study (conducted on a sample of single-parent, African American families), parenting variables were mediated through the child's self-regulation, and thus were indirectly connected to cognitive and social competence. Black et al. (1996) also examined competence among children in African American families, although their sample involved low-income, urban families. They conducted hierarchical multiple regressions in which parental nurturance and control (along with child age and context of data collection—feeding or play) were used to predict the child's interactive communication and affective regulation. Although their results were somewhat weaker than what others have reported, parental nurturance contributed significantly to the prediction of child communication, and parental control contributed significantly to the prediction of child affective regulation.

Diaz et al. (1991) considered child competence within the framework of parental teaching style, or scaffolding (Vygotsky, 1978). They compared low- and high-risk families, finding that high-risk mothers were more likely to employ controlling teaching strategies. However, in their study, a cognitive component involving maternal attributions of child competence proved to be the strongest predictor of the child's successful task performance.

Parenting and Competence: Prior OSLC Research with School-aged Children

The link between family interaction and the development of competence is highly relevant to the coercion model. For example, competence has often been viewed as the converse of antisocial behavior (e.g., McCord, 1991). In the aforementioned research on competence, there is considerable conceptual overlap between the parenting variables related to competence and the coercion theory parenting constructs. For instance, control (as described in a number of the previously discussed competency studies) and discipline (as described in coercion theory) share a number of characteristics, as do warmth and positive reinforcement. Additionally, Brody and Flor's (1998) measure of maternal involvement in school may be seen as an analogue for monitoring, and their concept of "no-nonsense parenting" within African American families is defined in similar terms as "effective discipline" (Patterson, Reid, & Dishion, 1992). The similarity between these parenting measures and the coercion theory constructs, and the strength of the relationship between these parenting measures and competence, leads us to hypothesize that discipline, monitoring, and the use of positive reinforcement plays a central role in the development of child competence.

Patterson et al. (1992) examined the relationship between discipline, monitoring, positive reinforcement and three child measures related to competence: academic skills, peer relations, and self-esteem. Academic skills may be seen as a component of cognitive competence, and peer relations may be seen as an aspect of social competence. Self-esteem, though not easily categorized within cognitive or social competence, may be both a precursor and a sequela of both forms of competence.

Analyses were conducted on data from the Oregon Youth Study (OYS). The research strategy for this study included data collection from two cohorts of youth and their families, thereby allowing for an examination of the replicability of the results. Correlations among the measures when the boys were age 10 are shown in Table 3.1. Significant correlations were obtained between parent discipline and academic skills and between parent discipline and peer relations (these results were replicated across both cohorts). Monitoring was significantly correlated with academic skills, peer relations, and self-esteem in Cohort 1, but not in Cohort 2. Positive reinforcement was significantly correlated with academic skills across both cohorts, with peer relations in Cohort 2, and with self-esteem in Cohort 1.

Shifting to a multivariate analysis strategy, Patterson et al. (1992) conducted a series of regression analyses in which a variety of family management variables were regressed on measures of child behavior. The family management variables included monitoring, discipline, positive reinforcement, problem solving, and parental involvement. Data were analyzed by cohort; results are shown in Table 3.2. The parenting variables accounted for 12% and 21% of the variance in the

Table 3.1. Correlations Between Child Behaviors and Parental Monitoring, Discipline, and Positive Reinforcement in the OYS Sample.

| Child Behavior | Parenting Skill | | | | | |
| | Monitoring | | Discipline | | Positive Reinforcement | |
	Cohort I	Cohort II	Cohort I	Cohort II	Cohort I	Cohort II
Academic Skills	.36***	.15	.29**	.32**	.23*	.18*
Peer Relations	.30**	.16	.36***	.45***	.03	.16*
Self-esteem	.35***	.18	.15	.18	.18*	.14

*p < .05. ** p < .01. *** p < .001.

Table 3.2. Multivariate Analyses for the Relation Between Family Management Skills and Child Behaviors in the OYS Sample.

Child Behavior	Parenting Skill[a]					
	Monitoring	Discipline	Reinforcement	Problem Solving	Involvement	R^2
Academic Skills	.29	.22	.09	.14	-.09	.21
	.10	.28	.01	.10	-.04	.12
Peer Relations	.25	.32	-.14	.06	.02	.19
	.06	.47	-.13	.07	.12	.24
Self-esteem	.28	.04	-.02	-.25	.18	.22
	.02	.16	-.08	-.05	.46	.23

[a]Standard partial betas for Cohort I (upper row) and Cohort II (lower row).

academic skills measure, 19% to 24% of the variance in the peer relations measure, and 22% to 23% of the variance in the self-esteem measure. These values fell short of the goal to account for 30% of the variance in key criterion variables. An examination of the standard partial beta weights for each of the predictors revealed discipline as the strongest predictor of academic skills and peer relations (but not of self-esteem).

Social Contextual Factors, Parenting, and Competence

Although the OSLC results are consistent with other research examining the role of parenting in the development of competence, the relationships between independent and dependent variables are weaker than those obtained in models predicting antisocial behavior from the same parenting constructs. There may be a variety of reasons for this. First, there may be less variability in OSLC measures of positive outcomes, which would result in a restriction of range and would decrease the magnitude of the relations among measures (Stoolmiller, 1998a). Second, the assessment of competence employed in these analyses is limited in comparison to those typically incorporated into analyses examining negative outcomes using the coercion model: It is based on the report of a single informant—the parent—in response to items on a single questionnaire. Our experience with the development of latent construct measures (see Patterson & Capaldi, 1991) suggests that more adequate measures of competence, involving multi-agent, multi-method assessment procedures, would provide for much more powerful tests of models involving the prediction of competence.

A third reason for weakened relationships involves the age of the children in the sample and the cross-sectional nature of this data. Although competence is clearly an outcome of interest throughout childhood and adolescence, the contextual interactional processes may be critical during infancy and early childhood. As children age, competence may be more self-reinforcing, requiring less input from parents. To examine this issue, it would be necessary to explore data gathered earlier in childhood than were available for Patterson et al. (1992). It would be especially interesting to examine longitudinal data to compare the strength of these competence models and the relative contributions of parenting variables within the models at different ages.

Fourth, there is a tendency to conceptualize competence and antisocial behavior as opposite ends of a single continuum. Though somewhat logical, there are inherent problems in this approach. Competence does not preclude antisocial behavior, and not all of those children who exhibit low levels of antisocial behavior are socially and cognitively competent. For example, in reporting on adult follow-up data from the Cambridge-Somerville Study, McCord (1991) found that 15% of the sample demonstrated behavioral maladjustment (e.g., criminal behavior or schizophrenia) and high achievement (e.g., high occupational status), suggesting a pattern of high antisocial behavior and high competency. Conversely, 29% of the sample demonstrated healthy behavioral adjustment and low achievement, suggesting a pattern of low antisocial behavior and low competency. To better understand the development of competence, we propose that competence and antisocial behavior be conceptualized as separate constructs. Viewed as such, analyses might focus less on whether the absence of coercive parenting produces competent behavior. Rather, analyses might focus on the extent to which the degree of competence and the degree of antisocial behavior result from particular interactional processes in the social context of the family.

Fifth, contextual factors may play a greater role in the prediction of competence than they do in the prediction of antisocial behavior. It is possible to account for a great deal of variance in antisocial outcomes through family management variables alone, but these variables may insufficiently explain how competence develops. In such analyses, the roles of social referencing, attachment, and parental teaching style may play a more proximal role in the development of child competence.

Our examination of competence in early development includes a discussion of research evaluating the prediction of child adjustment outcomes from social referencing, attachment, and scaffolding variables. We focus primarily on data from the toddler and preschool years and hypothesize that, at these younger ages, early social contextual factors may have their greatest impact on the development of competence. We provide a description of how each factor relates to social competencies and how each relates to aggression and coercive behavior. We also examine the relationship between each contextual factor and parenting behavior when there is data to support this link (e.g., in the attachment and scaffolding research). We conclude with a conceptual developmental model that articulates the relationships between early social contextual factors, parenting variables, and child competence, suggesting directions for future research to help evaluate this model and its component parts. Throughout our discussion, we rely on multi-method data, when available.

Social Referencing

The concept of *social referencing* refers to the phenomenon in which people respond to situations or stimuli according to emotional cues from others around them (Feinman, 1992). Social referencing, a behavior that appears as early as 1 year of age, may be linked to psychosocial adjustment through its effects on children's abilities to detect social cues. We hypothesize that children who more effectively look to others for emotional support and guidance may be more likely to develop social competence in family and peer interactions. The ability to solicit support may facilitate the accomplishment of tasks and therefore the child's sense of competence. Conversely, children who less effectively look to others for support and guidance may be at particular risk for later disruptive behavior. Deficits in the ability to accurately detect and interpret cues of emotion and intention in others has been linked to social aggression in children (Crick, 1994), which is a primary characteristic of antisocial children.

Social Referencing and Social Competence

Pears (1997) examined the social referencing behavior of 18- to 21-month-olds ($N = 41$) who were divided into groups of children at low or high risk for the development of behavior problems. The high-risk children—offspring of the OYS participants (Patterson et al., 1992)—were considered at high risk for the development of behavior problems on the basis of their fathers' prior delinquency rates, the young age of their parents, and their family's low socioeconomic status. The parents of the low-risk children—drawn from the community to be an age-matched control sample—were older, had more education, and had higher socioeconomic status than the parents of the OYS children.

In the Pears (1997) study, all of the children were presented with an ambiguous stimulus (e.g., a motorized ball that bounced around at random and produced a high-pitched laughing sound). The frequency of the children's social referencing to and positive affect sharing with their mothers in response to the stimulus was compared between groups. The groups were also compared on their latency to look to the parent after the ambiguous stimulus was presented.

Although the low- and high-risk children did not differ on the frequency of their social referencing, the low-risk children initially looked to their mothers about twice as quickly as the high-risk children. Furthermore, low-risk children were significantly more likely to share positive affect with their parents than were high-risk children. The fact that low-risk children were significantly quicker to look to their parents suggests that low-risk children may be receptive and comfortable using their parents as resources for emotional support. Conversely, the high-risk children's latency to look at their mothers and the low frequency of shared affect looks suggests that these children might be reluctant to interact with their parents emotionally. A hesitancy to seek out and detect cues about emotion and intention in others may, in turn, lead to a misattribution of hostile intent in others. The tendency to misattribute has been found to differentiate socially aggressive children from their non-aggressive peers (Crick, 1994). The roots of such problem behaviors as social aggression may therefore extend back to social referencing behavior in toddlerhood.

These results have implications for our consideration of the development of competence. The shorter social referencing response latencies of low-risk children suggests confidence that their parents will serve as reliable sources of information. Such confidence would most likely develop with repeated instances of parents providing cues that facilitate the achievement of desired outcomes. To the extent that a child has such a parent or caregiver, that child may develop a greater sense of competence than a child whose parent or caregiver is unavailable or provides unreliable social cues.

The link between social referencing behavior and later social competence has been demonstrated in a longitudinal study of the same children used in the above study (Pears, 1999). The high- and low-risk children, whose social referencing was measured when they were 18 to 21 months old, were brought back into the laboratory at 48 months of age to participate in play groups with their same-age peers. Their behavior during the playgroups was coded in vivo. Behavior was aggregated into a measure of the proportion of time that the children spent engaged in positive social behaviors, such as talking, sharing, and playing normatively, and the proportion of time that the children spent engaged in negative social behaviors, such as physical aggression, verbal aggression, and directive behavior. The child's frequency of social referencing at 18 months significantly predicted the child's positive social behavior towards peers at 48 months—higher rates of child social referencing resulted in higher proportions of child positive social behavior.

These results suggest that social referencing may affect some social competence outcomes in children. Children who look to their parents for cues about how to respond when they are 18 months old might become better detectors of emotional cues in their peers and, hence, have more competent relationships with their peers. Using the same sample, positive correlations were found between the frequency of social referencing at 18 months and emotion recognition and the ability to take the affective perspective of another person at 36 months (Pears, 1999). Social referencing may generate self-confidence and the ability to successfully rely on peers for emotional support later in childhood.

To summarize, it appears that social referencing behaviors in infancy and toddlerhood may represent one variable related to the development of competence and antisocial behavior, specifically in terms of peer relations. Further studies are needed to examine the relationship between social referencing behaviors and parenting styles. Parents who are more supportive, reinforcing, and effective at discipline may have children who are more able to rely on them for social cues; alternatively, parents who engage in coercive interactions with their young toddlers may essentially train their children to look elsewhere for emotional support.

Attachment Style

The parent-child attachment relationship is a second domain in which competent social interactions with a caregiver are hypothesized to lead to competent family and peer interactions later in childhood. The attachment paradigm has been widely used within developmental psychology for studying individual differences in child adjustment. Bowlby (1969) noted that the survival of infants depends on their abilities to maintain proximity to and contact with their primary caregivers. According to Bowlby, from the very beginning of life, the infant uses behaviors, such as crying or fussing, to keep his or her attachment figure near. Over the span of the first 12 to 18 months of life, infants learn which of their own behaviors elicit desired responses from the caregiver; infants adapt their own behaviors to fit those of their caregiver, resulting in parent-child attachments of varying quality.

The parent-child attachment relationship is thought to influence the likelihood that a child will be aggressive towards peers and that peers will respond negatively. Thus, attachment may affect the development of antisocial behavior—as discussed in chapter 5, one of the hallmarks of the antisocial child is aggressive behavior towards peers. Conversely, aggressive children also exhibit deficits in their prosocial behavior (Patterson, 1982; Patterson et al., 1992). Researchers have found that insecurely attached children are more likely to be aggressive and negative towards their peers than are securely attached children (Cohn, 1990; Park & Waters, 1989; Troy & Sroufe, 1987; Turner, 1991; Youngblade & Belsky, 1992). However, studies have differed on which insecure attachment group tends to be more aggressive. Some studies have found that insecure-avoidant children are more likely to aggress against their peers (Troy & Sroufe, 1987); other studies have found that insecure-ambivalent children are more aggressive (Cohn, 1990).

The most common procedure for assessing attachment in 12- to 18-month-old children is the Strange Situation (Ainsworth & Wittig, 1969), in which young children participate in a series of increasingly stressful separations from and reunions with their caregiver. Children are rated based on their responses to this series of separations and reunions: Secure (e.g., infants who explore freely in the caregiver's presence and use the caregiver as a source of comfort if distressed by separations); Insecure-Avoidant (e.g., infants who explore without sharing affect with the caregiver and avoid physical contact or ignore the mother even during reunion episodes); or Insecure-Ambivalent (e.g., infants who are wary of the unfamiliar, show little exploration, and are ineffective in gaining comfort from the caregiver during reunions because of anger or resistance to contact).

The Preschool Assessment of Attachment (PAA; Crittenden, 1995), an attachment classification system developed for preschoolers, is designed to take into account the changes that occur between toddlerhood and the preschool years and how these changes affect the attachment relationship. As children become more verbal and able to negotiate separations with the caregiver, their reactions to these separations change. In the PAA, children are classified as Defended, Aecure, or Coercive. Preschoolers who are classified as defended are similar to toddlers classified as Insecure-Avoidant in the Strange Situation. They do not seek to negotiate separations and reunions with their caregivers; instead they attempt to handle all of their emotional responses by themselves. Secure preschool children are similar to the children classified as secure in the Strange Situation. These children negotiate with their caregivers, communicate their feelings effectively, and receive aid from their caregivers in managing these feelings. Coercive preschoolers are similar to the children classified as insecure-ambivalent in the Strange Situation. They do not attempt to negotiate with their caregivers; instead, they use intense affect (often anger or helplessness) to elicit the desired response from their caregivers. This behavior pattern is similar to that in the coercive family interactions observed by Patterson (1982).

While there is some continuity from the Strange Situation classification system to the PAA 30-month classification, there are some important distinctions between the two insecure attachment classifications. In a study of 96 children who were classified at 18 months using the Strange Situation and at 30 months using the PAA, Fagot and Pears (1996) found that a significant proportion of children switched from Insecure-Avoidant to Coercive (see Table 3.3 for n/attachment classification information). Fagot and Pears offered an explanation for the movement from the Insecure-Avoidant to the Coercive attachment style. They stated that an initial strategy for an infant faced with either an unresponsive, inappropriately intrusive parent or a threatening, inconsistent parent may be to withdraw and avoid.

Table 3.3. Attachment Classification for the Same Children at 18 and 30 Months of Age.

18 Months—Strange Situation	N	30 Months—Crittenden PAA Classification		
		Defended	Secure	Coercive
Insecure-avoidant	38	18	2	18
Secure	49	5	36	8
Insecure-resistant	9	0	0	9
Total	96	23	38	35

Note. PAA = Preschool Assessment of Attachment

However, as the children grow older, those with insensitive parents may withdraw even further, becoming defended, while children with inconsistent but potentially explosive parents may develop a coercive, threatening interactive style.

Attachment, Social Competence, and Antisocial Behavior

To examine the relationship between attachment and peer relations in toddlers, Fagot and Kavanagh (1990) measured attachment classification (using the Strange Situation) in 81 children at 18 months. Subsequently, parent reports of problem behaviors was collected at 24, 27, 30, and 48 months using the Child Behavior Checklist (CBCL; Achenbach, 1985) and a telephone interview for parents of toddlers (Kavanagh, 1986). In addition, the children's coercive interactions were observed in home and peer playgroup settings at 18 and 30 months.

Analyses suggested that teachers and observers of the children's peer playgroup behavior rated the Insecure-Avoidant girls as more difficult to deal with and as having poorer peer relationships. However, there were no significant relationships between attachment and parent-reported child coercive behavior or between attachment and observed coercive behavior in the home and playgroup settings (Fagot & Kavanagh, 1990). One explanation for why the teacher and observer ratings showed a relationship between attachment and coercive behavior (in girls) and why the parent and coded behavioral ratings did not is that the teachers and observers see the children in a different setting than the parents. They may have observed interactional styles that were not identified by the behavior coding system and that only manifested themselves outside of the home setting. Teachers and observers also used broader rating scales that asked for a rating of a relationship, rather than just aggressive, noncompliant behavior, so they may have picked up on other behaviors that made these Insecure-Avoidant girls more coercive to deal with.

A second study highlighted the negative effects of having a coercive attachment style. Fagot and Pears (1996) examined the peer play behaviors of 30-month-olds ($N = 96$) whose attachment had been classified using the PAA. The children had attended playgroups at the University of Oregon between the ages of 18 and 30 months. Their play behavior with peers had been coded in vivo for aversive and prosocial interactions. Children classified as Coercive at 30 months of age had significantly fewer prosocial interactions with peers than did children who were classified as Secure or Defended—means for prosocial interactions for the Secure, Defended, and Coercive groups were .22, .16, and -.25, respectively.

When these children were 7 years old, their teachers were asked to fill out the Teacher Report Form (TRF) of the CBCL (Achenbach, 1991a) and the Walker-McConnell Scale of Social Competence and School Adjustment, a questionnaire measure of peer competence, peer acceptance, and social skills (Walker & McConnell, 1988). Coercive children were rated higher on internalizing and externalizing behavior on the TRF than were Secure or Defended children. In addition, using the Walker-McConnell teacher ratings, children who had been classified as Secure at 30 months received more positive peer ratings than children in the Coercive group. Secure children were rated as having fewer problems with their peers than were Coercive children. Being well liked by peers and having fewer problems with peers are characteristics of social competence (see Table 3.4).

Fagot and Pears (1996) noted that Coercive children more clearly fit the profile of disobedient risk-takers than did Defended children. Coercive children, who are likely to have been Insecure-Ambivalent as toddlers, are thought to develop intense and exaggerated affect in order to elicit the attention of inconsistent caregivers (Crittenden, 1995) Thus, these children are more likely to resemble children caught in the coercive cycle of using negative affects and behaviors to get their way from caregivers (Patterson, 1982). Defended children, on the other hand, are predicted to withdraw and become affectively inhibited, so they are less likely to become aggressive (Crittenden, 1995).

Other studies have found that Insecure-Ambivalent children, who are believed to become Coercive, are the group most likely to receive negative reactions from their peers. Jacobson and Wille (1986) found that, over time, peer responses to children who had been classified as Insecure-Ambivalent became more resistant and disruptive. Fagot (1997) studied the play behaviors of 156 toddlers whose attachment had been classified using the Strange Situation at 18 months. The children classified as Insecure-Ambivalent were less likely to receive positive responses from their peers when they made a positive initiation and were more likely to receive negative reactions to their positive initiations. Thus, the peers of Insecure-Ambivalent children may treat these children differently from a very young age (see Table 3.5).

Table 3.4. Attachment Classification for the Same Children at 18 and 30 Months of Age Preschool Attachment Classification and Teacher Ratings at Age 7.

	Crittenden PAA Attachment Classification at 30 months (N)			
	A (22)	B (35)	C (33)	Comparisons
Teacher ratings of Problem behavior on the TRF				
Externalizing (M raw score)	53	51	60*	C > B, A
Internalizing (M raw score)	55	54	62*	C > B, A
Teacher ratings of Peer Behavior on the Walker-McConnell				
Positive peer scale sum	3.6	3.8	3.2*	B > C
Peer problems scale sum	7.1	6.8	9.3*	B < C

Note. A = Defended; B = Secure; C = Coercive; PAA = Preschool Assessment of Attachment; TFR = Teacher Report Form.

*$p < .05$.

Table 3.5. Peer Responses to Toddler-Initiated Behaviors as a Function of Toddler Attachment Classification.

	Attachment classification						
	A		B		C		
Playgroup behavior	M	(SD)	M	(SD)	M	(SD)	F (2, 153)
Peer positive to child positive	.06	(0.72)	.17	(1.23)	-.54	(1.07)	3.78*
Peer negative to child negative	.03	(0.94)	-.06	(0.76)	-.00	(0.70)	0.92
Peer negative to child positive	.45	(1.20)	-.13	(1.06)	.65	(0.48)	4.35*

Note. Mean values in the table are z-scores. A = Insecure-avoidant; B = Secure; C = Insecure-ambivalent.

*Group C is different than Group A and than Group B, $p < .05$.

Taken together, these associations between attachment and peer relations help to link attachment and the development of coercive and competent behavior. Recent studies at OSLC have indicated that children in the Insecure-Ambivalent/Coercive attachment category tend to have the *least* competency with peers, although Insecure-Avoidant/Defended children may also be at risk for incompetent peer relations. Secure children clearly demonstrate the most socially competent behavior. These links to coercive and competent peer interactions are an essential step in the cycle of coercion that characterizes antisocial families. Unfortunately, little research has measured antisocial behavior and social competencies as separate domains in which to examine how children of secure and insecure attachments fare.

Attachment and Parenting

Not only does attachment have an influence on children's social competencies and antisocial behavior, but it also relates to effective parenting skills. Research has demonstrated that the behavior of the mothers of children in each attachment category varies (Ainsworth, Blehar, Waters, & Wall, 1978; Crittenden, 1995). Mothers of Secure children tend to be responsive to their infant's needs and to be willing to negotiate with their young child, helping them learn to handle their emotions on their own. Mothers of Insecure-Avoidant toddlers and Defended preschoolers tend to be less responsive to their children's needs, often rebuffing their attachment-seeking behaviors. This accounts for the children's later inability to use their caregivers to soothe them or help them manage their emotions. Finally, mothers of Insecure-Ambivalent toddlers and Coercive preschoolers tend to be inconsistent in their responses to their children. Thus, their children may not be sure whether to approach or avoid the caregivers and may not be able to control their emotional responses because they have received inconsistent feedback.

Attachment style also appears to be related to parent's ability to teach their children to solve problems effectively. This is another area in which attachment may affect the development of antisocial behavior, as children who display problematic behaviors often have poor problem-solving skills (Patterson, 1982; Shure & Spivack, 1972). Researchers have found that the parents of insecurely attached children display less support and a lower quality of assistance to their children during problem-solving tasks than do mothers of securely attached children (Frankel and Bates, 1990; Matas et al., 1978).

Fagot, Gauvain, and Kavanagh (1996) replicated and extended these results by differentiating between the two groups of insecurely attached children. They examined the teaching behaviors of the mothers of 93 children who had been classified using the Strange Situation categories at 18 months. The mothers and their children engaged in two problem-solving tasks when the children were 30 months of age. Mothers were told to give their children as much assistance as they thought that the children needed. The researchers found that mothers of insecure-ambivalent children gave less assistance on the tasks and showed more disapproval than did mothers of securely attached children.

Pears and Fagot (1995) examined the behavior of mothers whose children were classified using the PAA at 30 months. The children and their mothers were involved in two problem-solving tasks. The mothers of Coercive children demonstrated less appropriate assistance to their children during a difficult problem-solving task than did mothers of Secure children (as measured by observational ratings). During a task that should have been relatively simple for the children to solve, mothers of Defended children gave their children significantly more direction than did mothers of Secure children.

In their study of 96 children and their mothers, Fagot and Pears (1996) found that mothers of Coercive children used fewer instructional behaviors in the home than did mothers of Defended and Secure children (see Table 3.6). Mothers of Coercive children also tended to respond positively to their children's passive behaviors more often than did mothers of Defended and Secure children. However, mothers of Coercive children responded to their children's prosocial behaviors and attempts to communicate with positives less frequently than did mothers of securely attached children. Finally, mothers of Coercive children responded negatively to children's passive and negative behavior more often than did mothers of children in the other two groups. When the children's academic achievement was measured at the age of 7 years, Coercive children fared significantly worse at math than children in the other two groups and significantly worse at reading than Defended children—school failure is a prototypical behavior pattern in antisocial children (Patterson, 1982). These results suggest that mothers of Coercive children spend less time instructing children and are fairly indiscriminate with their reinforcement behaviors, tending to respond positively to passive behavior rather than rewarding appropriate behaviors.

Findings from these studies on the relation between attachment and parent's teaching behaviors also suggest that Insecure-Ambivalent (and later, Coercive) children may not receive adequate instruction from their parents in problem-solving skills. This is not surprising, given the likelihood for these parents to be inconsistent in their parenting. The lack of instruction and inconsistent parenting, in turn, may affect the child's achievement and interpersonal relations.

Scaffolding

In the toddler and preschool years, young children are rapidly developing new linguistic and cognitive skills. At this learning point, parents' cognitive teaching styles may be a critical components affecting children's social and cognitive competencies.

Table 3.6. Conditional Probability of Maternal Responses to Child Behavior in the Home at 30 Months of Age by Attachment Classification

Mother response to child behavior observed at 30 months	Crittenden PAA Attachment Classification (N)			
	A (23)	B (38)	C (35)	Comparison
Instructional to				
Passive	.16	.15	.09*	A, B > C
Negative	.18	.13	.09	
Prosocial	.21	.15	.10**	A > C
Communication	.45	.29	.28**	A > C
Positive to				
Passive	.07	.07	.10*	C > A, B
Negative	.04	.04	.09	
Prosocial	.21	.27	.14**	B > C
Communication	.12	.15	.09*	B > C
Negative to				
Passive	.03	.03	.06*	C > A, B
Negative	.02	.04	.06*	C > A, B
Prosocial	.01	.01	.01	
Communication	.01	.01	.01	

Note: A = Defended; B = Secure; C = Coercive; PAA = Preschool Assessment of Attachment.

*$p < .05$; **$p < .01$.

Fagot and colleagues have studied this time period extensively, focusing on an aspect of positive parenting called *scaffolding*. Parental scaffolding is meant to characterize the notion that a child's problem solving is guided by an adult or by a more experienced partner who structures and models ways for the child to solve a problem. The structure provided in the communication serves as a scaffold for the learner, providing a bridge between old and new knowledge. This notion of scaffolding has been largely influenced by Vygotsky's (1978) notion of the zone of proximal development.

Scaffolding and Cognitive Competence

To examine parental scaffolding skills and how they relate to children's cognitive competencies, Fagot and Gauvain (1997) measured mothers' observed instructional interactions with their 18-month-old child. Observed maternal cognitive assistance and support were measured during a series of puzzle-type tasks when the child was 30 months old. Children's cognitive performance was measured when the children were 5 years old by assessing the number of errors the child made on a solo puzzle task. The solo puzzle task was similar to the puzzle task (with parental assistance) at 30 months. Cognitive performance was also assessed by teacher ratings of the children's learning problems using the TRF of the CBCL (Achenbach, 1991a) and by scores on the Arithmetic and Vocabulary subscales of the Wechsler Preschool and Primary Scale of Intelligence (WPPSI; Wechsler, 1967). The results suggest that maternal scaffolding at earlier ages was related to *each* of these three cognitive competency outcomes. For example, observed maternal cognitive assistance at 30 months was related to fewer child performance errors in the laboratory task and to fewer learning problems as rated by the child's teacher. In addition, children whose mothers had given them more cognitive assistance at 30 months performed better on the WPPSI Arithmetic and Vocabulary subscales. These results suggest that parental scaffolding skills can have an effect on the development of children's cognitive competencies later in childhood. These relationships between parental scaffolding and child competence are especially pronounced here, as the authors found correlations across quite different domains of measurement—teacher report, a solo-task, and a standardized intelligence task. Next, we questioned whether or not parental scaffolding also predicts children's competencies in the social realm.

Scaffolding and Social Competence

Preliminary evidence supports the hypothesized link between parental scaffolding skills and children's social competence within the family. Fagot (1998) examined the cooperative and affectively positive behavior of 3-, 5-, and 7-year-olds in families where parents provided significant social structure and scaffolding interactions with their child. Parent-child dyads were observed during hypothetical vignettes: The parent was presented with a common social situation and was asked to help prepare their child for this situation. Topics included going to a birthday party, visiting friends with a baby, and going to a petting zoo. The frequency of problem solutions that parents offered in their conversations with the child was coded. Problem solutions were coded because they represent a type of scaffolding behavior manifested by parents during a social-interactional task. The analyses of parental problem solutions suggested that children who were provided with more problem solutions were more cooperative with their mothers and fathers and displayed more positive affects with their mothers. These findings suggested that, within the family, effective scaffolding in the parents was related to socially competent behavior in the child. Our next goal was to examine whether this pattern of correlations holds outside of the family and into the peer realm.

To examine the prediction of competence in children's peer relations, Leve and Fagot (1997) measured parental warmth and parental scaffolding using observational methodology with children at 18 months and at 5 years ($N = 159$). The warmth and scaffolding measures constituted an effective parenting construct. Children's prosocial peer relations were then assessed using a multi-measure strategy at 7 years. The 7-year-old positive peer construct included (1) teacher–reported peer competence, (2) positive observed peer behavior during laboratory interactions with a friend, and (3) observed scaffolding skills during laboratory interactions with a friend. A multiple group structural equation model was run to assess whether the prediction model differed for boys and girls; the best-fitting model is presented in Figure 3.1. The model suggests that the Time 1 effective parenting construct predicted children's positive peer relations at age 7, $\chi^2 (18) = 26.76$, $p = .08$, GFI = .90. The relationship between effective parenting and positive peer relations was only significant for boys. Therefore, it may be that boys learn a style of interaction from their parents that is then generalized to their

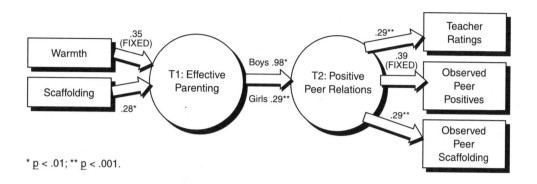

Figure 3.1. Longitudinal prediction of positive peer relations from effective parenting.

interactions with others. There is evidence that children learn negative behavioral interactions with peers from coercive, negative interactions with parents (Dishion, 1990a); these results suggest that the counterpart is also true: Children (at least boys) learn prosocial interactional skills after experiencing positive, scaffolding interactions with their parents.

Scaffolding and Parenting Variables

In addition to affecting social and cognitive competence outcomes, scaffolding behavior is also hypothesized to relate to a parent's positive attributes. Fagot and Gauvain (1997) examined the relationship between parenting style and a parent's use of scaffolding behaviors with a sample of 93 preschool-aged children. Positive and negative maternal behaviors toward the child were observed in the home for 5 hr when at 18 months. Maternal positive behaviors included making favorable comments, engaging in positive physical play with the child, and smiling at the child; negative behaviors included criticizing, verbally punishing, and harshly directing the child. At 30 months, maternal scaffolding behaviors were measured during a series of difficult puzzle-type tasks that the child and parent were asked to complete together. Maternal scaffolding was characterized by the amount of guidance and support mothers gave their child during these tasks. Sample behaviors included providing affective feedback (positive and negative), cognitive assistance, and positive support. The authors found that observed positive parenting interactions during the home visits at 18 months correlated positively with mother's positive support at 30 months ($r = .28$). In addition, mother's negative interactions at 18 months correlated positively with parental disapproval during the scaffolding tasks ($r = .26$), suggesting that negative parent-child interactions set the stage for ineffective scaffolding later in childhood. These results provide a link between the parenting measures described in the coercion model and the scaffolding research: Effective scaffolding may be a skill that coercive parents lack.

A Conceptual Developmental Model of Competence
Beginning in Early Childhood

Our review of the research conducted at OSLC suggests that several early contextual factors play a role in the development of social and cognitive competencies early in childhood. Specifically, work reviewed in this chapter provides evidence to suggest that social referencing, attachment, and scaffolding are each related to children's social competence and that scaffolding is related to the development of children's cognitive competence. How can this realm of research best be integrated with the extensive body of research on the coercion model? We know from coercion theory that inadequate discipline and poor parental monitoring are predictive of antisocial behavior. However, these measures have been less predictive of young children's competency. We also know that scaffolding, attachment, and social referencing are best measured in early childhood and that they may not be strong predictors of competency in later childhood and adolescence. In contrast, discipline, monitoring, and positive reinforcement constructs appear to be best measured in middle childhood and adolescence. To integrate these two bodies of literature, a developmental model must take into account the possible fluctuations of different predictors expressing themselves at different ages of the child. The predictors may also express themselves differentially depending on the strength of antisocial behavior and/or the competent behavior currently being exhibited by the child. For example, improving social referencing skills or training the parent(s) to improve their scaffolding skills with a child who is demonstrating high levels of antisocial behavior in adolescence may not be effective strategies for decreasing the antisocial tendencies of the child. Using those techniques with a young child who has yet to exhibit antisocial behavior, however, may buffer against future antisocial behavior.

To develop a model that integrates social contextual factors and coercion theory in early childhood, it is imperative to recognize that antisocial behavior and competent behavior are not opposite ends of a single continuum (e.g., Luthar & McMahon, 1996; Masten, Morison, & Pelligrini, 1985; McCord, 1991; Parkhurst & Hopmeyer, 1998; Rodkin, Farmer, Pearl, & Van Acker, 2000). Antisocial youth may have a full complement of social skills and social competencies but may not exhibit them in a peer group that engages in antisocial behavior. Researchers have demonstrated that there may be popular prosocial boys and popular antisocial boys (Rodkin et al., 2000). A child possessing social competence, cognitive competence, *and* antisocial behavior may engage in a different type of delinquent behavior than a child who is antisocial but lacks cognitive and/or social competence. Similarly, the same independent measures may predict delinquency as strongly as they predict nondelinquency (or vice versa). For example, a large-scale study of risk and protective factors in 7-, 10-, and 13-year-old boys suggested that risk and protective factors often co-occurred in the same model (Stouthamer-Loeber, Loeber, Farrington, Zhang, Van Kammen, & Maguin, 1993). The contingency coefficients were significant on the protective and risk sides in 43% of the comparisons made. This includes variables such as school motivation, academic achievement, peer delinquency, and parental supervision. Though several variables were identified as having a risk effect only, the authors were unable to identify any variables as having a protective effect only.

A proposed developmental model integrating coercion theory and research on competencies is shown in Figure 3.2. The figure divides children's outcome behavior into four quadrants: high competence and high antisocial (upper right); high competence and low antisocial (upper left); low competence and low antisocial (lower left); and low competence and high antisocial (lower right). Three separate diagrams are shown, one for each of the following time periods: Toddler/Preschool, Elementary School, and Adolescence. As noted by the symbols in each quadrant in the figure, children enter the Toddler/Preschool period with differing levels of competence and antisocial behavior (measured as aggressive and noncompliant behavior). Factors influencing these two domains at different stages of development appear within the arrows at the left of the figure. In the Toddler/Preschool period, we hypothesize that the social contextual factors of attachment, social referencing, and scaffolding play a large role in predicting which children fall in each quadrant. We have listed temperamental factors as a likely precursor to behavior at this age (see chapter 2 for a discussion of the link between temperament research and the coercion model). These are certainly not the only factors influencing children's

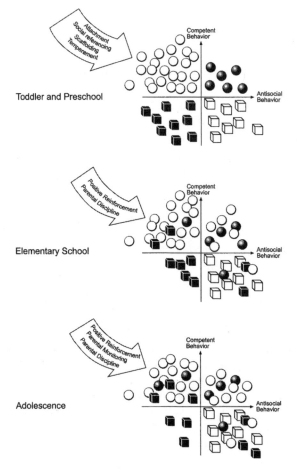

Figure 3.2. Hypothesized model of competence and antisocial behavior from early childhood through adolescence.

levels of antisocial and competent behavior. Results from the research reviewed in this chapter, however, suggests that they may be key predictors of early competent and antisocial behavior that can be integrated into the coercion model (other contributing factors may include parenting skills, peers, SES, and genetics, discussed throughout this volume).

As is suggested by the literature cited in this chapter, children with a coercive attachment style and a parent with ineffective scaffolding skills have a greater likelihood of a falling into the high antisocial behavior and low competence quadrant (lower right). Some children—who may exhibit aggressive tendencies stemming from temperamental characteristics but may exhibit cognitive competencies stemming from their parents' effective scaffolding skills—may fall into the high antisocial and high competence quadrant (upper right). Having effective social referencing skills, a secure attachment, and a flexible, resilient temperament may increase the likelihood of children falling into the high competence and low antisocial quadrant (upper left). Lastly, a group of children may not engage in antisocial behaviors with their family and peers but may lack specific social and cognitive competencies (lower left quadrant). Though such children may have poor social referencing skills and parents who provide ineffective scaffolding, they are resistant at this early age to the negative effects (e.g., poor peer relations) that these contextual factors may perpetuate.

As children transition into the school system (the second diagram in the figure), some remain in the same quadrant while others shift into neighboring quadrants because of the importance of parental discipline and positive reinforcement during this time period. We hypothesize that attachment, social referencing, and scaffolding become less predictive as parental discipline and reinforcement factors become more important. The parent-child interaction patterns present in insecurely attached toddlers and preschoolers may be early precursors to the types of coercive family interactions found in antisocial youth. Conversely, the interaction patterns practiced in families with securely attached toddlers and preschoolers may lead to effective and responsive parental discipline in the elementary school years. For example, following the figure, note that several children from the low antisocial and low competence quadrant (lower left) during the Toddler/Preschool period have transitioned into the high antisocial and low competence quadrant (lower right) during the Elementary School period. Such children may be exposed to ineffective parental discipline and a lack of positive reinforcement during this time, eventually eliminating any resistance the children had to negative social contextual factors during the Toddler/Preschool period.

Similarly, the hypothesized model suggests that a group of children move from the low antisocial and high competence quadrant (upper left) in the Toddler/Preschool period to the high antisocial and high competence quadrant (upper right) during Elementary School. We suggest that ineffective discipline and a lack of positive reinforcement during this period causes otherwise competent children to engage in antisocial, coercive interactions with their parents. These same children may be at a greater risk of moving into the lower right quadrant (high antisocial and low competence) in adolescence as the coercive cycle perpetuates itself (see chapter 4).

In the Adolescence period, not only do parental discipline and positive reinforcement continue to be important contributors to children's antisocial behavior and competencies, but parental monitoring also becomes critically important. In adolescence, we hypothesize that many children will have moved out of the low competence and low antisocial quadrant altogether (lower left quadrant, solid black squares) and into either the high competence and low antisocial or the low competence and high antisocial quadrant. The few children who remain in the low competence and low antisocial quadrant may be internalizers or very shy and withdrawn from social interaction but who refrain from antisocial behavior such as using drugs. By adolescence, two primary outcomes are hypothesized for the children who have moved out of the low competence and low antisocial quadrant. First, a group of these children will have been exposed to effective discipline and monitoring to push him/her in the low antisocial and high competence trajectory. A second group of children will have been exposed to ineffective discipline, a lack of positive reinforcement, and poor parental monitoring, thus pushing them toward the high antisocial and low competence trajectory. Similarly, the influence of poor parental monitoring, a lack of positive reinforcement, and ineffective discipline at this age causes some children to move from the high competence and low antisocial quadrant to the high competence and high antisocial quadrant; the adolescent learns coercive interactions patterns at home and extends them to the school and peer realms.

Preliminary Tests of the Hypothesized Model during the Toddler Period

To examine the effects of experiencing the precursors of social competency and of antisocial behavior, Fagot (1997) measured children's attachment classification via the Strange Situation using a sample of 156 families with 18-month-olds. The children were classified as Secure, Insecure-Avoidant, or Insecure-Ambivalent. The following were measured at 24 months: observed parental negative/positive reciprocity with the child, children's observed child negative/positive behavior with the parents, and children's observed negative reciprocity in playgroups. A series of hierarchical regression analyses were conducted to predict children's observed negative reciprocity in playgroups. First, the observed child behaviors in the home (negative/positive) were entered, followed by observed parental negative and positive reciprocity to the child. Next, the child's attachment classification (secure vs. insecure) was measured. Attachment was entered last to assess whether it added anything above and beyond the observed parent-child interactional exchanges theorized as important in the coercion model. The parent-child interactions together accounted for 31% of the variance, and attachment classification failed to account for any additional variance. The same measures were again entered in the same order to predict children's positive reciprocity in playgroups. Attachment was a significant predictor of positive peer interactions, with the full model accounting for 15% of the variance in children's positive peer reciprocity. The parent-child interactional exchanges failed to reach significance. This provides some validation to the hypothesis that attachment may play an important role in predicting young children's social competencies; whereas coercive parent-child interactions are key in predicting children's negative reciprocity (or antisocial behavior) with peers. However, the prediction of social competence (vs. antisocial behavior) accounts for much less of the variance in child behavior.

There is great potential in research to clarify the relationship between antisocial behavior and competence, to articulate trajectories of youth according to these domains of functioning, and to demonstrate how parenting and other factors impact those trajectories beginning in early childhood. At one level, such research will broaden the scope of coercion theory to incorporate both positive and negative outcomes. At another level, this research will allow for more developmentally sensitive prevention and intervention approaches and will facilitate the targeting of particular constellations of problems that may be marked by greater and lesser degrees of competence and antisocial behavior, respectively.

4

Reinforcement and Coercion Mechanisms in the Development of Antisocial Behavior: The Family

James Snyder and Mike Stoolmiller

A considerable amount of research time and effort at the Oregon Social Learning Center has been spent watching what children say and do during interaction with their parents and siblings at home and with their peers at school. The assumption is that the daily social environments experienced by children powerfully influence their display of aggressive, antisocial behavior. More specifically, the fundamental hypothesis is that the frequency of antisocial, aggressive behavior and its development over time are linked to its functional value in the daily social environment. In many ways, such an approach is not unusual. Most professionals interested in changing behavior attempt to ascertain how often and when a specific class of behaviors occurs, and the relation of those behaviors to other events. Such information serves to generate hypotheses about the function or cause of the behaviors and how to go about changing them. These activities are fundamental to a scientific approach to behavior change.

However, the observational approach to understanding antisocial behavior occurring at OSLC is unique in several ways. First, the child's interaction with the family and peers is observed in relatively naturalistic environmental settings. Second, coding systems are used to create detailed behavioral records requiring minimal inference from observers. Third, the resulting behavioral records describe the moment-by-moment (micro) social actions and reactions of individuals as they occur in real time. Fourth, these moment-by-moment data are then used in sequential analyses to discover and describe action-reaction patterns or contingencies between the behaviors of individuals to generate hypotheses about social influence. Fifth, the viability of these patterns and contingencies as potential explanations are tested using the criterion that they must accout for substantial variance in individual differences in aggression and antisocial behavior. And finally, methodological and statistical issues somewhat unique to observational data have also been addressed.

A number of scientific strategies could potentially be used to understand the origins of aggressive, antisocial behavior, and to formulate interventions to alter that behavior. The emphasis at OSLC on sequential, micro-level analyses of social

The support provided by Grant RO1 MH57342 (NIMH, U.S. PHS) to the first author in preparing this chapter is gratefully acknowledged.

interaction in the natural environment may not seem the most obvious or useful way to accomplish that task. The moment-by-moment social actions of children and the reactions of other people at home and in school may seem banal, fleeting, and weak. Surely the forces that shape antisocial behavior are more powerful, pervasive and obvious. The assumption at OSLC is to the contrary: The cumulative experiences of the child captured in these moment-by-moment actions and reactions as they are repeated over time are very powerful engines serving as a primary mechanism in the development of antisocial behavior.

This chapter provides a rationale for efforts to identify microsocial mechanisms within families that drive the development of antisocial behavior. It summarizes data concerning microsocial processes in family environments that have been collected over the last three decades and evaluates the contribution of these data to our understanding of the origins of antisocial behavior. It presents a specific focus on siblings, including coercion models in a genetically informative twin sample. It covers important methodological and statistical issues peculiar to working with microsocial observational data. Finally, the implications of these data for developing effective preventive and clinical interventions are discussed.

Rationale for Research on Social Interaction

Scientific understanding of the origins and causes of antisocial behavior is incomplete (Brown, 1997; Robins, 1992). Given that antisocial behavior is a pressing social and mental health problem, the task is to build an understanding of antisocial behavior at the same time we are trying to prevent and treat it. Consequently, research concerning the origins of antisocial behavior and efforts to develop effective interventions has a kind of boot strapping quality in which each area informs the other. This dialectical process has resulted in incremental progress over time.

Using an operant perspective, much of current treatment of antisocial children and adolescents is based on the assumption that children perform antisocial behavior to the degree that it is socially functional. The frequency of aggressive behavior should be related to the likelihood that it is positively reinforced or serves to avoid punishment (Patterson, 1982). Treatment entails teaching parents and teachers how to rearrange contingencies to decrease aggressive behavior and to increase more desirable, skilled behavior (Barkley, 1981; Forehand & McMahon, 1981; Patterson, Reid, Jones, & Conger, 1975). Observations of family interaction obtained before and after treatment have shown that behavioral parent training programs are effective (Brestan & Eyberg, 1998; Kazdin, 1987). These clinical efforts are buttressed by studies comparing the interaction of conduct problem children with family members to that of children who do not have such problems. These studies found that the interaction of conduct problem children relative to that of their counterparts was characterized by more frequent and extended aversive or aggressive interchanges; the problem child was a source of high levels of coercion, but also a frequent victim of coercion (Patterson, 1982; Reid, 1978; Snyder, 1977; Wahler & Dumas, 1986). By the mid 1980s, we knew that antisocial children resided in and contributed to highly aversive social environments at home and at school, but we did not know how those environments were created and how they were sustained. How could high frequency exchanges of aversive behavior be functional or reinforcing? How could knowledge of reinforcement contingencies be used to formulate more effective interventions? Answers to these questions were delayed.

Beginning in the 1980s, several shifts in basic and applied research on antisocial behavior occurred in response to presses within the scientific and policy communities, leading to a decreasing emphasis on research concerning the role of micro-level mechanisms in the development of antisocial behavior. First, behavioral-reinforcement theory went out of vogue. Alternate explanations concerning the mechanisms associated with antisocial behavior were derived from cognitive, attachment, and more recently, emotion regulation theories (Maccoby, 1992). Second, there was a shift from cross-sectional research with small, selected samples to longitudinal research using large, representative samples of children and families. The goal of this research was to describe the developmental pathways leading to serious and persistent antisocial behavior, and to identify risk factors that contributed to movement along that pathway. Most of this research used global, macro-level measures of antisocial behavior and its potential social causes. Third, increasing emphasis was placed on prevention given that it is very difficult to change antisocial behavior once it has progressed to persistent and serious forms. Using findings from longitudinal, epidemiological research, efforts are made to modify risk factors in order to delay the onset or alter the trajectory of antisocial development (Conduct Problems Prevention Group, 1992; Kellam & Rebok, 1992; Reid, 1993).

The macro-level, multi-modal, multi-setting, large-sample gestalt of these shifts in theory, methodology, and research strategy shifted the search for micro-level mechanisms into the background. It may seem that research on day-to-day micro-level social mechanisms is less relevant given this bigger picture. The experimental prevention-longitudinal strategy and data appears to have moved us beyond watching the daily interaction of children in family, school, and peer settings. Although initial results are slowly coming in, it appears that preventive interventions for antisocial behavior constructed on attempts to reduce macro-risk factors identified in longitudinal research have reliable, but modest, short-term effects (Brown, 1997).

The modest effects of preventive intervention suggest that we do not yet fully understand the origins of antisocial behavior. It is our assertion that research identifying micro-level processes by which aggressive, antisocial behavior is shaped in day-to-day interactions with peers, parents, and siblings is a critical missing link needed to translate the findings concerning macro-level risk factors identified by longitudinal and epidemiological research into highly detailed, specific strategies needed to create more powerful interventions. Specification and measurement of the microsocial processes by which interventions are hypothesized to have their effects on antisocial behavior would also provide a more precise and informative test of the causal status of risk factors derived from epidemiological and longitudinal research.

Microsocial research plays an important translator role. In longitudinal and research, self-reports, rating scales, and interview responses are typically used to define risk factors associated with antisocial behavior. Using multiple informants and methods, these measures are combined to form constructs (with minimal measurement bias and direct estimates of measurement error) that powerfully *predict* individual differences in the levels, growth, and progression of antisocial behavior (e.g., Forgatch, 1991; Patterson, 1996; Patterson, Reid, & Dishion, 1993). However, measures that have considerable *predictive* validity do not necessarily have good *clinical* or *treatment* validity. Rating scales, self-reports, and responses to interview questions are relatively global, static, and indirect in that they ask informants to aggregate information across time and situations. The frequency, duration, intensity, topography, and sequential arrangement among events are lost. Global measures use a relatively low power lens to provide a broad contour picture containing minimal detail. Data most relevant to specifying interventions for antisocial behavior and to understanding the processes by which those interventions have their effects require a higher power lens that provides more (molecular) detail. Put in another way, risk variables identified in longitudinal and epidemiological research generally locate malleable targets of intervention (e.g., parent discipline, association with deviant peers), but are like black boxes in that we don't know exactly how these risk factors operate in the daily social experiences of children and adolescents. But knowledge of microsocial processes is precisely what is needed to formulate more powerful interventions. Macro-level relative to micro-level causal models are often conceptually and statistically simpler but less useful in that they pinpoint only an *array of possible intervention targets and strategies* (Haynes and O'Brien, 1990). Measurement of moment-by-moment social interaction processes specifies the mechanisms by which risk factors operate to influence developmental trajectories of antisocial behavior.

Intervention strategies used in preventive and clinical trials are based on relatively detailed, micro-level theories about the processes by which a specific strategy has its effects on a target behavior. Intervention entails a rearrangement of the environment at a situational, sequential, moment-by-moment level. Macro-level measures often fail to map in sufficient detail onto the micro-level processes posited by intervention theory to mediate behavior change (Follette, 1995). As a consequence, it is difficult to articulate the details of intervention based on global risk factors and to ascertain the degree to which intervention successfully alters the processes that serve as the active ingredient for change.

Consider an example of a global risk factor found in longitudinal research to be a robust predictor of antisocial behavior and parental discipline. In longitudinal studies, parental discipline is typically measured via rating scales completed by observers, parental responses to interview questions, or child reports of perceived parental actions. Discipline is then expressed as a single score based on a sum of items derived using a specific method or on a statistical combination of scores using multiple methods and informants. The resulting score varies along some scale and is variously labeled in terms of the degree to which discipline is harsh, punitive, inconsistent, non-contingent, hostile, cold, etc. This global definition of discipline suggests that intervention might usefully focus on improving discipline so that it is less harsh, less punitive, more consistent, more contingent, and less cold. But, it is really unclear which of the characteristics described by these labels should be targeted, and how behavior-environment relationships should be rearranged so that there is less harshness, more contingency, etc. The specific behavioral referents and the temporal sequencing of child and parent action-reactions comprising discipline as a social phenomenon are unavailable. There is no cumulative record of how the parent responded to child noncompliance or hitting, or how the child responded to parental commands or verbal corrections. Discipline really entails repeated parent-child social encounters or sequences of actions and reactions. It is also at this level that parents are taught how to engage in better discipline. Without such detail, it is difficult to specify how, in intervention, discipline might be altered or improved, what it should look like, or the degree to which it was successfully altered in order to test its causal role in the development of antisocial behavior. Behavioral parent training assumes that rearrangement of parental reinforcement contingencies for child misbehavior is critical to bringing about change, but it is unclear whether this rearrangement makes discipline less harsh, inconsistent, non-contingent, etc.

Similarly, association with deviant peers has been shown to be a powerful risk factor for the development of antisocial behavior and drug use (e.g., Dishion, Patterson, & Griesler, 1994). Although we can accurately measure the degree to which a child's friends are deviant, we have minimal information about the mechanisms in social interaction by which children reciprocally select one another as friends or associates. We can measure how children may show increased antisocial behavior after a period of association with deviant peers, but the processes by which deviant or constructive behavior is encouraged or discouraged during the extensive social interactions of the child with his or her peers is largely unknown. Association among deviant peers and the behavior shaping occurring within those relationships are potentially powerful targets for intervention, but sufficient detail is lacking about the processes to formulate intervention to alter peer association and behavioral shaping. The lack of knowledge concerning specific linkages between risk factors and developmental outcomes, and the consequent inability to specify intervention could be made for a host of other risk factors for antisocial child behavior: parental psychopathology, single-parent households, residing in poor, high crime neighborhoods, and failures to bond with normative agents and organizations. Micro-level research on social mechanisms and processes that operate daily in family, classroom, and playground settings provides an important and necessary complement to macro-level longitudinal research on developmental trajectories and risk factors for antisocial behavior. Micro-level research serves as a critical translating bridge between developmental research and intervention trials.

Microsocial Processes and Antisocial Behavior

The basic assumption in coercion theory is that individual differences in antisocial behavior are the result of cumulative daily social experiences of children with persons in their natural environment. If this is the case, it should be possible to differentiate the social interaction of aggressive and non-aggressive children with parents, siblings, peers, and teachers. As recently as the middle 1960s and 1970s, reviewers (e.g., Frank, 1965; Jacob, 1975) indicated that few variables had been identified which could reliably distinguish normal and disturbed families. Beginning in the 1970s, researchers affiliated with OSLC embarked on a series of cross-sectional comparisons of the family and peer interaction of children defined as either aggressive or non-aggressive according to clinic referral, parent rating scales, or teacher checklists. Two tactics differentiate this series of studies from most previous efforts. First, behavioral coding systems were developed to capture the moment-by-moment social behavior that family members directed toward one another or that occurred in child-peer interaction (Dishion et al., 1983; Dishion et al., 1993; Reid, 1978) at a very fine-grained level (e.g., aversive, negatively-valenced verbal and nonverbal behavior: criticism, name calling, commands, teasing, hitting, negative gestures, etc.). These coding systems provided a description of sequential behaviors exchanged by family members or in peer groups along a real time line. Second, a search for patterns, structure or, sequential relationships between behaviors occurring in the interaction of children with family members or peers was made. Building on the work of Raush (1965), the notion was that social influence occurring in relationships is indexed by calculating conditional probabilities between the behavior of one person and that of another. Based on information theory, social influence occurs in so far as the behavior of one person reliably alters or predicts the behavior of another person relative to its base rate occurrence (Hetherington & Martin, 1979; Gottman, 1979). Rates and frequencies of the behavior of children, parents, siblings, or peers provides information about how much or how often behavior occurs, but sequential or conditional probabilities provide information about when or why behavior occurs (Patterson, 1982).

Cross-Sectional Research on Patterns of Family Interaction

It should be noted at the onset that any differences observed in comparing the interaction of aggressive and non-aggressive children in family or peer settings does not prove that these daily social experiences cause aggressive, antisocial behavior, but the failure to find differences would certainly serve to falsify the basic assumptions of coercion theory. Given that caution, a number of empirical differences have been observed in the interaction of aggressive children with parents and siblings relative to that of non-aggressive, normative children. A summary of the findings derived from 10 different samples of families with aggressive and non-aggressive children obtained at the Oregon Social Learning Center and affiliated research centers between 1975 and 1995 are shown in Tables 4.1 and 4.2. The data in the tables refer to between-group (aggressive children vs. controls) mean differences in conditional probabilities reflecting the social interactional contexts in which aversive behavior was observed during the interaction of the target child with family members. Startup refers to the conditional probability that a family member will initiate an aversive behavior directed toward a second member given the second member was not aversive: Probability ($X_{\text{time } t+1}$ aversive | $Y_{\text{time } t}$ not aversive). Reciprocate refers to one family member responding in kind to the aversive behavior of another family member: Probability ($X_{\text{time } t+1}$ aversive | $Y_{\text{time } t}$ aversive). Continuance refers to the probability that a family member will persist in aversive behavior regardless of the action of the other member: Probability ($X_{\text{time } t+1}$ aversive | $X_{\text{time } t}$ aversive).

The observational data in Tables 4.1 and 4.2 show considerable variation across studies in the absolute levels of startup, reciprocate, and continuance, reflecting differences in sample characteristics and behavioral coding systems from which the data were derived. The tables show that irritable actions and reactions are moderately frequent occurrences in most families, but there are clear differences in that some families seem to be able to manage and dampen irritability, whereas it is exacerbated and amplified in others. The data show that aggressive, antisocial children reside in and contribute to highly aversive family environments. Aggressive relative to non-aggressive children are 1.5 to 5 times more likely to engage in unprovoked aggression, to reciprocate the aversive behavior of another family member, and to persist in aversive behavior once they have initiated it (Table 4.1).

Table 4.1. Differences in Social Interaction Patterns of Aggressive and Non-Aggressive Children: Target Child Behavior in Cross-Sectional Studies.

Sequential Pattern	Non-aggressive	Aggressive	Reference
	Child Toward Mothers		
Startup	.13	.23	Snyder, 1977
	.01	.04	Patterson, 1982
	.05	.11	Patterson et al., 1992
	.08	.16	Snyder et al., 1995
Reciprocate	.18	.26	Snyder, 1977
	.09	.22	Patterson, 1982
	.10	.25	Patterson et al., 1992
	.17	.30	Snyder et al., 1995
Continuance	.12	.25	Patterson, 1982
	.10	.10	Patterson et al., 1992
RPM Physical Aggression	.0002	.0022	Patterson, 1986
	.0031	.0103	Snyder et al., 1994
	Child Toward Fathers		
Startup	.10	.18	Snyder, 1977
	.00	.02	Patterson, 1982
	.04	.04	Patterson et al., 1992
Reciprocate	.15	.27	Snyder, 1977
	.08	.16	Patterson, 1982
	.08	.09	Patterson et al., 1992
Continuance	.05	.24	Patterson, 1982
	.06	.07	Patterson et al., 1992
RPM Physical Aggression	.000	.0032	Patterson, 1986
	Child Toward Siblings		
Startup	.01	.03	Patterson, 1982
	.05	.07	Patterson et al., 1992
Reciprocate	.10	.19	Patterson, 1982
	.32	.39	Patterson, 1984
	.12	.13	Patterson et al., 1992
RPM Physical Aggression	.0014	.0075	Patterson, 1986

Fathers, mothers, and siblings in families of aggressive relative to non-aggressive children are 1.25 to 3 times more likely engage in unprovoked aggression, to respond in kind to aversive child behavior, and to persist in aversive behavior once they have initiated it (Table 4.2; the one exception is the study by Patterson et al., 1992, which compared clinic-referred to high-risk children). Families with aggressive children are highly coercive social systems. All family members contribute to this coercion in relation to the target child, and the exchange is clearly bilateral and systemic. The observed differences in aversive interaction among family members with and without aggressive children represent a relatively robust finding (with typical effect sizes > .50), and have been found in multiple samples using different methodologies. Similar findings have been observed by investigators at other

Table 4.2. Differences in Social Interaction Patterns of Aggressive and Non-Aggressive Children: Parent and Sibling Behavior in Cross-Sectional Studies.

Sequential Pattern	Non-aggressive	Aggressive	Reference
Mothers Toward Child			
Startup	.13	.20	Snyder, 1977[a]
	.02	.05	Patterson, 1982
	.11	.18	Snyder et al., 1995
Reciprocate	.22	.27	Snyder, 1977[a]
	.28	.35	Reid et al., 1981[a]
	.16	.20	Patterson et al., 1982
Continuance	.12	.25	Patterson, 1982
	.15	.37	Snyder et al., 1995
Physical Aggression	.0002	.0050	Patterson, 1986
	.0001	.0046	Snyder et al., 1994
Fathers Toward Child			
Startup	.01	.03	Patterson, 1982
Reciprocate	.08	.12	Patterson, 1982
Continuance	.05	.24	Patterson, 1982
Physical Aggression	.0008	.0032	Patterson, 1986
Siblings Toward Child			
Startup	.01	.03	Patterson, 1982
Reciprocate	.19	.25	Patterson, 1982
Continuance	.21	.27	Patterson, 1992
Physical Aggression	.0012	.0070	Patterson, 1986

[a]Based on estimates from 10-sec. interval coding systems.

research sites (e.g., Forehand, King, Peed, & Yoder, 1975; Gardner, 1989; Robinson & Eyberg, 1981).

The sequential relation between the aversive behavior of one person and that of another is not simply coincidental. Experimental manipulations involving an increase in the aversive behavior of one family member result in a concomitant increase in the likelihood of a subsequent aversive response by another family member (Patterson, 1979, 1982). The home is replete with aversive expression and experiences for aggressive children, consonant with the Patterson's notion that they are both victims and architects of a coercive system. This is not a one-way street; children actively contribute to their own socialization.

Aversive social events not only occur more often in the family environments of aggressive versus non-aggressive children, but once initiated, these aversive events tend to snowball and have a life of their own. In the daily social experience of aggressive, antisocial children, one person is fairly likely to initiate aversive behavior, a second to respond in kind, and the initiator to continue being aversive especially if the second person reciprocated the initial aversive behavior (Patterson, 1974, 1976; Patterson & Moore, 1979). The conditional probabilities of startup, reciprocate and continuance within families are correlated on the order of .20 to .60 (Patterson,

1982). Aversive events do not occur in a random, unconnected fashion. Stoolmiller (1992) showed that the temporal distribution of aversive events during social inter-action is accurately described by a negative binomial distribution. This distribution contains a mathematical term called a contagion parameter that indicates, as the word suggests, that once an aversive event occurs, there is an increasing likelihood of the reoccurrence of such events for a period of time. Patterns of aversive inter-action are not ephemeral events; the conditional probabilities describing the coercion process in families are reliable (r's = .30 to .70) over a two to eight week period (Pat-terson, 1984).

Coercive Interaction, Escalation, and Hitting

Longitudinal research has shown that, as children continue on a developmental tra-jectory of antisocial behavior from preschool to middle elementary school, low level aversive behaviors such as noncompliance, whining, and defiance are transformed into less frequent, higher amplitude behaviors such as bullying, hitting, lying, and stealing. Still later, during adolescence, bullying and hitting may progress to rob-bery and assault, and lying and stealing into fraud and burglary. Long duration, extended coercive exchanges may contribute to this progression. As parent-child coercive interactions become increasingly organized and extended in time, there is an increased likelihood of escalation—an aversive action in a sequence will evoke an aversive reaction that is more intense and noxious than the evoking action. Once caught in a long coercive exchange, escalation may become a primary tactic in such exchanges because the use of more noxious, painful behavior than that of the other person may induce capitulation. Consequently, extended coercive interchanges dur-ing family interaction play a critical role in increasing the variety and severity of children's antisocial behavior.

Support of this role for escalation requires evidence for several linked hypothe-ses. First, the observed interaction of aggressive relative to non-aggressive families should be characterized by longer duration coercive episodes or by a higher frequency of extended coercive episodes. Observational data support this hypothesis. Reid (1986) found that 3–4% of all coercive episodes in aggressive families were longer than 12 seconds compared to 1.5% of all episodes in non-aggressive families. Snyder et al. (1994) and Patterson (1982) reported that the average length of coercive episodes in aggressive families was 1.5 times that of non-aggressive families. Patterson (1982) also reported that the probability that a coercive episode would be extended, once initiated, was .30 for aggressive families and .11 for non-aggressive families.

The second hypothesis is that the noxiousness of behavior increases as a coercive episode is extended in duration. Observational data also support this hypothesis. Reid (1986) found that the likelihood of abusive behaviors (threats, humiliation, and hitting) increased in a linear fashion with the length of observed episodes regardless of family type, from a mean probability of .13 for episodes of less than 11 seconds, through a mean probability of .20 for episodes with durations between 12 and 23 seconds, to a mean probability of .33 for episodes greater than 23 seconds in length. Loeber (1980) and Patterson (1982) reported small but statistically reliable increases in the mean noxiousness of behaviors at each progressive step in coercive parent-child episodes. Snyder et al. (1994) found correlations between coercive episode length and the level of noxiousness reached in those episodes to be .25 to .30 for non-aggressive families and of .35 to .40 for aggressive families. Although escalation is positively related to the duration of coercive episodes in all families, it is a more powerful and pervasive phenomenon in aggressive than in non-aggressive families. The proportion of coercive episodes in which family members escalate is greater in aggressive (53%) than in non-aggressive families (37%). Aggressive family members escalate to a higher level of noxiousness and are more likely to re-escalate after another member de-escalates than are members in non-aggressive families (Snyder et al., 1994). In fact, aggressive children show a very short latency to escalation and escalate to higher levels than their mothers and siblings (Patterson, 1980; 1982).

A third, linked hypothesis is that frequent and high-level escalation during coercive episodes is associated with progressions toward the performance of increasingly serious antisocial behavior. One relatively unambiguous criterion for serious antisocial behavior is physical aggression. Note in Tables 4.1 and 4.2, that aggressive children and members of their families hit each other at 3 to 10 times more often than their non-aggressive counterparts. Sibling interaction appears to be a particularly powerful training ground for physical aggression; the rate of hitting is 2 to 5 times greater during child-sibling interaction than parent-child interaction. Several studies suggest that hitting occurs during long duration coercive episodes and coincides with escalation during those episodes. Patterson (1986) found that a composite of startup and reciprocate during child sibling interaction correlated on the order of .20 to .50 with the concurrent observed rate of child physical aggression toward siblings. Snyder et al. (1994) extended these findings to mother-child interaction. The rate at which mothers and children were observed to be physically aggressive toward one another was correlated (r's > .60) with the probability with which they escalated and with the level to which they escalated during coercive sequences. Patterson et al. (1992) identified a developmental progression such that the occurrence of physical aggression in family interaction (the third step in the progression) was preceded in 50 to 70% of the families by frequent and extended coercive episodes. Escalation may be a particularly important process in the development of later violent in contrast to property crimes. Loeber, Weissman, and Reid (1983) found that children who were arrested for assault during adolescence engaged in much higher rates of aversive behavior than their parents relative to children who were later arrested for stealing.

Coercion and escalation are bilateral processes. All members in families with aggressive, antisocial children contribute to and reside in a highly disputatious, hostile environments in which pain and coercion are primary strategies of social influence and control. Coercion is an insidious form of social influence. Because it is so powerful, its continued use often results in its transformation into a sharper and more caustic tool. Although powerful and effective in controlling other's behavior in the short run, it is self and relationship destructive in the long run.

The Search for Reinforcement in the Natural Environment

Research suggests that there is a reliable relationship between the coerciveness of the social environment in which an individual resides and the frequency with which that individual engages in aggressive, antisocial behavior. However, the reason why mutually noxious, hostile environments are created in family relationships is not obvious and perhaps even counterintuitive. Why do family members show high levels of irritability and aggression toward one another when it seems so punishing? Why do children and their siblings argue and fight with one another with such frequency? What explains variations in levels of reciprocal coercion, escalation and physical aggression we observe in the family relationships of different individuals? So far, we have described *what* is happening in the family that contributes to the development of aggressive, antisocial behavior, but not *why* it occurs.

There is no shortage of theories that account for coercive behavior. Individual differences in irritability and coerciveness may reflect genetic differences in emotionality and impulsiveness (e.g., Rowe, 1994). Irritable, aggressive parents and children share genes and live under the same roof, creating highly coercive family systems. Early training in coerciveness may then generalize and be re-created in other relationships and settings. Cognitive theories suggest that irritability and coercion are the result of biased or incomplete processing of social information such that the actions of others are misconstrued as aversive; the formulation and selection of responses to those actions lead to hostile and coercive reactions by family members (e.g., MacKinnen, Lamb, Belsky, & Baum, 1990). Other cognitive theories suggest that irritable, coercive actions, and reactions in family interaction result in a failure by the child to internalize socially accepted standards to control their own behavior (Maccoby, 1992) or result from a generalized view of other people as hostile and unpredictable (Landy & Peters, 1991). Theories focusing on emotion suggest that coercive, aggressive interaction in family and peer relationships is the result of an inability to self-control negative affect (Snyder et al., 1997) and of difficulty in accurately reading and adeptly responding to the affective communications of others (Dix, 1991). We will return to genetic theories later in this chapter when we focus on siblings.

Our work is based on a different explanation. Borrowing from an operant perspective, coercion theory hypothesizes that socially aggressive and antisocial behaviors are performed in so far as they are functional in escaping or avoiding punishment in the natural environment (Patterson & Reid, 1970). More specifically, aggressive responses during extended, escalating coercive interchanges are performed in so far as they successfully terminate other family member's attempts to alter or control one another's behavior (negative reinforcement). Hitting a sibling in response to the sibling's teasing will be performed if it terminates the teasing. A child's noncompliance to parental commands will promote similar behavior in the future if it deflects the command. Coercive behavior may be highly functional in gaining social attention, desired materials, and preferred activities (positive reinforcement). Throwing a tantrum in a grocery store is likely to reoccur if it leads to getting a candy bar. Acting goofy in church will be repeated if it leads to siblings' laughter. In many cases, both positive and negative reinforcement may operate simultaneously to powerfully select and shape aversive behavior.

Initial data derived from observational studies of parent-child interaction in the natural family environment did not support a reinforcement hypothesis. The rates of aggression of individual children were not reliably correlated (< .30) with rates of parental positive reinforcement provided for that aggression, nor were there reliable differences between the rates of parental positive reinforcement of child coercive behavior observed in the interaction of clinic-referred versus normative, comparison families (Patterson, 1982). Taplin and Reid (1977) reported that behavioral parent training resulted in a decrease in father- but not mother-delivered positive consequences for child coercive behavior, and in an increase in mother- but not father-delivered positive consequences for prosocial child behavior. These changes did not occur in families not exposed to treatment. However, even this partial support for the reinforcement hypothesis was diminished when a pre-post, cross-lagged panel correlations indicated that changes in child coercive behavior were not associated with changes in parental reinforcement.

Observational studies of family interaction repeatedly found that parents of conduct problem versus normative children were more likely to respond to child coercive behavior in an aversive manner. This could be interpreted as attempts to punish child coercion, but such attempts were powerfully associated with an increased probability of the immediate reoccurrence of child coercive behavior—a so-called punishment-acceleration effect (Patterson, 1979; 1982). It simply may be that negative reinforcement or escape conditioning provides a better account of the mutual coercion process in families than does positive reinforcement. This notion is buttressed by data indicating that interventions for children with aggressive behavior based solely on ignoring or extinction of aggressive behavior and positive reinforcement of prosocial behavior are not effective (Forehand, 1977).

The role of negative reinforcement in promoting coercive interaction was first examined in a series of experimental studies. Devine (1971) randomly assigned mother-child dyads to one of two conditions. In each condition, mothers were instructed to create an aversive state by withdrawing attention from their young children. Mothers in one condition were then asked to systematically reinstate attention contingent on child coercive behavior, and the mothers in the second condition were asked to systematically provide attention contingent on child positive social behavior. Three trials of these contingencies were sufficient to reliably and dramatically increase the duration and decrease the latency of the reinforced child response-coercive for the first condition and prosocial for the second condition. Woo (1978) and Patterson (1982) replicated these findings using single-subject reversal designs replicated across multiple mother-child dyads. In each case, the probability of children's coercive responding (complain, whine, provoke) to maternal aversive behavior (commands, restraint, or attention withdrawal), increased dramatically relative to baseline after as few as fifteen trials.

These experimental manipulations suggest that negative reinforcement may play a powerful role in shaping coercive behavior. However, it is necessary to demonstrate that negative reinforcement operates in a similar fashion during family interaction in the natural environment. Initial efforts to demonstrate a relationship between the rate of child coercive behaviors and the utility of those behaviors in terminating parent aversive social intrusions were mixed. Patterson (1979) reported zero order correlations between the rate per minute at which each of 33 children engaged in coercive behavior and the rate at which this coercive behavior was negatively reinforced by their parents. However, Patterson (1979) found support for negative reinforcement in predicting the probability with which an individual child used each of seven coercive behaviors (e.g., tease, hit, humiliate, whine, threatening command) and the utility of each of those behaviors in terminating aversive parental actions. The correlation for clinical families was highly significant (.93), but was not significant for non-clinical, comparison families (.53). Although the like-lihood of parental negative reinforcement of child coercive behavior was higher in clinic-referred (.22) than in non-referred comparison (.15) families, this difference was very small (Patterson, 1982).

Research concerning the role of positive and negative reinforcement of coercive behavior during social interaction in the natural environment went into a period of dormancy for several years. Although coercion and reinforcement continued to be central aspects of family-based treatment and prevention of child conduct problems, and served as a primary metaphor for organizing and explaining much of our lon-gitudinal research, progress in empirically substantiating the role of reinforcement in the development of antisocial behavior was stymied by four methodological issues. The first issue had to do with defining a contingent relation between a response and an event following that response in the absence of experimental control over the response-event relation. The second issue involved determining which social events, when put in a contingent relation with a behavior, might serve as reinforcers for that behavior. The third issue involved the unit of analysis. Reinforcement may or may not occur each time one individual responds to the behavior of another. We were simply making educated guesses about which social actions might serve as reinforcers, how to identify contingencies, and where those contingencies might occur in the auto-correlated matrix of sequentially ordered behaviors comprising natural family interaction. The fourth issue involved specifying the relationship between the rate of a response and the rate of reinforcement for that response. We had been work-ing under the assumption that there was a direct, linear relationship: The more frequently a response is reinforced, the more frequently it will be performed; reinforcement strengthens behavior. However, this assumption was a flawed. This empirical and methodological state of affairs led reviewers to conclude that the role of reinforcement in the performance and shaping of aggressive behavior was either relatively unimportant or untestable, and that other, typically cognitive explana-tions, were more promising (Maccoby, 1992; Maccoby & Martin, 1983; Robinson, 1985).

Some progress has subsequently been made in solving the methodological prob-lems in assessing reinforcement contingencies in the natural environment. The first methodological problem requiring a solution was to develop a set of rules by which to identify reinforcement contingencies as they occur in the stream of social interaction in the natural environment. An answer to this problem was available from experimental research in animal classical conditioning (Rescorla, 1988) and in operant conditioning of infants (Watson, 1979). A contingency between a response and a consequence occurs when the response is both necessary and sufficient to occa-sion that consequence. In a perfect contingency, the consequence only occurs after the response, and the response always generates the consequence (if, and only if the, response . . . then the consequence). The sufficiency of a response in producing a consequence can be defined operationally as the conditional probability of the con-sequence given the response. The necessity of a response in producing a consequence can be indexed operationally by comparing the just defined conditional probability (consequence given response) with the unconditional probability of the consequence. Each of these probabilities is easily calculated if the behaviors occurring during the interaction of two individuals can be reliably coded in the temporal order in which they occur.

The second problem, identifying social events that serve as reinforcers, was addressed in the following manner. We made the simplifying assumption that it is possible to identify a priori, a set of social events that, as the result of common social and cultural experience, are perceived as positive or aversive in valence by most of the people most of the time. Events commonly ascribed as positive would typically serve as positive reinforcers for a response when those events occurred in a contingent relationship with that response. Events commonly ascribed as aversive would typically serve as negative reinforcers for a response when those events were withdrawn contingent on that response. This approach avoids circularity in defining reinforcing events (Meehl, 1950). In so far as the ascribed valence and reinforcement value of these events are not generalized across people and settings, this assumption would increase error variance and lead to rejection of the hypothesis. Snyder and Patterson (1986) provided support for validity of this assumption by showing that when parents responded to child compliance to a parental command with positively valenced behavior, the child was more likely to comply the next time the parent issued a command. When parents responded to child compliance with a negatively valenced behavior, the child was less likely to comply to the next parental command.

The third problem had to do with where to look for contingencies in the stream of social interaction. This involves a guess about what is a meaningful unit of behavior in relation to reinforcement—when to lump and when to split. It is also necessary to partial out antecedent stimulus control. As described earlier in the chapter, the data indicate that coercive behavior on the part of one person is very likely to beget coercive behavior by another, and that these coercive behaviors tend to accumulate or aggregate temporally into extended, mutually coercive exchanges that escalate and lead to physical aggression. We took advantage of this empirical phenomenon to define our unit of analysis. These aggregated, extended exchanges can be construed as a unit called conflict that occurs when two or more people direct aversive behavior toward each other during social interaction. The individuals involved in the conflict experience an ongoing aversive state supplied by the behavior of the other party to the conflict, creating the condition for a negative reinforcement contingency when the conflict ends. Each behavior made by parties during the conflict comprises a series of behavioral tactics, each of which can lead to conflict termination (e.g., offset of the aversive state or negative reinforcement) or can fail to terminate conflict (e.g., no offset of the aversive state or non-reinforcement). Over a series of conflicts, each of the various types of behavioral tactics made by an individual accumulates a functional value relative to the other tactics in being associated with conflict termination. The frequency at which each of the behavioral tactics is performed by an individual during social conflicts, and the frequency at which each of these tactics immediately precedes conflict termination can be observed. These two frequency counts can then be used to define the conditional probability of conflict termination for each tactic.

For this to be workable, conflict needs to be carefully defined. There is fairly strong agreement in the research literature (Shantz & Hobart, 1995) that the onset of a conflict occurs when an aversive behavior by one person is reciprocated by a second person. It takes two to fight. The offset of a conflict has been less consistently defined. Logically, if it takes two to begin, it must take at least two to end; there must at least be reciprocated non-aversive behavior involving both parties to the conflict. However, observational data suggest that aversive behavior has considerable momentum. Like hot coals that often flare up, conflicts are very likely to reappear for at least a short period time after their apparent resolution. Sequential and temporal analyses suggest this high probability flare-up period is about 30 to 60 seconds in duration. If there is no recurrence of aversive behavior during this time, the probability of an aversive behavior exchange returns to its baseline value. These findings on the termination of conflict apply to interaction between peers (Cairns & Cairns, 1994), marital couples (Griffin, 1993), and between parents and children (Snyder & Patterson, 1986). About 4 to 5 behaviors occur in a typical 30-second period of social interaction. Consequently, we used a criterion of four consecutive non-aversive behaviors or 30 seconds without interaction to define conflict termination.

The matching law (Hernnstein, 1974; Williams, 1986) provides a clear description of the relation between rates of responding and reinforcement for that responding, addressing the final methodological problem. This law states that the frequency of reinforcement an individual receives for a specific response (such as aggression) relative to the frequency of reinforcement received by that individual for other responses (such as praise, talk, requests) determines how frequently the individual will perform a specific response (aggression). There is a rough match between the functional value of each of an array of responses and the relative rate at which each of that array of responses is performed. Reinforcement is a within—not a between—individual mechanism. On reflection, this makes intuitive sense. The subject decides how to respond based on the functional (reinforcement) value of each of a set of responses he or she could possibly make in a particular situation. How well a response works for the subject compared to how well it works for other people is irrelevant. From a matching perspective, responses in an individual's repertoire are not strengthened but rather are selected on the basis of their functional value in adapting to the ambient social environment.

The matching formulation of the role of negative reinforcement in coercive or conflictual social exchanges results in a model which hypothesizes that an array of behavioral tactics, both coercive (hitting, threatening, disapproving) and constructive (asking questions, giving information, acknowledging), can be used to respond to the aversive behavior of another person. The likelihood with which each of these various tactics will be used by a party during conflict depends on the previous utility associated with each tactic relative to other tactics in bringing about a termination of the conflict (e.g., negative reinforcement). The utility of a given tactic is simply defined by counting how often the tactic is associated with conflict termination and dividing by the frequency at which it occurs during conflict sequences. The relative probability of the tactic entails comparing this conditional probability (termination given tactic) to the base rate probability of conflict termination. Note that these procedures are exactly the same as those used to define a contingent relation in observational research.

In order to test the negative reinforcement hypothesis using these advancements in methodology and theory, researchers observed 10 hours of the interaction of each of 20 mother-child dyads. Half of the children evidenced serious conduct problems, the other half did not (Snyder & Patterson, 1996). Conflict sequences were identified for each dyad during the first 5 hours of interaction, and the relative functional utility (or negative reinforcement value) of each of six constructive and four coercive tactics in terminating conflict were calculated separately for each mother and child. These utilities were used to predict the relative probability with which those tactics were used by each mother and child during the second 5 hours of inter-action. Congruent with the matching law, the relative reinforcement utility of each of the tactics during the first 5 hours was linearly correlated with the relative probability with which they were performed during the second 5 hours of observed interaction. Bivariate scatter plots of this relationship for two children are shown in Figure 4.1. The median correlation for conduct problem children was .65 and for their mothers was .59. The median correlation for normative children was .60 and for their mothers was .54.

These data have several interesting implications. It is clear that individuals' per-formance of coercive behavior during family interaction is finely tuned to the ambi-ent functional values of that behavior in the immediate social environment—in this case, termination of conflict or negative reinforcement. Reinforcement is a bilateral process. Children and parents shape each other's behavior, and consequently con-tribute to coercive family environment. From a matching law perspective, negative reinforcement or escape conditioning during parent-child conflict not only selects and shapes coercive behavior, but constructive behavior as well. Conflict can serve as a source of learning skillful as well as coercive responding. Negative reinforcement operates in normative, non-problem mother-child dyads as well as in those contain-ing a child with conduct problems. It is not specific to pathological responding or pathological families and serves a general mechanism or process in socialization. The relative rate of reinforcement of constructive versus coercive tactics differentiates the learning that occurs in families with a conduct problem child relative to that in normative families. As shown in Table 4.3, coercive (.46) relative to constructive (.29) tactics work best for conduct problem children. Conversely, for normative children,

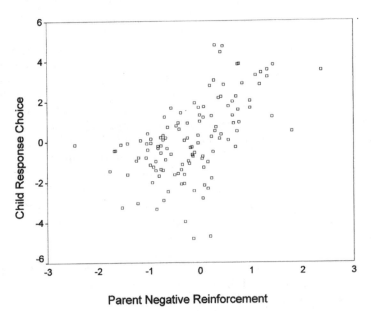

Figure 4.1. Bivariate scatterplots of the relation of the functional utility of conflict tactics and the performance of those tactics for two children.

Table 4.3. The Relative Reinforcement Utility of Conflict Tactics in Families With and Without Conduct Problem Children.

Coercive Tactics	Prob. (Neg. Reinf.)	Constructive Tactics	Prob. (Neg. Reinf.)
		Conduct Problem Children	
Negative Verbal	.50	Positive Verbal	.27
Command	.42	Talk	.31
Noncomply	.21	Comply	.26
Negative Nonverbal	.48	Positive Nonverbal	.23
		Neutral Nonverbal	.14
		No Response	.29
Total Coercive	.46	Total Constructive	.29
		Normative Children	
Negative Verbal	.30	Positive Verbal	.25
Command	.32	Talk	.38
Noncomply	.30	Comply	.27
Negative Nonverbal	.25	Positive Nonverbal	.23
		Neutral Nonverbal	.08
		No Response	.39
Total Coercive	.30	Total Constructive	.38

constructive (.38) relative to coercive (.30) tactics have a higher functional utility in terminating conflicts with their mothers. The same mechanism leads to very different lessons in problem and non-problem families.

A second step is needed to relate these matching law findings to individual differences in aggressive, antisocial behavior. In addition to knowing individuals' response choice of constructive versus coercive tactics during conflict, we need to know how often conflict occurs in order to predict individual differences. Snyder and Patterson (1996) demonstrated that a combination of the functional utility of coercive responding during conflict and the frequency of conflict calculated on the basis of one 5 hour period of observation predicted the frequency of coercive responses during a second five hours of observation both for children (multiple $r = .81$) and mothers (multiple $r = .73$). Negative reinforcement may be involved in shaping the topography of coercive behavior as well as its frequency. Snyder et al. (1994) found that negative reinforcement for escalation during a specific conflict sequence was positively and reliably associated with more intense aversive responses during a subsequent conflict for both mothers (median $r = .42$) and children (median $r = .47$).

The data from these studies were very encouraging, but were derived from a very small, select sample. Recently, we have replicated the association between negative reinforcement and coercive family interaction in a longitudinal study of a clinical sample of 53 families (Snyder, Schrepferman, & St. Peter, 1997). The relative probabilities of the referred child's coercive behavior toward parents and siblings and the relative probability with which parents and siblings negatively reinforced that behavior during conflict episodes were derived from observations of family interaction in the home prior to intervention. There was a reliable path (.49) from parental negative reinforcement to a coercion construct defined by child startup and reciprocate to the parents and accounted for 24% of the variance in child coercion construct. In a similar fashion, there was a reliable path (.52) from sibling negative reinforcement to child startup and reciprocate toward siblings, accounting for 27% of the variance in child coercion toward siblings. This replication provides increased confidence concerning the negative reinforcement-coercion link and extends it to sibling as well as parental relationships. However, the generality of the reinforcement-coercion linkage needs to be tested in a larger sample of families reflecting a full range of conduct problems in both boys and girls.

Linking Coercive Family Processes to Subsequent Development of Child Antisocial Behavior

Cross-sectional research provides considerable empirical support for coercion theory. Members in families with conduct problem children engage in very frequent bouts of reciprocal coercive behaviors of considerable intensity and duration. Additionally, the use of coercive behavior appears to be associated with its utility (relative to more constructive tactics) in turning off aversive social intrusions by other family members. However, coercive family interaction may simply reflect transient phenomena indicating that the behavior of individuals is sensitive to the quality of the ambient social environment and its immediate functional utility in adapting to that environment. The cross-sectional nature of many of these studies makes inferences about cause and effect ambiguous. Two interpretations are equally plausible. The presence of a conduct problem child in the family may generate high levels of coercive interaction (as indexed by startup, reciprocate, continuance, escalation, and hitting), or coercive interaction may cause child conduct problems. The link between negative reinforcement and child coercion may simply reflect shared method variance. Short of experimental manipulation, establishing the relevance of coercion and reinforcement mechanisms requires that those mechanisms longitudinally predict an antisocial behavior construct defined by multiple agents and methods sharing minimal method variance with the observational predictors.

The linkage of coercive discipline to subsequent child antisocial behavior has been established in a number of longitudinal studies at the OSLC, described in other chapters. Additional discussion is also presented in the sibling section of this chapter. However, a few exemplars of these studies will be described in detail here to make explicit the longitudinal linkage between coercive process and child antisocial behavior. Using the clinical sample just described, Snyder et al. (1997) showed that coercive child behavior toward parents and siblings, and the parents' and siblings' negative reinforcement of that coercive behavior accounted for 33% of the variance in a construct defined by police contacts, out of home placement, and school discipline problems during the subsequent two years. Child-parent and child-sibling coercion and reinforcement each made unique contributions to the prediction. More recently, Schrepferman and Snyder (2000) have found that the non-occurrence of police arrests during the two years after treatment in this clinical sample was reliably associated with pre- to post-treatment shifts in parent negative-reinforcement contingencies that favored constructive relative to coercive child responses during parent-child conflict

Bank and Patterson (1992) tested a model in which observational measures of coercive child interaction with parents, siblings, and peers at ages 9 to 10 were used to predict concurrent antisocial behavior measured by parent, teacher, and peer report. Coercive interaction reliably predicted concurrent antisocial behavior. Bank and Patterson then showed that coercive interaction at ages 9 to 10 predicted child antisocial behavior measured by police contacts and child self-reported delinquency at age 14 after controlling for antisocial behavior at ages 9 to 10. This is a very powerful demonstration of the role of coercive interaction for several reasons. Each of the constructs was defined by different informants or methods; their covariation cannot be explained by shared method variance. Coercive interaction predicted change in antisocial behavior over time. Coercive family interaction during childhood is related to a wide array of developmental outcomes. Bank, Patterson and Reid (1996) reported that child startup and reciprocate toward parents and siblings at ages 4 to 12 was correlated with juvenile delinquency, adult arrests, hostility toward women, and an array of mental health problems 10 years later.

The Critical Role of Siblings

The role of siblings deserves some special attention for a number of reasons. First, sibling studies in general are a powerful analytic tool for understanding family environmental effects. This has been clearly demonstrated in behavior genetics where the sibling study is a mainstay. Because siblings are nested within families, the sibling study allows a decomposition of the variance of any outcome into between family or shared and within family or nonshared effects. In addition, if siblings of at least two different levels of genetic relatedness are included in the sample, for example full biological siblings and half siblings, then additive, genetic influences may also be studied. The utility of the between and within decomposition is that it can be applied to child outcomes, even if predictor data is not available, to generate clues about where to look in the family environment for effects. For example, large between-family effects on an outcome like antisocial behavior implicates some aspect of the family environment that is strongly correlated across siblings. Large within-family effects suggest that either some aspect of the family environment that is largely uncorrelated across siblings is important, or environmental determinants outside the family, which are usually not correlated across siblings, are important. This approach can also be expanded to include specific, environmental predictors producing a decomposition of the overall predictor effect on the outcome into shared and nonshared components as will be demonstrated later in this section. The sibling study is not utilized often outside of behavior genetics, which is unfortunate because it has additional attractive advantages besides estimation of shared and nonshared variance components.

Another important advantage of the sibling study is that it preserves more of the family system for study and analysis. It seems trite to say that the family is a complex system, but the implications of this obvious fact are often ignored. Clearly, the more of a complex system, like the family, that is included in a study, like siblings, fathers, grandparents, etc., the higher the potential for important insights into the system's operation. A traditional barrier to sibling studies that is often mentioned is the problem of statistical dependence introduced by sampling siblings within families. In recent years, however, there has been a virtual explosion of statistical techniques devoted to the analysis of dependent data such that this is no longer a realistic concern. To be sure, statistical difficulties are not the only challenges inherent in a sibling study. Except for twin studies, sibling studies also automatically introduce sampling complexities involving age, gender, and birth order. These challenges are not insurmountable, however, but they do need to be balanced against the ultimate value added from the additional scientific information available from the sibling study over the traditional one child per family study.

Finally, empirical evidence is beginning to accumulate that indicates that sibling influences are potentially more proximal determinants of child problem behavior outcomes than parenting variables, especially in adolescence. This is not to say that parents do not play a crucial role in the socialization of their children, because they do, but a key part of that role may be the orchestration of harmonious sibling relationships. It is surprising how little empirical literature is actually available that examines the simultaneous influences of siblings and parents on child outcomes. We turn now to reviewing some of the evidence generated in our own lab and note links with the existing sibling literature.

Sampling Issues

Early work on siblings was based largely on contrasting a group of families that were recruited for clinical studies on the effectiveness of parent training for conduct problems with an approximately equal number of apparently normal families that were matched to the clinic families on background demographics. The data that were employed generally came from 6 to 10 one hour observation sessions that for the clinical groups served as a baseline for judging improvement over time in the identified problem child. There are two important things to note about this sort of design. First, it is an extreme group's design that oversamples the high end of the child antisocial distribution. Thus, relative to a more representative population-based sample, effect sizes and correlations would be expected to be somewhat bigger. Second,[1] the clinic families selected themselves into the study on the basis of the parent's, usually the mother's, perception that one particular child in the family had behavior problems so severe that treatment was highly desirable. Of course, the existence of high levels of behavioral problems in the child was verified by direct observation before the family was admitted to the study. But, because free therapy was at stake, this screening process may have also motivated the parents to make their child look as bad as possible during the baseline screening period by being extra coercive toward the child.[2] But, even if the parents were not purposely faking bad, these families were somewhat unique in their perception that one particular child, as opposed to multiple siblings, had a behavior problem. The demand characteristics of the screening process and the selection bias probably had the effect of magnifying the uniqueness of the family processes swirling around the problem child as compared to deviant families in the general population under more naturalistic conditions where no particular child is singled out as the problem child. In the review that follows, references to the clinic and normal samples will be to these early samples. Later work on siblings was based on more representative sampling although high crime neighborhoods were targeted to increase the level of antisocial behavior in the samples. Two samples will be referred to the Oregon Youth Study Planning (OYSP) sample and the Oregon Youth Study (OYS) sample. The OYSP involved three grade cohorts, fourth, seventh and tenth grade boys (the target child) and their families and data was collected at one point in time. The OYS involved two grade four cohorts of boys (the target child) and their families separated by 1 year and data collection is ongoing as the OYS is a long-term longitudinal study. The OYSP and OYS samples were recruited in the same way from the same neighborhoods and schools. The important sampling differences between the clinic and normal comparisons on the one hand and the OYSP and OYS on the other should be kept in mind when comparing results.

Early Work

Several interesting findings emerged in very early work that suggested that sibling interaction was a key ingredient in the development of serious antisocial behavior. Patterson and Cobb (1973) found that they could identify a network of antecedent behaviors that reliably elicited teasing and hitting on the part of the problem child. Both behaviors were associated with the same network of stimuli. Later analyses demonstrated that the family members most involved in the coercive episodes involving hitting and teasing were siblings (Patterson, 1977). The sibling responses also tended to increase the likelihood of more problem child hitting and teasing.

Arnold, Levine, and Patterson et al. (1975) found that siblings in 27 clinic families had Total Aversive Behavior (TAB) scores, a summary rate-per-minute score of 14 different kinds of aversive behavior, of .56, whereas the identified problem child's TAB score was nonsignificantly higher at .75, and the correlation between the two scores was .74. Perhaps more interesting, Arnold et al. also observed that when 18 of the 27 families applied the behavior management techniques learned in therapy to the siblings and across the entire sample of 27 families, siblings showed significant reductions in coercive behavior. Evidently, parents have a strong tendency to be consistent in their discipline practices across siblings within a family.

The early sibling work, however, was sporadic, and it was not until 1984 that Patterson began to weave the disparate threads together into several papers that focused specifically on siblings. These papers were significant, because they proposed that the contributions of siblings to the development of antisocial behavior within families, although long neglected, were probably as important as the contributions of parents.

Is Coercion A Family Affair?

As discussed earlier in this chapter, coercion definitely runs in families. Patterson (1984b) provided some interesting details on the differences in other family member's levels of coercion, including and excluding interactions with the identified problem child. According to Tables 4.4 and 4.5, mothers and fathers in the clinic sample were no more coercive than normals if their interactions with the problem child were excluded, but this was not true for siblings. Regardless of the problem child's contribution, the proportion of the sibling's behavior that was coercive in the clinic sample was about twice the corresponding proportion in the normal sample, and this difference was significant for both male and female siblings.

There were no significant within, family differences in proportions of aversive behavior by male or female siblings directed at other family members for any of the groups, clinical or normal (Patterson, 1984b). This finding, however, should be contrasted with findings from the matching law reported below. Between group effect sizes, however, all were rather large, although small sibling sample sizes prevented some of the comparisons from reaching the .05 level of significance. Mean shifts for the significant comparisons ranged from .64 to 1.21 within group standard deviations. Thus, siblings in clinic families were in general more coercive to other family members than siblings in normal families by a substantial amount.

Findings for familial levels of sibling coerciveness from Patterson (1984a; 1984b) are summarized in Table 4.4. As can be seen, the problem child is only slightly more coercive than his male and female siblings, and the proportions of sibling coercive behavior are affected very little by the specific contribution of the problem child.

When the proportions of coercive behavior by siblings of the problem child to other siblings are tabulated, as in Table 4.5, again there is very little difference between the problem child and his siblings. In other words, if the children of a normal family were playing in one room and the children of a clinic family were playing in the other, it would be easy to tell clinic from normal, but it would be far more difficult to guess which is the problem child in the clinic family. The early OSLC data strongly suggest that child behavior problems are strongly familial, and not just because one particular child is out of control in his/her interactions with the others.

Additional findings concerning sibling reactions to each other and the determinants of extended coercive chains strongly implicate siblings as mutual influences in each other's coerciveness. For example, Patterson (1984b) reported that regardless of whether the sibling was older or younger than the problem child and regardless of the context defined by the sibling antecedent behavior, there were strong group differences in the proportions of coercive behavior of the problem child toward the sibling. The effect size for the group comparison was 1.35 within group standard deviations, a very large effect across all sibling antecedents. Patterson (1984b), however, reported even bigger differences between the clinic and normal samples for the conditional probability of the problem child performing two successive coercive behaviors, given he was interacting with his siblings regardless of the age of the sibling (younger vs. older than the problem child). The effect size for the group comparison was 1.74 within group standard deviations. Evidently, longer sequences of coercive behavior discriminate better between clinic and normal samples than the overall base proportion of coercive behavior. The final finding of interest was that sibling aversive behavior during a coercive episode with the problem child was rather strongly correlated with the overall rate of coercive episodes or chains for the problem child. Thus, siblings appear to make strong contributions to the overall level of coerciveness of each other because of the frequent and extended conflicts they get into in clinic families.

As further evidence of the symmetry of conduct disturbances among siblings in clinic families, Patterson (1986) noted that although there were significant elevations of the three irritability variables, startup, reciprocate, and continuance, in clinic samples compared to normals, there were no substantial differences between sibling reactions to each other within samples, although one sibling was identified as the problem child.

Two of the three irritability variables, reciprocate and startup, for both target child and sibling were used to predict ratings of fighting for the target child provided by peers, teachers, and mothers in the OYSP. The target child irritability variables

Table 4.4. Proportions of Coercive behavior for Male and Female Siblings of the Problem Child (PC) in Clinic and Normal Samples, with and without PC interactions included in analysis.

	Clinic		Normal	
	With PC	Without PC	With PC	Without PC
Male Sib	.11	.10	.05	.06
Female Sib	.09	.09	.04	.05
PC[1]	.13		.05	—

[1]PC = Problem Child.

Table 4.5. Proportions of Coercive behavior for Siblings and PC in Clinic and Normal Samples towards other siblings in the family.

	Clinic			Normal		
	Brother	Sister	PC	Brother	Sister	PC
Male Sib	.16	.09	.14	.04	.05	.05
Female Sib	.09	.11	.11	.05	.02	.03
PC[1]	.14	.13	—	.05	.04	—

[1]PC=Problem Child

were, not surprisingly, more highly correlated with the ratings of his fighting than the sibling measures, but sibling counter aggression predicted target child fighting .35, .37, and .15 for fourth, seventh and tenth graders respectively with the first two correlations being significant at the .05 level. A similar and pivotal finding reported was that the sibling reciprocate measure correlated .64 and .42 with the Elliott self-report measure of Delinquency Life Style for the target child in the seventh and tenth grader samples respectively. The magnitude of these correlations suggests that sibling relationships are important for understanding adolescent delinquency. Patterson (1984a) also reported for the OYSP across all grade cohorts that the correlation of the target child fighting score with target child reciprocate toward his siblings, mother, and father were respectively .47, .30 and .22. The correlation of the target child fighting score with the siblings, mother, and father reciprocate toward the target child were respectively .31, .23, and nonsignificant. Note that the relative ordering of the magnitude of the correlations is the same in both cases, and the sibling data are more predictive of fighting than the parent variables.

In summary, siblings appear to be intimately involved in mutual coercive interactions of each other and coercion theory holds that this is a basic training mechanism for later delinquency. In the clinic versus normal comparisons, the only way the problem child stood out from his siblings was in his embattled relationship with his mother. We turn now to a discussion of gender differences and a reanalysis of the matching law data originally presented in Patterson (1984b).

Early work at OSLC concentrated on boys, and thus, gender differences did not figure prominently. The sibling work, however, presented an opportunity to explore potential gender differences, albeit in small samples. Patterson (1984b) reported a matching law analysis of sibling preferences for attacks on mothers. The data in the original figures are replotted in Figure 4.2. The match was very good for the relative likelihood of female sibling attack of mother with the relative likelihood that mother, as opposed to other family members, would pay off the female sibling for her attack. Recall that the matching law holds that siblings will distribute their attacks across family members in the same proportion that family members provide payoffs for those attacks. For example, if in a given family the relative payoffs for the female sibling to attack mother, father and problem child are 20%, 40%, and 40% respectively, then the female sibling will attack mother, father and problem child in the same relative proportions.

There is, however, a problem to note about matching law analyses applied to naturalistic observational data. The independent variable, the relative likelihood of reinforcement for a sibling attack, is actually a subset of the dependent variable, the relative likelihood of a sibling attack. This built-in part-whole relationship will automatically produce an impressive correlation. Thus, the striking scatterplots in Figure 4.2 need to be interpreted with that caveat in mind. But, having noted that, Figure 4.2 shows that the match is not as good for the male sibling attacking mother as the female sibling. The male sibling plot shows all but two of the points are underneath the dashed line, defining a perfect match. The matching law has been extended to handle cases of nonlinearities, so-called over- or undermatching, and response preferences that are independent of the relative rate of reinforcement, so-called bias. As argued by Baum (1979), matching law data can be fit using the power family of curves to quantify over-or undermatching and bias. The extended version of the matching law, sometimes referred to as power matching as opposed to simple matching, makes the gender differences more apparent and potentially interesting by converting bias and over-or undermatching into statistical parameters that can be estimated and subjected to hypothesis testing.

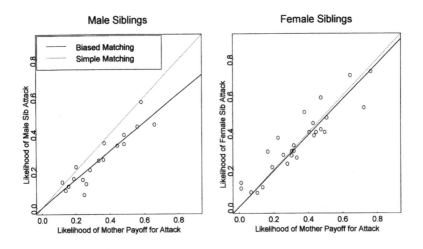

Figure 4.2.   Matching law scatterplots for male and female siblings.

The general relationship for power matching can be derived from a quadratic regression model:

$$y = b_0 + b_1 x + + b_2 x^2$$

If neither b_0 nor b_2 are significantly different from 0, it suggests that under- or over-matching is absent. More specifically, if the quadratic term is nonsignificant, it suggests that $a = 1$ and the log transformation is unnecessary because the power matching law simplifies to $y = b x$, which is a simple regression equation without an intercept and can be fit with a standard linear regression program. In addition, if b_1 is not significantly different from 1, it suggests that bias is also absent and simple matching holds. Of course, if b_2 was significant, then fitting the model in equation 2 becomes more attractive as a way of estimating a.

When this equation was fit to the male sibling data in Figure 4.2, neither b_0 nor b_2 were significantly different from 0, as might be anticipated from the plot of the data, suggesting the lack of over- or undermatching, or equivalently that $a = 1$. When the quadratic term was dropped from the model, the intercept b_0 was not significantly different from 0 but the slope, b_1, was significantly less than 1 suggesting that the male siblings were negatively biased against attacking mothers. When the intercept was dropped from the model, the estimate of the bias was .85 with a standard error of .038. The t test for the null hypothesis that the bias is equal to 1 is $(1-.85)/.038 = 3.95$, which is highly significant with 17 degrees of freedom. For the data in Figure 4.2 for female siblings, neither b_0 nor b_2 were significantly different from 0, as might be anticipated from the plot of the data, suggesting the lack of over- or undermatching, or equivalently that $a = 1$. When the quadratic term was dropped from the model, the intercept and slope were not significantly different from 0 and 1 respectively, suggesting that simple matching holds for the female siblings attacking mother. When the intercept was dropped from the model, the estimate of the bias was .98 with a standard error of .038. The t test for the null hypothesis that the bias is equal to 1 is $(1-.98)/.038 = .53$, which is not significant with 26 degrees of freedom. The t test for the hypothesis that the slopes are equal across gender groups is equal to $(.98-.85)/\text{sqrt}(.038^2 + .038^2) = 2.42$, which is significant at $p = .02$.[3] To get an idea of the magnitude of the gender difference back on the raw scales of relative rates, the simplest approach is to compute the ratio of b for females to males that gives the proportionate difference in relative rate of attacks on mothers for females versus males at any given level of relative rate of reinforcement. This calculation is $.98/.85 = 1.15$, which suggests that at any given level of relative reinforcement, female siblings are 15% more likely to attack mother than male siblings. Or equivalently, male siblings require a higher level of maternal payoffs to reach the same level of attacks as female siblings. For example, to achieve a relative rate of attack of .50, male and female siblings require, respectively, relative rates of reinforcement of .59 and .51. The nature of this gender difference is unknown. Wearden and Burgess (1982) noted, however, that biases in matching law analyses of animal behavior show up clearly when the response manipulanda (such as a lever for one response and a key for the other) are different for the two choices. The obvious parallel here is that mother's gender makes the choice of who to attack asymmetric for the male and female sibling. It would be interesting to see if gender differences replicate for attacks on fathers and specifically if there is a preference for same-sex victims. It is also interesting to note that the pattern of preferences for same-sex parental victims by male and female siblings are present in Tables 6 and 7 in Patterson's original report (1984b), which give mean likelihoods of coercive behavior directed at various family members by siblings, but the pattern is vanishingly small and nonsignificant. It could be that relative rates of reinforcement have to be considered, as in the matching law, for gender differences to emerge clearly as they do in Figure 4.2, above.

After Patterson's groundbreaking sibling studies in 1984, sibling research went into hibernation for more than 10 years until Lew Bank began a new round of studies using the OYS sample. In the meantime, a number of highly influential papers emerged from behavioral genetics that proposed that shared family environmental influences were unimportant for most major child outcomes of interest, that environments encountered by siblings within families were virtually uncorrelated leading to almost no sibling resemblance beyond that due to shared genes, and that what little environmental influences on child development existed, all were nonshared or within family in nature (Plomin & Daniels, 1987; Scarr, 1992). In addition, other theorists pushed one step further and proposed that the lack of shared family environmental influences meant that parenting practices were unimportant, that parents contribute little more to their child's development than genes and that socialization is due to peer influence outside the home (Harris, 1995; Rowe, 1994). Findings from predominantly clinical populations at OSLC and in other labs supporting the importance of family environment and parenting were dismissed as representing processes only relevant for a small proportion (5–25%) of families at the extreme, disturbed end of the family environmental distribution (Plomin et al., 1997; Rowe, 1994; Rowe, 1997; Scarr, 1992).

The early sibling work by Patterson in 1984 on clinical populations does not support the above views, although it does suffer from the limitation of unknown or limited generalizability, as noted by behavior geneticists. The work in the OYSP, however, is consistent with the earlier clinical work concerning the key role of parents and siblings in the development of antisocial and delinquent behavior. And, because the OYSP is a well-defined population sample, the results generalize to mixed working and middle-class populations that comprise the vast majority of the families with children in America. Bank's work, to be discussed below, also addresses some of the new issues raised by behavioral geneticists.

Bank, Burraston, and Patterson (1997) reported a series of SEMs and regressions in the OYS sample that demonstrated that both sibling negative interaction and ineffective parenting made important contributions to predicting future child adjustment. The impact of parent effectiveness at grades four and six on the average arrest rate across grades seven, eight and nine was mediated by sibling negative interactions at grades four and six. Perhaps even more importantly, they found that by grade twelve, the interaction between sibling negativity and parent effectiveness (both from grades four and six) was significant in predicting cumulative arrests by grade twelve. The nature of the interaction indicated that OYS boys with the highest number of cumulative arrests tended to have both highly negative sibling relationships and ineffective parenting at grades four and six. Negative sibling interaction was also significantly predictive of deviant peer affiliation and positive peer relations at grade twelve over and above parent effectiveness and stability effects of early measures of the dependent variables. Negative sibling interaction was not predictive of depressed mood or academic achievement, either univariately or in combination with other predictors. Negative sibling interaction was significantly correlated with grade twelve antisocial behavior, but the effect was mediated by the stability effect of antisocial behavior. Of course, a weakness of the findings discussed above is that the influence of shared genes cannot be controlled or estimated. However, OSLC has recently developed a twin sample in which a genetically informative analysis can be made to explore some of these issues.

A model similar to that used by Pike, McGuire, Reiss, Hetherington and Plomin (1996) is shown in Figure 4.3 for the OSLC twin data. The OSLC twin sample is described in greater detail in Leve (in press). Shared, nonshared, and genetic variance components were, respectively, 40%, 30%, and 30% for child antisocial behavior (assessed by a composite of direct observation, observer global ratings, and maternal ratings). This result does not support the positions of Plomin et al. (Plomin, Chipeur, & Neiderhiser, 1994; Plomin & Daniels, 1987) or Scarr that most important environmental influences on child outcomes are nonshared or within family. The overall variance components are obtained by squaring and summing all paths to either of the sibling outcome variables representing the same source of variance (e.g. genetic variance is .522 + .182 = .30). The overall amount of variance in child antisocial accounted for by maternal discipline (assessed by direct observation) was .23, which was highly significant. This variance component is obtained by squaring and summing all paths from mother discipline to either sibling outcome measure (e.g. .2022 + .1812 + .4002 = .23). The environmental portion of this variance was .20, which represented 87% of the total variance and this too was highly significant. This result does not support the positions of Rowe or Harris that parenting is unimportant for understanding

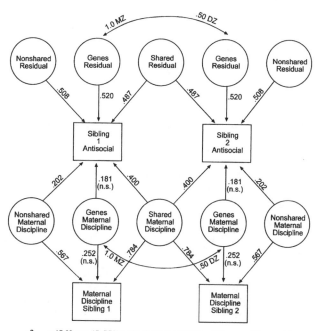

$\chi^2_{(11)} = 15.63$, $p = .15$, BBN = .933, BBNN = .977, CFI = .979, $n_{MZ} = 74$, $n_{DZ} = 75$

Figure 4.3. The Oregon Social Learning Center Twin Model.

childhood antisocial behavior. The genetic portion of the variance accounted for by maternal discipline (.03) was quite small and nonsignificant. Note that this does not replicate some of the findings being reported from the NEAD project in which so called genetic effects on environmental measures are detected (Plomin, Reiss, Heatherington, & Howe, 1994). The shared and nonshared portions of the total environmental variance were, respectively, 80% and 20%; and the shared effect was significantly greater than the nonshared effect. Thus, the model in Figure 4.3 does not support the currently popular view that shared family influence is unimportant for most developmental outcomes. The model in Figure 4.3 also suggests that, of the remaining environmental influences that are not measured and included in the model, shared family influences are probably substantially more important than nonshared influences because the nonshared residual variance estimate of $.508^2 = .258$ for child antisocial also includes random measurement error. For example, if the reliability of the composite sibling antisocial measure was .80, probably a generous reliability estimate, then only $.508^2 - .20 = .058$ of the .258 nonshared residual variance is left to be potentially explained by additional environmental predictors. In contrast, $.487^2 = .237$ of the sibling antisocial measure is still potentially explainable by shared family influences. Direct sibling influences are a natural candidate for a large part of the remaining shared effect and would be consistent with the prior work at OSLC on microsocial sibling influences on coercive and delinquent behavior described above.

Potential reasons for why results with the OSLC twin data do not replicate results coming out of the NEAD project or adoption studies such as the Colorado Adoption Project (CAP) may include the use of direct observation for maternal discipline, a greater range of family environments, or both. Stoolmiller (1999; 1998) has shown that the restricted range of family environments that accompanies behavior genetic adoption studies can result in serious underestimation of shared family effects and overestimation of genetic and nonshared effects. The NEAD study, although not an adoption sample, is still predominantly an advantaged, middle-class sample, due most likely to the selection criteria used of requiring families to be maritally stable for at least 5 years.

Getting Reliable Estimates of Microsocial Processes

The final topic in this chapter on microsocial processes in families addresses a perennial question that comes up in connection with observing behavior: How much observation is necessary to get a reliable estimate of a rate or proportion? In the first part of the chapter, we argued that observing microsocial processes was a potentially powerful tool for elucidating mechanisms by which more global constructs come to be related the way they are. In a sense, micro data allows us to open the black box and see the inner workings that coercive family process. Observational data, however, have some very attractive additional advantages. Patterson (1982) reviewed a large body of evidence that demonstrated that observational measures derived from microcoded behavior had the highly desirable properties of being objective, sensitive and accurate. The few limitations that emerged from this work included a) observation tends to dampen the amplitude of deviant behavior of those being observed, b) if parents want to, they can make their child look bad by giving more commands, c) expectation biases can be induced in behavior coders, but only if experimenters go to great lengths (e.g., by telling coders what to expect and then immediately reinforcing them after the coding session for seeing the right thing). The properties of objectivity, sensitivity, and accuracy may be particularly important in intervention studies when all the naturalistic raters are part of the intervention and cannot be counted on to give unbiased reports of behavior change (see Stoolmiller, Eddy, & Reid, 2000, for more discussion of this issue). The strengths of observational data, however, are also its limitations. Because it is so objective, sensitive, and accurate, observational data picks up everything that is going on during the observation session, much of which may be irrelevant or nonrepresentative. In a sense, it is like a very sensitive microphone that picks up all the noise in a lecture hall, not just the speaker, but coughing, rattling of paper, shuffling of feet, etc. Another, and perhaps the most crucial, limitation of observation data is its expense. The cost of collecting observation data on large samples is high and has led to the proliferation of cheaper self- and natural-rater reports via questionnaires. This is unfortunate because the ratings of natural observers including the self are often problematic because of systematic biases and distortions (Fergusson, Horwood, & Lynskey, 1993; Eddy, Dishion, & Stoolmiller, 1998). Random measurement error is easily dealt with using standard psychometric tools, but systematic bias is a much more serious problem and difficult challenge.

The limitations and expense of observational data make it crucial to understand efficient ways of analyzing this data. The consequences of misunderstanding the psychometrics of these data are very expensive null results that could lead to the abandonment of observational data as an assessment tool. Fortunately, much of standard psychometrics can be directly imported and applied to observational data. The lack of systematic distortions and biases actually make standard latent variable modeling an ideal tool to use with observational data.

The first important point about observational data is that day-to-day variability in microcoded behavior is large. People behave differently today than yesterday, and they will behave differently tomorrow than today. Observational data faithfully pick up all this day-to-day variability because of it strengths. Jones, Reid, and Patterson (1975) did an elegant generalizability study of the currently popular OSLC microcoding system on the clinic and normal comparison groups described above. They found a small proportion of the variance in coercive types of behavior, about 5%, was due to coders in both the clinic antisocial group and the normal group of boys. More importantly, they found that essentially all the remaining variance in the normal group and most of the remaining variance in the antisocial group was due to the interaction of subjects by occasions which implies very little trait-like and mostly state-like quality to the behavior. The antisocial group also had a significant amount of variance due to individuals, which corresponds to trait variance. Neither group showed a significant proportion of variance due to individual by time interactions, which means that the level of individual differences in change over time was consistent with a random error mechanism. Incidentally, Jones et al.'s results are inconsistent with a theory that views antisocial behavior as a continuously and normally distributed trait in the population. The normal boys, who presumably have lower levels of the antisocial trait, should have also shown stable individual differences in antisocial behavior, but at a lower mean level.

There are many potential reasons for such day-to-day variability, and most current developmental theories would see this variability as irrelevant for important developmental child outcomes. We are aware of no popular developmental theory that places large emphasis on the one-time occurrence of rare events. This is not to say that rare events are never interesting or important and cannot be studied with observational data, but they are not the focus of coercion theory or most other developmental theories. A good analogy is the relationship of the weather to something like plant growth. The weather in Eugene is highly variable on a day-to-day basis, but stable patterns over longer time periods exist in terms of rainfall and sunlight, and these patterns have important developmental consequences for plants (and allergy sufferers) in Eugene.

An efficient way of dealing with day-to-day variability in observational data is to sample over occasions and use a latent variable model to partial out variance specific to occasions. This is formally identical to the multi-method multi-trait approach that is currently popular in SEM. Minor statistical complications are involved. Some scale transformation is usually necessary to render the data more normally distributed, especially if the behavior is not common, and sometimes it may be necessary to use latent variable methodology for censored variables if the time of observation at each occasion is short and a floor effect is introduced (see Stoolmiller, Eddy, & Reid, 2000; or Oord & Rowe, 1997 for more details on problems with censoring). We will now demonstrate with an example, a way of dealing with variability in observation measures due to occasions.

The data for this example is drawn from the OYS at the first wave when the boys were in fourth grade. Three 1-hour sessions of home observation were conducted over about a 3 week period. Behavior was microcoded using the FPC (Dishion, et al. 1983). The 3 sessions were coded by a different coder each time to eliminate the possibility of coder effects. Coder effects in this kind of design are confounded with occasion effects, but when coder effects are estimated separately by having a random subset of the sessions coded simultaneously by two different coders, the correlation is usually about .85–.90. Thus, similar to Jone's findings cited above, coder effects are not a substantial proportion of the total variance and the occasion effects are not due to deficiencies in the coding system or coder training. A measure of maternal discipline skill was derived for each individual session based on an a priori definition of which codes in which affective valences were thought to constitute irritable discipline. A proportion score and a rate score were combined to form each individual session score for maternal discipline. We will now demonstrate different ways of handling variability due to occasions and their consequences on the estimate of the correlation between maternal discipline and child antisocial behavior.[4] In Figure 4.4, Model 1, when each of the three session scores for maternal discipline is correlated with the child antisocial construct score, the average of the 3 correlations is .267. This estimate of course, does nothing to correct for unreliability due to occasions. In Model 2, when the three session scores are combined first into an overall construct score and then correlated with antisocial, the correlation rises to .324, a 21% increase over Model 1. The averaging across sessions before computing the correlation, of course, helps boost the reliability of the aggregate measure by magnifying the true score variance relative to the error variance. Model 3 shows a simple latent variable approach to handling unreliability. The proportion and rate scores are respectively aggregated across sessions to form two indicators for the latent variable, which is then correlated with, antisocial. The two factor loadings are constrained to be equal to each other as are the two error variances for simplicity. As can be seen in Figure 4.4, Model 3, the model fits reasonably well and the correlation rises again to .360, a 35% increase over

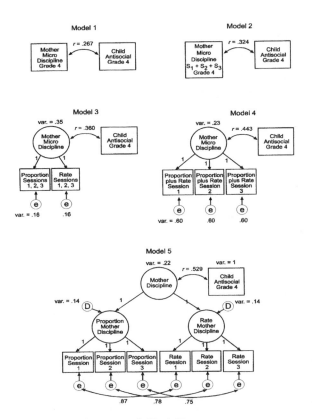

Figure 4.4. Models for observed maternal discipline measures.

Model 1 but only an 11% increase over Model 2. Model 4 shows an alternative and preferred parameterization that aggregates the rate and proportion measures within a session to form a single indicator for each session for the latent variable. Even with equality constraints on the factor loadings and error variances as in the previous model, this model fits reasonably well and the correlation with antisocial rises again to .443, a 66% increase over Model 1, a 37% increase over Model 2, and a 23% increase over Model 3. The reason Model 4 is preferred over Model 3 is that because Model 3 aggregates across sessions, covariance between the rate and the proportion due to occasions is being incorporated into the latent variable, which results in an inflation of the variance of the latent variable with occasion effects and an attenuation of correlations of the latent variable with any other variables of interest. Because occasion variance is large, the difference between Model 3 and 4 is appreciable. The inflated covariance due to occasions is easy to spot in the correlation matrix shown in Table 4.6 by comparing correlations on the main diagonal to the off diagonal elements in the submatrix of nine correlations between the proportions and rates.

The final model to be considered is Model 5 in Figure 4.4. This model disaggregates the rate from the proportion measure of maternal discipline at each session to create 2, first order maternal discipline scores. A second order factor captures that common variance between the proportion and rate latent scores after occasion effects are removed at the first order by using correlated error terms. Note that the model fits reasonably well and the correlated errors capturing the occasion effects are very large in magnitude and highly significant. More importantly, however, the

Table 4.6. Correlations among rate and proportion scores of maternal discipline for individual home observation sessions from Oregon Youth Study, Wave 1.

Prop 1	1.00					
Prop 2	.30	1.00				
Prop 3	.25	.41	1.00			
Rate 1	.62	.16	.18	1.00		
Rate 2	.19	.52	.29	.50	1.00	
Rate 3	.11	.14	.55	.43	.51	1.00

estimated correlation with antisocial behavior rises again to .529. This represents increases of 98%, 63%, 47%, and 19% respectively over Models 1, 2, 3, and 4. The advantage of Model 5 over models 1 and 2 is quite dramatic.

It is also instructive to perform some simple reliability calculations based on model 5. The reliability of a single proportion score as a measure of maternal discipline is the ratio of the variance of second order factor to the total variance of the proportion score, which is .22 / (.22 + .14 + .70) = .21 and the implied correlation with child antisocial is .24. For a single rate score, the estimated reliability is .22 / (.22 + .14 + .59) = .23 and the implied correlation is also .24. The reliability of either 1st order factor as an indicator of maternal discipline is .14 / (.14 + .22) = .61 and the implied correlation with child antisocial is .41. Thus, the correlations with child antisocial increase by 71% and 121% respectively for the first and second order factors over a single rate or proportion score.

The reliability of a composite based on aggregating a given number of proportion scores, say k, can be computed using the formula

$$Reliability = \frac{k\ var\ (F\ )}{var\ (V\ ) + (k-l)\ var\ (F\ )} \qquad (1.4)$$

where var(F) is the variance of the latent second order factor and var(V) is the variance of the observed observational measure. The reliability for three sessions turns out to be .46, which is disappointingly low, and the implied correlation with child antisocial would be .34. This is an improvement over a single proportion but is still inferior to the results obtained for the first order latent proportion score. Where equation 1.4 was plotted against k the number of items for maternal discipline based on the proportion score from the results of Model 5, it can be a reliability of .80 is achieved at about 15 sessions. Lest the reader think that the maternal discipline proportion measure is unusual, reliability curves for two other microsocial variables, a conditional rate measure of maternal negative reinforcement of child coercion from a standardized lab task, and a child rate of physically aversive behavior as observed during a 10 minute recess on a school playground (Stoolmiller, Eddy & Reid, 2000) were also calculated. Both measures would require a large number of sessions (substantially more than were actually collected) to achieve a reliability of .80, which is usually considered acceptable reliability.[5] In our experience, shorter individual sessions of observation usually lead to lower reliability for a given measure, which is fairly intuitive. Less obvious is that when more complicated measures are computed, such as conditional probabilities or z scores for two- or three- step sequences or negative reinforcement at the end of a conflict chain as described earlier, these variables tend to have even lower reliability then simple rates or proportions based on the same amount of time of observation. This probably reflects the difficulty for coders of correctly coding whole sequences of events rather than just a single occurrence, but these more complicated processes may also show more natural day-to-day variability than simple rates and proportions. Regardless of the cause, the consequences to the investigator are clear; adequate reliability is even harder to achieve for the most theoretically interesting microsocial variables.

It is important to understand the statistical consequences of low reliability. Reliability has absolutely no effect on the probability of a type I error. It remains at whatever alpha level the researcher adopts regardless of the reliability of the variables involved. To see this, consider trying to detect a group difference with a normally distributed outcome variable with zero reliability. Regardless of the true effect size, the scores for both groups will be nothing but random normal noise. But this is precisely the null hypothesis which statistical theory says will be falsely rejected with a probability of alpha. As demonstrated above, however, low reliability does lead to dramatic attenuation of effect sizes, both mean shifts and correlations. This implies that for given sample and population effect sizes, the probability of a type II error will increase as the reliability of the measures involved decreases. Thus, low reliability leads to null results, which in turn can lead to the premature abandonment of promising lines of research, or worse yet, promising intervention strategies for helping people. This problem will be particularly acute for detecting statistical interactions or moderator effects. Although reliability of .80 may be adequate for detecting most main effects that would be of practical interest, it is not adequate for detecting important higher order effects. For example, Aiken and West (1991) found that within the framework of the normal theory linear model (e.g. ANOVA or regression models), a drop in reliability from 1.0 to .80 or .70 for the two predictors involved in an interaction lead respectively to obtained effect sizes of one half and one third their true values for the interaction. The implication for the maternal discipline measure based on three sessions with a reliability of .46 in the OYS with 200 cases is that even very strong interactions will probably go undetected.

So what can be done to remedy these problems? First, if research resources are very generous and the design of the study does not make it impractical, then many sessions of observation can be collected to achieve acceptable reliability. We assume, however, that this will rarely be the case. Thus, latent variable methodology and sampling across at least two or three occasions is imperative when working with behavioral observation. A perhaps easier and cheaper alternative might be to conduct multiple observation sessions on a random sub-sample to obtain a reliability estimate that is used for the entire group (Allison & Hauser, 1991). This is clearly an area of research design that needs more work to identify cost-effective and efficient designs, although some work has already appeared (Brown, Indurkhya, & Kellam, 2000). This approach is feasible with methodology that is now available except for testing models that include interaction. It is highly desirable to use latent variables to model interaction because of the problems induced by low reliability. Unfortunately, the methodology to handle interactions is not well developed within the SEM framework. Although strategies have appeared, they tend to (a) be very difficult to implement, (b) they do not provide good standard errors, or (c) they provide good standard errors only for huge sample sizes, or (d) all of the above. Monte Carlo techniques such as the Gibbs sampler or bootstrap resampling may offer some promise for the future. These are important methodological developments for the most efficient utilization of observational data.

Summary And Implications For Intervention

Longitudinal and epidemiological research clearly indicate that family environments characterized by harsh or inconsistent discipline, poor monitoring, and an inability to solve problems are strongly associated with increased risk for antisocial outcomes. The availability of these global labels is beguiling because they suggest we know exactly how to intervene to reduce risk. The premise of this chapter that the global risk factors are like black boxes which locate important influences in a general sense, but we need to look inside the boxes to understand the mechanisms by which influence is created and exerted in order to develop effective preventive and clinical interventions.

We have opened the black box and looked at the mechanisms and processes describing the daily social interactions of families associated with increased risk for child antisocial behavior. Coercive interaction between children and their parents and siblings appears to be an important engine in social development, and it occurs in all families. Coercive interaction occurs as parents attempt to correct, guide, and discipline their children. It occurs when siblings face off in competition for attention and squabbles over materials and status. Resolution of conflict and bilateral repair of social interaction are important family processes that contribute in a substantive manner to subsequent child development. Aversive intrusions and disagreements provide the opportunity for learning constructive means of resolving conflict and repairing social interaction as well as for the shaping of caustic, coercive, and aggressive behavior. Which lesson is learned depends on the contingencies that are operating in the daily family environment. The behaviors used by family members to respond to aversive events and conflict are selected and honed by short-term negative reinforcement contingencies. If counter-coercion, escalation, and hitting work, they will be used. Negative reinforcement of coercive responses to conflict is an insidious process associated with the development of conduct problems, delinquency, adult criminality, and a host of other behavior problems. Aversive social intrusions also provide an opportunity for the development of constructive conflict management, communication, and problem-solving skills. In so far as these constructive responses are functional in the short-term resolution of conflict, they will be repeated and shaped in future social encounters. Aversive social events and negative reinforcement are an integral in promoting socially skilled as well as antisocial behavior.

The promise of research on social interaction is that it informs intervention. Current data have several implications for clinical and preventive interventions. Standard parent training interventions teach parents to track and reinforce positive behaviors with social attention and other reinforcers, and to track negative behavior, set clear limits and consistently enforce those limits with non-physical punishment (e.g., time out, response cost). The data reviewed in this chapter are certainly consistent with this approach, but provide considerably more detail. The goal of intervention is not to reduce aversive social events and conflicts to zero. Parents cannot socialize their children using solely positive tactics (explanations, empathy) and reinforcers. As effective socialization agents, parents set rules, teach compliance, and discourage immature and aggressive behavior. Sometimes, "no" means "no" regardless of the child's acceptance of parental rationales and explanations. Even normative, skilled children with easy temperaments throw tantrums, are defiant, non-comply, tease their siblings, and hit.

Some parents say "no" and deal with child misbehavior in ways that promote the child's self-control, rule-following, and social skills, whereas other parents respond in a manner that leads to child aggression and antisocial behavior. Our research on family interaction elaborates the basic approach used in parent training in the following way: (1) Skillful parents appear to be able to intervene, teach, and correct in ways that entail fewer aversive intrusions, to stay calm, and to focus on the problem at hand. They clearly describe the desired behavior, provide explanations, and state contingencies. This reduces but does not totally mitigate child coercive responding. (2) When they or their children become aversive, skillful parents are able to de-escalate, to delay responding, and to engage in problem-solving talk and actions that cue similar child responses. Once the occasion for conflict occurs, skillful parents try to dampen the aversive exchange and look for agreement and cooperation. (3) Skillful parents persist in this constructive form of teaching, even if interaction has evolved into a conflict, until the child engages in constructive responses and desired behavior, and then use negative reinforcement to promote both child self-control and skillful conflict resolution. Skillful parents model and teach but do not fight. They do not back down from child threats, tantrums, and defiance, but calmly persist until the lesson is taught. Skillful parents do not get so caught up in coercive interaction that they fail to engage in constructive behaviors to cue similar behavior by their children, and provide consistent reinforcement contingencies when desired behavior occurs. This is a more complex set of skills than standard parent-training protocols suggest, and these skills must be maintained in the face of an aversive social environment, personal distress, or arousal. Good parenting is like singing an aria, playing a piano, fly fishing, or operating a complex machine. It takes concentration, timing, sensitivity to feedback, and fine feed-forward control.

Although parents as adult socializing agents are responsible for promoting constructive child behavior, children contribute in a reciprocal, active manner to the process. Successful socialization of children who are temperamentally difficult or who have learned from past social experience that coercion works will require even higher levels of parental skills. These children may show a lower tolerance threshold for aversive events, have difficulty dampening their own behavior, and be less sensitive to reinforcement contingencies than their normative counterparts. The selection and shaping of behavior during discipline and conflict episodes, either constructive or coercive, is bilateral and mutual. The relative lack of involvement of children in standard parent training interventions belies the impact that children have on their parents' behavior. It may be useful to develop interventions in which children are primed to be more responsive to changes in parent behavior. Simultaneous intervention with the child and the parent in a manner that complements and reinforces the effects of the other may provide a sufficient increase in the power of intervention to offset the increased cost of doing so.

The manner in which parents engage their children during teaching and discipline encounters is as important as achieving the lesson that is the focus of the encounter. Parental intervention impacts child socialization at two co-occurring levels. At one level, children need to be taught not to hit and tease, and to comply and be polite. This is the primary focus of standard parent training. At the second level, parents are simultaneously teaching their children to communicate, to problem solve, and to resolve conflict. Successful socialization entails not only achieving children's adherence to social rules and norms, but also fostering children's ability to accept corrective feedback and to repair interaction when conflict occurs. In fact, what lessons are taught is inextricably intertwined with how they get taught. Intervention requires that we use sophisticated procedures to help parents learn and use these complex, dual-level skills.

Our understanding of the social processes that promote antisocial behavior is still limited. The matching formulation of reinforcement has a metaphorical status when applied to social interaction in the natural environment. Alternate formulations that better fit the bilateral, systemic reinforcement processes that occur in the family are needed. We are likely to better understand social processes under conditions of change. Our next task is extensive observations of family interaction during intervention with clinical or at-risk samples and to ascertain the dynamic changes in bilateral and iterative family interactions associated with short- and long-term changes in child antisocial behavior. There are a number of other processes and mechanisms, including social information processing and emotion regulation that are operating inside the black box of daily family interaction. We need to observe the operation of these additional mechanisms and processes and to understand mediating and moderating effects among these mechanisms, coercion and reinforcement. Despite this complexity and size of this continuing task, we have developed the methodology and made sufficient progress to be on the cusp of an exciting and productive research agenda needed to foster the development of a new generation of more effective family interventions.

1. Assuming the linear model with constant error variance is valid across the entire range of the relevant predictor which is itself a questionable assumption. See Stoolmiller, Patterson, and Snyder (1997) for evidence of a nonlinear relationship, specifically a positive quadratic relationship between parent discipline and child antisocial behavior.

2. It has been shown that when an experimenter instructs parents to purposely make their child look bad during behavioral observation sessions, they usually succeed and they tend to accomplish the goal by increasing their rate of directives. The increase in directives usually leads to more parent-child arguments and conflict than normal.

3. In a few cases, the male sibling in Figure 4.2, plot on the left, came from the same family as the female sibling in Figure 4.2, plot on the right, which introduces an obvious lack of independence for some of the observations. For simplicity, this complication was ignored. Most likely, the correlation between siblings would be positive and thus, the standard errors are somewhat underestimated making the statistical tests slightly liberal.

4. We have taken some liberties with the data that we would not ordinarily do to simplify the example and focus it more clearly on the problem of variability due to occasions. First, the models are based on analyzing the correlation matrix of the measures which discards information about the means and variances. Second, a number of other effects that are apparent upon close examination of the data are ignored. Briefly, these include the fact that there was a modest first session effect such that the rates and proportions of maternal discipline were somewhat lower at the first session then the next two, and that the correlation of the maternal proportion scores with child antisocial behavior was somewhat higher than the corresponding correlation for the rate score. Although these effects are interesting, they are relatively small compared to the occasion effects that the example is intended to illuminate.

5. A plot of the reliability curves by k sessions for each of the three measures can be obtained from the second author of this chapter.

5

Reinforcement and Coercion Mechanisms in the Development of Antisocial Behavior: Peer Relationships

James Snyder

Family relationships make an early, important, and ongoing contribution to the development of child antisocial behavior. However, peers provide an additional, unique, and powerful context that influences individual differences in the social growth of children. Peer relationships complement those in the home in that they involve interaction among individuals of roughly equal developmental and relational status. Exposure to an array of peers with diverse characteristics in school and neighborhood settings extend children's social experience and provide an opportunity for children to make choices and locate social niches compatible with their own repertoire. Peer relationships provide an additional, complex, and iterative set of daily social experiences and contingencies that shape social behavior during childhood and adolescence. In recent history, social, educational, and economic changes have dramatically increased the amount of time children spend with peers, often without adult supervision, and consequently the potential influence of peers on children's social development. One issue to be addressed in this chapter is the degree to which peers make a unique contribution to the development of child antisocial behavior, violence, drug use, and early sexual activity.

Child-parent and child-peer relationships are different not only because of the developmental and role status of the participants, but also because of the elective versus obligatory nature of the relationships (Dishion & Patterson, 1997). Parent-child and sibling relationships are, to a large extent, closed and obligatory. Family members do not freely select one another, have minimal opportunity to avoid relationships with each other, and consequently engage in substantial amounts of ongoing interaction. In peer relationships, individuals are free to selectively affiliate with one another. Each individual can elect to spend considerable time with one person and avoid others, and can choose to minimize already established relationships and move on to others. A second issue addressed in this chapter is niche finding—how and why children select peer associates and friends, and the manner in which this selection influences their developmental outcomes.

Neither peer nor family relationships stand still developmentally. As a child matures, relationships which are initially closed and obligatory often become more open and elective. Young children's range of experience with and choice of peers and non-familial social agents are somewhat limited—to the school and classroom to which they are assigned, and the immediate neighborhood in which they are raised. The nature of relationships with teachers, with parents and siblings to some to degree, and with peers to a substantial degree, changes during middle childhood and adolescence. During this period, children normatively spend less time at home with parents and siblings, and move into increasingly open middle school and high school settings that provide exposure to and choice among a larger number of peers with more diverse behavioral characteristics. Teachers can often be selected or avoided. Children gain access to their own transportation, extend the size of their neighborhoods, and spend increasing amounts of time with peers outside of immediate adult supervision. All relationships, including those with family members, become more open and less obligatory. Reflecting these developmental shifts, the influence of peer relationships on developmental outcomes described in this chapter is considered separately for earlier childhood and for later childhood and adolescence.

Longitudinal, macro-level research clearly documents the important role of peers in the development of antisocial behavior. This role occurs along two simultaneous and related tracks, the importance of which shift as the child matures. The first track involves establishment of relationships with and a reputation among the general peer group and occurs during preschool and early elementary school years during children's initial experiences in the peer group. Children who lack social skills and engage in frequent aggressive behavior as a result of family socialization are likely to be rejected by the normative peer group (Patterson, DeBaryshe, & Ramsey, 1989). Such rejection puts the child at increased risk for subsequent antisocial behavior (Asher & Coie, 1990). The second track entails selection of compatible peer associates and friends. Once such selective affiliations are established, mutual shaping of response repertoires occurs such that associates and friends become increasingly similar behaviorally. Antisocial children are likely to select one another as affiliates (Cairns & Cairns, 1994), and association with deviant peers has been shown to be a powerful and robust predictor of subsequent antisocial behavior and drug use (Dishion, French, & Patterson, 1995). The development and implementation of effective clinical and preventive interventions for antisocial behavior depends on an increased understanding of peer relations and influence at macro- and micro-levels. At a macro-level, we need to know how children's reputation or status in general peer groups, and their selective peer associations and friendships are related to the development of antisocial behavior. At a micro-level, we need to understand the processes by which children acquire their status or reputation in the peer group, by which they select friends and peer associates, and by which peers alter, shape, and maintain social behavior. This chapter focuses on both micro- and macro-level analyses of peer influence, but emphasizes micro-processes.

Social Processes in Peer Relationships

Somewhat different processes are likely to operate in obligatory, closed relationships than in those that are open and elective. Coercion and negative reinforcement serve as powerful mechanisms in the development of antisocial behavior in closed, obligatory relationships. This was evidenced in the previous chapter on the role of coercion and negative reinforcement in the family. Coercion and negative reinforcement may also be critical mechanisms by which young children's relationships with the normative peer group and teachers powerfully contribute to the development of antisocial behavior. In school, young children are exposed to a limited set of classmates and one or two teachers, creating relatively closed, obligatory relationships that entail extensive and recurring interaction over time. Given that a child lacks skills and is uncooperative and aversive, such extensive, recurring interaction in a limited choice setting is likely to serve as a powerful breeding ground for coercive interaction engineered by negative reinforcement. However, coercive interpersonal processes also operate in the selective peer relationships and friendships of older children and adolescents, especially those of antisocial individuals.

Although coercion and negative reinforcement in open, elective relationships contribute to individual differences in antisocial behavior, they become less powerful. The child and the co-participants in such relationships are likely to avoid or escape from a specific elective relationship when it becomes the source of recurring, intensively aversive encounters and to seek out relationships with individuals who provide more frequent positive reinforcement. With increasing freedom and choice about how to distribute social time over peers, activities and settings, individuals gravitate toward activities, settings, and people that provide higher relative ratios of positive to aversive social experiences (Conger & Simons, 1995; Gottman, 1991).

Within elective peer relationships, partners are likely to shape one another's behavior via positive reinforcement. Positive reinforcement in elective relationships can support "good" (e.g., school achievement and other normative activities—Kindermann, 1993) or "bad" (e.g., delinquency and drug use—Dishion, Patterson, & Griesler, 1994) behavior, depending on the behavioral characteristics of peer affiliates. In summary, the working hypothesis is that positive reinforcement serves as an increasingly important mechanism in the development of antisocial behavior as children grow older. It mediates children's choice of friends and peer affiliates. Once such affiliations are established, it serves as the mechanism by which behavior is shaped within the relationship.

Another developmental shift has implications for peer-based contingencies associated with the shaping and growth of antisocial behavior. Beginning in the preschool years and continuing through adolescence, individuals' receptive and expressive verbal capacities evolve to increasingly sophisticated levels. Children's own verbal behavior takes on an increasingly powerful role, relative to external social contingencies, in regulating and influencing their social behavior. Moreover, the content of verbal behavior is importantly shaped by external social contingencies such that reinforcement contingencies play a dual role, exerting influence on behavior indirectly via social responses to stated behavioral intentions, and directly via others' responses to the behavior itself (Branch & Hackenberg, 1998; Hayes & Wu, 1998). Reactions by peers to what children say they will do or have done as well as what they actually do become increasingly important in shaping social behavior. The content of these statements can be supportive of antisocial (e.g., "He really pisses me off; I'm going to kick his ass!") or constructive (e.g., "I feel really angry when he does that; I need to stay away from him.") behavior. How others react to verbalized behavioral intentions and reports about one's own past behavior influences the subsequent performance of those behaviors.

The indirect effect of social reinforcement of verbal intentions and reports on antisocial behavior occurs in both closed, obligatory and in open, elective relationships. However, it is likely to be particularly powerful in the open, elective relationships in that the children select as affiliates peers whose verbal and overt behavior are compatible with their own. Children who are coercive and antisocial are likely to select peers as close associates who are similarly coercive and antisocial in talk and in action. Dyad partners will then not only reinforce one another's antisocial actions, but will model and reinforce each other's verbal reports of past antisocial behavior or of verbal intentions about subsequent antisocial behavior. On the other hand, a child who is skilled and engages in socially approved activities is likely to select as close associates peers who are similar behaviorally and who verbally endorse such activities. They then shape and amplify one another's positive social behavior both via direct reactions to the behavior and via approval of verbal reports about the past or future performance of that behavior.

In summary, as children move out of the relatively obligatory, closed family relationships of young childhood, become increasingly involved in elective, open relationships with peers during later childhood and adolescence, and develop increasingly sophisticated verbal repertoires, new social processes may begin to operate, and old social processes may shift in importance. It becomes necessary to explain how children select their social environments as well as how they are shaped by those environments (Buss, 1987). Shifts in the expression of antisocial behavior despite its continuity (Patterson, 1993) are likely accompanied, or perhaps driven, by shifts in processes and mechanisms.

Peer Relationships and the Development of Antisocial Behavior During the Early to Mid-Childhood

Peer Rejection, Coercion, Conflict, and Negative Reinforcement

As they make the transition from the home to day care, preschool, and school environments, children are systematically exposed to a large number of non-related age mates. This transition provides children's first peer culture. Children's initial accommodations and social behavior in this new setting are likely to reflect their socialization at home. Children who fail to acquire social skills and rule following and are uncooperative and aggressive in the family demonstrate a similar lack of skills and aggressiveness with peers (Dishion, Duncan, Eddy, Fagot, & Fetrow, 1994; MacKinnen-Lewis, Volling, et al., 1994; Putallaz, 1987). As a result, they are often disliked and rejected by many of their peers, a social status conferred as early as preschool (e.g., Vitaro, Tremblay, Gagnon, & Bouvin, 1992) and replicated in later childhood (Patterson, Dishion & Bank, 1984) and early adolescence (e.g., Dishion, 1990). This status is quickly re-established in newly forming peer groups (e.g., Coie & Kupersmidt, 1983; Dodge, 1983). Because of their noncompliance, lack of skills, poor academic performance, and aggressiveness, these children are also described in negative terms by non-familial adult caretakers and teachers.

Peer dislike and rejection, academic deficits, and rejection by teachers are early social failures that increase children's risk for a number of concurrent and prospective forms of maladjustment, including antisocial behavior and aggression, early ini-

Table 5.1. Differences in the Social Interaction Patterns of Aggressive and Nonaggressive Children: Interaction With Peers and Teachers.

Sequential Pattern	Non-aggressive	Aggressive	Reference
	Child Toward Peers		
Startup	.09	.22	Shinn et al., 1987
	.02	.09	Snyder, 1984
	.02	.06	Snyder et al., 1983
Reciprocate	.09	.22	Shinn et al., 1987
	.04	.40	Snyder, 1984
	.27	.37	Snyder et al., 1983
Continuance	.23	.42	Snyder, 1984
	Peers Toward Child		
Startup	.07	.16	Shinn et al., 1987
	.02	.07	Fagot, in press
	.11	.19	Snyder et al., 1983
	.08	.13	Snyder, 1984
	Teacher Toward Child		
Startup	.08	.21	Snyder et al., 1983
	.01	.04	Snyder, 1984
Reciprocate	.34	.44	Snyder, 1984

Note: Estimates of reciprocate and continuance are not available for all relationships.

tiation into drug use, and depression (e.g., Kupersmidt & Patterson, 1991; Dishion, 1990). Rejection by normative peers also facilitates association with deviant peers (considered in more detail below). Association with deviant peers, in turn, appears to mediate the association of peer rejection to multiple forms of later child maladaptation (Dishion, Patterson, Stoolmiller, & Skinner, 1991).

Coercion and negative reinforcement are central processes by which peer dislike and rejection increase risk for the development of antisocial behavior. The peer environment and the school classroom are replete with aversive social events. A basic developmental task faced by children making the transition to school entails learning how do deal with disagreement, competition, and conflict in a manner that promotes positive peer relationships and friendships.

Aggressive children have considerable difficulty in accomplishing this task. Data concerning aggressive and nonaggressive children's observed interaction with peers and teachers are shown in Table 5.1. Aggressive relative to nonaggressive children are much more likely to initiate unprovoked verbal or physical aggression (labeled startup) toward their peers, to reciprocate peer aggression, and to continue in aggression once they have initiated it. These patterns of behavior undermine the establishment of constructive, cooperative peer relationships, and are likely to result in dislike and rejection by the larger peer group. However, this coerciveness is not a one-way street. As shown in Table 5.1, aggressive relative to nonaggressive children are 12 to 3 times more likely to be recipients of peer-initiated verbal or physical aggression, consistent with data provided by Dodge (1980). With time and the establishment of a negative reputation among peers, the peer interaction of aggressive children becomes increasingly organized around aversive behavior exchange and conflict, to which both parties contribute (Price & Dodge, 1989).

As shown at the bottom of the Table 5.1, teachers are similarly predisposed to treat aggressive children more aversively than they treat nonaggressive children. Fewer observational data have been collected at OSLC and its affiliated research centers that explicitly compare the coercive interaction of aggressive and nonaggressive children with peers and teachers than with family members, and nearly all of the data (with the exception of Shinn, Ramsey, Walker et al., 1987) have been derived from preschool-aged children. However, a very large number of empirical studies of peer relationships replicate these findings (e.g., Dodge, 1983; Dodge, Schlundt, Schocken, & Delaguch, 1983; Raush, 1965).

Our observational research suggests that about one out of every 10 social behaviors exchanged among peers are coercive, comparable to that of siblings in the home. Aversive social events occur, on the average, once every 2 minutes on the school playground (Snyder, 2000). Once a coercive behavior has been initiated, the likelihood that it will be reciprocated and continue is quite high (see Table 5.1). Patterson, Littman, and Bricker (1967) reported that the typical preschool-aged child is involved in an average of 3.4 conflict episodes with peers per hour, and that the typical conflict episode entails the exchange of five aversive social acts. Frequent, extended coercive interchanges among peers provide the opportunity to learn that aggression is functional in dealing with other people. Frequent aversive exchanges among peers may reflect the equality of the participants in terms of developmental status, the sharing of limited space and resources, and reduced supervision of children's behavior resulting from the lean adult to child ratios found in day care and school settings. Preschool and early elementary school settings provide social conditions that may lead to the rapid shaping, reinforcement, and amplification of coercive, antisocial behavior in children whose repertoires on entry to those settings are already characterized by frequent aggression, tantrums, and noncompliance.

Aggressive children are the instigators and targets of a higher frequency of aversive responses in the peer group than are nonaggressive children, both in terms of initiating coercive behavior and in responding in kind to the aversive behavior of others. Startup, reciprocate, and continuation of aggressive behavior are highly intercorrelated (rs = .40 to .80; Snyder & Brown, 1983). This suggests that coercive interactional events tend to cluster temporally, creating conflict sequences. The occurrence of conflict sequences creates the conditions for negative reinforcement (see previous chapter), which then may serve as the mechanism by which aggressive behavior is maintained and shaped in school, playground, and neighborhood settings.

The hypothesis is that, in so far as coercive relative to constructive tactics are useful for a child in terminating conflict with peers, the more likely coercive tactics will be used in relating to peers. Snyder and Brown (1983) provided a partial test of this hypothesis based on observed conflict sequences derived from the interaction of 10 aggressive and 10 nonaggressive preschool-aged children with their peers. The results are consistent with the negative reinforcement hypothesis, as shown in Table 5.2. For aggressive children, conflict termination was positively associated with the use of verbal aggression (prob. = .69) and negatively associated with talk (prob. = .44) relative to the base rate probability of conflict termination (prob. = .56). For

Table 5.2. A Comparison of The Relative Utility of Coercive and Constructive Conflict Tactics by Aggressive and Nonaggressive Children in Terminating Conflict With Peers.

Conflict Tactic	Aggressive Children Pr. Conflict		Nonaggressive Children Pr. Conflict	
	Termination	z statistic	Termination	z statistic
Verbal Aggression	.69	4.31	.43	-5.72
Talk	.44	-4.76	.74	3.57
No Response	.56	.64	.79	4.33
Baserate	.56		.68	

Note: Any z-statistic with a value greater than 1.96 is significant at + $p05$.

nonaggressive children, conflict termination was positively associated with talk (prob. = .74) and no response (prob. = .79), and negatively associated with verbal aggression (prob. = .43) relative to the base rate of conflict termination (prob. = .68). Aggressive children were most frequently reinforced by their peers for using coercive behavior, and nonaggressive children for using nonaversive, constructive behavior.

Peer victims may also provide positive as well as negative reinforcement for coercive behavior and attacks. Child aggression is highly functional in attaining access to desired activities and materials and in establishing one's status among peers, especially for males (Maccoby, 1998; Olweus, 1994). Consistent with this notion, Patterson et al. (1967) found that children whose aggressive behavior toward a peer victim was reinforced by the victim were likely to target the same victim using the same aggressive behavior during the next episode of aggression. In contrast, children whose aggressive behavior was resisted by a peer victim were likely to target a different victim, use a different aggressive behavior, or both during the next aggressive episode. Patterson and his colleagues (1967) also found that children who were frequently victimized and showed low rates of aggression initially became more aggressive over time to the degree that their counterattacks were successful in turning off bullies' aggression. Victims whose counterattacks were unsuccessful in terminating peer aggression did not become more aggressive over time and continued to be victimized at high rates. Children perform behaviors in the peer setting in so far as those behaviors are functional in attaining desired materials, activities, and status.

The role of the peer group in the development of aggressive behavior has a systemic quality. Perpetrators are often reinforced for their coercive efforts, and victims are faced with the choice of learning to defend themselves with counter-coercion or of continued victimization. Patterson et al. (1967) report a median correlation of .50 between the frequency at which young children are aggressive and at which they are victimized in the peer group, and Snyder and Brown (1983) report similar correlations between the rates at which children are initiators and recipients of aversive behavior. There is considerable reciprocity—children get what they give. This bilateral, systemic effect further suggests that there should be considerable temporal stability in children's aggressiveness in the peer group. Patterson et al. (1967) report that the median cross-time correlation for individual differences in observed aggression over the school year was .70.

Coercive behavior and negative reinforcement appear play a powerful role in maintaining and shaping aggressive, antisocial behavior in the peer setting during the preschool and elementary school years. For at-risk children, verbal and physical aggression becomes a salient, practiced means of relating to peers, begetting repeated rejection, and counter-coercion by normative peers. Paradoxically, even though it begets rejection and counter-coercion by peers, such aggressive behavior is highly functional in the short run. In the long run, however, this behavioral trap places the aggressive child at considerable risk not only because it maintains and amplifies aggressive behavior, but because it initiates a series of developmental progressions in which the aggressive child selects social niches that promote further aggression and in which there is decreasing access to social environments that promote skilled, normative social behavior. The causal role of peer coercion and negative reinforcement inferred from correlational research has been supported by recent prevention trials indicating that alteration of contingencies on the playground leads to substantial reductions in peer aggression (Stoolmiller, Eddy, & Reid, 2000).

Selective Peer Affiliation, Friendships, and Positive Reinforcement

As they move into extensive contact with peers in school, playground, and neighborhood settings, children begin choosing friends and close affiliates. Children are selective about how they distribute their social time among peers. This implies that the amount of social influence exerted by specific peers varies with the amount of time the child spends with those peers, and the type of influence being exerted depends on the characteristics of the target child and his or her close peer associates. Choice occurs even during preschool and early elementary school years, though the range of choice is limited by the children's placement in specific classrooms and schools and by the amount of mobility in the neighborhood allowed by parents or caretakers. The range of choice increases with child age and maturation, and progresses toward increasingly large and diverse peer contacts during middle school and high school.

Peer reports by older children and adolescents concerning membership of individuals in selected social-affiliative networks indicate that nearly all children are a part of such networks regardless of their behavioral characteristics (e.g., Cairns & Cairns, 1994). There is relatively little information about selective affiliation and peer choice by younger children (Hinde, Titmus, Easton, & Tamplin, 1985; Ladd, Price, & Hart, 1990), with the exception of generalized sex-segregation (Daniels-Bierness, 1989; Maccoby, 1998). Snyder, West, Stockemer, Gibbons, and Almquist-Parks (1996) assessed the selective peer affiliations of younger children by observing the amount of time each child spent with each of his or her classmates on the playground and by obtaining each child's preference ratings for each classmate. Snyder et al. (1996) found that 4- to 5-year-old children's distribution of social time among peers was highly skewed; each child spent about 50% of playground time with two or three peers. Children as young as 4 years of age, when exposed to an at least partially open social environment, make explicit affiliate choices and form intensive, continuing relationships with a small number of peers out of those available in the immediate environment. This selectivity is more differentiated than simple same-sex segregation. Active peer selection operates well before the middle childhood years.

When entering a newly forming peer group comprised of unfamiliar children, children probe the social landscape to locate compatible peers. Our working assumption is that individuals gravitate toward individuals with whom interaction produces positive social experiences and avoid individuals with whom interaction generates aversive social experiences. Put in more formal learning theory terms, children will distribute their social time among the array of available peers in proportion to the relative rate of positive reinforcement generated during interaction with each of those peers (Snyder, 1995).

In order to test this hypothesis, Snyder et al. (1996) used observations of the social interaction of each child in several newly forming preschool classes with each of his or her classmates during the first month of the school year to calculate the probability of receiving positive social consequences from each classmate relative to the base rate of positive consequences received from all classmates. During the second month of the school year, the amount of time each child spent in social interaction with each of his or her classmates on the playground was observed, and each child's preference rating for each classmate was obtained. Using a short-term longitudinal design, these measures were replicated on the same set of children later in the school year. The bivariate relationship between the relative probability of positive reinforcement received from each peer and the amount of association time with and preference for each peer was calculated for each child, following a matching law formulation of individual choice described in the previous chapter. Children's selective behavioral affiliations with both same-and-opposite sex classmates were strongly related to the relative rate at which they were reinforced by those classmates both at the beginning (rs from .70 to .85) and later (rs from .65 to .85) in the school year. This matching process applied to opposite- as well as same-sex relationships despite strong same-sex preferences.

Peer relationships in a classroom, or in other open settings comprised of elective relationships, is not a totally stable system. Selective affiliations are adjusted and realigned over time according to ongoing and iterative social experiences. A perturbation in one part of this system is likely to ripple throughout the system. Snyder et al. (1996) found that the continuity in peer affiliations over the 2 month period was reliable but modest, ranging from .22 (for females with males) to .68 (for males with males). Strong mutual affiliations (defined as a reciprocated preference and >15% shared association time on the playground) were relatively stable, the probability that a strong mutual affiliation would persist over a 2 month period was .61 for boys and .68 for girls. Mechanisms that mediate initial peer selection should account for change as well as continuity in those affiliations over time. According to the reinforcement formulation, shifts in a child's peer affiliations over time should be predicted by changes in the relative rate of positive consequences received from each of those peers. Snyder et al. (1996) tested this model by calculating the correlation between the relative rate of reinforcement received by each child from each of his or her peers at one time point with the child's selective affiliation with those peers in 4 weeks later, after partialling out the child's earlier peer affiliation scores. The partial correlations were sizable and highly reliable (range of rs = .65 to .80) for opposite as well as same-sex relationships.

These findings are consistent with a reinforcement-matching formulation. Children allocate their time among and express a verbal preference for peers based on the functional (reinforcement) value of those peers based on recent social experience. Children spend most of their time in relationships that provide the best payoffs. This accounts for same-sex segregation and preference and for selective affiliations within same- and opposite-sex groups. However, children continue to spend a small amount of time surveying remaining, less reinforcing social relationships in order to stay in contact with shifts in contingencies. As the functional value among relationships change over time, so does affiliation. Such flexibility and openness to environmental change is highly adaptive (Raush, Barry, Hertel, & Swain, 1974). Our understanding of the processes by which children make peer choices and establish selective affiliations is certainly incomplete and in need of replication. This matching-reinforcement process may also account for peer affiliation and preference in older children and adolescents (Conger & Kileen, 1974).

Research has repeatedly indicated that individuals, when operating in an open environment offering elective relationships, select and affiliate with others who are behaviorally similar to themselves (as well as similar in external characteristics such as age, sex, and race) Such findings are observed across the life span and in the context of various types of relationships (Caspi & Herbener, 1990; Kandel, Davies, & Baydar, 1990). The source of such behavioral homophily in peer selection is not clear, and identification of processes by which it occurs would provide a powerful tool in intervention. It is our working assumption that children and adolescents form strong associations on the basis of positive payoffs, and that such payoffs are maximized when partners are behaviorally compatible. From this person-environment fit perspective, the selection of close affiliates on the basis of behavioral similarity reflects a matching-reinforcement process; children are most likely to be reinforced at high rates by peers who are behaviorally compatible. This formulation applies to the aggregation of children in social dyads or in larger peer networks and to aggressive, antisocial, as well as skilled, norm-endorsing children.

To test this hypothesis, Snyder, Horsch, and Childs (1997) divided a sample of preschool children into groups who were highly aggressive (above the 90th percentile relative to normative samples) and less aggressive (below the 90th percentile). Both low and high aggression children distributed their association time with peers on the playground and indicated differentiated self-reported preferences for specific peers to a similar degree and used the same reinforcement-matching process to select peer affiliates. Highly aggressive children locate and establish social niches in the peer environment in a manner comparable to that of less aggressive children. Given highly aggressive children also frequently engage in behavior that is aversive to peers, the degree to which they successfully find peer niches and the characteristics of the peers with whom they affiliate become an interesting issue. Snyder et al. (1997) found that 43% of highly aggressive children and 86% of less aggressive children established strong mutual affiliations (defined by mutual positive preference scores and observed mutual association of total playground time > 15%). Highly aggressive children were more likely (78%) to be involved in strong unilateral peer relationships (non-reciprocated preference and association) than were less aggressive children (55%). Strong mutual affiliations showed more temporal continuity (probability of persistence = .70) than strong unilateral affiliations (probability of persistence = .24) over a 2 month period. There were no differences in the temporal persistence and intensity of unilateral or mutual affiliations of high and low aggression children. Highly aggressive children have more difficulty in successfully establishing mutual close peer relationships than do less aggressive children, at least during the preschool-aged years. Once established, mutual affiliations are relatively enduring regardless of the child's aggressive status. High relative to low aggressive children are more often involved in non-reciprocated peer relationships that dissipate over time. Aggressive children are not without friends or a peer network, but their friendships and peer networks are more difficult to establish, more tenuous, and less stable.

Given that strong peer affiliations are established by aggressive children, the next question concerns the behavioral characteristics of their close peer associates. Snyder et al. (1997) found that 50% of strong mutual affiliations of highly aggressive children were with peers who are also highly aggressive compared to 12% of those of less aggressive children. The unilateral affiliations of highly aggressive children were more likely to be with other highly aggressive peers (38%) than those of less aggressive children (24%). In the context of matching-positive reinforcement processes, more and less aggressive children established behavioral affiliations with specific peers who were similar to themselves in aggressiveness. This suggests that selection on the basis of positive reinforcement is compatible with, and possibly the vehicle for, behavioral homophily among child dyads.

As suggested previously, close peer associates and friends provide the social context for a good deal of positive exchange. But, approximately half of all coercive exchanges experienced by preschool children occur during interaction with close mutual or unilateral peer affiliates. Interactions in peer dyads containing one or two highly aggressive children relative to dyads comprised of non-aggressive children were twice as likely to involve coercive behavior. The mean duration of coercive episodes in dyads containing one or two aggressive children was twice as long, and the mean intensity level of coercive behavior was 1.5 higher than that of non-aggressive dyads (Snyder et al., 1997). Aggressive children are contributing to and experiencing a high dosage of coercive social exchange with peers, both in the general peer group as a function of their negative reputation and rejection, but also in the more selective relationships they establish within the larger peer context, very often with other highly aggressive children. The amount of time children spent interacting with aggressive peers had a powerful impact on their subsequent performance of aggressive behavior, as measured by playground observation and global teacher ratings. As shown in Figure 5.1, children who spent minimal association time (< 15%) with aggressive peers showed decreases in aggression over a subsequent 2 month period. In contrast, children who showed moderate (15% to 30%) or substantial time (> 30% of total social time) associating with aggressive peers showed increases in aggressive behavior during the following 2 months. Association with highly aggressive peers, often in elective close unilateral or mutual affiliations, influences individual differences in short-term growth of aggressive behavior. Although aggressive children can locate and select friends who, because of their behavioral compatibility, are reinforcing, both the children's and their friends coercive repertoire are likely to lead to frequent and extended disagreements and conflicts, even in their close peer relationships. Frequent and extended coercive exchange among peers predicts growth in aggressive behavior as early as the preschool years.

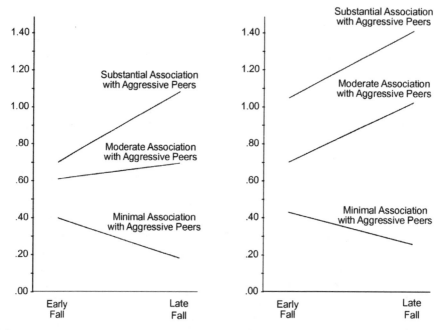

Figure 5.1. Association with aggressive peers and temporal changes in child aggressive behavior.

Peer Relationships and the Development of Antisocial Behavior During Pre-adolescence and Adolescence

Association With Deviant Peers and Adolescent Growth In Deviant Behavior

Longitudinal data from multiple samples clearly and repeatedly indicate that there is considerable growth in multiple forms of deviant behavior beginning at ages 12 to 14, which continues through middle adolescence and, in some cases, late adolescence and young adulthood. These forms are highly inter-correlated and include antisocial behavior, arrests, violent acts, substance use, risk taking, sexual intercourse, and early childbearing (e.g., Dishion, Poulon, & Skaggs, 2000; Farrington, 1986; Gottfriedson & Hirschi, 1990; Huizinga, Loeber, & Thornberry, 1993; Jessor & Jessor, 1977; Moffitt, 1993; Patterson, Dishion & Yoeger, 2000; Patterson & Yoeger, 1999). Such growth may reflect biological maturation and the establishment of social autonomy consonant with normative adolescence. However, there are clear individual differences in the developmental trajectory of these behaviors, and their early onset and persistence substantially increase individuals' risk for continuing maladjustment during adolescence and early adult years (Dishion et al., 2000; Moffitt, 1993; Patterson, 1996; Patterson & Yoeger, 1993).

Association with deviant peers during late childhood and early adolescence has repeatedly been found to be one of the most powerful, proximal predictors of individual differences in the onset, persistence, and progression of antisocial behavior, drug use, criminal activity, and sexual behavior in several longitudinal studies in our own work in Oregon (Capaldi, Crosby, & Stoolmiller, 1996; Dishion, Capaldi, & Yoeger, 1999; Dishion, Capaldi, Spracklen, & Li, 1995; Patterson & Dishion, 1984; Patterson, Dishion, & Yoerger, 2000; Snyder, Dishion, & Patterson, 1986) and documented by other investigators (e.g., Coie, Terry, et al., 1995; Elliott & Menard, 1996; Kandel, 1982; Vitaro, Tremblay, Kerr, Pagani, & Bukowski, 1997).

The increasingly powerful influence of peers on behavior during pre-adolescence and adolescence is the result of several converging normative transitions. Progression to middle school and high school brings with it exposure to a larger number and a broader array of peers with whom to associate. Children spend increasing amounts of time with peers without the direct supervision of adults (Larson & Richards, 1991). As part of biological and cognitive maturation, adolescents push for autonomy (Steinberg & Silverberg, 1986) and come into increasing conflict with parents and other adults (Montemayor, 1982). Peer influence does not necessarily have negative developmental connotations. Peers may support positive as well as deviant behavior. The nature and power of peer influence depends on a combination of factors: The characteristics of the peer associates and friends with whom a youth identifies and spends time, parental and other adult supervision of peer choice and free-time activities, and the amount of time adolescents spend wandering with peers in unorganized activities without adult supervision (Osgood, Wilson, Bachman, O'Malley, & Johnston, 1996; Stoolmiller, 1994). During this adolescent transition, there is considerable variation in peer-induced risk for growth in antisocial and other forms of problem behavior. The contexts and processes by which such risk is inbued has been the focus of considerable attention in our empirical work.

Peer Associates, Friends: Selection and Deviancy Training

During elementary school, children who lack skills, are highly aggressive, and who are rejected by the normative peer group begin to systematically associate with other rejected, highly aggressive children (Dishion et al., 1991; Ladd, 1983; Snyder et al., 1997). This aggregation of deviant peers into small social networks accelerates during the transition to more impersonal middle school and high school settings which contain a larger pool of compatible age mates and decreased monitoring by adults. In both our work (Dishion, Andrews & Crosby, 1995; Dishion et al., 1994; Dishion et al., 1995; Dishion & Skaggs, 2000; Poulon, Dishion, & Skaggs, 1999) as well as that of other researchers (Billy, Rodgers, & Udry, 1984; Kandel, 1978; Poulin, Cillisen, et al., 1997), friendships and other intensive peer affiliations have been observed among adolescents who are similar in terms of deviant behavior, including arrests, antisocial behavior, smoking, alcohol use, and early sexual activity.

Behavioral similarity between adolescent friends and among members of adolescent cliques is the result, in part, of an active selection process based on behavioral compatibility (Cairns & Cairns, 1994; Kandel, 1978). The social processes by which such compatibility is recognized and probed has not been unambiguously specified. Preliminary evidence suggests that preference and selective affiliation are quickly established during initial encounters in newly-forming peer groups, and are made on the basis of the relative rates of positive social reinforcement exchanged during these initial encounters (Conger & Kileen, 1974; Hops, Albert, & Davis,

1997) similar to the processes described for younger children earlier in this chapter. In friendships and peer networks of deviant adolescents, the social exchange of positive reinforcers is likely to be organized around deviant talk and activities (Dishion, Patterson, & Griesler, 1994).

Adolescent friends and peer associates who spend time together serve as potent models, collaborators, and reinforcement agents for one another such that their behavior becomes increasingly similar over time (Kandel, 1978; 1986), especially in the absence of parental or other adult supervision. The choice of peers, activities, and settings determines opportunities and support for drug use, delinquency, and antisocial behavior. Given continuing exposure to deviant peers, unsupervised wandering, and antisocial activities, an individual's behavior is shaped in a manner that promotes the contagious spread and growth in new, more varied, and serious forms of deviant behavior. These peer association-shaping mechanisms are likely to be central to the metamorphosis and growth of antisocial behavior in pre-adolescence and adolescence, extending and amplifying the developmental trajectory of children with early-onset antisocial behavior (Patterson, 1996; Patterson & Yoerger, 1993). These mechanisms may also provide the impetus for adolescent-onset or late starting antisocial involvement (Patterson & Yoeger, 1997). Given the powerful and proximal role of peer influence, an understanding of the processes by which shaping of antisocial behavior, drug use, and other problem behaviors occur in adolescent friendships and cliques is critical to the development of effective preventive and clinical interventions.

Our hypothesis is that mutual positive social reinforcement among deviant friends and peer associates plays a central role in the shaping, amplification, and diversification of antisocial behavior. Peer reinforcement may operate to directly shape and encourage deviant behavior as it occurs in the natural environment (e.g., peers laugh when one child pushes another, a peer says "Cool!" after a child successfully shoplifts a CD). Peer reinforcement may also encourage deviant behavior indirectly by shaping and encouraging talk about previous antisocial actions (war stories—"Let me tell you about the time when I snuck out of the house . . . ") or about future intentions to engage in antisocial behavior (jacking up—"I know this guy who we can buy some dope from tonight and then can get blasted . . . "). Peer talk provides information, scripts, and verbal rehearsal relevant to increasing variety and expertise in antisocial behavior. The extent to which such talk is met with a positive social response during peer interaction will determine its power in promoting antisocial behavior. Criminal behavior and drug use during childhood and adolescence frequently involves dyads or groups (Howell, Krisberg, and Jones, 1995) such that reinforcement during the commission of deviant behavior or crime is likely to take both direct (behavioral) and indirect (talk) forms, providing mutual instruction and immediate feedback as well as modeling and practice during the commission of the deviant act.

Dishion and his colleagues have diligently tested the role of positive reinforcement processes in shaping antisocial behavior in close peer relationships, building on efforts begun some 30 years ago. Buehler, Patterson, and Furniss (1966) observed the likelihood at which female delinquents in a group residential setting were reinforced for deviant versus normative or socially conforming talk and behavior. Initial observations indicated that girls' rule breaking and aggressive behavior, and verbal criticism of adults and adult rules led to positive social reactions from peers

70% to 90% of the time, and that socially conforming talk and actions were reinforced by peers at a much lower rate. Much of the peer reinforcement took non-verbal rather than verbal form, especially for antisocial behavior. In a more thorough analysis, the reactions of peers and adult staff to delinquent girls' talk and behavior were systematically observed for a week. Peers in the residential institution reacted positively to delinquent girls' antisocial talk and behavior 65% of the time, whereas normative talk and behavior was reinforced 33% of the time. Adult staff members responded positively to normative talk and behavior 79% of the time, and to antisocial talk and behavior 17% of the time. However, peers relative to staff provided twice as many social reactions to girls' talk, and efforts by the staff to engage girls in problem solving were met with negative reactions 58% of the time.

In a recent study building on these earlier findings, Dishion, Andrews, and Crosby (1995) observed the conversations between 13-year-old boys and their self-identified male friends. Half of the boys had been identified as antisocial 3 years earlier. Dishion and his colleagues found that the friends of antisocial relative to non-antisocial boys were more likely also be antisocial. The rate of antisocial talk in the conversations of antisocial boys with their best friends was 1.7 times more often than that observed in the friendship dyads of non-antisocial boys. The duration of antisocial talk in the friendship dyads of deviant boys was 350% greater. Normative talk was 70% less than that of boys in the normative dyads. Antisocial dyads spent 30% of their conversational time in antisocial talk. This supports the notion that boys select one another on the basis on similarity in antisocial behavior, and once antisocial boys establish a relationship, they spend a considerable amount of their social time recalling or planning antisocial activities.

In a replication and extension of these findings, Dishion, Spracklen, Andrews, and Patterson (1996) observed the conversations of 186 high-risk adolescents and their best friends. Three hypotheses were tested. First, adolescent friendships involving at least one antisocial member (defined by a history of arrest) would engage in more rule-breaking talk than those in which neither member was antisocial. Second, friendship dyads with an antisocial member would provide more reinforcement for antisocial talk than friendships without antisocial members. Third, based on a matching-reinforcement model, the relative rate of antisocial talk occurring during conversations in dyads would be reliably correlated with the relative rate of positive social responses provided by dyad members for such talk. All three hypotheses were supported.

Friendships involving two antisocial boys contained nearly 3 times as much rule-breaking talk as friendship dyads containing one antisocial boy; It was 4.5 times as much as friendships in which neither boy was antisocial. Friendships involving two antisocial boys engaged in only half as much normative talk as the other dyad types. Dishion et al. (1996) used sequential analyses to assess the reactions of friends to rule-breaking and normative talk in each of the dyad types. As shown in Figure 5.2, positive reactions in friendship dyads involving two antisocial boys were primarily engendered by rule-breaking rather than normative talk (bottom of the figure). In friendship dyads where neither partner was antisocial, positive reactions occurred primarily in response to normative talk (top of the figure). In friendships comprised of one antisocial and one non-antisocial boy, positive reactions occurred in response to normative talk and, to a lesser degree, rule-breaking talk (middle of the figure).

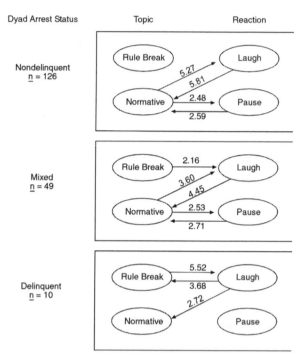

Figure 5.2. Sequential transitions between topics and reactions (lag 1) within male adolescent friendship dyads.

These data suggest that different contingencies are offered by friends for one another's talk depending on the behavioral characteristics of the youth in that friendship. Antisocial friends provide social contingencies that promote rule-breaking talk whereas non-antisocial adolescent friends provide contingencies that promote and sustain normative talk. In further support of this interpretation, Dishion et al. (1996) found the relative rate at which friends responded positively to rule-breaking talk during conversation accounted for 84% of the variance in the rates of rule-breaking talk. A scatter plot showing the relationship between rule-breaking talk and reinforcement of such talk is shown in Figure 5.3. The data in the scatter plot indicate that the content of conversations among adolescent friends is closely tuned to their friends' reactions, consistent with a matching-reinforcement model.

Rule-breaking talk and its social reinforcement among adolescents is not simply a a transient phenomenon during this developmental period. There is considerable cross-time stability in the rate of rule-breaking talk of adolescents and their best friends, and this stability does not vary as new friendships are formed and old ones are terminated change (Dishion, Eddy, Haas, Li, & Spracklen, 1997). Rule-breaking talk and its positive reinforcement are not innocuous, but rather serve as a source of deviancy training that has powerful, diverse, and persisting developmental effects. Peer deviancy training has been found to predict growth in arrests, violent behavior, drug use, and sexual activity over the subsequent 2 to 4 years of development (Dishion, Capaldi, et al., 1995; Dishion, Eddy, et al., 1997; Dishion, Spracklen, et al., 1996). For example, Patterson, Dishion, and Yoeger (2000) have shown that the impact of early involvement with deviant peers at age 10 on growth in arrests,

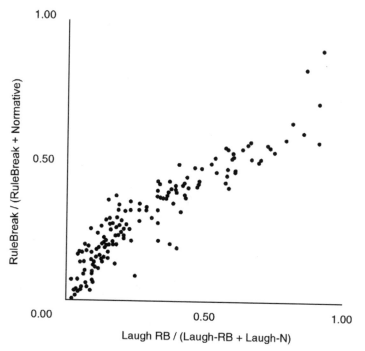

Figure 5.3. A matching law analysis of rule-breaking discourse in boys' friendship dyads (n = 181).

substance use, and sexual intercourse from ages 10 to 18 is fully mediated by deviancy training at age 14 (see Figure 5.4). In this analysis, deviancy training was defined as sophisticated construct comprised of the rate of reinforcement of deviant talk, the degree of association with deviant peers, the level of antisocial behavior of peer associates, and the amount of time spent with peers. Fifty-three percent of the variance in the growth construct comprised of measures of the three forms of maladjustment were accounted for by deviancy training. As a whole, Dishion's research on deviancy training provide very powerful findings. In each study, true growth in a variety of negative developmental outcomes, each derived from different sources, and reflecting ecologically valid and socially salient problems, have been prospectively linked to peer deviancy training.

Stronger causal inferences concerning the relationships of association with deviant peers and deviancy training to the development of antisocial behavior have been derived from experimental, controlled intervention trials. Dishion and Andrews (1995) and Dishion, McCord, and Poulin (1999) report that the delivery of preventive interventions in formats entailing the systematic aggregation of at-risk youth have negative, iatrogenic, long-term effects relative to youth who received no intervention or family-based intervention. Adolescents targeted using peer-group interventions evidenced more growth in tobacco use, teacher-reported delinquent behavior, arrests for index crimes, alcohol use, and other mental health problems. These iatrogenic effects occurred despite efforts to minimize peer deviancy training during intervention sessions with careful monitoring and contingency management. Descriptive reviews (O'Donnell, Manos, & Chesney-Lind, 1987) and meta-analyses

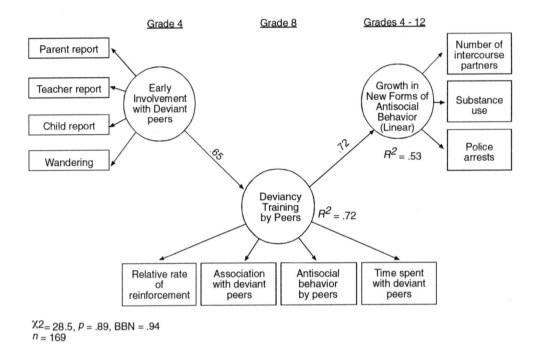

Figure 5.4. Deviance training as a mediator between involvement with deviant peers and growth in antisocial behavior.

(Lipsey, 1992) indicate that the iatrogenic effects of peer-based interventions with high-risk youth may be common. Contexts which aggregate large numbers of deviant youth in close proximity or in common activities engender deviant peer group association, deviancy training, and ultimately promote growth in problematic behavior. These contexts may result from social interventions such as ability tracking in schools, mental health services, preventive interventions, group home placement, and incarceration of juveniles. They may also result from social and economic forces which lead to aggregation of poor, single-parent, or otherwise under-resourced families in specific neighborhoods.

Peer Associates and Friends: Relationship Quality and Support

The negative impact of selection of and association with deviant friends and peers may appear to be at odds with the positive functions ascribed to friendships, social networks, and social support in the broader literature in developmental and social psychology (Hartup, 1996). In fact, friendships and cliques involving deviant peers do provide mutual support and a sense of belonging, but are organized around deviant activities (Cairns & Cairns, 1994). The interaction of antisocial adolescents with their friends is characterized by a level of positive engagement comparable to that observed in friendship dyads comprised of normative youth (Dishion, Andrews, & Crosby, 1995). Antisocial as well as normative adolescents perceive their friendships as relatively positive (Poulin, Dishion, & Haas, 1998).

However, there is evidence that the quality of friendships among antisocial youth is lower than that among normative youth (Brendgen, Little, & Krappman, 1997; Dishion, 1990; Dishion, Andrews, et al., 1995; Poulin et al., 1998). There is more coercion, bossiness, and negative reciprocity. Friendships are shorter in duration, and often end in acrimony. Compared to perceptions of their friends, antisocial youth ascribe a more positive and less negative quality to their friendship. Dyadic coercion and perceptual discordance about the quality of the relationship increases as youth are more antisocial. The lack of social skills and reliance on coercive means of relating to others is characteristic of antisocial individuals in family and in peer relationships during childhood are still apparent in their friendships and peer cliques during adolescence. If a youth is antisocial, the relative lack of positive relationship qualities with close friends is associated with growth in antisocial behavior (Poulin et al., 1999). A history of marginal peer relationships, troubled friendships, and reliance on deviance to establish new relationships come at considerable cost. It is harder to locate compatible individuals, and there is reduced access to normative activities and individuals. It is more difficult to sustain relationships. Short-duration, often-coercive close relationships are primarily organized around deviant talk and activities, further exacerbating the negative developmental process.

The Ongoing Role of Families

While families may exert less influence as children move into adolescence, gain access to open settings containing a more diverse set of peers, and increase their autonomy, families continue to play critical roles in adolescent development. Parental monitoring is particularly important in channeling and modulating peer influence. Good monitoring entails knowledge of a child's peer associates, whereabouts, and activities when the child is not in the home. Good monitoring involves the negotiation of clear limits and rules that regulate a child's exposure to negative influences and activities, and parental willingness and skillfulness in responding contingently to violations of those limits and rules (Patterson, 1982). Effective monitoring grows out of earlier parent-child relationships in which there is good problem solving, a sense of mutual involvement, and infrequent coercion (Dishion et al., 1995). Monitoring is particularly important in environments characterized by high densities of deviant individuals and replete with opportunities for deviant activities (Wilson, 1980).

Our research has shown that poor parental monitoring consistently accounts for substantial variance in deviant peer association, both indirectly via child antisocial behavior and more directly via its influence on a child's opportunity to associate and have unsupervised time with antisocial peers (Dishion et al., 2000; Dishion et al., 1991; Patterson & Dishion, 1984; Snyder et al., 1986). In a series of elegant analyses, Stoolmiller (1994) demonstrated high correlations among developmental growth trajectories for unsupervised wandering, association with deviant peers, and antisocial behavior from age 10 to age 14. Kilgore, Snyder, and Lentz (2000) report that parental monitoring may contribute importantly to children's exposure to deviancy-producing experiences in school, neighborhood, and home contexts as early as kindergarten. The causal status of monitoring in reducing antisocial behavior and deviant peer contact has also been established in preventive and clinical trials (Dishion & Andrews, 1995; Eddy & Chamberlain, 2000; Forgatch, 1991). Improvement in monitoring as the result of intervention is clearly associated with reductions in child antisocial behavior

Sibling relationships are often considered prototypes for peer relationships. In fact, siblings appear to contribute to deviancy training in a manner that is similar to peers and may, in fact, facilitate contact with deviant peer groups. Bullock and Dishion (2000) have observed that sibling pairs in high-risk relative to normative families engage in more collusion, or planning to conspire in antisocial behavior, even in the presence of their parents. Like peer deviancy training, sibling collusion involves the endorsement and reinforcement of rule-breaking behavior. Sibling collusion contributes to growth in antisocial behavior after controlling for deviant peer association (Bullock & Dishion, 2000). In addition to mutual endorsement of deviant behavior, siblings' self-reported rates of co-participation in delinquent acts are highly correlated (Rowe & Gulley, 1992). Bank, Snyder, & Burraston (2000) have found that siblings often share common peer groups, and that these shared peer contacts are a vehicle by which older siblings introduce younger siblings to a variety of deviant behaviors, including delinquent acts, drug use, and sexual activity. An unexplored inference is that younger siblings' exposure to older siblings' peers may play an important role in early onset antisocial behavior, and its later escalation during early-adolescence.

Peer relationships are active social fields that strongly impact child developmental trajectories. The nature of behavioral influence exerted in peer relationships is clearly tuned to the ambient social reinforcers occurring in those relationships. Social rewards in deviant peer relationships, both for talk and action, prepare and encourage youth to engage in variety of antisocial behaviors and to seek additional and subsequent relationships that support such behavior. Thus, as one peer relationship is replaced by another, the deviancy training process continues. It is the social function of deviant behavior rather than the specific individuals with whom youth develop friendships that appears to be critical to peer influence. Youth seek peer relational and activity niches congruent with their own repertoires, and in so doing, establish and iteratively recreate experiences that amplify and diversify that repertoire. In the case of individuals on an antisocial developmental trajectory, these niches and experiences provide continued impetus for continuity and growth in various forms of deviant behavior.

Association with deviant peers does not arrive, de novo, in late childhood and adolescence. Rather, it is a product of previous and ongoing failures in socialization and of coercive training in the home (Ramsey, Patterson, & Walker, 1990), and of relational difficulties, mutual coercion, and rejection in peer and school settings. Recent evidence also suggests that selective association and friendship choice and rule-breaking talk and its reinforcement by peers may begin in the early grade school years. Thus, two peer social processes that promote progression and growth in antisocial behavior may be operating from kindergarten through high school. The first process entails a coercive relational style facilitated by negative reinforcement contingencies, rejection by normative peers, and low-quality, short-duration friendships. The second process involves selective affiliation and friendship formation among deviant children and adolescents, and deviancy training in the forms of collusion and co-participation, facilitated by positive reinforcement contingencies. Using a metaphor from John Reid, adding social failure and coercion training in the peer setting to that already established in the home, and then adding deviant peer selection and the deviancy training processes occurring in friendships among antisocial individuals are like hooking second and third engines to the train of antisocial development—it becomes much more powerful and attains greater momentum.

Peer relationships are embedded in other social contexts, and the course of peer relationships and their influence on child developmental trajectories are impacted by those contexts. The quality of parent-child relationships and parental monitoring influence the nature, extensiveness, and direction of peer influence. Early sibling relationships may serve as developmental prototypes for peer relationships, and sibling relationships during childhood and adolescence may provide training, opportunity, and practice in deviant behavior. Peers to whom individuals are exposed and from whom they select friends or associates are not a random sample drawn from a huge peer urn. In fact, larger social and economic forces place children in geographic locations, neighborhoods, and schools that limit or bias the behavioral characteristics of individuals comprising the peer group (a smaller, more select urn). The characteristics of the peer group and the manner in which it contributes to child socialization may be different in inner city Chicago than in rural Wyoming, or in an affluent Los Angeles suburb than in a blue-collar neighborhood in Pittsburgh, Pennsylvania.

We think the same social processes and mechanisms operate in peer groups in all of these locales, just as probability theory applies to different colored marbles drawn from large and small urns. However, the direction in which peers influence child development (including antisocial behavior) not only depends on the dynamics within a specific peer group (e.g., rejection vs. acceptance, and peer selection and shaping), but also on the characteristics of the peer group (e.g., concentration of antisocial children) determined by larger social and economic forces. Peer rejection, coercion, and negative reinforcement, and peer selection/shaping and positive reinforcement operate in each locale, but the direction and power of these social processes in promoting or mitigating antisocial behavior may vary depending on the locale. The concentration of unskilled, antisocial children in a given locale is very important. The behavioral correlates of rejection versus acceptance within the larger peer group, the extent to which coercive processes operate, the ease at which affiliations with deviant peers can be established, and the contingency relationships between reinforcement and behavior within those affiliations may be different in locales with high versus low concentrations of antisocial youth (e.g., Raush, 1965; Wright, Giammarino, & Parad, 1986).

Much of our peer research has used samples residing in locales that are characterized by relatively high concentrations of children at considerable risk for antisocial behavior (from high crime neighborhoods, from single-parent families with incomes below the poverty level, in residential or treatment settings serving antisocial children). Undoubtedly, there are settings containing even higher concentrations of high-risk or antisocial peers. Systematic comparisons of the means by which coercion, negative reinforcement, deviant talk, and positive reinforcement operate differentially or result in different net effects in peer locales with higher versus lower concentrations of at risk children have yet to be made.

Individuals' own history of antisocial behavior provides an additional, complementary context. As individuals proceed along a developmental trajectory characterized by more varied and more serious antisocial behavior, they are increasing unable to access activities, persons, and settings that provide the opportunities for acquisition of skills, knowledge, and experience requisite to economic and social success, either because of their choice or because of active exclusion by normative individuals and organizations. Antisocial behavior is a function of the larger contexts in which individuals reside, and the contexts in which people reside are also a product of antisocial behavior. Peer influence depends on elective niche finding and on non-elective social and economic forces which influence the concentration of deviant peers in the child's social environment, including educational, residential, or specialized intervention settings.

This preliminary sketch of the contexts, relationships, and processes relevant to peer contributions to antisocial behavior is probably only a rough approximation of the "real picture." But the sketch suggests that very powerful, and sometimes insidious processes and contingencies, are at work in peer relationships, which create conditions that account for individual differences in the onset, persistence, and severity of antisocial behavior. Continuing clarification of the details of the picture are likely to have powerful implications for how we can go about creating educational settings, social programs, and preventive and remedial interventions that foster positive child and adolescent development.

6

Contextual Risk Across the Early Life Span and Association with Antisocial Behavior

Deborah Capaldi, David DeGarmo, Gerald R. Patterson, and Marion Forgatch

Environmental factors have long been considered to be key to understanding the etiology of delinquent behavior (Wilson, 1983). Sociologists (Laub & Sampson, 1991) and psychologists (Farrington, 1978; Loeber & Dishion, 1983) have come to view family variables as prime determinants for antisocial and delinquent behavior. These family processes are embedded within larger contexts that affect the family such as employment changes (Freeman, 1983), divorce (Capaldi & Patterson, 1991; Hetherington, Cox, & Cox, 1981), large family size, criminality of parents (Farrington, 1979), psychiatric disorder of parents, urban residence, and disorganized and high-crime neighborhoods (Offord, Boyle, & Racine, 1991; Rutter & Giller, 1983).

Whereas there is substantial agreement that the contributions of family and contextual variables are significant, there is little consensus about how these variables fit together in determining criminal outcomes. The relation between contextual variables and antisocial and delinquent behavior is often considered in an additive fashion. The risk associated with particular predictors and the degree to which additional risk factors indicate higher risk for antisocial behavior has been the focus of many studies. Although this approach is useful for predictive purposes, it does not illuminate the processes that relate the contextual factors to the antisocial behavior. A second approach that is commonly taken is to examine the association between a particular contextual factor (e.g., marital conflict, parental depression, divorce) and children's behavior problems. Though these studies generally pay much more attention to the processes involved, it is often difficult to determine whether the potentially causal association is with the contextual factor under study or the association of both with contextual factor(s) not considered. Some of these studies control for socioeconomic status (SES), which helps strengthen findings, but other unconsidered contextual factors may be crucial. In a review of the effects of parental depression on children, Rutter (1990) considered one of the main challenges for future research was to determine the extent to which effects on children derived from the parental depression itself, rather than from associated risk factors including other forms of parental psychopathology. Research designs should take into account the potential causal associations among contextual factors, as well as consideration of the processes that relate context to child behavior.

Life-span theory suggests that individual characteristics relate to selection of contexts, either intentionally or unintentionally. Parent psychopathology is seen as relating to most other contextual factors causally (e.g., that antisocial behavior relates to divorce) and sometimes reciprocally (e.g., the association between stressful events and depression). In the present report, we contend that many of the effects of contextual variables on the development of antisocial behavior in childhood and adolescence are mediated through family and peer process variables (Figure 6.1). The implication is that much of the effect of context on antisocial behavior will be through contextual associations with social interactions among family members or with exposure to, and interactions within, the deviant-peer group. There may be a good deal of overlap among contextual variables in terms of their impact on family or peer processes. One of the hypotheses to be tested is that there is significant covariation among contextual variables.

Each of the contextual variables identified in the general model in Figure 6.1 has been shown in one or more studies to covary significantly with either antisocial or delinquent behavior in boys. These variables include parental antisocial behavior (Bank, Forgatch, Patterson, & Fetrow, 1993; Capaldi & Patterson, 1991; Farrington, 1979; Lahey et al., 1989; Patterson, 1999b), divorce, parental or family structure transitions (Cherlin et al., 1991; Capaldi & Patterson, 1991; Forgatch, Patterson, & Ray, 1996; Hetherington, Cox, & Cox, 1979), stress, depression (Forgatch, Patterson, & Skinner 1988; Snyder, 1991), neighborhood (Wilson, 1987), employment (Farrington, Gallagher, Morley, St. Ledger, & West, 1986), and occupation and education as indicators for SES (Elliott, Huizinga, & Ageton, 1985). Parental substance use is not presented as a separate contextual factor in Figure 6.1 because it is conceptualized as an indicator of antisocial behavior. It is one aspect of antisocial behavior that may have a very disruptive effect on parenting. Parent psychopathology, including antisocial behavior and depression, is depicted as underlying other contextual factors and parenting practices, because the effect of such pathology permeates family life. Marital conflict or aggression is not specifically

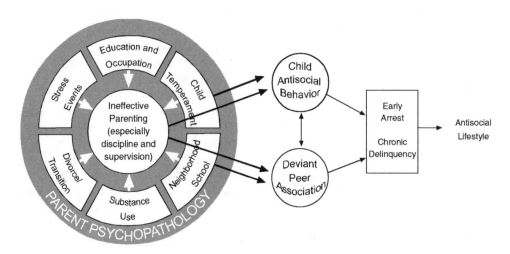

Figure 6.1. A mediational model for the association of family context and antisocial behavior.

included in Figure 6.1, but may be associated with poor parenting skills. This contextual factor is currently receiving attention for its possible relation to children's behavior problems (Grych & Fincham, 1990). We posit that parents with higher levels of antisocial behavior will engage in aggressive interactions with their partner and will also tend to use coercive and inconsistent discipline with their children, thus failing to inhibit antisocial behaviors. Findings regarding this hypothesis will be presented later in the chapter.

Whereas each of the contextual variables in Figure 6.1 has been shown to be associated with antisocial outcomes, many of the studies cited previously also demonstrated a mediational relation between context and outcomes. In each case, the mediational process was through either family or deviant-peer group interactions. We believe that two different processes account for the association between stable or trait-like versus state-change contextual factors and boys' antisocial behavior. Contextual factors such as SES and antisocial personality have been found in many studies to be relatively stable characteristics of parents. Both contextual factors have been found to be consistently related to poor child adjustment (Capaldi & Patterson, 1991; Farrington, 1978; Offord et al., 1991). These stable contextual factors identify parents who are at risk because they never learned parenting skills and/or learned some inappropriate parenting behaviors (e.g., coercive techniques and harsh, abusive discipline).

Less stable state characteristics (e.g., stress and depression) are hypothesized to disrupt or diminish parenting by taking the parents' time and attention from their child or by producing depressed or irritable mood states. Patterson (1982) has argued that a wide range of contextual factors can disrupt parenting practices by increasing negative social exchanges between the parent and child during times of family stress, and that prevention of these negative social exchanges might prevent increases in antisocial behavior for the child. An early test of mediational theory was provided by Elder, Caspi, and van Nguyen (1986) who showed that the effect of economic hardship on child outcomes was mediated by disruptions in parental discipline. Evidence for an association between state characteristics and parenting practices is often difficult to establish because such characteristics are often related to the more stable parental characteristics (previously discussed). As such, the magnitude of their independent causal role is often questionable. Chronic family problems (e.g., parent antisocial behavior) have been found to predict both family stress and poor child adjustment (Cohen, Burt, & Bjorck, 1987; Gersten, Langner, Eisenberg, & Simcha-Fagan, 1977). Quite complex theoretical and empirical models are thus needed to test such associations.

The Antisocial Parent and Family Risk Context

We have argued that the individual parent is not simply a passive reflector of contextual effects. To a large degree, parents' behavior actively creates or changes their family context (Bank et al., 1993; Capaldi & Patterson, 1991; Patterson, 1999b; Patterson & Capaldi, 1991). For example, the father who is chronically unable to hold a steady job contributes to the family's economic problems. We have identified parental antisocial behavior as being a strong risk indicator related to poor parenting skills and other contextual deficits. This personality trait may impact a wide range of contextual variables such as income, employment, stress, depression, and divorce/parental transitions. Thus, it is hypothesized that the antisocial trait of the parent has both a direct and an indirect effect on parenting practices: The direct effect because the trait is associated with failure to acquire skill in parenting and with the acquisition of inappropriate parenting, and the indirect effect because it is related to negative contextual factors that also impact the family and diminish parenting. Antisocial parents are more likely to use threats and scolding and be inconsistent in their discipline practices (Patterson, Reid, & Dishion, 1992). The coercive interpersonal style also places the parents at risk for marital conflict, divorce, and multiple marital transitions that may exacerbate their ineffectiveness in discipline confrontations, monitoring, and family problem solving.

Whereas much of the effect of contextual variables on child antisocial behavior is mediated by parenting skills, contextual factors may have some direct effects, especially under more extreme conditions. For example, poverty may place a family in a high-risk context that severely limits opportunities for positive adjustment. Sociohistorical changes indicate some direct effects of context. For example, anthropological studies have suggested that contact with Western cultures may be followed by structural changes in primitive societies that produce increases in adolescent antisocial behavior (Schlegel & Barry, 1989). Due to contextual change, what once had been effective parenting may no longer serve. In very high-risk environments, such as high-crime areas of inner cities, even exceptionally skilled parents may not prevent their child's engagement in criminal activity. A social environment in which parents with a reasonable level of skill and commitment may expect to raise a normal, healthy child is a prerequisite of the mediational model, which was tested in a moderate-sized metropolitan area.

Neighborhood Influences and Deviant-Peer Association

An extrafamilial association of context and process, which is expected to be strongly related to antisocial behavior, is that adolescents in neighborhoods and schools with a high deviant-peer density will be more likely to become involved with deviant peers and delinquency.

This community-level hypothesis is based on sociological theory regarding community disorganization. Sampson and Groves (1989) tested Shaw and McKay's community disorganization theory (Shaw & McKay, 1942). According to this theory, crime varies between communities according to the ability of the community structure to realize the common values of its residents and maintain effective social controls. Five aspects of the community structure (i.e., economic level, mobility, ethnic heterogeneity, family disruption, and urbanization) are posited to affect crime levels through social disorganization. This is evidenced by lack of ability to control teenage peer groups, the low density of local friendship networks, and the low level of participation in formal and voluntary organizations. Sampson and Groves showed that all five dimensions of community structure were significantly related to local friendship networks, organizational participation to a lesser degree, and especially to the presence of unsupervised peer groups in the neighborhood. Unsupervised peer groups were the strongest predictor of various indices of community crime. We argue that the strongest factor in control of unmonitored youth peer groups is parental supervision of their own adolescents, including supervision of their group leisure-time activities. However, the Shaw and McKay model identifies community-level factors that affect the ratio of antisocial or delinquent peers to prosocial peers in a neighborhood.

Youth who are not already antisocial by early adolescence may be more likely to become involved with the deviant peer group in neighborhoods in which the deviant peer density is high. This hypothesis has not been tested on the OYS sample, partly because the sample selection process led to homogeneity of neighborhoods. West (1982) found evidence for a specific effect of neighborhood on individual arrest rates. He showed that delinquency rates for boys declined after their families moved out of London, relative to boys who stayed in London in higher crime neighborhoods. Wilson (1987) found that when controlling for SES youth in cities needed more monitoring than youth in the suburbs to prevent them from engaging in delinquent acts.

Therefore, training by antisocial peers is seen as a highly important extrafamilial process in the development of antisocial behavior. Parents can influence this process with strong family management skills, but this task can be made exceedingly difficult in neighborhoods with high densities of deviant peers and few resources for prosocial activities. In extreme cases, the density of deviant peers and the severity of their antisocial behaviors may overwhelm the parents' attempts at family management. Reiss (1986) argued that in disorganized, high-crime neighborhoods, parental authority and control is replaced by that of peers, and the strong peer-control system forms an antisocial subculture.

Antisocial Behavior in Girls

Unfortunately, most of our work regarding context has pertained only to boys because the OYS sample contains only male participants. Antisocial girls have received less research attention in the past, in part because of the lower levels of antisocial behavior in girls. Girls receive lower ratings for externalizing problems in childhood (Achenbach, 1991a; 1991b) and have lower arrest rates than for boys at adolescence. By one estimate, arrests for boys outnumber arrests for girls by 4:1, arrests for violent index crimes by 9:1, and for the most serious index property crimes by 11:1 (Chesney-Lind & Shelden, 1992).

Despite recent growth in research on conduct disorder (see Keenan, Loeber, & Green, 1999 for a review) fundamental questions remain unanswered, including the nature of the developmental pattern for onset of antisocial behavior in girls. Although girls' aggressive and troublesome behavior shows some stability, it shows less stability over longer periods than boys' behavior and has been found less predictable in recent work with models that explain significant variance in boys' behavior (Block & Gjerde, 1993; Caspi, Lynam, Moffitt, & Silva, 1993; Fagot, 1995a; Shaw, Keenan, & Vondra, 1994; Tremblay, Masse, Perron, & Leblanc, 1992). Part of the problem in explaining girls' antisocial behavior is that the chronic, persistent type of delinquency associated with stable antisocial behavior has a very low base rate for girls and is therefore more difficult to predict. Girls' delinquency appears more likely to be the experimental kind associated with later onset and desistance after adolescence. Robins (1966; 1986) and others (Silverthorn & Frick, 1999; Zoccolillo, 1993) have found that the majority of girls appear to have an onset of these problems in adolescence. This kind of delinquency in boys is also less predictable from childhood behavior.

Women who were conduct disordered in childhood have been found to be at lower risk than men for an externalizing diagnosis in adulthood (39% versus 73%), but at much increased risk for internalizing diagnoses (73% versus 26%) (Robins, 1966; 1986). Although most criminal activity may not continue into adulthood for girls, many of the negative adult outcomes of antisocial behavior that have been found for boys have also been found for girls (Pajer, 1998). Adolescent delinquency predicts later impairment and poor care of children in adulthood (Otnow-Lewis et al., 1990; Robins, 1986). Measures of antisocial behavior in mothers have been associated with younger age at first birth, poor child-rearing practices, and poor child adjustment (Capaldi & Patterson, 1991; Serbin et al., 1998). Therefore, antisocial behavior in girls is seen as perpetuating the cycle of family problems associated with antisocial behavior into the next generation. Lack of positive parental behaviors (Kavanagh & Hops, 1994) and sexual abuse (Chesney-Lind & Shelden, 1992) may be risk factors, especially pertinent for girls. Robins (1966) showed that girls referred to a clinic for antisocial behavior came from somewhat more disturbed homes than referred boys. In general, we expect that this consideration of contextual factors relating to antisocial behavior in childhood should apply to girls as well as to boys.

OSLC Studies of Contextual Effects

Bronfenbrenner (1988) argued that full models for the relationship between contextual factors and child behavior should consider the particular context, the process by which it affects the child, and the characteristics of the child that interact with the contextual factors and processes. We are in close agreement with this perspective. A strong association between parental skills and childhood antisocial behavior was discussed in chapter 4 and will also be discussed in chapter 9. Here we will review the association between these factors and familial context.

Social disadvantage. Larzelere and Patterson (1990) tested the hypothesis that the effect of social disadvantage on child antisocial or delinquent behavior is mediated through poor parental management. Social disadvantage, as indexed by SES (parental education and occupation), was assessed at grade four and delinquent behavior at grade seven. Delinquency was assessed by both self-report and arrest records. The association was best described as mediated by the family management practices of monitoring and discipline with no significant direct path from low SES to child delinquency. The model accounted for 46% of the variance in delinquency. Findings by other researchers support a mediational model for the effects of social disadvantage on delinquency. Laub and Sampson (1988) reanalyzed data from the well-known longitudinal study by the Gluecks (e.g., Glueck & Glueck, 1959) and showed that the effects of contextual variables (e.g., parental criminality and alcoholism, broken homes, and overcrowding) on delinquency were mediated through maternal supervision, parental discipline, and parental attachment.

Stress and negative emotion. Most families are occasionally subjected to severe stress (e.g., a major illness, unemployment, a drop in income, or divorce). Such changes in contextual state may be accompanied by disruptions in parenting practices that, in turn, lead to child adjustment problems.

Stressful events are hypothesized to relate to disrupted or diminished family management, mainly by affecting parental mood states that cause increased negative emotion, especially irritability and depression (Conger, 1991; Frijda, 1986; Patterson, 1982, 1983; Snyder & Huntley, 1990; Wahler & Dumas, 1983). Daily variations in stress have been shown to covary with daily variations in parental irritability (Patterson, 1983). Increased irritability leads to less effective discipline confrontations as shown in the observation study by Snyder (1991).

Negative emotions (e.g., anger and contempt) have also been associated with poor parenting; namely, poor supervision, problem solving, and parent-child relationships. Capaldi, Forgatch, and Crosby (1994) found for the OYS sample that direct observation of strong negative parental emotion (anger and contempt) during family problem-solving interactions related to poor problem-solving outcome and poor parent-child relationships, whereas neutral and positive emotion were related to positive outcomes. Forgatch and Stoolmiller (1994) found that observed negative parental emotion was related to poorer parental monitoring or supervision.

It is also likely, although not tested here, that stress may focus parental attention away from child rearing to concerns such as finding a job, surviving an illness, or establishing a relationship with a new partner. It is hypothesized that reduced attention would adversely affect supervision, positive parental involvement, and consistency of discipline.

Evidence has been found that depression in mothers interferes with parenting skills in a variety of ways. Depressed mothers are found to be less responsive to their children's concerns, less likely to initiate actions that address these concerns, less likely to engage in cooperative problem solving with their child, more likely to use hostile discipline, and less effective at socializing cooperative and compliant behaviors (Cox, Puckering, Pound, & Mills, 1987; Downey & Coyne, 1990; Kochanska & Kuczynski, 1989; Kochanska, Kuczynski, Radke-Yarrow, & Welch, 1987; as referenced in Dix, 1991; Radke-Yarrow, 1998). Mothers' depression has been related to aggressive behavior problems in children (Weissman et al., 1984; Zahn-Waxler, Cummings, McKnew, & Radke-Yarrow, 1984). Hammen and colleagues (Burge & Hammen, 1991; Hammen, 1992; Hammen, Burge, & Stansbury, 1990) have examined the effect of stress and maternal depression on parent-child interactions and child behavior. They found that there is a reciprocal relation between stress and depression, and that both adversely affect parent-child interactions; stress being related to more negative, critical behavior, and depressed mood to less task involvement.

A study by Conger (1991), which was replicated for the OYS by Patterson (1991), showed that the impact of certain stressors for intact families (a drop in income, severe illness, or death in the family) on child adjustment was mediated by parental depression. Stress was related to higher levels of parental depression; this, in turn, was related to poor family management practices. For single-parent families, measures of stress were found to relate directly to poor discipline practices (Forgatch, Patterson, & Skinner, 1988).

An additional stress factor that can affect parental mood states and diminish parenting is the child's antisocial behavior itself. Forgatch et al. (1996) found for the Oregon Divorce (ODS1) a sample in which there was a feedback effect from the boys' antisocial behavior through maternal stress to less effective discipline practices. The coercive and aggressive child elicits strong negative affect, such as anger, from his or her parent. Parents of antisocial children may reduce unpleasant interactions by avoiding the child. In fact, these parents may even have given up trying to control their child's behavior, and prefer that the child spend as much time as possible out of the house and away from them. As previously discussed, interactions charged with negative emotion and parental rejection diminish family management skills, including discipline and supervision, and result in further increases in the boys' antisocial behavior.

Parents at Risk for Family Structure Transitions and Unskilled Parenting

The importance of considering the relation between contextual factors in determining possible causal processes can be seen in considering the large body of research on the relation between divorce and troubled behavior in children (e.g., Hetherington et al., 1979, 1981; Wallerstein & Kelly, 1980). Early research in this area focused on the risk status of the single-parent versus the two-parent family and the effect on the parents and child of the stress and disruption of the divorce. The presence of a stepfather was generally considered to have an ameliorating effect on antisocial behavior, at least for boys (Hetherington et al., 1981; Santrock, 1972; Tooliatos & Lindholm, 1980).

Capaldi and Patterson (1991) reconceptualized the contextual variable of family structure as the number of parental transitions experienced by the family since the child's birth (0 = intact families with two biological parents, 1 = first separation, 2 = first stepfather, 3 = further transitions such as second separation, second stepfather, etc.). It was hypothesized that parents' antisocial and unskilled behavior put them at risk for marital transitions and ineffective parenting skills. Maternal antisocial behavior was assessed by arrest record, driving license suspensions, Minnesota Multiphasic Personality Inventory (MMPI) hypomanic and psychopathic deviate subscales, substance use, and age at first birth. Evidence that antisocial behavior predicts relationship transitions has been found by other researchers. In an analysis of the Gluecks' data, Sampson and Laub (1990) showed that childhood temper tantrums and adolescent delinquency significantly predicted later divorce. Figure 6.2 shows the structural equation model used to test this hypothesis for the OYS sample that was run on a matrix from which SES and income had been partialled out. The contextual and family management variables were assessed at grade four, and the boys' adjustment was assessed at grade six.

As hypothesized, mothers' antisocial behavior was significantly related to the number of relationship transitions they had experienced since the son's birth and to poor supervision and participation in fewer activities with their sons. These skill deficits were, in turn, related to a summary measure of their sons' poor adjustment that included peer rejection, deviant-peer association, antisocial behavior, low academic skills, depression, low self-esteem, and substance use. The path from transitions to parent involvement was nonsignificant with mother antisocial behavior in the model. Poor discipline practices did not load on the parenting factor when SES and income were partialled out of the model.

The number of parental family structure transitions was found to be significantly related to the boys' delinquency, measured by arrest records collected 3 to 4 years later (grade seven or grade eight). Eleven percent of the boys in the intact group, 23% in the first-time-separated group, 38% in the first-time-stepfather groups, and 32% in the multiple-transition group had been arrested at least once. Boys with one transition showed twice as many first arrests as boys with no tran-

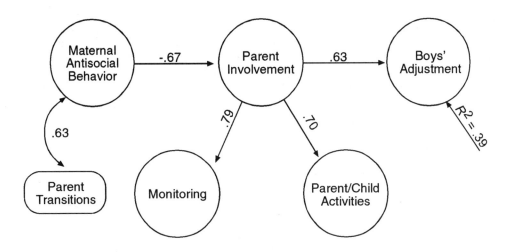

Figure 6.2. Mediated model for mother's antisocial behavior and parental transitions.

Note. From "Relation of parental transitions to boys' adjustment problems: I. A linear hypothesis; II. Mothers at risk for transitions and unskilled parenting," by D. M. Capaldi, and G. R. Patterson, 1991, *Developmental Psychology, 27*, p. 501. Copyright 1991 by the American Psychological Association, Inc.

sitions, and boys with two or more transitions showed three times as many first arrests as those with no transitions.

The prevailing model in relating parental divorce to antisocial child behavior has been a stress model hypothesizing that divorce upsets the child and disrupts the parents' family management skills, leading to increases in the child's antisocial behavior. This model may explain some proportion of the child's behavior problems. In fact, for the OYS sample, divorce has been associated with subsequent poor supervision (Patterson & Capaldi, 1991). The Capaldi and Patterson findings, however, suggest that because mothers' antisocial behavior is related both to transitions and to poor parenting, the transition groups probably showed lower levels of parenting skills and poorer sons' adjustment than the intact group *prior* to the transition. This interpretation is supported by the finding of Block, Block, and Gjerde (1986) that preschool boys from subsequently divorcing families were more aggressive and impulsive than boys whose parents did not divorce later.

Stable Versus Dynamic Contextual Effects

Although longitudinal studies have shown that both stable and transitory contexts are linked to poorer parenting practices, several questions remain unanswered concerning how different contextual factors are interrelated and how they are associated with transitional processes over time. As discussed, stable conditions, such as social class, may predict more transitory contextual factors that disrupt the family social environment. This is consistent with a social causation perspective that posits that a disadvantaged social position creates more stress and disruptive family events (Lorenz et al., 1997). Another perspective, that of social selection based on the failure model (Capaldi, 1991; 1992; Patterson & Capaldi, 1990), suggests that antisocial parents are selected into more socially disadvantaged conditions and are also at risk for stress and disruptive events because of their antisocial behavior. The interdependence of contextual variables may reflect a series of bidirectional influences. Prolonged disadvantaged social conditions (e.g., unemployment, downward social mobility, increased stress) can lead to further risk of relationship transitions, disruptive social interactions, and negative life events (Lorenz et al., 1997; Patterson & Forgatch, 1990). All these conditions, in turn, can amplify antisocial characteristics and, therefore, disrupt family interactions (Elder & Caspi, 1988; Patterson & Forgatch, 1990).

To understand how stable and dynamic processes are interrelated, the timing of contextual changes should be examined within longitudinal frameworks. It is important also to disentangle short-term adjustment from longer-term adjustment outcomes associated with acute and chronic contextual factors. In this section, both the Oregon Divorce Study (ODS) and Linking Interests of Families and Teachers (LIFT) studies provide examples of modeling the impact of stable and dynamic contextual factors on parenting and child adjustment, as represented in the theoretical model shown in Figure 6.1.

In the ODS 2, DeGarmo, Forgatch, and Martinez, (1999) showed that maternal education, maternal occupation, and income levels prior to divorce predicted standardized reading and math achievement scores for boys in elementary school. In testing a mediational model of parenting practices, a latent construct of effective parenting, measured as observed discipline and problem solving, mediated the effects of maternal education on achievement scores. However, in the presence of parenting practices, occupational status had a direct effect on boys' achievement, maternal education had a direct effect on skill-building activities in the home environment, and income had a direct effect on appropriate school behavior. These findings suggest that individual components of larger socioeconomic contexts play unique roles in predicting family management and long-term developmental outcomes within transitional families.

To test the hypothesis that family structure changes are detrimental to effective parenting, DeGarmo and Forgatch (1999) used 444 families from the LIFT sample to model the effect of transitions on parenting and to examine contexts as predictors of transitions. Predictors included mother's age; maternal depression using the Center for Epidemiological Study of Depression (Radloff, 1977); the number of parental arrests based on court records (e.g., for the average of mother and father for two-parent families); and SES using the Hollingshead Index of Social Status (Hollingshead, 1975). Baseline family structure was scored using Capaldi and Patterson's (1991) operationalization (e.g., coded 0 for intact families; 1 for never-married or first-time divorced, single mothers; 2 for first-time stepfamily; and 3 for biological mothers who had experienced multiple transitions). Mother-initiated conflict and problem-solving outcomes were based on the observational measures of parenting used in DeGarmo et al. (1999). Analysis of the LIFT sample supported Capaldi and Patterson's linear hypothesis, that is, more transitions at baseline were significantly associated with higher levels of mother-initiated conflict and lower levels of problem solving.

Independent of transitions, maternal depression was associated with higher conflict and lower problem-solving scores. This latter finding was consistent with previous studies of family interactions with depressed individuals (Forgatch et al., 1996; Hops et al., 1987). Findings from the LIFT study also indicated that maternal antisocial personality indexed by maternal arrests was associated with more conflict, whereas higher levels of SES were associated with better problem solving. Growth curve analyses revealed that, over the 2-year study period, parenting improved as a normative developmental trend. The LIFT families significantly decreased in their mother-initiated conflict bouts and significantly increased in their family problem-solving outcomes.

A unique feature of this particular study of family structure was that transitions were modeled as a time-varying covariate of observed maternal parenting using hierarchical linear modeling (HLM: Bryk & Raudenbush, 1992; Raudenbush, 1995). For the 84 families who experienced a transition during the study, the aggregate trajectories showed that parenting improved, as was the case with the entire sample. However, at the time of the transition, there was an increase in family conflict and a decrease in problem solving. The overall net effect for the transitional families was a hindering of the improvements in parenting exhibited by the sample over time. The net growth rates for the entire sample and the growth rate for the transitional families are shown in Figure 6.3 (DeGarmo & Forgatch, 1999). Compared to the whole sample over the 2-year period, parenting for the transitional families improved at a significantly slower rate than for the rest of the sample.

To understand the interrelations of contextual factors in the population-based LIFT sample, DeGarmo and Forgatch (1999) examined predictors of family structure transitions. Both transitions at study entry (baseline) and the cumulative number of additional transitions at each wave during the first 2 years of LIFT were modeled as the dependent variables. Contextual factors significantly associated with baseline transitions were maternal depression, parental arrests, lower SES, and being a younger mother. Younger mothers, as well as those who showed higher levels of depressive symptoms, were likely to experience additional transitions during the first 2 years of the study. Intact families experienced fewer transitions during the study compared with other family types. In total, 11% of intact families, 33% of the first-time, single-mother families, 20% of the first-time stepfamilies, and 37% of the multiple-transition families experienced a transition in the 2-year study period. Therefore, as on the OYS, a prior history of transition was a risk factor for further family disruption. Indeed, family structure was the strongest predictor of future transitions in a multivariate analysis.

In summary, evidence consistent with both social causation and selection perspectives was provided by findings in the LIFT sample. Both SES and parental antisocial behavior were associated with parental transitions, however, neither of these variables predicted additional transitions during the study. These findings also indicate that both relatively stable contexts (SES, antisocial personality) and more transitory contexts (depression, parental transitions) are unique predictors of parenting practices, as well as of the likelihood of having an additional transition. One limitation in this analysis was that parental antisocial behavior was estimated from parental arrests in the state of residence, rather than by a more comprehensive construct as used in the OYS. A more comprehensive

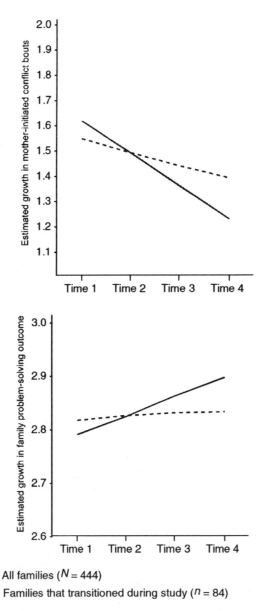

Figure 6.3. Overlay of linear growth trajectories for LIFT sample and subsample of families that transitioned during the study.

Note. From E. M. Hetherington (Ed.), *Coping with divorce, single parenting and remarriage: A risk and resiliency perspective* (p. 235), by D. S. DeGarmo and M. S. Forgatch, 1999, Contexts as predictors of changing parenting practices in diverse family structures: A social interactional perspective to risk and resilience. Hillsdale, NJ: Erlbaum. Copyright 1999 by Erlbaum. Reprinted with permission.

measure of parental antisocial behavior may have predicted additional transitions during the study period for the LIFT sample.

These findings emphasize the importance of considering possible causal associations among contextual variables. The intervention model would be profoundly different for antisocial parents who never learned appropriate parenting skills and may have developed some abusive parental behaviors, compared with parents whose skills were adequate until they became disrupted by the relationship transition. Furthermore, the findings showing greater risk for families experiencing multiple transitions imply that first-time single mothers and younger mothers may benefit more from preventive interventions than would single mothers with multiple transitions.

Structural Interrelations of Contextual Variables

Associations among seven contextual variables from the first wave of data collection for the OYS (grade four) are summarized in Table 6.1. Some variables were composite scores, namely, SES (occupation and education), parental antisocial behavior (driving license suspensions, arrests, MMPI psychopathic deviate and hypomanic scales, substance use, and mothers' age at first birth), stress (life events and daily hassles), and depression (self-report scales). Income and number of parental transitions were based on parental self-reports. Parental antisocial behavior, SES, stress, and depression were a mean of mothers' and fathers' scores in two-parent families. The seven contextual factors showed a consistent pattern of association. Of the 21 correlations among these seven variables or constructs in Table 6.1, 18 were significant at least the .01 level. As discussed earlier, parental antisocial behavior was associated with difficulty in holding a job and with parental transitions.

To what extent do the seven interrelated contextual factors form a single dimension? Table 6.2 summarizes the factor loadings for a forced one-factor solution. All the contextual factors loaded .37 or higher on the single factor, again demonstrating their high interrelation. A family that is at risk on one contextual dimension is likely to be at risk on several. Families with multiple contextual risk factors will be particularly at risk for deficits in family management skills and, consequently, for antisocial behavior in sons. Though contextual risk factors overlap, additional risk factors explain further variance in behavior. Capaldi (1989) showed that SES, income, and parental transitions each accounted for unique variance in a summary

Table 6.1. Correlation Matrix of Contextual Variables/Constructs.

	Family Income	Parental Antisocial Behavior	Parental Transitions	Parental SES	Parental Stress	No Employed Parent	Depression
Income	—						
Antisocial	-.46**	—					
Transitions	-.46**	.45**	—				
SES	.26**	-.22*	-.16	—			
Stress	-.29**	.25**	.25**	-.14	—		
Unemployment	-.45**	.33**	.28**	-.30**	.16	—	
Depression	-.25**	.31**	.26**	-.19*	.49**	.14*	—

**p < .001. *p < .01

Table 6.2. Forced 1 Factor Solution of Contextual Factors.

Income	-.71
Parental antisocial behavior	.65
Parental transitions	.60
No employed parent	.51
Parental depression	.48
Parental stress	.46
SES	-.37

construct of boys' adjustment. Measures of parenting practices would account for additional variance.

The data clearly indicated that all of the contextual variables examined were significantly interrelated. The findings do not tell us why they are interrelated. Again, the interrelations may indicate a bidirectional relation between the parental antisocial trait and the other contextual variables (a social selection model), or reflect a social causation model (i.e., prolonged unemployment causes downward social mobility, increased stress, and depression and leads to risk for transitions). The associations among the contextual variables again emphasize the importance of multivariate designs for the study of contexts. Examination restricted to just one contextual variable would give a very limited perspective.

Contextual factors in early and late onset of arrest. Capaldi and Patterson (1994) examined the degree to which contextual factors differentiated three groups of boys in the OYS sample: (a) no juvenile arrest, (b) early arrest (prior to 14 years of age), and (c) later juvenile arrest (14 to 18 years of age) (Patterson, Capaldi, & Bank, 1991; Patterson & Yoerger, 1993). Groupings and analyses were based only on juvenile arrest records. Because early arrest is related to risk for chronic offending, the findings of such an analysis have important prevention implications. Capaldi and Patterson (1994) hypothesized that early-onset boys would be at significantly greater risk, as defined by the seven contextual factors assessed at grade four that were previously presented. Five of the seven constructs differentiated among the three groups in a multivariate analysis of variance. Parental depression and stress were nonsignificant. Contrasts comparing the late and early arrest groups indicated that the families of boys who were arrested prior to 14 years of age showed higher risk for parental antisocial behavior, parental transitions, unemployment, and low SES than boys arrested later. Most of the early onset youths appeared to come from families who showed multiple contextual risk factors. The no-arrest group showed low contextual risk. Poor parental discipline was also found to be associated with juvenile arrest, and the poorest discipline was found for the early arrest group.

In summary, the analyses reviewed regarding the role of context in the childhood onset of antisocial behavior in boys supported the theory that a major effect of contextual variables is through their relationship to the parents' family management practices. These models did not consider genetic effects that are expected to make a contribution to the child's poor adjustment in addition to the effect of unskilled parenting (Scarr, 1985).

Protective Factors During Family Transitions

We have examined contexts as risk factors, and now turn to the question of how positive contextual factors may ease the process of family structure transitions. Specifically, support and problem solving within the adult social environment are evaluated as an independent resource that enhances the parent-child relationship. As couples share responsibility for socializing a child, a marital or cohabiting partner is the primary source of parental support. Belsky and Vondra (1989) have suggested that when marital support is absent, social networks become more important for single mothers and become the principal source of parental support. Simons and Johnson (1996) argued that nonspousal support is unlikely to substitute for, or function as, parenting support from spouses; therefore, its impact on parenting may be indirect, through the mother's well-being. A series of recent reports from the ODS1 and ODS2 studies have addressed the question of how interactional processes in adult-confidant relationships (e.g., intimate partners, friends, and family members) function to help mothers maintain higher quality parenting as they experience marital transitions (DeGarmo & Forgatch, 1999).

Our perspective predicted a stronger effect of social support on parenting for more proximal and specific measures of support (Dunkel-Schetter & Bennett, 1990). For example, support provided in the context of discussing and trying to resolve parenting and personal problems is more proximal to parenting practices than are global assessments of support networks or perceived availability. Therefore, we developed a latent construct measuring interpersonal support (DeGarmo & Forgatch, 1997b), including supportive behaviors and process rated from the Problem-Solving System (Forgatch, Fetrow, & Lathrop, 1988) and emotional support scored from the code for Specific Affect (SPAFF: Gottman, 1989).

Confidant support was examined in the ODS1 study at the 4-year follow up. Controlling for maternal distress (family stress and depression or life-events stress) and confidant type, a direct effect from observed confidant support to parenting practices was found (standardized beta = .55, p < .05, DeGarmo & Forgatch, 1997a). Parenting practices were measured as observed problem solving and discipline, scored during mother-child interactions on different days in a different setting. Confidants could be either intimate partners or friends. The direct effect of support on parenting was replicated in the ODS2 study at baseline using measures of perceived confidant support (standardized beta = .36, p < .05) (DeGarmo & Forgatch, 1999). Therefore, independent samples indicated that specific measures of support during discussions of parenting and personal problems showed a direct association with parenting.

A final model tested the effects of contexts including repartnering, SES (education and occupation), and mother's antisocial personality (arrests, substance use, and subscales 4 and 9 on the MMPI) on confidant-mother problem solving, using the ODS1 sample 4 years following baseline. It was hypothesized that problem-solving outcomes would be the mechanism accounting for the relationship between confidant support and parenting practices. This model is shown in Figure 6.4 (from Forgatch & DeGarmo, 1997).

Confidant support enhanced the problem-solving outcomes. Those outcomes, in turn, contributed to effective parenting practices, which predicted lower levels of child antisocial behavior. Problem-solving solutions mediated the effect of support

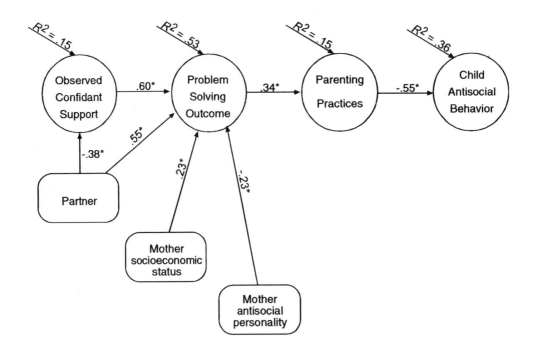

Figure 6.4. Progression model linking confidant support and contextual factors to child adjustment.

Note. From "Adult problem solving: Contributor to parenting and child outcomes in divorced families," by M. S. Forgatch, and D. S. DeGarmo, 1997, *Social Development, 6*, p. 247. Copyright 1997 by Blackwell Publishers Ltd. Reprinted with permission.

on parenting. The effects of repartnering following divorce provided interesting results. Partners were observed to be less supportive during problem-solving discussions than were other types of confidants, but were found to produce better problem-solving solutions. Perhaps partners were less unconditionally supportive in their behaviors and affect than were friends and family. Because intimate partners may be more directly involved in the mother's personal and parenting issues, they may be more solution focused than friends or family. SES was associated with better problem solving, which was consistent with the longitudinal LIFT data presented previously. Antisocial mothers had poorer problem-solving outcomes; however, it was surprising to note that adult problem-solving outcomes mediated the effect of maternal antisocial qualities on parenting practices.

Taken together, these data indicated the importance of problem solving and the quality of confidant relationships for parent and child outcomes during stressful family transitions. Higher quality interactions and relationships within the adult social environment of divorced and repartnered mothers served as a protective factor for parenting.

Intergenerational Transmission of Contextual Risk

Contextual outcomes in young adulthood. Contextual risk may be transmitted from one generation to the next, particularly by the greater risk for ongoing antisocial behavior and associated adjustment failures of children who have been raised in at-risk families. Cicchetti and Schneider-Rosen (1986) presented an organizational model of development that posits that normal or successful development is a series of interlocking social, emotional, and cognitive competencies, with early adaptation promoting later adaptation. The concept of hierarchical integration describes the process of adaptation and cumulative development (Cicchetti, 1990). We posit that conduct problems interfere with this development of competencies, thus causing a developmental chain reaction of failures (Capaldi, 1991, 1992; Patterson & Capaldi, 1990). Conduct problem boys are noncompliant, and thus do not learn as well as nonconduct problem boys, either in home or in school settings. In addition, their aggressive and abrasive behaviors result in negative reactions and rejection by others (e.g., parents, teachers, and peers). This combination of lack of competence and negative reactions from others results in pervasive failures in adjustment. In delineating basic principles of child development, Sroufe (1990) also posited that some developmental pathways represent adaptational failures that are associated with an increased likelihood of later failures. Kellam and Rebok (1992) in their life-course social-field framework see continuities in behavior as associated with earlier learning, successes, failures, and potential for change in interactions in new social fields (e.g., the work place). Thus, stability in risk contexts is seen as associated with developmental failure and continued engagement in antisocial behaviors.

One mechanism by which childhood conduct problems are associated with ongoing contextual risk seems to be through accelerated developmental trajectories, whereby conduct problems are associated with taking on adult roles at an earlier age than is normative for the peer group. Newcomb (1987) has described the process whereby risk or problem behaviors are associated with more rapid movement into adult roles as *pseudomaturity*. Similarly, Burton, Obeidallah, and Allison (1996) have described the accelerated life courses of inner-city African-American adolescents. High school drop out may be a large factor in such acceleration, because such young men are likely to enter employment earlier.

Evidence that conduct problems in childhood are predictive of continued adjustment failures and contextual risk in young adulthood, along with accelerated entry into adult roles, was found in prediction to outcomes in the 2 years following the senior year of high school, at 18 to 21 years of age for the OYS men (Capaldi & Stoolmiller, 1999). Problems in young adulthood included continued antisocial behavior with higher frequencies of arrests, as well as continued risk for associated psychopathology in the form of depressive symptoms and substance use. Consistent with the hypothesis that the association of contextual risk and adjustment is mediated through process variables, continued risk was also seen in the area of association with deviant peers. New problems included failures to graduate from high school, enter higher education, attain and keep employment, or keep a driver's license, along with an early exit from the family-of-origin home (prior to 18 years of age) and very early fatherhood. These findings indicate that these young men were essentially recreating in young adulthood some of the contextual disadvantages of their parents (e.g., lower SES levels, more unemployment, and higher levels of psychopathology). These factors would lead to the prediction that they will also experience higher stress levels, already seen in such factors as more drivers' license suspensions. These findings are in keeping with a reanalysis of the data from the Berkeley Growth Study showing that the antisocial child is at significant risk for downward mobility (Caspi & Elder, 1988). From a longitudinal perspective, a boy's antisocial behavior is a better predictor of future social status than is a measure of his family's SES.

Similar findings regarding prediction of contextual risk and continued behavioral problems in young adulthood have been found for girls who showed conduct problems in childhood. Robins (1986) found that conduct problems in childhood predicted life events such as changes in residence, job loss, and break up with spouse/partner and friends in adulthood for both boys and girls. Bardone, Moffitt, Caspi, Dickson, and Silva (1996) found that conduct-disordered girls developed antisocial personality disorder symptoms by 21 years of age, including illegal behavior. Contextual risk into young adulthood for these girls was seen in substance dependence, dependence on multiple welfare sources, school dropout and leaving home, multiple cohabitation partners, and mutual violence with a partner, as well as early pregnancy and childbearing. Thus, the continuity of contextual risk associated with developmental failure that was found for the young men in the OYS sample has been found in prospective studies of young women.

Aggression toward a partner. A further area of problematic outcomes in young adulthood for men with higher levels of conduct problems, which have considerable consequence for context for the next generation, is seen in their relationships with intimate partners. Capaldi and her colleagues (Capaldi & Clark, 1998; Capaldi & Crosby, 1997) found that young men with a history of antisocial behavior are more likely to date young women with higher levels of antisocial behavior, and to be both psychologically and physically aggressive toward their partners. Consistent with an accelerated pathway to adult roles, such men also engaged in sexual intercourse at earlier ages (Capaldi, Crosby, & Stoolmiller, 1996) and were more likely to have a partner with whom they could participate in the OYS Couples' Study at 18–20 years of age. It appears that prosocial young men tend to establish intimate relationships at later ages than conduct problem young men.

The intergenerational transmission paradigm has predominated in explanations of spousal violence for almost 20 years. The major contextual risk factor that has been identified in studies of husband-to-wife violence has been witnessing such violence in the family of origin (Hotaling & Sugarman, 1986). Aggression between parents may be observed and directly modeled in later relationships with partners (Rosenbaum & O'Leary, 1981; Stets, 1991; Straus, Gelles, & Steinmetz, 1980), or this process could be mediated via the child's antisocial behavior. These models, especially the former with no mediating factor, are commonly hypothesized in the etiology of violence toward partners. A second model of the intergenerational transmission of violence posits that physical abuse toward the children themselves teaches them that violence is a tactic to use in family relationships. Thus, these children are likely to behave aggressively toward both their spouse and children when they grow up (Straus et al., 1980).

We hypothesize that the main social learning mechanism involved in the intergenerational transmission of violence involves unskilled parenting, especially ineffective and coercive discipline practices, and low levels of parental monitoring. These, in turn, are associated with the development of antisocial behavior that includes in young adulthood coercive, aggressive, and violent tactics toward their intimate partners. The association of parental dyadic aggression and the child's later aggression toward a partner is hypothesized to be attributable mainly to the fact that antisocial parents are more likely to be aggressive toward their partners as well as unskilled and coercive in raising their children (Capaldi & Patterson, 1991; Patterson & Capaldi, 1991).

Capaldi and Clark (1998) compared prediction from two family process constructs, namely, parental dyadic aggression and unskilled parenting for the young men in the OYS. Models were tested hierarchically, starting with the simple direct effects of the family process predictors and then adding mediational effects via boys' antisocial behavior (Baron & Kenny, 1986). Finally, comprehensive models were tested including all five constructs: parental antisocial behavior, parental dyadic aggression, unskilled parenting, boys' antisocial behavior, and the young men's aggression toward a partner. Parental antisocial behavior was assessed at grade four, the family process constructs in late childhood to early adolescence (grades four–eight), the boys' antisocial behavior in mid-adolescence (grade ten), and aggression toward a partner in young adulthood (17 to 20 years of age). We predicted that parental dyadic aggression would be associated with boys' antisocial behavior. However, we hypothesized that unskilled parenting practices would make the major contribution to the development of the boys' antisocial behavior. We expected poor parenting practices and parental conflict to be highly associated measures of the use of coercive and unskilled tactics within the family.

The findings provided support for the hypothesis that family-of-origin process factors were related to later aggressive behavior toward an intimate partner by the young men in the OYS sample, to the degree that they were associated with his development of antisocial behavior by adolescence. The development of antisocial behavior is thus seen as the key social learning factor in the intergenerational transmission of family aggression and violence. As parental antisocial behavior was strongly associated with aggressive behavior toward their own intimate partners, the association was found across two generations. Poor parenting practices were found to have a stronger association with the sons' later aggression toward a partner, via his antisocial behavior, than was parental dyadic aggression. Findings for the hypothesized mediated intergenerational model are shown in Figure 6.5. The evidence was consistent with the hypothesis that any indirect association of parental dyadic aggression with later aggression toward a partner occurred mainly because of the association of both family constructs with parental antisocial behavior. The possible indirect causal role of the parental dyadic aggression, however, was not completely ruled out in the models tested. Both of these family process constructs assess an unskilled and coercive interpersonal style.

The finding, that the association of the family process factors and the boys' later aggression toward a female intimate partner was best described as being mediated by the boys' development of antisocial behavior, is crucial to understanding the intergenerational transmission of aggression and to designing prevention programs. Most research on intergenerational transmission generally does not consider this

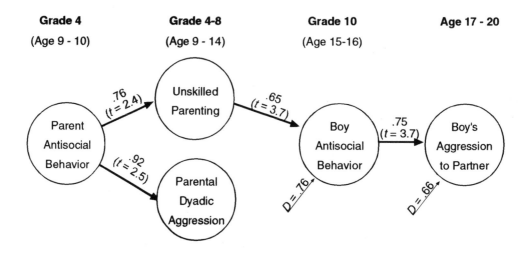

Figure 6.5. Mediational social learning model of the intergenerational transmission of family aggression and violence.

Note. From "Prospective family predictors of aggression toward female partners for at-risk young men," D. M. Capaldi and S. Clark, 1998, *Developmental Psychology, 34*, p. 1177. Copyright 1998 by the American Psychological Association.

mediating factor. This can lead to fallacious conclusions about the nature of intergenerational risk and the nature of the interventions that might help prevent aggression toward a partner.

Mediational Effects on Continuity of Contextual Risk

The childhood and adolescent model posited that the effect of contextual factors on antisocial behavior was mediated through family and peer process. In young adulthood, relationships with partners and peers may partially mediate the effect of prior behavioral characteristics on continuity of contextual risk and problem behaviors. Thus, we would predict that desistance from association with deviant peers would result, for example, in reduction or cessation of criminal involvement, improved employment prospects, and decreased substance use.

For the OYS sample, a preliminary analysis of the effect of intimate relationships on desistance of criminal activity was conducted. It was hypothesized that men who are less severely delinquent would be more likely to desist. Therefore, a stronger effect was expected for non-FBI index offenses than for index offenses. The OYS young men were placed into five groups according to their participation in the Couple's assessment in late adolescence and young adulthood as follows: (a) No participation at T1 or T2, (b) T1 participation only, (c) T2 participation only, (d) T1 and T2 participation with a different partner both times, and (e) T1 and T2 participation with the same partner at both times. The mean age of the OYS young men at T1 was 18.7 years, and at T2 was 21.3 years of age. Nonparticipation in the Cou-

Table 6.3. Nonindex Offense Change Scores from Ages 17-18 to Ages 20-23.

	Offense change scores (1)
No partner (n = 33)	+21.4
T1 partner only (n = 11)	-2.6
T2 partner only (n = 50)	-16.0
T1 and T2, different partner (n = 60)	-28.6
T1 and T2, same partner (n = 46)	-19.7

ple's Study was due almost entirely to not having a partner. The change score for self-report index and nonindex offenses over this period was calculated and an analysis of variance was conducted. Self-report of offenses are a more sensitive index than arrests, because the ratio of police contacts to self-report offenses has been estimated at around 3-10:100 (Elliott & Voss, 1974; Erickson & Empey, 1963; Gold, 1966). The index offense scale contained 10, and the nonindex scale 23 items, including assault and minor theft.

As expected, little systematic change was seen for index offenses. Mean change scores for the groups for nonindex offenses are shown in Table 6.3. Findings indicated that the group of young men who were not in relationships that were sufficiently lengthy to participate in the Couple's assessment *increased* nonindex offenses by an average of 21 offenses between the ages of approximately 17–18 and 21–23 years. Young men who were in relationships at T2 showed a reduction in offenses over the same period. Note that the relatively small group of young men who were in a relationship only at T1, but not at T2, showed little reduction in nonindex offenses at T2. Overall, the effects appear to be quite large and meaningful in terms of reduction in crime. These findings are particularly interesting as they indicate that just the presence of a relationship, regardless of the characteristics of the partner, may be a protective factor for criminal activity. The change scores seem to indicate that young men who are not in a relationship in late adolescence to early adulthood are at risk to increase their criminal activities, which is counter to the overall developmental trend that is sharply decreasing at this age (Empey, 1978).

The examination of relationship factors may thus prove fruitful in explaining changes in behavior and contextual risk in young adulthood. Different dimensions of young-adult context and adjustment may be associated with different aspects of the relationship. For example, perhaps merely the presence of a relationship will prove to have the strongest association with desistance of less severe criminal activity, whereas partner characteristics (e.g., prosocial skill levels) may relate to improvement for more severe criminals. A further possibility is that the more severely antisocial young men will not show improvements until rather late, perhaps in the mid- or late 20s.

Early Fatherhood and Risk for the Next Generation

As previously mentioned, men with higher levels of antisocial behavior were also likely to become fathers at an early age. Fatherhood prior to 20 years of age was found in univariate analyses to be associated with the same factors that have been associated with the developmental pathway of antisocial behavior and developmental failure, namely, contextual risk (low SES, low income, and parental antisocial behavior) and also the academic failure and antisocial behavior of the young father himself (Fagot, Pears, Capaldi, Crosby, & Leve, 1998). A profound marker of the continuance of risk context for the next generation was apparent in that only 40% of the children born to these young men prior to 20 years of age lived with both their mother and father at around 18 months of age. Thus, many of these children were being raised in single-mother or stepfather homes. Furthermore, 40% of the children had no contact at all with their biological father. Evidence was also seen for the early emergence of coercive parenting, in that the at-risk fathers showed higher levels of negative behavior during interaction with their toddler on a parent-child puzzle task.

Evidence has been found in other studies for similar risk for early parenthood in girls who showed higher levels of conduct problems in childhood. Bardone et al. (1996) found twice the rate of pregnancy by 21 years of age for young women who had been conduct disordered in childhood, and over three times the rate of childbearing (30% vs. 8%). Serbin et al. (1998) found twice the rate of adolescent motherhood for girls who had been aggressive in childhood. Observed maternal unresponsiveness to their child was associated with their own childhood aggressive behavior.

Of course, conduct problems are not the only factor associated with intergenerational transmission of contextual risk. Living in the same or similar high-risk neighborhood in adulthood to the one in which they were raised, regional recessions and restriction of employment opportunities and similar events may be associated with intergenerational transmission of contextual risk. However, evidence from the OYS indicates that the highest levels of intergenerational transmission of contextual risk factors are seen for those young men who showed higher levels of conduct problems in childhood and adolescence.

Discussion

In the studies described in the first section of this chapter, we emphasized that the family and peer processes, which are proximal to childhood and adolescent onset of antisocial behavior, are embedded in a larger matrix of distal contextual variables. Contextual factors impinging on the family are causally associated, sometimes in a chain reaction. Thus, unemployment will also be associated with lower family income, greater stress, depression, and less stable families (more parental transitions). Antisocial men and women with associated problems, such as lower academic achievement and poor job skills, are at risk for being caught in a cycle of contextual factors that place themselves and their families at risk.

It appears that contextual factors are associated with parenting behaviors that place the child at risk for antisocial behavior because (a) they are indicators of stable characteristics of parents that are associated with their failure to learn skilled parenting and their learning of detrimental behaviors (e.g., harsh approaches to discipline) and (b) they represent state changes (e.g., stress) that are associated with the disruption of parenting. The coercive interpersonal styles, risk for life failures, and lack of parenting skills of antisocial adults place them in contexts that continue to elicit negative emotion, disrupt family functioning, and lead to antisocial behavior in the next generation. However, evidence for positive processes that help protect against the negative effects of contextual risk on parenting was found in social support for mothers who experienced divorce. This suggests that preventive interventions with mothers who have experienced parental transitions should include the positive use of social support.

The studies presented in the second half of the chapter provided prospective evidence that the cycle continues into the next generation. Children who developed antisocial behavior show patterns of associated developmental failure and an array of associated contextual risk factors in young adulthood. Effects of cumulative continuity (Caspi & Herbener, 1990) were seen in the prediction to an array of negative outcomes in late adolescence and young adulthood. The young men in the OYS who had higher levels of antisocial behavior were entering adulthood with substantial disadvantages. Cumulative continuity is further seen in that the environmental options of such young men are restricted in young adulthood, and they are more likely to find ecological niches that support antisocial behavior. For example, we have shown that young men with higher levels of conduct problems are more likely to date young women with higher levels of conduct problems (Capaldi & Crosby, 1997). These findings indicate that it is hard to overemphasize the importance of childhood conduct problems for adjustment failures in young adulthood for men, and also for continued and pervasive contextual risk. The consequences for the young man, his intimate partners, and for the children whom he fathers are profound.

Acknowledgments

We gratefully acknowledge the support for this project provided by Grants R37 MH 37940 and RO1 MH 50259 from the Prevention, Early Intervention, and Epidemiology Branch of the National Institute of Mental Health (NIMH), U. S. Public Health Service (PHS); Grant P30 MH 46690 from the Prevention, Early Intervention, and Epidemiology Branch NIMH and from the Office of Research on Minority Health (ORMH); and Grant RO1 MH 38318 from the Child and Adolescent Treatment and Preventive Intervention Research Branch, Division of Services and Intervention Research, NIMH, U. S. PHS

Note. Sections of this chapter are substantially adapted on the chapter from D. Fowles, P. Sutker, & S. H. Goodman (Eds.), *Experimental personality and psychopathy research* (pp. 165–198), by D. M. Capaldi and G. R. Patterson, 1994, Interrelated influences of contextual factors on antisocial behavior in childhood and adolescence for males, New York: Springer Publications. Copyright 1994 by Spring Publishing Company. Adapted with permission.

7

A Developmental Model for Early- and Late-Onset Delinquency

Gerald R. Patterson and Karen Yoerger

This chapter is a brief overview of several decades of OSLC studies that define a theory of delinquency. The theory is developmental in that it traces two trajectories of antisocial behavior, each characterized by an orderly sequence of stages. One trajectory leads to early arrest (prior to age 14) and adult crime and the other to late-onset arrests and desistence from adult crime. Which trajectory characterizes a child is shown to have major implications for adult adjustment. The primary focus in this chapter is to understand the mechanisms, both within and outside the family, that maintain the trajectories. This, in turn, requires an explanation of how it is that antisocial behaviors undergo dramatic changes in form at several developmental stages. A key assumption is that the developmental models inform prevention trials as to why, when, and how to intervene.

Changes in Overt and Covert Forms of Antisocial Behaviors

The developmental model presented here takes the position that growth in antisocial behavior is discontinuous rather than continuous (Patterson, Shaw, Snyder, & Yoerger, 2001). If one assumed that growth is a continuous function, then it would be expected that various observers and reporters would see aggressive events increasing as a function of age. Even a quick review of the literature shows that this is not the case (Nagin & Tremblay, 1999). Whether representing parents, teachers, observers, or child self-report, the data showed that the rates of aggression significantly decrease between ages 2 and 12 years. As we shall see, during adolescence some forms of antisocial behavior increase as a function of age. An understanding of what is increasing, what is decreasing, and why this occurs becomes one of the keys to constructing a developmental model of aggression.

A pattern of findings from various studies suggests that the development of antisocial behavior in children may be discontinuous in nature (Patterson et al., 2001). At this point, we are aware of two periods of almost explosive growth punctuated by a long interval of quiescence between ages (about) 2 through 12 years. The findings suggest that the first growth process may be initiated as early as 12 months through about 2 years of age. Following a period of no growth, indeed negative growth, there is an interval beginning in adolescence characterized by dramatic

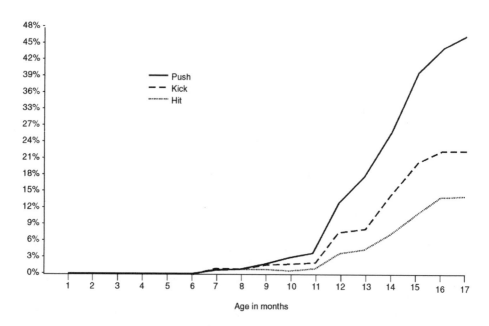

Figure 7.1. Cumulative onset of physically aggressive behavior (Tremblay et al., 2001).

increases in new forms of antisocial behavior. The toddler growth spurt is characterized, primarily, by overt forms; whereas the adolescent growth spurt is characterized by massive growth in covert antisocial behavior accompanied by additional growth in new forms of overt antisocial behaviors.

Tremblay et al. (in press) collected questionnaire data from 511 mothers of 17-month-old infants (boys and girls) on the occurrence of pushing, hitting, and kicking behaviors together with a retrospective account of when these behaviors first occurred. The findings are summarized in Figure 7.1. Forty-six percent of the mothers reported that their infants pushed, about 24% reported kicking, and 15% hitting. At 17 months of age, boys with siblings were about twice as likely to report kicking as were boys without siblings. The findings are consistent with observation studies that showed siblings played a key role (Bank, Burraston, & Snyder, 2001) and particularly so in the acquisition of physical aggression (Patterson, 1984, 1986).

Additional findings from the Tremblay et al. (in press) study showed that beginning at 27 months and maintaining through 132 months, the slope for hitting, biting, and kicking behaviors was essentially negative. Fewer than 5% of the children were said to frequently engage in these behaviors. What is particularly interesting is the fact that these high-amplitude (severe) behaviors occur as early as 17 months. Alternatively, the original coercion model implied that the longer the child was in the coercion process the more likely he or she was to engage in escalating processes that produced increasing severity in the form taken by the antisocial behaviors (Patterson, 1982). Loeber also proposes developmental pathways that begin with minor problems, such as "annoys others," but over time the progression expands to include violence and rape (Loeber, 1991; Loeber et al., 1993). There is now good reason to doubt that the time-in- process hypothesis is correct. There is increasing evidence of the kind provided by Tremblay and colleagues that the more severe forms of overt antisocial behaviors (hit, bite, kick, attack) are already in place by 2 years of age. For example Shaw's longitudinal analyses of maternal ratings beginning at age 2 years showed the now familiar negative slope in antisocial behavior (Patterson et al., 2001). But more to the point, the analyses of three longitudinal data sets covering the interval from age 2 through 18 years showed negative growth for a subset of more severe overt items, such as attack and fighting.

The hypothesis that emerges suggests that there is no detectable growth in the frequency or severity of overt antisocial events during a quiescent period from about age 2 through 12 years. The quiescent hypothesis also includes the assumption that, during this interval, covert forms of antisocial behavior occur only infrequently and also show no positive growth. It should be noted, however, that there is an important sense in which the problem child may be said to be getting worse during the quiescent interval. With each passing year in the coercion process, the child's arrested socialization becomes increasingly apparent. For example, academic difficulties become apparent by the 2nd or 3rd grade, and rejection by normal peers is evident within a few weeks of school entrance. The clear signs of social incompetence and failure plus the warning signs provided by juvenile forms of aggression lead responsible adults to begin referring the child for testing and special classroom placement. It is when the child becomes involved in the adolescent growth spurt for deviant behavior that the process of labeling becomes a matter of acute importance and a major concern to the community.

Data describing the quiescent interval are summarized in Figure 7.2 for both overt and covert ratings. The findings are based on a longitudinal study by Reid,

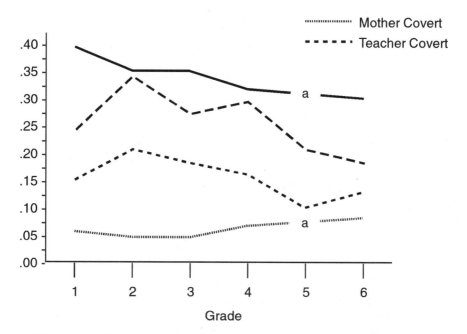

Figure 7.2. Overt and covert antisocial behavior during quiescent interval.

Eddy, Fetrow, and Stoolmiller (1999) for a sample of moderately at-risk families. The overt antisocial scale contained 19 items for mothers and 23 items for teachers. The covert scale for both mothers and teachers had 11 items (Patterson et al., 2001). Both sets of items were taken from the Child Behavior Checklists (CBC-L; Achenbach & Edelbrock, 1979). Data are presented here for boys rated by both mothers and teachers. It can be seen for the interval from grade 1 through grade 6 that all four sets of ratings are consistent with a no-growth hypothesis. In a repeated measures MANOVA, the linear coefficient for maternal ratings of overt antisocial behavior was -.07, highly significant at p < .00. Although teachers generally perceived fewer overt antisocial behaviors than did mothers, teachers' ratings showed a very similar linear coefficient, -.08, significant at p < .01.

Mothers perceived very low levels of covert antisocial behavior, and the linear coefficient (.01) was not significant. The findings are consistent with the quiescent-interval hypothesis as are the data from teachers' ratings. Although teachers see almost twice as much covert antisocial behavior as do mothers, they also perceive a significant decrease as a function of age of child. The linear coefficient was -.06, with a p < .02. The findings offer general support for the hypothesized quiescent interval during which time there is little evidence for growth in either overt or covert forms of antisocial behavior.

The mechanisms that maintain these early forms of overt antisocial behavior are detailed in earlier chapters of this volume. Generally speaking, the models assumed that the coercion process is initiated as the result of an interaction between several variables. One set defines biological variables (birth weight, pre- and post-natal complications, genes) associated with a difficult to raise infant and a relatively noncontingent caregiver (chapter 2). The evidence is steadily mounting that shows coercive parents tend to be deficient in cognitive skills as well (Azar et al., 1984; Beauchaine, 1999; Fagot, Gauvain, & Kavanagh, 1996). The unskilled caregiver inadvertently reacts to the child in such a way that the relative rate of childhood socially competent behaviors will be low, and the relative rates of deviant behaviors will be high. The caregiver's lack of skills can be amplified further by contextual forces that impinge from the environment, such as, divorce, unemployment, illness, and poverty (see chapter 6). We would now like to add one further concept to this set of models. It concerns the bidirectional relationship between context and microsocial processes.

In chapters 2 and 6, we hypothesized that the effect of contextual variables on child outcomes is mediated by the extent to which child and caregiver's microsocial processes are disrupted and become coercive. Recent formulations have given the relationship between microsocial process and context a definite bidirectional cast (Patterson & Granic, 2001). The earlier formulations emphasized deviant child behaviors and limited social competency as natural outcomes of the microsocial exchange. We had overlooked yet another, very important, outcome. Parent-child coercive social exchange is accompanied by a selection process that serves as a feedback loop to strengthen the long-term trajectory to adult crime. For example, the selectivity might determine the social experiences encountered by the child in the school setting. We hypothesized that the child is an active agent in this process, not a passive *tabula rasa*. The child's coercive interpersonal style leads to rejection by many normal peers. This leads him or her to select settings and individuals who maximize the payoffs that he or she can receive, given a limited repertoire of skills. Typically, this would consist of younger children and also children who reinforce his or her deviant behaviors and, on the short term, ignore his or her coercive interpersonal style. The child also selects playground areas that are not readily supervised by adults and stays away from organized games or activities that require a high order of skill.

For the younger child, the settings and individuals selected in the school serve only as an adjunct to the basic training in antisocial behavior that is being carried out by parents and siblings in the home. We suspect (James Snyder, personal communication, August 2000) that, even in the elementary school grades, deviant peers are providing positive reinforcement for deviant behaviors. However, given the limited time allocated to unsupervised peer interaction, the effect on the overall deviancy may be minimal and serve mainly as a support for the familial microsocial processes. For younger problem children who reside in school settings where the adults are in control, the deviant peer contribution does not produce new forms of antisocial behavior, nor does it appreciably increase the rates of overt antisocial behavior. However, epidemiological studies of inner-city schools emphasize the fact that in some school settings the adults are not in control (Kellam, Rebok, Ialongo, & Mayer, 1994). The effect of such a setting may increase both overt and incubate new forms of antisocial behavior. The fact that the settings are controlled by peers rather than adults could mean that more time is available for unsupervised interactions with deviant peers and accompanied by rich schedules of reinforcement for deviancy. If this were the case, then the teacher reports of overt antisocial behaviors should show a positive slope. However, teacher ratings for very large samples did not show such an increase for either males or females from grades one through six (Kellam et al., 1994).

We hypothesized that a similar feedback loop operates during adolescence. At this point, the selectivity effect is profoundly amplified. The key lies in the fact that in our society, adolescence is viewed as a mandate for large amounts of time unsupervised by adults. Programmatic studies by Dishion and his colleagues showed that the microsocial process occurring during the interaction of deviant peers is heavily laced with mutual reinforcement for deviancy talk. These studies are reviewed in detail in chapter 5. The key concept concerns significant growth in new forms of covert antisocial behavior during the interval from early to midadolescence. In what immediately follows, we will briefly explore three hypotheses concerning growth in covert antisocial behavior and its hypothesized dependency on prior development in overt antisocial behavior. High levels of overt antisocial behavior during childhood are thought to be a necessary prelude for growth in new forms of covert antisocial behavior. In turn, early overt behavior and later massive growth in covert antisocial behavior are thought to be significant predictors for adult arrest.

The first hypothesis concerns the relationship between early forms of overt and later growth in covert antisocial behavior. In a longitudinal study by Reid et al. (1999), data were collected annually for 5 years from mothers and teachers of 144 first grade boys and 186 fifth grade boys. A structural equation model (SEM) showed that teacher and parent ratings converged to define the latent constructs for overt at grade one and for covert antisocial behavior at grade six. The analyses showed an acceptable fit between the data set, the a priori theoretical model, and a path coefficient approaching 1.0. Given that the constructs were defined by only two indicators, a more conservative estimate of the relation between the two constructs would be a conditional probability for high-covert activity at grade six, given high levels of overt activity at grade one. This probability was .54, strongly supporting the hypothesis that over a 5-year interval, early high levels of overt antisocial predict high covert antisocial behavior. These variables identify two of the key events in the early-onset trajectory to adult crime. In the same vein, data from the OYS showed that 10-year-old boys who scored high on a construct for overt antisocial behavior were, as adolescents, most likely to show dramatic growth and sustained covert antisocial behavior (Patterson and Yoerger, 1997b).

The second hypothesis concerns the positive growth for covert behavior during the adolescent interval. A prior analysis of a 5-item covert scale from the OYS showed positive growth that began at about age 13 and continued through about age 17 (Patterson & Yoerger, 1997a). A reanalysis of the data for ages 10 through 18 used an expanded 10-item covert scale to estimate a linear coefficient of .10 (a positive slope) with a $p = .00$. Using the same 10-item scale, maternal ratings for the fifth grade cohort from the Reid et al. (1999) study showed a linear coefficient of .03 ($p = .00$) for ages 10.5 through 14. Examination of the teachers' ratings for a slightly different covert antisocial scale in the Reid et al. sample showed a linear coefficient of .06 ($p = .00$). Clearly, more studies are required; it seems particularly important to obtain further data from teachers. The hypothesized growth in covert behavior during the adolescent interval rests on a single replication.

Boys who maintained high overt antisocial scores through preadolescence were hypothesized to be the individuals who would show the most growth in covert antisocial behaviors. In an ANOVA, boys from the Reid et al. grade five sample, who scored above the mean on maternal ratings of overt antisocial behavior at grades seven, eight, and ten, showed significantly larger increases in covert antisocial behavior between grades five and ten ($F = 8.30$, $p < .01$).

Although early forms of overt antisocial behavior provide a significant base for predicting both juvenile and adult arrests, we hypothesized that measures of growth in covert antisocial behavior would augment predictions of long-term antisocial outcomes. To test the hypothesis with the OYS sample, both parent and teacher ratings were used to define the overt and covert antisocial constructs at each age from grade four through grade ten. Given a score on overt antisocial behavior at grade four that was at or above the median, the likelihood of three or more juvenile arrests was .39. Given both a high overt score at grade four and an increase (difference score above 0) in covert behavior between grades four and ten, the likelihood of chronic offending was .55, and the likelihood of an adult arrest (by about age 23) was .57. However, given a high overt score and a decrease (or no change) in covert antisocial behavior, the likelihood of chronic juvenile offending fell to .26.

These findings support a model that suggests early high levels of overt antisocial may be a necessary prerequisite for both juvenile chronic and adult offending. To illustrate the relationship further, police arrest data were collected annually for the OYS sample from grades four through twelve. Figure 7.3 summarizes the risk of police arrest each year for each of four different patterns of overt and covert variables. The likelihood of a police arrest for individuals who scored low on the overt (grade four, teacher and parent ratings) scale remained low and only reached about 0.12. However, boys who showed considerable growth in covert antisocial behavior during adolescence, but with no history of overt antisocial behavior (by definition, late-onset boys), showed a steady but low level progression in risk of arrest, reaching .21 only late in high school. Similarly, boys with a history of overt but no fol-

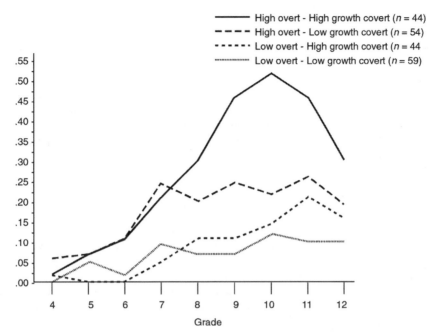

Figure 7.3. Contribution of overt and covert antisocial behavior variables to predicting annual arrest.

lowing growth in covert antisocial behavior hovered at the 0.20 level. A later section of this report shows that the majority of individuals in this group then dropped out of the crime process.

The most dramatic pattern was defined by a history of overt antisocial behavior followed by intense growth in covert antisocial behavior. The resultant risk for police arrest was identifiable as early as grade six and increased at an almost constant rate to a peak at grade ten. We assumed that this increase, and the decrease that begins with grade ten, was determined by the degree of involvement with deviant peers. However, the interpretation of the decrease is complicated by the change from minor to adult status that accompanied the boy's 18th birthdays.

The pattern of high early overt antisocial behavior and later growth in covert antisocial behavior is analogous to results from the three longitudinal studies reviewed in Kelley, Loeber, Keenan, and De Lamatre (1997). They reported that boys who advanced along an overt antisocial trajectory to serious delinquency also engaged in covert forms of antisocial behavior. For this group, the covert and overt antisocial pathways were highly correlated.

Early-Onset Trajectory to Antisocial Behavior

Two Paths to Juvenile Offending

It has become clear to a number of investigators that juvenile delinquents do not constitute a homogeneous class of individuals. Rather, there may be several trajectories, each with different outcomes as adults (Loeber & Stouthamer-Loeber, 1998). For example, DiLalla and Gottesman (1989), Moffitt (1993), and Pulkkinen (1986) differentiate between transient and persistent offenders. Each path is hypothesized to be driven by different mechanisms. For example, Farrington and Hawkins (1991) demonstrated that childhood-based measures could significantly differentiate persistent from transient offenders.

Alternatively, a group of investigators, including the present authors, have examined the feasibility of differentiating between early arrest (by age 14 or 15 years) and late-onset arrest (Farrington & Hawkins, 1991; Patterson, Capaldi, & Bank, 1991; Patterson, DeBaryshe, & Ramsey, 1989; Patterson & Yoerger, 1997a; Simons, Wu, Conger, & Lorenz, 1994; Stattin & Magnusson, 1991).

Early Onset

In the Oregon version of the early-onset model, we assumed that there is an orderly progression from high rates of childish forms of overt antisocial behavior that may begin as a toddler and progress to more advanced forms. Later stages in the sequence form a progression that includes early arrest, chronic juvenile offending, and adult chronic offending. The first event in the adolescent segment of the early-onset trajectory is defined by a latent construct for antisocial behavior assessed by multiple indicators at grade four.

As shown in Figure 7.4, the likelihood of a boy assessed as antisocial at grade four being arrested prior to age 14 is .45. For boys who scored at or above the median on the antisocial construct, the odds of an early arrest were 13.6 times greater than for boys who scored low (Patterson, Forgatch, Yoerger, & Stoolmiller, 1998). Given

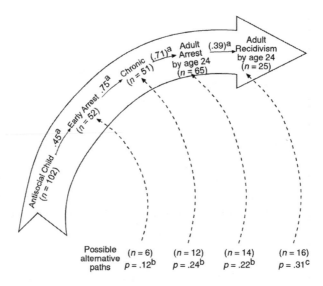

Figure 7.4. Early onset trajectory to adult crime.

an early arrest, the odds of being a chronic (three or more juvenile arrests) offender are 39.7 times greater than for non-early-onset individuals.

For the OYS sample, the likelihood of an adult arrest, given chronic juvenile status, was .71. This closely replicates the figure of .74 found in the Swedish longitudinal study by Stattin and Magnusson (1991). It is also in the range of comparable values noted by the Blumstein, Cohen, Roth, and Visher (1986) review of three longitudinal studies. The goal is to identify the small set of adults who commit the bulk of crimes for their cohort. We assumed that the majority of them have passed through the progression from antisocial childhood behaviors, through early-onset to chronic juvenile offending, and then to adult chronic offending. Keeping with this idea, the Stattin and Magnusson (1991) study showed that all but two of the adults who had committed 10 or more crimes had passed through early arrest (prior to age 15), and all had two or more arrests as adolescents (age 15 to 20 years). In a similar vein, the meta-analyses by Gendreau, Little, and Goggin (1996) showed that pre-adult arrests were among the best predictors of adult recidivism.

The trajectory assumption carries with it the notion that the progression is transitive (e.g., an individual at an advanced stage has passed through each of the prior stages). In the OYS sample of the 52 early-onset boys, 46 had also previously been identified as antisocial; and of the 51 chronic offenders, 39 had been arrested early. Of the 65 arrested as adults, 36 had also been chronic juvenile offenders. Patterson, Forgatch, Yoerger, and Stoolmiller (1998) examined the pattern of movement through the trajectory. The data showed that 96 of the 103 antisocial boys moved in an orderly transitive pattern through the three steps. Of the 51 chronic offenders, 71% moved through all three points. The findings were consistent with the idea of a single major path to chronic juvenile and chronic adult offending. However, these descriptive data cannot speak to the question of whether a single model can explain how the process starts, what maintains it, and what determines movement from one stage to another. Is a different model required for each stage as implied in the Farrington and Hawkins (1991) study? Or is a different model required for each trajectory, as suggested by the programmatic studies by Loeber and his colleagues (Loeber and Farrington, 1998; Loeber & Stouthamer-Loeber, 1998)?

The Oregon delinquency model takes the position that both the early- and late-start trajectories represent variations on the same underlying theme. The underlying theme as outlined in this volume assumes a complex relation between contextual variables, such as divorce, poverty, and depression, as being mediated by inept parenting and deviant peer socialization together with their concomitant reinforcement contingencies. This implies that contextual, parenting, and peer variables should account for much of the variance in determining early onset as shown in Patterson, Crosby, and Vuchinich (1992). Variables from the same model should also account for variance in the late-onset model (Patterson & Yoerger, 1993). There are three variables separating early- from late-onset trajectories. (1) The most important variable is timing. We hypothesized that the early-onset process begins during preschool years, whereas the late onset begins in mid-adolescence, (2) the level at which the disruptions occur for parenting and peer processes differ. We assumed that all of the processes are more disrupted for early- as compared to late-onset trajectories. (3) The levels of social incompetence were assumed to be significantly

Table 7.1. Variables Collected at Grade 4 Predicting Early Onset and Adult.

Grade 4 context	Discriminate Function Analysis Differentiating Early from Late Onset			Differentiating Adult Desisters from Nondesisters		
	Function 1	$F(1,94)$	p	Function 1	$F(1,94)$	p
Discipline	0.66	8.99	.00	.44	4.03	.05
One or both parents employed	-0.55	6.11	.02	-.60	7.37	.01
Parental transitions	0.44	2.98	.09	.59	7.28	.01
Parental SES	-0.42	3.63	.06	-.31	1.95	.17
Parental antisocial behavior	0.44	3.56	.05	.29	1.72	.19
Income	-0.23	1.07	.30	-.24	1.20	.28
Parental depression	0.30	1.79	.18	.23	1.11	.30
Supervision/monitoring	0.15	0.47	.50	-.14	.43	.52
Parental stress	0.27	1.42	.24	.20	.86	.36
Canonical R	0.42			.43		
Eigenvalue	0.22			.22		
Significance of Power of Function (χ^2)	17.49 ($p = .04$)			17.92 ($p = .04$)		

higher for the early- as compared to late-onset delinquency and significantly higher for late-onset delinquency as compared to nondelinquency.

Data from the OYS were used to test the hypothesis that challenging contexts and inept parenting practices could significantly discriminate between the two trajectories. It was further hypothesized that these differences would be in place by late childhood. To test these hypotheses, the contextual and parenting variables were assessed at grade four and employed in a discriminant function to differentiate early from late onset (defined by when the first arrest occurred; Capaldi & Patterson, 1994). As shown in Table 7.1, the parenting and contextual variables employed in a discriminant function loaded significantly on a single factor that significantly differentiated early- from late-onset families. The canonical correlation of .42 attests to the power of this factor. The loadings vary slightly from the original report because of subsequent court record updates and data corrections.

As compared to boys with late-onset delinquency, early-onset boys usually come from families characterized by parents who use ineffective discipline practices, and who themselves tend to be antisocial and unemployed. There were also borderline trends for the families of early-onset boys to be low socioeconomic status (SES) and characterized by frequent marital transitions. There seems little question that boys with early- as compared to late-onset delinquency come from environments that are significantly more disrupted, placing them at significantly greater risk for delinquent behaviors.

Patterson and Yoerger (1997a) used data from the OYS to test the hypothesis that boys with early-onset delinquency were less socially skilled than were late-onset boys. We assumed that the skills of boys with late-onset delinquency would fall some-

Table 7.2. Testing the Limited Social Skills Hypothesis (from Patterson & Yoerger, 1997a).

Variable	Mean			Scheffe		
	Early onset N = 53	Late onset N = 60	Not delinquent N = 93	Early vs. not	Late vs. not	Late vs. early
Child social skill	-.61	.07	.30	X[a]		X
Poor peer relations	.58	-.01	-.32	X	X	X
Academic achievement	-.30	-.10	.24	X	X	
Self-esteem	-.30	.12	.09	X		X

[a]Tests were significant at .05 level or better.

where in between those of boys with early-onset and nondelinquent trajectories, exemplars of what DiLalla and Gottesman (1991) call "marginally adjusted."

As shown in Table 7.2, data collected at grade four significantly differentiated boys with early-onset from those with late-onset delinquency by their limited levels of social skill (teacher, parent, and peer ratings), more disrupted peer relations (parent, teacher, and peer ratings), and lowered self-esteem (child report). The findings support the hypothesis that in late childhood, it was already possible to identify boys with early-onset delinquency as less socially skilled and more deviant than late-onset boys, and both at-risk groups were significantly less skilled than were nondelinquents.

The data showed that, compared to nondelinquents, the late-onset boys had poor peer relations and lower academic achievement (parent, teacher, tests). The findings were in general agreement with a prior investigation by DiLalla and Gottesman (1991) in showing that late-onset boys tended to be more like nondelinquents than they were like boys with early-onset delinquency. In a similar vein, Caspi and Moffitt (1995) concluded that transient adolescent offenders tended to be more like normal boys than like chronic offenders. As we shall see in a later section, late onset is analogous to Moffitt's transient offenders in that most of them desist from crime as adults.

Family and contextual variables seem to serve as important determinants for how development unfolds by age 10 years. The programmatic studies by Shaw and his colleagues discussed in chapter 2 suggest that these same variables may tell us how the process is initiated during the toddler stage. However, it is not clear that the process that creates deviant outcomes in childhood is in any way related to the process that maintains deviancy during adolescence. We hypothesized that disadvantaged context and poor family management practices make significant contributions to maintaining the deviancy process during adolescence.

In the Oregon model, we hypothesized that a single model might account for the maintenance within the trajectory (Patterson, Forgatch, Yoerger, & Stoolmiller, 1998). As a very conservative test, we hypothesized that variables identifiable during childhood would predict to each of the three stages in the trajectory portrayed earlier in Figure 7.4 (childhood antisocial behavior, early-onset arrest, and chronic arrest). In the univariate logistic regressions shown in Table 7.3, measures collected at grade four on social disadvantage, family transitions, and discipline and moni-

Table 7.3. Contextual and Parenting Variables as Predictors of Future Trajectory Stages (Patterson, Forgatch, Yoerger, & Stoolmiller, 1998).

Variables	Child Antisocial		Early Onset		Chronic Offender	
	ß	p	ß	p	ß	p
Social disadvantage	0.47	.002	0.65	.001	0.66	.001
Marital transitions	0.23	.106	0.56	.001	0.49	.003
Parental monitoring	-0.64	.000	-0.44	.009	-0.44	.009
Parental discipline	-0.97	.000	-0.66	.000	-0.63	.000

$N = 202$

toring practices significantly predicted the early-onset and chronic juvenile stages of the trajectory. This is consistent with the idea that they may function as maintenance mechanisms for the trajectory. As we shall see in a later section, the deviant peer group also makes an important contribution to maintenance in these stages.

The extent to which an individual penetrated the sequence was related to the level of disruption in context and family processes measured during childhood and to a time-dependent measure of the degree of involvement with deviant peers. The more disrupted the family or the context in which they lived and the greater the availability of deviant peers at that point in time, then the greater the risk of moving to a more advanced stage (Patterson et al., 1998). The findings were consistent with the idea of a single trajectory to chronic offending explained by a single model.

Changes in Form: The Metamorphosis

Findings from trajectory studies pose an interesting problem. One of the most salient features of the trajectory concerns the change in form describing the transition from overt antisocial behaviors that define childhood behavior problems to delinquent acts described in police arrest data. Breaking into a house has a topography that is quite different from taking money from mother's purse. Rape and physical assault seem to belong in a different class from that of temper tantrum. Most theories fail to specify the precise nature of this transformational process. Given a developmental sequence that moves from childhood behavior problems to adult crime, how does one explain the changes in form that make up this progression?

The general assumption entertained by many investigators, including the present writers, is that a metamorphosis takes place during the interval from late childhood to early adolescence. In the Oregon studies, we assumed that the driving mechanism for these dramatic changes was to be found by studying the microsocial details of the intensive interactions with deviant peers. Although Burgess and Akers (1966), Elliott, Huizinga, and Ageton (1985), Thornberry (1990), Thornberry and Krohn (1997), and Patterson and Dishion (1985) had all stressed the key role played by deviant peers in fostering crime, they remain relatively silent about the nature of the process that brings it about. At best, each investigator established a correlation of some kind between time spent with deviant peers and negative outcomes, such as crime, substance use, and early sexual activity. If discussed at all, it was generally assumed that the changes were due to peer-induced changes in attitudes, values, and standards (Elliott et al., 1985).

Some astute observers (Burgess & Akers, 1966) hypothesized that the key mechanism involved reinforcers supplied by members of the deviant peer group, however, it was left to the programmatic studies by Dishion and his colleagues to identify the microsocial process that attends these exchanges (Dishion & Patterson, 1997; Dishion, Patterson, & Griesler, 1994; Dishion, Spracklen, Andrews, & Patterson, 1996;). The Dishion studies (detailed in chapter 5) were based on grade eight data from videotaped laboratory interactions between the adolescent and a close friend. The tapes were coded to measure the relative rates of reinforcement supplied by peers for deviant and for prosocial behaviors. Questionnaires and interviews were also used to estimate the extent to which the peer was antisocial and the amount of time the target child spent with antisocial peers. These variables served as indicators for a deviancy-training construct. Assessments collected at grades four to twelve specified a latent construct for growth in new forms of deviancy (Patterson et al., 2000). Greater involvement in deviancy training meant higher relative rates of reinforcement for deviant talk, more time spent with peers, and a higher ratio of deviant peers.

Data from the OYS also showed that parents, teachers, and child self-reports of early involvement (grade four) with deviant peers predicted heavy involvement (.85, path coefficient) in grade eight in deviancy training. Heavy involvement with deviancy training was, in turn, predictive of simultaneous training in several new forms of deviant behavior, including substance use, health-risking sexual behavior, and police arrest. In fact, an individual growing at a fast rate in use of substances was very likely growing at comparable rates in other new forms of deviancy as well (e.g., rates of growth were intercorrelated and defined a latent construct for new growth). The deviancy-training construct accounted for 53% of variance in new growth.

Other studies have also found that peers in a nursery school setting (Patterson, Littman, & Bricker, 1967) and adolescents in correctional institutional settings (Buehler, Patterson, & Furniss, 1966) positively reinforce deviant behaviors. It seems reasonable to assume that the amount of growth in deviancy would depend upon the availability of deviant peers and the amount of unsupervised time spent with them. The studies by Osgood, Wilson, Bachman, O'Malley, and Johnson (1996) of routine activities stressed the importance of amount of time spent in routine unsupervised activities as predictors for criminal careers.

Patterson (1993) used the OYS to examine the contribution of changes in deviant peer involvement and unsupervised activities (wandering) as contributors to growth in substance use and truancy during adolescence. As shown in Figure 7.5, when the study began at grade four, those boys already involved with deviant peers showed elevated intercepts for the new forms of antisocial behavior—truancy and substance use. Initial involvement with deviant peers also predicted (.58) accelerated growth in these new forms. However, increasing involvement with deviant peers and in unsupervised time were also significant contributors. Including covariates that assess changes in deviant peer involvement generates a model that accounts for 54% of variance in new growth.

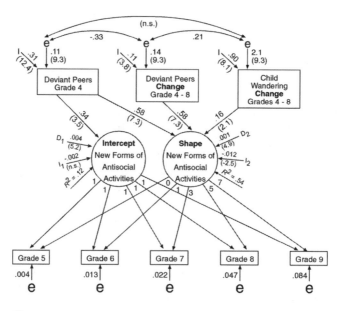

$\chi^2_{(27)}=34.59$, $p = .15$, BBN = .892, BBNN = .973

Figure 7.5. A growth model for changes in form (Patterson, 1993).

Our Iowa colleagues, Simons, Wu, Conger, and Lorenz (1994), replicated several of the key features of the early-onset model in a study based on four waves of data from a sample of rural families. The early-starter group was identified by their self-reports of serious delinquent acts prior to age 14. They found the expected relation between disrupted parenting and both oppositional-defiant child behavior and social disadvantage. As would be expected from the early-onset model, both disrupted parenting and oppositional-deviant child behaviors predicted T1 involvement with deviant peers. Time 2 child oppositional behavior also predicted T2 involvement with deviant peers. The relation between oppositional child behavior and self-report arrests was mediated by involvement with deviant peers.

There is thought to be yet another dimension to the contributions made by deviant peers. It has been known for some time that the bulk of juvenile crime is committed by groups of two or more individuals. Zimring (1984) reviews some of the earlier studies, starting with Shaw who showed that 8 out of 10 boys committed their offenses in the company of one or more of their peers. Modern studies show variable rates depending somewhat on age and type of crime; for example, 90% of gun robbery episodes involved groups as compared to 60% for assault and 78% for homicide. This is not to say, of course, that all juvenile crimes are committed in the company of fellow travelers. For example, earlier findings by Knight and West (1975) showed that recidivists were more than twice as likely to have committed serious crimes by themselves.

These findings imply that the setting in which juvenile crime is committed is most likely defined by social exchanges among two or more persons. The social interactional perspective is that a good share of the interactions with family and peers are overlearned and, therefore, unlikely to be controlled by direct cognitive processes

(Patterson, 1982, 1997). Given a matrix of overlearned networks of controlling stimuli for the majority of juvenile delinquent activity, it is difficult to see rational choice theory as offered by Wilson and Herrnstein (1985) as a viable explanation for crime. While hot-wiring a car, at what point does the young adolescent step out of the rapid-fire exchange with peers and reflect on the subjective calculus of cost and benefit? In the same vein, it is difficult to imagine that while picking the lock to the door, the adolescent sequentially engages in the several steps involved for direct cognitive processes as outlined in social informational processing (Dodge, Pettit, Bates, & Valente, 1995). We submit that the group process provided by the company of one's peers is more likely a proximal cause for crime than any existing cognitive theory.

A Model for Late-Onset Offending

The details of the late-onset offending model are presented in Patterson (1994) and Patterson and Yoerger (1993; 1997a). As already noted, the general assumption is that both early- and late-onset individuals can be identified during late childhood, or perhaps much earlier; but that remains to be seen. Late-onset individuals are characterized by their marginal levels of deviancy (antisocial behavior) and their marginal levels of social competency. Presumably, their families are embedded in marginally disadvantaged contexts, and their parents are marginally skilled in managing their families. In fact, the late-onset model might best be characterized as the "marginality model," an idea originally suggested by DiLalla and Gottesman (1989). They contrasted persistent and transitory offenders and found that, in many respects, transitory offenders were intermediate between persistent and nonoffenders (e.g., marginal adjustment). In keeping with the marginality assumption, the findings from Tables 7.1 and 7.2 described earlier showed that the late-onset boys were, in fact, less antisocial than the early-onset boys but more antisocial than were nondelinquent boys. The peer relation variable also showed significant support for the marginality model. In keeping with the hypothesis, late-onset boys as compared to early-onset boys were also shown to be more socially skilled and to have better peer relations and higher self-esteem.

We hypothesized that coercive processes in the families of early-onset delinquents are accompanied by commensurately lower support for socially competent behaviors. The effect of this dual failure for the early-onset group became evident as early as the third or fourth grades when these boys were obviously failing in school, rejected by peers, and significantly depressed. We hypothesized that families of the late-onset boys would be characterized by significantly higher rates of relative reinforcement for prosocial behavior and significantly less coercive exchange than early-onset boys. As a result, by the time the late-onset boys reach midadolescence, they have developed a set of work and relational skills that will produce reliable reinforcement for nondelinquent activities. This, in turn, implies that their delinquent careers will be relatively brief. We hypothesized that the measures of childhood social skills plus measures of young adult work and relational skills would significantly predict which of the late-onset individuals will desist from further delinquent activities. We will explore the findings for desistance in a later section.

In the general model for late-onset boys, the deviant peer group plays the key role in actually training for covert antisocial and delinquent behaviors (see chapter

5). This emphasis on the role of deviant peers as the mediating mechanism between family process and late-onset arrest is in direct contrast to nonessential roles assigned deviant peers by both Hirschi (1969) and more recently Moffitt (1993).

Thus far, there have been only two applications of SEM to the late-onset model. The small sample from the OYS of boys, who were average or lower on the antisocial score assessed at grade four, was used to test the assumption that disruptions in monitoring might increase the boys' associations with deviant peers during early adolescence (Patterson & Yoerger, 1997a). The findings in Figure 7.6 show that challenges in family life (e.g., recent unemployment, severe illness, divorce, change in residence, pubescence occurring between ages 11 and 12) were significantly associated (.38, path coefficient) with less effective monitoring and with increases (.33, correlation) in family conflict. As predicted, increasing family conflict and disrupted monitoring contributed to increased involvement with deviant peers, accounting for 56% of the variance in that construct.

As shown by Montemayor and Flannery (1989), Paikoff and Brooks-Gunn (1990), and others, conflicts with parents typically increase during early adolescence. Does this imply an increase in risk for negative reinforcement and training for the adolescent to become coercive? We do not have a definitive answer to this question. However, ratings of overt antisocial behavior would reflect such a process. However, contrary to this expectation, findings for overt antisocial behavior show

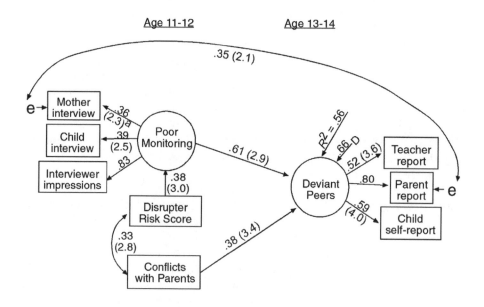

$\underline{N} = 80$

$\chi^2_{(16)} = 15.36$, $p = .50$, BBN = .893, BBNN = 1.0l0, CFI = 1.000

[a]values within parentheses are t-test scores

Figure 7.6. Parenting and late-onset delinquency (Patterson & Yoerger, 1997a).

strong negative slope during all of adolescence for both early- and late-onset anti-social boys and for nonoffenders alike (Patterson & Yoerger, 1997a). Our best guess is that preschool is the most productive interval for training in coercive skills, and that growth in coercive skills is not one of the by products of interaction with deviant peers.

The second attempt to model late-onset delinquency was carried out by our Iowa colleagues (Simons et al., 1994). From their sample of rural Iowa families, they selected a subgroup of adolescents who had not committed (self-report) two serious delinquent acts by the age of 14 years (e.g., potential late-onset cases). They exam-ined several hypotheses. The key idea was that for late-onset individuals, coercive oppositional (antisocial) behaviors would not play a central role in selecting deviant peers or in risk for police arrest. This is unlike expectations for early-onset delin-quency, where the antisocial construct plays such a key role. The model predicts a significant path from ineffective parenting to deviant peer involvement and from deviant peers to self-reported serious crimes. The findings supported all three hypotheses.

Early and Late Growth

We were interested in comparing the growth in deviancy for early- and late-onset individuals (Patterson, 1999). For example, is the rate of growth in deviancy roughly equivalent for the early and late onset, or is it that early-onset deviancy is not only growing at a faster rate, but also reaches greater extremes of severity?

Based on earlier findings by Wolfgang (1977), we had thought that the higher frequency of offending for early onset implied higher risk for more severe crimes, his data indicated that frequency correlated significantly with severity. A prior analysis of OYS data by Capaldi and Patterson (1996) showed that, given three or more arrests, the probability of a violent crime was .47. The comparable figure from the Farrington (1991) analyses of the London cohorts was .49. Kelley, Loeber, Keenan, and DeLamatre (1997) also reported that frequency and violence are cor-related. The OYS data showed that both chronic nonviolent and chronic violent offenders resided in families characterized by highly unskilled family practices and negative contextual variables. In the Capaldi and Patterson (1996) study, the fre-quency of self-reported nonviolent offending accounted for 40% of the variance in self-reported violent offending. We concluded that frequency and severity of offend-ing are correlated.

We were interested in the question of early- and late-onset differences in sever-ity. Up to age 18 years, severity of crime did not increase as a function of age. For both groups, about a fourth to a fifth of all of their arrests included a felony. The data for both groups showed no noticeable increase in severity over time. By 18 years of age, the 52 boys in the early-onset group had accumulated 488 charges; the mean of 9.39 was significantly ($p = .000$) greater than the corresponding mean of 3.66 for the 58 boys in the late-onset group. Data in Figure 7.7 show that the early-onset group started earlier and continues longer. However, as shown in Figure 7.7, once the late-onset group enters the training process, the acquisition slopes for the two groups are very similar. About 22% of the crimes in both groups were serious (e.g., felonies), and the proportion seemed to hold for both groups at each point in time.

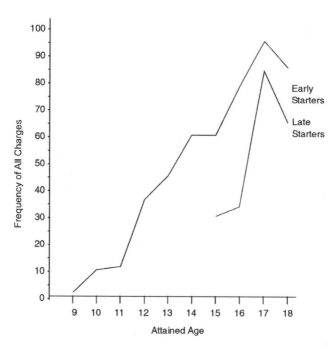

Figure 7.7. Frequency of criminal charges by attained age.

One would also expect that the early start for the growth in new forms of antisocial behavior, such as substance use, health-risking sexual behavior, and arrests (official records), would be higher for the early- as compared to late-onset groups. In keeping with these hypotheses, there were borderline trends for early-onset boys to show higher rates of substance use and an increased number of intercourse partners (Patterson, 1999).

We hypothesized that these differences in frequency reflect the contribution of differences in timing. However, the Dishion studies suggested that they might also reflect the contribution of differences in intensity of training for deviancy. To directly test the timing-training intensity hypotheses, indicators for the deviancy-training construct were combined to form a single composite score. The mean deviancy training score for the early-onset group was .35 (.71 SD) and for the late-onset group, it was -.33 (.58 SD). The scores imply that the early-onset group received more intensive contacts, interacted with peers who were more deviant, and received higher rates of relative reinforcement for deviancy. The deviancy-training variable correlated .47 (p = .00) with the total frequency of arrests during adolescence.

A multiple regression analysis was used to test the relative contribution of timing and training intensity, two variables accounting for arrest frequency during adolescence. The multiple correlation was .51; the beta for deviancy training was 2.90 (p = .00); and for age of onset; it was −2.60 (p = .02). Clearly, both timing and deviancy training make unique and significant predictions to overall arrest frequency.

There is one further dimension of criminal behavior that merits comment. It is a phenomenon commented upon but seldom analyzed. It has to do with the episodic

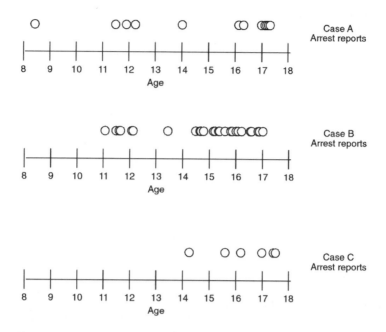

Figure 7.8. The episodic nature of juvenile crime.

nature of arrest data (Chaiken & Rolf, 1985), which, in turn, implies that undetected criminal activity may also be episodic (LeBlanc & Frechett, 1989). The OYS data for police arrests for three cases covering the interval from age 8 to 18 years are shown in Figure 7.8. Cases A and B are exemplars of early onset in that their first arrests occurred prior to age 14 years. Case C is an example of late-onset arrest. Each of them fits the pattern noted by LeBlanc and Frechett (1989), where periods of high criminal activity are followed by periods of relative inactivity.

In keeping with the general delinquency model, we hypothesized that a burst of activity would covary with periods of involvement with deviant peers. Ratings of deviant peer involvement were collected annually from parents and teachers. Findings from logistic regression analyses are summarized in Table 7.4. The data showed that concurrent measures of deviant peer involvement were significantly predictive of police arrest at each grade from six through twelve.

Adult Adjustment

By the time the OYS boys were about 23 years of age, 65 (32%) had been arrested at least once as an adult. Forty-one of them had been arrested two or more times. Fourteen had no prior record of juvenile arrests. For the current model, this means a false negative error (14/65) of 22%. This is in keeping with a comparable figure of 25% for the Philadelphia cohort study (Wolfgang, 1977) and 15% for the LeBlanc and Frechett (1989) study.

It will be another few years before the OYS sample of arrested adults provides a sufficient database for modeling determinants. However, we assume that the

Table 7.4. Logistic Regressions of Police Arrest on Concurrent Measures of Involvement with Deviant Peers.

Grade	ß	Exponentiated ß
6	1.60**	4.93
7	2.61***	13.63
8	1.76***	5.83
9	1.26***	3.53
10	1.53***	4.60
11	1.41***	4.08
12	1.29***	3.63

$**p < .01; *** p < .001$

forthcoming model will be a logical extension of the model that served for juvenile crime. Presumably, a history of exposure to unskilled family management and disadvantaged context will be significant predictors, but estimates of adult contacts with deviant peers will make the major contribution to criminal activity. In keeping with the idea that the adult stage is an extension of the juvenile stage, data from the OYS showed that, given a grade four overt antisocial construct score at or above the median and a covert antisocial difference score above zero (grades four to ten), the likelihood of an arrest as an adult was .57 (Patterson et al, 2001). The reader will recall that the two variables had also been significant predictors of juvenile chronic offending (probability of .55). In a similar vein, the likelihood of an adult arrest, given prior status as a chronic (three or more arrests) juvenile offender, was .71. The Patterson and Yoerger (1999) analyses also showed that the contextual variables, SES and marital transitions assessed at grade four, were significant predictors for adult arrest, just as they had been as predictors for childhood antisocial and delinquent behavior.

Given status as early-onset juvenile offender, the likelihood of arrest as a young adult was .65; this is in dramatic contrast to the comparable value of .29 for late-onset boys. The majority (71%) of the late-onset boys were identified as desisters (no adult arrest through about age 23 years). In fact, the majority of desisters (70%) came from this group. Although late-onset offenders account for 53% of the juvenile offenders in the OYS, they account for only a small subset of the chronic juvenile (24%) and adult recidivists (two or more arrests, 29%). The Oregon model hypothesizes that contextual and parenting variables that predicted early and late onset should significantly predict adult arrest and desistence. The most conservative test of this hypothesis would be to use childhood measures of these variables to predict the adult outcomes. The data testing this hypothesis are summarized in Table 7.1. It can be seen that the significant prediction across the 13-year span offer strong support for the hypothesis. The variables that most significantly differentiated arrest desistance were parent employment, transitions, and parental discipline. All three of these had been among the top five variables differentiating early- from late-onset delinquency.

Our hypothesis is that the majority of midlife (age 30 to 35 years), high-rate, chronic offenders will have moved to this status through the life-course trajectory traced out in Figure 7.4: first, overt antisocial child, then early arrest, chronic juvenile arrest, young adult arrest, and finally adult chronic offending. This hypothesis is consistent with findings from several studies. For example, the meta-analyses by Gendreau et al. (1996) showed that pre-adult offending was a significant predictor of adult repeat offending. The large-scale longitudinal study by Stattin and Magnusson (1991) found that 74% of juvenile chronic offenders had been arrested as young adults (age 21 to 29). In the same study, a very small group of adults accounted for the bulk of adult offenders. Eighty-three percent of those who had committed 10 or more offenses as adults had first passed through (a) early arrest, then (b) continued adolescent offending, and finally (c) adult recidivist offending.

The general pattern of findings is consistent with the hypothesis that adult offending is an extension of the models that predicted juvenile offending. The findings reiterate the assumption that there is a single trajectory and perhaps a single set of models that explain the initiation and maintenance through this trajectory.

Implications for Prevention

Knowing the details of the main path followed by the majority of chronic juvenile and adult offenders strongly emphasizes the need to initiate prevention trials some years prior to first arrest. By the time the first arrest occurs, the individual is already carrying the full burden of school failure, rejection by normal peers, and an obvious lack of skills required to survive in either the world of work or the world of enduring human relationships. Our best guess, based on current analyses of growth in antisocial behavior, is that the most cost efficient time to intervene may be in the first 2 or 3 years of life. As a secondary issue, the evaluation of prevention trials should include both prosocial and deviant intraindividual growth patterns as criterion measures.

The models point to the need for parents and deviant peers to occupy the central focus for the prevention-intervention trials. The prevention trials described in this volume make a strong case for the causal status of parenting practices and the reinforcement contingencies they control. The fact that in randomized prevention trials (chapter 11) the magnitude of change in parenting correlates significantly with the magnitude of change in child outcomes clearly implicates parenting practices as causal mechanisms.

Be that as it may be, most investigators are clearly aware of how difficult it is to work with parents. In our experience, it requires at least 2 years of intensive training and experience before even a gifted clinician can put these ideas into clinical practice. For these reasons, many chose to focus on training teachers rather than parents (Embry, Flannery, Vazsonyi, Powell, & Atha, 1996; Greenberg, Kusche, Cook, & Quamma, 1995; Grossman et al., 1997). At the present time, we have no information as to the relative utilities that follow one strategy or another. If we ignore the family and focus our efforts on reducing aggression only in the school setting, does this effectively reduce the overall societal rates of delinquency? One would think that it might. However, would the results be stronger if both the home and school settings were altered? Again, one would think so. But these are questions for the next round of prevention trials. These are far more interesting questions than those confronting us just one short decade ago when it was not at all clear what the answer was to the question, "Does anything at all work?"

Some Preliminary Models for Societal Rates of Delinquency

A theory of delinquency must eventually address the problem of why societal rates change over time or why one community might have a higher prevalence of delinquent individuals than another. This has traditionally been the province of sociology. For example, Cloward and Olin's (1960) formulation about the contribution of social and economic status to delinquency represented a broad stream of theorizing labeled as strain theory. This body of literature was reviewed by Kornhauser (1978). From this perspective, it was assumed that adolescents are pressured to engage in delinquent acts because they experience marked differences between their aspirations and their actual opportunities for achievement. Unfortunately, strain variables, by themselves, did not account for much of the variance associated with national differences in crime rates. For example, impoverished countries, such as Mexico and India, do not have crime rates as high as do many of the Western industrialized countries, such as the United States (James, 1995).

The Kornhauser (1978) review also focused on the role that strain variables might play in accounting for individual differences in rates of delinquency. Her review and the later one by Elliott et al. (1985) showed very low returns. For example, when adolescent reports of the discrepancy between opportunity and aspiration served as a measure of strain, they accounted for only a small amount of variance in self-report measures of delinquency. In some studies there was no relationship, and in others the correlations were actually negative.

This section briefly sketches out a possible application of the early-, late-onset delinquency model to account for differences in societal rates. As the data showed, the early-onset trajectory defines multiple stages that place the individual at increasing risk for adult arrest. For this reason, the following discussion will focus on accounting for the prevalence of early-onset individuals. The discussion is highly speculative in that, as yet, we have not attempted empirically based testing.

As the models are applied to predicting prevalence of police arrest, they seem to be hierarchically arranged; the strongest predictor would be a high prevalence for extremely antisocial 9- and 10-year-old boys. Capaldi and Patterson (1991) and Patterson (1999) showed that, in the OYS high-risk sample, status as a single mother is just one point on a progression. Although children of single parents were more at risk for early arrest (.29) than were those from intact families (.13), risk increased further with each additional transition from single-parent to stepparent to multiple transitions. Children from stepparent families were at three times more risk (.32) than those from intact families and by themselves accounted for 36% of boys with early arrests. Risk for children from the multiple-transition group was .39. In the high-risk OYS sample, children from transitional families accounted for 80% of all the boys with early arrests.

In the hierarchy of models for accounting societal rate, the next most proximal variable would be the prevalence of unskilled parenting. This, in turn, raises the prevention-oriented question of just how it is that one might identify a subgroup of families most at risk for unskilled parenting and, in turn, for producing antisocial children. We assumed that the subset of families most at risk would be those in transition from intact to single parent, single parent to stepfamily, and stepfamily to multiple transitions. Furthermore, we hypothesized that transition families most at risk would be socially disadvantaged and involve an antisocial parent.

Families in Transition

This section briefly outlines the role of family transitions in determining aggregate rates for prevalence of antisocial boys. For example, Lykken (1995) cited evidence showing a seven-fold increase in risk of offending for boys from father-absent as compared to father-present homes. There was also strong evidence for an increase in prevalence of broken homes. Lykken reported a five-fold increase in the proportion of births to unmarried mothers and a doubling of the divorce rate since 1960. Burgess (1994) notes a three-fold increase in single-mother households. What is it that brings these increases about? Although there is no clear set of empirical findings that accounts for all of the increases in single parent-households, Patterson (1999) offers a brief review of some economic factors thought to determine changes in prevalence for these families. McCord (1989) points out that the broken home constitutes one of our most enduring theories about the cause of crime. Her review of studies of industrialized countries consistently identified broken homes as a correlate of crime.

The problem with this hypothesis lies in the fact that most broken homes do not produce delinquents. Rutter and Giller (1983) carefully reviewed the considerable body of studies and concluded that the relation between broken homes and delinquency was at best inconclusive. A later review of 50 longitudinal studies by Wells and Rankin (1991; cited in Utting, Bright, & Henricson, 1993) reached a similar conclusion. The weak correlation between delinquency and broken homes holds whether viewed from the individual difference or the aggregate rates perspective. For example, aggregated rates of divorce do not covary with aggregated rates of crime as shown in the review by Utting et al. (1993). They found a seven-fold increase in divorce in Britain over the last 30 years. During the interval from 1960 through 1970, both crime and divorce rates increased. However, although crime rates continued to rise during the 1980s, the divorce rates remained relatively stable. The problem is to determine which broken homes are at risk to produce antisocial boys and which are not.

From the perspective of the coercion model, it would be hypothesized that the broken homes at greatest risk for producing antisocial children would be single mothers, stepmothers, and multiple-transition mothers who were ineffective in their parenting skills. Others might emphasize the emotional turmoil engendered by this repeated rupturing and repartnering of relationships that produces children who are out of control and failing in school, the two most frequent outcomes of divorced families (Cherlin et al., 1991; Hetherington, Cox, & Cox, 1979; Stolberg & Anker, 1983). McCord (1989) noted the single-parent deficits in supervision and in affection as possible causes for higher crime rates in some single-parent families.

In her development of a transition model, Forgatch and her colleagues offered yet another set of explanations. She proposed that the stressors associated with transitions increase the irritability and negative emotionality of the single mother. Presumably, socially disadvantaged and antisocial mothers are particularly likely not only to be inept in their parenting, but to also experience stressors that reduce social support networks and further disrupt parental discipline and family problem solving (DeGarmo & Forgatch, 1997, 1999; Patterson & Forgatch, 1990). These models were replicated and extended in a second longitudinal study of divorced families reported in (Forgatch, Patterson, & Ray, 1996).

The Forgatch transitions models imply that antisocial single mothers may not only be at risk for ineffective parenting, but also more likely to generate stressful separations and react more irritably to the stress once the process is underway. The series of hypotheses are: (a) that antisocial parents were more likely than nonantisocial adults to divorce, (b) more likely to have an antisocial child prior to the divorce, and (c) more likely to experience multiple transitions. The assumption that antisocial parents are at greater risk of divorce is indirectly supported by Lahey et al. (1988) and also by findings from the OYS (Patterson & Capaldi, 1991). In the latter, during the first 2 years of the study, 24 initially intact or single-mother families were involved in one or more transitions. Seventy-one percent of the mothers from those families scored high on an antisocial behavior composite score (drug use, driver's license suspension, Minnesota Multiphasic Personality Inventory [MMPI] scores for Psychopathic Deviate and Hypomania; Hathaway & Monachesi, 1953).

These considerations led us to hypothesize that maternal antisocial behavior would covary with transition frequency, such that in high-risk (socially disadvantaged) samples, the more transition experienced, the higher the risk of antisocial behavior. This hypothesis was tested by using four different measures that constitute the indicators for a latent construct for maternal antisocial behavior: (a) pregnancy prior to age 19.9 in keeping with findings from Emery, Kitzmann, and Aaron (1993) and others who found that antisocial adolescents are more likely to have early pregnancies; (b) high MMPI scores on Hypomania and Psychopathic Deviate in keeping with the studies that showed these two scores predicted delinquency (Hathaway & Monachesi, 1953); and (c) substance abuse and (d) arrest or license suspension (Patterson & Capaldi, 1991). For each indicator, the cut point was set at the 70th percentile. Ten percent of the mothers in intact families scored at or above the cut point on two or more of the indicators and could be said to be antisocial. The proportion was 14% for single-parent families, 40% for stepfamilies, and 57% for families with multiple transitions. The four indicators showed the expected increase in prevalence of antisocial mothers with increasing transition frequency.

Thus far, it has been suggested that for a socially disadvantaged sample of transition families, those who have an antisocial mother, might be screened for prevention trials designed to reduce early-onset delinquency. As noted earlier, the most proximal predictor for societal rates of early arrest was thought to be based on a composite measure (parents, teachers, peer) of childhood antisocial behavior assessed at ages 9 or 10 years. A latent construct for childhood antisocial behavior should provide a cost-efficient means for identifying which transition families are most at risk of producing a boy who will be arrested prior to age 14 years. Combining the two pieces of information provides a solid basis for predicting individual differences in early-onset arrest. For example, about 29% of the intact families with extremely antisocial boys were at risk for early arrest. About 57% of the antisocial boys from stepfamilies were arrested early. It seems that for single mothers, some combination of at-risk neighborhoods, social disadvantage, and maternal antisocial behavior may best serve as a means for identifying greatest risk for disrupted parenting. If future studies support these speculations, the findings would have major implications for precisely where our prevention efforts should be centered. It would seem important to mount major efforts to support the parenting behavior of socially disadvantaged mothers in transitions with antisocial sons. In terms of a prevention science, the bulk of society's efforts should focus on the problem of deflecting individuals from developmental paths that move toward early-onset juvenile arrest. We believe that such a focus is also the most effective approach to reducing aggregate rates of juvenile offending.

Summary

A case was made for the utility of formulating two different trajectories to juvenile offending. The early-onset trajectory is thought to have its beginnings during the preschool interval, producing a child who is both socially incompetent and at risk for early arrest and a career in adult crime. The late-onset delinquency boys were found to possess marginal levels of social competency and marginal levels of deviancy, predicting one or two arrests after the age of 14 years. As adults, these boys were most likely to desist from adult crime.

The initial stage of the early-onset trajectory consists primarily of overt forms of antisocial behavior that are identifiable as early as age 17 months. The rates of overt antisocial behavior show a significant decline between ages 2 and 12 years, accompanied by very low rates of covert behavior that also show little or no growth during this interval. The next stage for this trajectory begins during early to midadolescence and is characterized by a rapid growth in covert forms of antisocial. Although parenting and contextual variables continue to play a significant role during this interval, the key role in the acquistion of covert forms is defined by the amount of unsupervised time and the availability of positive reinforcement provided by deviant peers for deviancy training.

The late childhood-adolescent segment of the early-onset trajectory was comprised of three stages: growth from overt to covert antisocial, first arrest prior to age 14 years, and chronic juvenile offending. Data showed that the majority of chronic juvenile offenders moved through all three stages. Given chronic juvenile offending, the likelihood of an arrest as a young adult was .71. We hypothesized that the majority of adult chronic offenders will be shown to have been chronic juvenile offenders.

The findings showed that measures of disadvantaged context and poor parenting practices assessed during childhood served as significant predictors to each of the childhood-adolescent stages. This was interpreted as meaning that the parenting practices, contextual, and deviant peer reinforcement variables may serve as maintenance mechanisms at all points in the trajectory. Time-dependent measures of the deviant peer involvement and the level of disturbance in family and context predicted which individuals penetrated further in the progression.

A key issue for delinquency models has to do with metamorphosis from childish forms of overt antisocial to serious delinquent acts. A deviancy training process was formulated that was defined by observed relative rates of reinforcement for delinquent talk and estimated prevalence of antisocial peers and time spent with them. The assumption was that once involved in the process, there was little difference between early- and late-onset experiences. The two groups ostensibly differed in terms of when they started (early or late), the level of deviancy, and the level of social skills each individual brought to the process. The fact that the late-onset boys were more socially competent leads to the prediction that they will more likely desist from delinquent activities. Eventually, they find prosocial activities more reinforcing than delinquent activities. We hypothesize that the early stages of training are evident to adult observers as reflected in the child's increased rating of covert antisocial acts. In keeping with this, the studies showed significant increases in covert antisocial activities during adolescence, with early-onset beginning this training sooner than did the late-onset boys.

Findings suggest that, given limited funds, prevention trials should be focused on the early-onset group. Trials should be initiated at least by age 9 or 10 years. Ideally they might be launched during the toddler stage. Presumably, the more effective prevention trials would focus on training parents to be more contingent, include work on academic skills, and careful monitoring to restrict the amount of time given to unsupervised activities with peers.

Acknowledgments

We gratefully acknowledge the financial support provided by Grants R37 MH 37940, Antisocial and Other Personality Disorders Program, Prevention, Early Intervention, and Epidemiology Branch, National Institute of Mental Health (NIMH), U.S. Public Health Service (PHS); RO1 MH 38318 Child and Adolescent Treatment and Prevention Intervention Research Branch, DSIR, NIMH U.S. PHS; and P50 MH 46690, Prevention and Behavioral Medicine Research Branch, Division of Epidemiology and Services Research, NIMH, U.S. PHS. I (Patterson) also wish to thank John B. Reid, not only for his thoughtful critique of an earlier draft of the manuscript, but for the gentle seduction he provided for my initiation into prevention science. Correspondence concerning this manuscript should be addressed to Gerald R. Patterson, Oregon Social Learning Center, 160 East Fourth Avenue, Eugene, OR, 97401; carleenr@OSLC.org.

8

Coercive Family Processes and Adolescent Depression

Betsy Davis, Lisa Sheeber, and Hyman Hops

It may, at first, confound the reader to encounter a chapter on adolescent depression within the context of a book ostensibly focused on aggression and antisocial behavior. However, the focus on depressive functioning in adolescents presented herein is not as mystifying as it might appear. There is some evidence that, analogous to pleiotropic phenomena in genetics, certain elements within family environments may produce more than one effect in children's behavioral functioning. Epidemiological studies have indicated that antisocial and depressive behavior co-occur within the lifetime of adolescents at a significant rate (Lewinsohn, Hops, Roberts, Seeley, & Andrews, 1993). Further, Fergusson and colleagues (1996) found little evidence that either disorder caused the other, but rather the covariation between the two disorders could be explained by the presence of common or correlated risk factors. It is our underlying hypothesis that a shared family mechanism, namely coercion, applies to the development and maintenance of depressive functioning in adolescents but that the details of how these processes apply to depression differ from those operating to impact antisocial behavior. Given that unipolar depressive disorders affect up to 3% of the general high school population at any one point in time and up to 20% of teens by age 18 (Lewinsohn, Rohde, Seeley, & Fischer, 1993) and, moreover, that depression can serve to negatively impact life trajectories by contributing to impaired relationship and occupational functioning (Bardone et al., 1996), a focus on investigating family processes linked to depressive functioning becomes paramount.

Goal and Structure of the Chapter

The goal of the present chapter is to present our research perspective and evidence of family mechanisms that support the development and maintenance of adolescent depressive behavior and other symptomatology. We will outline the various stages of our research relating family coercive interactional sequences to depressive behavior and denote the extent to which our research has evolved to address the weaknesses currently existing in the depression literature. We begin our presentation by outlining our theoretical perspective and the methodological developments it necessitated.

This is followed by a summary of our earlier work on the familial context of maternal depression, which formed the foundation upon which much of our subsequent research has evolved. In particular, it was in our examination of maternal depression that the basis of our functional framework for examining the presence of coercive processes and their relation to the maintenance of depression was developed.

Next, we present our more recent work focused on family processes associated with adolescent depression. Building on our original framework examining coercive processes in maternal depression, our focus parallels the work at the Oregon Social Learning Center on the development of adolescent antisocial behavior. The research we present highlights the generalizability of the coercive processes model to the understanding of adolescent depression.

Following our presentation of the traditional view of coercive processes, we present our current efforts to widen the view of the family relative to its contribution to child development. We have taken a paradigmatic shift away from a dyadic examination of family interactions to allow for the importance of triadic interactions, particularly the impact of specific dyadic interactions on third-party family members. We have conducted this work within the context of marital distress and conflict between parents, the child's response to these parent interchanges, and their impact on developmental processes. Our work presented here regarding adolescent depression was spurred by the importance of marital relationship quality to both the parent-child relationship and the child's level of functioning, as well as our recognition of the importance of considering the child as an active participant in the family system (Bell, 1968; Grych & Fincham, 1990).

To overlay the framework of coercive processes onto a triadic view of the family, we have had to take a broader view of coercion. From a child-response perspective, the potential for coercion occurs if parental conflict in the child's presence has the potential for eliciting the adolescent's negative affect and behavioral responses. In line with the dyadic performance theory upon which coercion theory was based (Patterson, 1982), the aversive parental behavior may produce an aversive response in the child which, in turn, may influence the behavior of the parents. Within a negative reinforcement paradigm, the power of the adolescent's behavior to reduce the parental conflict can be conceptualized as a set of pain control techniques that, if reinforced, set the stage for a sustainable behavioral repertoire.

Finally, to conclude our chapter, we will highlight unexplored issues and areas of research that will guide our continued focus on coercive processes in social interactions that will become part of our programmatic efforts to understand the onset and maintenance of depressive behavior.

Theoretical Perspective and History

Theoretical Underpinnings

An interpersonal approach to depression has had a long history (e.g., Ferster, 1973; Lewinsohn, Weinstein, & Shaw, 1969; Patterson & Rosenberry, 1969) and it is fitting to place our work within that perspective. The 1976 study by Coyne had an enormous heuristic value—generating and inspiring a large body of work on the reactions of people to depressed persons—and more importantly, creating a mind-set that encouraged other theorists to understand depression as an interpersonal process and not solely as a within person variable (e.g., Gotlib & Robinson, 1982; Hammen, 1991). This focus on depression as an interpersonal process laid the groundwork for microsocial examinations of the reciprocal influences between the depressed person and those in their social environment.

Our work has also been influenced greatly by social interactional (SI) theory (e.g., Cairns, 1979; Patterson, 1982). We were impressed with the usefulness of this perspective for investigating socialization practices (e.g., Fagot, 1978) and resulting developmental trends (e.g., Fagot, Leinbach, & Hagan, 1986) as well as problematic behavior patterns (e.g., Patterson, Reid, & Dishion, 1992). With the emphasis on behavior within a responsive social environment, SI theory suggests that interactional patterns within salient contexts are critical areas of study and key targets for change (Cairns, 1979; Lamb, Suomi, & Stephenson, 1979; Patterson & Reid, 1984). Further, within a social interactional perspective, an individuals' behavior is conceptualized as being under the control of the social environment and at the same time operating as a context for the behavior of other social agents (Hops, 1992).

Coercion theory, in particular, was developed within a social interactional framework for the study of aggressive behavior within families (Patterson, 1982). In coercion theory, the researchers postulated that escape or avoidance conditioning trains family members to be antisocial (Patterson, Reid, & Dishion, 1992). The work of Patterson and his colleagues (1982) on coercive processes in families of aggressive children highlighted the functional nature of aggressive behavior. In such families, members tend to exhibit higher levels of aversive behavior than do members of normal families. The aversive behavior is functional in reducing others' aversive attacks and in obtaining positive consequences such as maternal attention. Thus, aggressive behavior is negatively and positively reinforced by other family members. The problem is that often the successful behavior of the other person is itself aversive. Consequently, these subtle and frequent contingencies may shape and maintain very high rates of aversive behavior in all family members. Importantly, it has been demonstrated in more recent findings (Snyder & Patterson, 1995) that for coercion to operate within families one must consider the relative rate of reinforcement, as compared to the relative rate of everything else in the family environment, to more fully account for the individual differences observed in aversive or aggressive functioning. This type of process-oriented conceptualization of the family context has led us to consider whether we could develop a similar framework regarding the functions of depressive behavior and the social contingencies that reinforce and maintain the behavior.

Focus on Direct Observation

Over the course of our research we have used a variety of methods to study families but consider observations of family interactions as a necessary inclusion. Direct observation provides data on the social processes in families that are not otherwise available. Self-reports, while important, cannot produce meaningful information about the subtle contingencies that occur continuously within social interaction (Patterson, 1982). Data collected by objective observers of the stream of social interaction provide information on the molar aspect of these interactions (e.g., rates of aggressive or depressive) and when subjected to microsocial analyses can also identify social contingencies that may be controlling behavior. Such data can contribute to the development of theoretical models and allow for the testing of specific hypotheses in a scientifically rigorous manner (Jacob & Tennenbaum, 1988).

Our examination of the functional impact of behaviors displayed in social environments has been facilitated by the development of the LIFE coding system (Hops, Biglan, et al., 1987; for a review see Hops, Davis & Longoria, 1995). The LIFE system was originally developed to assess behaviors characteristic of depressed individuals as well as to facilitate the examination of functional relations between the behavior of the depressed person and that of their family members. Of particular relevance in the development of the LIFE code was the distinction between aggressive and depressive behaviors, a distinction upon which our research on interactional processes related to both marital distress and depressive symptomatology was predicated.

Within the LIFE code, aggressive behaviors include affective behavior suggestive of anger or irritation such as yelling or "eye rolling" as well as verbal criticisms, threats, or arguments. Depressive behaviors on the other hand, are defined by affective behavior suggestive of dysphoria such as crying, looking down, and speaking in a slow and quiet manner as well as by self-derogatory and complaining statements (so long as the complaint is not directed at the other interactants). It is not surprising that researchers have commonly collapsed across these two classes of negative behaviors as both have been demonstrated to be aversive to others in the social environment (Biglan et al., 1989; Coyne, 1976; Patterson, 1982).

Despite this similarity, however, aggressive behaviors are more overtly conflictual when compared to depressive behaviors. Thus, depressive behaviors may be more likely to elicit sympathetic responses and suppress aggressive responses in the short term, despite evidence that they may be associated with greater levels of aggressiveness and relationship difficulties over time (e.g., Biglan, Hops, & Sherman 1988; Biglan, Rothlind, Hops & Sherman, 1989; Hokanson, Loewenstein, Hedeen, & Howes, 1986; Hops, 1992). Hence, these two classes of aversive behaviors are best conceptualized as distinct forms of conflict behavior. It should be noted, in this regard, that although depressive behaviors include those that are commonly associated with depressive disorder, neither class of aversive behaviors is considered to be uniquely in the domain of a particular group of disordered persons. Both types of behaviors may be common to individuals experiencing any number of stressful circumstances including marital distress (Hops, 1992).

Perhaps the most common statistic for examining the interactive sequences of behaviors is the Allison-Liker z-score (Allison & Liker, 1982) which reflects the extent to which a specified sequence of behavior occurs more or less often than would be expected as a function of the base rate of each behavior. Z-scores are computed by comparing the unconditional probability of the consequent behavior of interest with the conditional probability of that behavior when it is preceded by a particular antecedent behavior. The z-score represents both the strength and direction of the sequential connection between the antecedent and consequent behaviors. A positive z-score indicates that the occurrence of an antecedent behavior increases the probability that the consequent behavior will be displayed; this is referred to as an elicitation effect. Conversely, a negative z-score indicates that the occurrence of an antecedent behavior decreases the likelihood of the consequent behavior; this is referred to as a suppression effect. Conditional z-scores have been used in our research on family processes to indicate when one family member is positively reinforcing (i.e., a positive z-score reflecting the elicitation of a positive behavior in response to an antecedent behavior) or negatively reinforcing (i.e., a negative z-score reflecting the suppression of a negative behavior in response to an antecedent behavior) another family member's behavior.

Framework and Findings

Based on the work of Patterson and colleagues (1979;1982) and a review of the literature, we developed a functional framework which laid a foundation for utilizing the underlying assumptions of coercion theory to better understand the social relationships of depressed individuals (Biglan, et al., 1988). Within our framework, the coercive process has three components. *First*, depressed people live in aversive social environments that are conducive to the development of depressive behavior. *Second*, the behaviors of depressed persons are aversive to others, constituting a salient stimulus for response. *Third*, depressive behaviors are functional in reducing others' aversive behavior as well as eliciting positive social consequences.

Reviews of the adult literature found support for the first assumption, namely, that depressed people live in aversive social environments. Depressed individuals have been found to experience more stressful events (e.g., Billings & Moos, 1983) as well as an absence of positive events (McPhillamy & Lewinsohn, 1974). Interactional studies in analogue settings have shown depressed individuals to receive more negative comments in conversations with a nondepressed counterpart as well as receive fewer reinforcing behaviors, such as directly supportive statements (Gotlib & Robinson, 1982; Howes & Hokansin, 1979). In our own work, we found higher rates of irritable affect in children of depressed mothers when compared to children of nondepressed mothers, particularly when maternal depression was paired with marital distress (Hops et al, 1987).

Second, there is evidence that the behavior of depressed people is aversive to others. In his seminal work, Coyne (1976) found that participants rated themselves as more depressed, anxious, hostile, and rejecting of others following telephone conversations with depressed persons compared to their feelings after conversations with nondepressed persons. Others studies have since noted that the behavior of depressed individuals is less positive and more negative in both marital interactions (e.g., Hatuzinger, Linden, & Hoffman, 1982) and family interactions (Hammen et al, 1987). We also found that depressed mothers were more aggressive than normal mothers in laboratory interactions (Biglan et al., 1985) and more dysphoric and less happy during family interactions at home (Hops et al., 1987).

Third, although fewer in number, studies have examined the functional characteristics of depressive behavior in adults. We compared three groups; families with a depressed mother, families with a depressed and maritally distressed mother, and families without any psychiatric history or current difficulties. We found that depressive affect and behavior were functional in reducing the aversive behavior of family members during laboratory and home interactions (Biglan et al., 1985, Hops et al., 1987). Analyzing the moment-by-moment sequential interactions, we noted that the probability of an aversive response by a family member was significantly lower immediately following a depressive behavior emitted by a depressed mother compared to a nondepressed one. In other words, the depressed mothers' depressive behavior suppressed the aggressive behavior of other family members thereby providing her some brief respite from family aversiveness. However, as there was some evidence that the level of aversiveness in the depressed families was higher than in nondepressed families, it appeared that these respites were short lived. Nonetheless, those brief respites, considered within a negative reinforcement paradigm, appeared sufficient to maintain the mother's depressive behavior over time.

Further demonstrations of the functional effects of maternal depressive behavior on children's aversiveness were found by Dumas, Gibson, and Albin (1989). Using sequential analyses in a study of depression and marital interaction, Nelson and Beach (1990) also found levels of depressive behavior highest among depressed wives. However, they also noted that suppression of spousal aggression by depressive behavior seemed to dissipate with longer durations of marital discord. Nelson and Beach (1990) suggest that over long periods of discord, husbands may habituate to their wives' depressive behavior. Clearly, more research is needed to evaluate this phenomenon within varying contexts and over time.

Evolution Toward Adolescent Depression

We have begun to extend the original coercive framework from a focus on maternal depression to the examination of the development and maintenance of adolescent depression within families. Currently, as regards our continuing search for understanding depressive behavior, we consider ourselves to be in the midst of an iterative process of model-building as outlined by Dishion & Patterson (1999) and supported in Coyne's (1999) recent commentary on the status of research on the interpersonal processes in depression. We have adopted a strong underlying theory upon which to examine the interactional behavior of depressed persons, spent considerable effort in developing and testing an observational coding system to tap important constructs related to family processes and depression (Hops, Davis & Longoria, 1995), and tested hypotheses related to coercive processes in family and their link to depressive functioning.

Across the span of our research endeavors, we have slowly been testing coercive hypotheses in different populations and samples. It should be noted that across our studies, the definitional basis of depression has differed somewhat based on its method of assessment. There have been studies involving depression as defined by both diagnostic interview for clinical disorder as well as self-report of distress/symptoms. Though we acknowledge that this approach is not without its critics, we conceptualize depression as representing a continuum ranging from low levels of distress to more problematic clinical levels. Our working hypothesis is that analogous family processes operate to maintain depressive functioning across these different populations. Of course, we recognize that this hypothesis is, in the end, open to empirical investigation; one that the continued gathering of evidence will either support or disconfirm.

Evidence of Coercive Family Interactions and Adolescent Depression

Our work on family processes in adolescent depression provides evidence related to the three components of coercive processes identified by Biglan et al. (1988); to wit, that such adolescents live in aversive social environments that are conducive to the development of depressive behavior, display behaviors that are aversive to others, and that these behaviors are functional in reducing family members' aversive behavior as well as eliciting positive social consequences.

Depressed Kids Live in Aversive Environments

We have recently conducted two studies that bear on the question of whether depressed adolescents are subject to aversive family environments that are conducive to the development of depressive behavior. In an initial investigation (Sheeber & Sorensen, 1998), we examined adolescent- and mother-reported family functioning as well as behavioral observations of mother-adolescent interactions in families with clinically depressed and healthy adolescents. The data from both sources and across methods converged, indicating that depressed adolescents experience less supportive and nurturant family environments than do their nondepressed peers. Consistent with past research, depressed adolescents reported that their families were less cohesive, that their parents were less accepting of them, and that they had fewer and less satisfying sources of social support. Mothers of depressed adolescents similarly described their families as less cohesive. Between group differences were also apparent in their observed interactions. As assessed with the LIFE coding system, mothers of depressed adolescents demonstrated less facilitative behavior than did their counterparts in families of healthy adolescents. The finding that reported deficits in supportive family interactions and relationships reflect the behavioral patterns of families with depressed adolescents is noteworthy in that with few exceptions, adolescents have been the sole reporter of both family support and depressive mood in earlier studies. Thus, these findings are important in that they suggest that these earlier findings were not primarily attributable to depressive biases in adolescents' reports.

Depressed adolescents and their mothers, compared to their counterparts in comparison families, also described their family interactions as being more conflictual, more negative and with more openly expressed anger. These results are consistent with adolescent self-reports obtained in previous nonclinic samples (e.g., Hops, Lewinsohn et al., 1990) as well as with reports provided by parents of younger children diagnosed with affective disorders (Fendrich et al., 1990). Observational data on the other hand, revealed that mothers of the depressed adolescents displayed more depressive but *not* more aggressive behaviors during the interaction relative to mothers of nondepressed adolescents. The absence of elevated rates of aggressive behavior on the part of depressed persons' family members is consistent with the findings from our earlier maternal depression study, in which evidence that depressed women were exposed to more aggressive environments was marginal (Biglan et al., 1985; Hops et al., 1987). In this regard, it is also notable that the evidence that families of depressed children display elevated rates of aggressive behaviors is quite limited as well (see Sheeber & Sorensen, 1998).

In a second, larger study (Sheeber et al., 1997) we investigated the direction of influence between family processes and adolescent depression. This was an important step because our earlier cross-sectional design precluded us from determining whether family characteristics are stable and elicit depressive symptomatology or whether they emerge as a consequence of interacting with a depressed person. In this investigation, the relation between family support, family conflict, and adolescent depressive symptomatology was examined over a one year period in a community sample of 231 female and 189 male adolescents and their mothers. Structural equation models were used to examine the relationship between adolescent depression and both family support and family conflict across time controlling for stability. The first stage of the analysis consisted of confirmatory factor analysis to develop multimethod, multisource factors that reliably measured the latent constructs of family support, family conflict, and adolescent depression including parent and adolescent report and behavioral observations. The adolescent depression construct, though composed of multiple measures, was based on adolescent report variables only.

Consistent with past research, the results indicated that the quality of family relationships was related to depressive symptomatology in community adolescents. Less supportive and more conflictual family environments were associated with greater depressive symptomatology both concurrently and prospectively over a one-year period. These results are also congruent with findings from clinical studies in which the quality of parent-adolescent interactions has been shown to predict the clinical course of depressive disorders (Asarnow et al; 1993; Sanford et al; 1995). Conversely, depressive symptomatology did not predict deterioration in family relationships over the one-year period. Thus, there was no evidence that disruptions in family relationships were reactive to depressive behavior on the part of the adolescent. These results are similar to those obtained based on adolescent self-report data (Hops et al., 1990) in which teenagers' negative perceptions of their family environment were found to be a stable characteristic of those prone to higher levels of depressive symptoms. Of course, these results apply within the range of family disruption and depressive symptomatology observed in this community sample only. It is possible that depressive behaviors of clinical severity may noticeably impact family functioning; this remains a consideration for future research.

Behavior of Depressed Kids Is Aversive to Others

Based on the initial study described above, we obtained some preliminary data suggesting that the behavior of depressed adolescents is aversive to those in their family environment. During the mother-adolescent problem-solving discussions, depressed adolescents displayed less facilitative and problem-solving behavior as well as more depressive behavior than did their healthy peers. They did not, however, display elevated rates of aggressive behavior. So, similar to their mothers, depressed adolescents evidenced specificity in the nature of the aversive behaviors demonstrated as well as a notable deficit in their display of positive behaviors that one would expect to be well-received by family members. This finding of elevated levels of depressive, but not aggressive behaviors is consistent with the results obtained by Slesnick and Waldron (1997) in a study of depressed adolescents.

In a second analysis, we specifically assessed whether mothers' mood was adversely effected by interactions with their depressed adolescents (Sheeber & Sorensen, 1998). Mothers completed the MAACL-R (Zuckerman & Lubin, 1985), a widely used measure of transient mood states (Marcus & Nardone, 1992), both prior and subsequent to the interaction, with the latter assessment targeting how they felt during the interaction. Repeated measures ANOVAS were conducted on mother ratings of "hostility," "depression," and "positive affect" in order to examine whether problem-solving discussions had a more negative effect on mothers' moods in the families of depressed adolescents. A significant group by time interaction emerged for mothers' scores on the hostility scale, with mothers of depressed adolescents only, reporting feeling greater hostility during the interaction than before it. This result is consistent both with evidence that depressed adults negatively impact those with whom they interact closely (e.g., Coyne et al., 1987) as well as with preliminary evidence that depressed youth elicit distressed reactions from unfamiliar adults (Mullins, Peterson, Wonderlich, & Reaven, 1986).

Behavior of Depressed Kids Is Functional Within the Family

We have, to date, conducted one investigation of whether adolescent depressive behavior has social consequences in the family environment—that is, whether parents may inadvertantly teach their children to behave in a depressed manner through a process of negative and/or positive reinforcement (Sheeber, Hops, Andrews, Alpert & Davis, 1998). Based on our earlier work (Hops, Biglan, et al., 1987), we hypothesized that this reinforcement process would be more likely to emerge in families of depressed than nondepressed adolescents, and might thus partially account for the development and maintenance of depressive symptomatology.

Problem-solving interactions were observed in a community sample that included 86 families where the adolescent reported elevated depressive symptoms and 408 comparison families. Sequential analyses suggested that parents of depressed adolescents may be inadvertently reinforcing depressive behavior. In particular, t-tests conducted on Allison-Liker lag 1 z-scores indicated that mothers of depressed adolescents were more likely than mothers of nondepressed adolescents to increase facilitative and problem-solving behavior in response to adolescent depressive behavior. Additionally, fathers of depressed adolescents were more likely than their counterparts in families of nondepressed adolescents to decrease aggressive and problem-solving behavior subsequent to adolescent depressive behavior.

The reduction of paternal aggressive behavior in response to adolescent displays of depressive behavior is consistent with findings regarding the suppressive effect of women's depressive behavior on the aggressive behavior of their spouses and children observed in earlier studies (Biglan et al., 1985; 1989; Dumas, Gibson, & Albin, 1989; Hops et al., 1987). The results regarding mothers' responses to depressive behavior, moreover, extend previous findings by indicating that adolescent depressive behavior may be subject to positive contingencies as well. Though Dadds et al. (1992) reported correlational data suggesting that child depression may constrain parents' aggressive behavior, to our knowledge this is the only study using sequential analyses to demonstrate that adolescent depressive behavior suppresses parental aggressive behavior. It should be noted here, that in a recent study, Slesnick and Waldron (1997) reported the unexpected finding that suppression of aggressive behavior was greater in families of *nondepressed* adolescents. This finding runs counter to hypotheses based on a reinforcement model and is somewhat difficult to interpret. This difficulty is exacerbated, moreover, in that mothers and fathers behaviors were combined and so differential responses as a function of parent gender may have been lost.

We had hypothesized that parental problem solving would be elicited by adolescent depressive behavior, and so the finding that the contingencies varied as a function of parental gender was unexpected. This effect may be attributable to heterogeneity in the behaviors comprising the problem-solving construct. As behaviors as diverse as commands, problem-statements, and proposals for one's own behavior change are included in the construct, the construct may encompass both supportive and aggressive behaviors. One possibility suggested by our pattern of results is that fathers and mothers engage in different aspects of this behavior; unfortunately, our codes do not have adequate specificity to examine this possibility. Additionally, taken as a whole, the sequential analyses suggest that adolescent depressive behavior served as a stimulus for action in mothers and inaction in fathers. This pattern of women engaging and men withdrawing in response to negative affect arising within conflict situations is consistent with observations of marital dyads (e.g., Gottman & Krokoff, 1989; Lindahl & Markman,1990).

In this investigation we also examined whether the pattern of parents inadvertently reinforcing depressive behavior would be observed only when the adolescent was currently experiencing depressive symptoms or whether it would be maintained when the adolescents' depressive symptomatology decreased. We considered this question to be relevant to understanding whether interactional patterns characteristic of families with depressed children are stable and thus potentially relevant to the etiology or maintenance of depressive symptomatology or whether they emerge as a consequence of interacting with the depressed child. It could be argued, for example, that because families have different levels of tolerance for the expression of negative emotion (Gottman, Katz, Hooven, 1996), the nature of parental responses to depressive behavior may be a relatively stable attribute that differentiates families and accounts for variability in depressive behavior. Alternatively, as depressive behavior elicits emotional and behavioral responses in others, it is possible that reinforcing responses to depressive behavior would occur only in the context of elevated symptomatology. That is, the sympathy and concern elicited by elevated depressive symptomatology results in more supportive responses to depressive behavior during a depressive episode but not when the depressive symptomatology declines.

To address this question, a repeated measures ANOVA was conducted on each of the Allison-Liker z-scores that differentiated depressed from nondepressed adolescents at year one. The group by time interaction, which addressed the question of whether change in family behavior from year one to year two varied as a function of the adolescents' depressive status, was nonsignificant for each of the sequences, suggesting that the observed interactional sequences are *not* state characteristics evident only during periods of elevated depressive symptomatology. Interestingly, the interaction term for analyses on the proportion of adolescent depressive behavior was also nonsignificant, indicating that formerly depressed adolescents continued to display higher levels of depressive behavior in interactions with their parents despite changes in their self-reported depressive symptomatology. It is feasible therefore, that presenting depressive behavior in the context of parent-teen interactions is a learned behavior that continues subsequent to the lessening of more intrapersonal depressive symptomatology. This continuity in teen depressive behavior may explain the lack of change in sequential interactions; and of course, the reinforcement of depressive behavior may explain its persistence.

Summary

It would appear that the contextual and functional relations that were identified in studies of adults and more specifically in our work with families of depressed mothers can be extended to those of depressed adolescents. In both, there is evidence of coercive processes existing in social environments that are highly aversive, setting the stage for the power of both negative and positive reinforcement paradigms that may be operating in the development and maintenance of depressive behavior. It should be noted in this regard that the aversive nature of family interactions, appears, at this point, to be a function of elevated depressive behaviors and deficits in prosocial and problem-solving skills, more so than of directly aggressive behavior. Our continued work with adolescents may also help to identify those processes early in the development of depressive behavior, given that the symptomatology takes a dramatic leap upwards during this period of time.

Family Systems Approach

We have begun to expand our view of family processes to examine triadic interactions that occur in the context of conflict between parents. Particularly, we are examining adolescent responses to marital conflict and the impact of their responses on their own subsequent functioning. Our focus on adolescent response to parental conflict to further the delineation of coercive family processes as one potential mechanism to explain the relation between these responses and later adjustment was done for several reasons. First, existing literature examining the impact of marital conflict on children produced evidence in support of the first two components of our functional framework. Namely that depressed individuals reside in aversive environments and that the behaviors of depressed persons are aversive to others, constituting a salient stimulus for response.

Second, we noted that the preponderance of studies on child response to marital conflict had heretofore utilized primarily self-reports of marital conflict and child responses. Thus, this literature was methodologically limited for directly examining interactional family processes that might assist in explaining the impact of marital conflict on child adjustment. Given that we had microsocial observational data on family interactions, we believed that we could test the validity of the associations based on self-report, but could also begin the process of moving the field towards more family-*process* oriented examinations.

Relatedly, we noted that the prevailing theoretical perspectives in the literature did not allow for the examination of influence between parent and child behavior to be reciprocal. Rather they focus on the unidirectional impact of marital conflict on the child, but do not allow for the child's response to subsequently impact the parents' behavior. This latter child-to-parent impact is central to the examination of the coercive process as a mechanism for explaining child adjustment.

In this section, we structure our discussion around the evolutionary process that led us to consider coercion as a mechanism within the triadic family unit and to explore the effect of marital conflict on the child. First, we present a brief synopsis of the literature to provide support for the first two components of our functional framework. Second, we present a theoretical discussion explaining our shift away from current theoretic models to one that is more conducive to more fully examining family interactional processes as mechanisms for explaining child functioning. Last, we present data supporting the delineation of coercive family processes as one potential mechanism explaining the relation between child responses and their subsequent adjustment.

Existing Evidence

As noted in the introduction to this chapter, there is abundant research demonstrating an association between marital conflict and child functioning (Peterson & Zill, 1986; Holden & Ritchie, 1991; Snyder et al., 1988; Emery & O'Leary, 1982; Porter & O'Leary, 1980; Johnson & O'Leary, 1987; Jouriles, et al, 1989; Jouriles, et al, 1988; Smith & Jenkins, 1991). From this literature it is clear that marital conflict contributes to an aversive family environment which, if surrounding the child, is predictive of both internalizing and externalizing problems.

Further, there is evidence to suggest that marital conflict elicits negative feelings and behaviors from children, thus setting the stage for potential responses from others in the child's social environment. Children display various behaviors in the presence of conflict, with distress being one of the most commonly reported child responses to simulated adult and interparental conflict (Cummings, 1987; Cummings, Iannotti & Zahn-Waxler, 1985; Cummings, Vogel, Cummings, & El-Sheikh, 1989; Cummings, Zahn-Waxler, Radke-Yarrow, 1981; Cummings, Ballard, & El-Sheikh, 1991; Cummings, Ballard, El-Sheikh, and Lake, 1991). Children also report anger and sadness in response to parent conflict (Cummings, Iannotti, & Zahn-Waxler, 1985; El-Sheikh, Cummings, & Goetsch, 1989; Cummings, Vogel, Cummings & El-Sheikh, 1989; Cummings, Ballard, El-Sheikh & Lake, 1991) as well as concern, shame, self-blame and fear (Cummings, Pellegrini, Notarius, & Cummings, 1989; Grych & Fincham, 1993). Given the consistent reports of child affective and behavioral reactions to parental conflict, it is clear that these responses can serve to set the stage for potential responding from others in the child's social environment, particularly the parents. In support of a coercive model of family interaction, a child response that results in a de-escalation of parental conflict behavior, provides evidence for the presence of negative reinforcement that may be contributing toward the maintenance of the child's behavior.

Further strengthening the potential for the child's response behavior to alter parent behavior is evidence that children do become directly involved, and intervene, in their parents' conflict. Children from maritally violent homes have been shown to be not only preoccupied with, but become enmeshed in, conflict involving their mothers (Cummings, Pellegrini, Noratius, & Cummings, 1989). Child involvement in interparental conflict has also been demonstrated in less extreme populations (Cummings, Zahn-Waxler & Radke-Yarrow, 1981). Jenkins, Smith, and Graham (1989) found that 71% of children reported that they intervened to stop their parents' quarrels and that greater frequency and severity of quarrels was associated with greater intervention. O'Brien, Margolin, John and Krueger, (1991) reported that boys from homes characterized by physically aggressive marital relationships were more likely to endorse interference strategies, involving both verbal and physical intervention, in response to simulated family conflict situations when compared to boys from low conflict homes.

Although limited in number, existing studies also support a relation between child response behaviors and their level of adjustment. Exposure to, and involvement in, parental conflicts have been related to both child withdrawal (Johnston, Gonzalez & Campbell, 1987) and internalizing problems (Jouriles, Murphy, et al., 1991). In more recent investigations, children's use of coping strategies that involve them in their parents' conflict predicted higher levels of self-reported anxiety, hostility, and lower self-esteem (O'Brien, Margolin, & John, 1995). Quite clearly the aversive event of marital conflict can drive a child to behave in ways that attempt to control the painful situation (Emery, 1982), with such responses being related to the child's functioning both concurrently and prospectively.

Theoretical Perspective

A focus on differential family processes may help to explain the presence or absence of child difficulties (Emery, 1988; Cummings & Davies, 1994), since not all children from high conflict homes develop problems. Unfortunately, there has not been much movement in this direction so far. As noted above, one potential reason may be due to the limitation in the prevailing theoretical perspectives which view the child's response as a mediational variable, with a unidirectional influence from conflict in the marital dyad to the child (see Figure 8.1; Grych & Fincham, 1990; Davies &

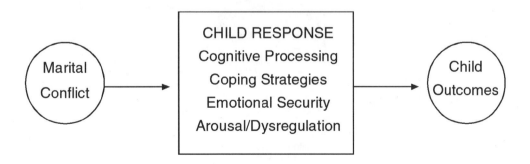

Figure 8.1. General structure of mediational models.

Cummings, 1994). Each of these models, while important and informative, does not allow for the bidirectional influence of the child's response on further parent behavior and hence may fail to identify and include important family processes that contribute, above and beyond properties of the marital conflict, to child problematic functioning. Consequently, prevention and intervention strategies relative to family therapy addressing child functioning may also be limited.

From our perspective, the central focus in studies of relations between interparental conflict, child response, and child adjustment should be the family unit that, in its smallest form, is triadic. Dividing the family system into dyadic pairs is antithetical to the understanding of the family as a social system in which the behavior of each member necessarily affects the behavior of every other member, a notion central to both systems (Minuchin, 1974) and social-interactional perspectives (Patterson, Reid, & Dishion, 1992). In our conceptual model (See Figure 8.2), the child's response behavior is now more fully centered upon the child as an integral member of the family system.

Within this framework the path of interest, in terms of defining mechanistic links to child functioning, stems from the child's response to marital conflict instead of conflict within the marital dyad. Thus, our focus draws attention to the interactional factors within the family that may help to maintain child response patterns and their association to subsequent child functioning. This focus views children as active participants in the family who not only are affected by, but have an impact on, the family as a system.

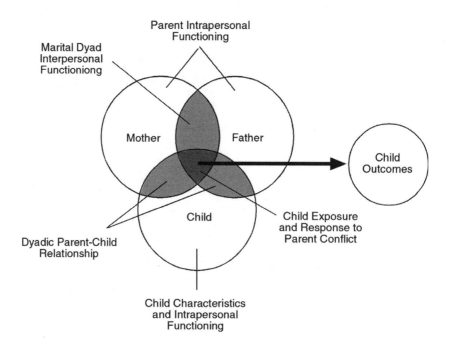

Figure 8.2. Family focused model.

Evidence of Coercive Systemic Processes
and Child Functioning

In the following studies, we attempted to show first that adolescent responses could be sequentially linked to parent conflict behavior and that such responses were associated with increases in adolescent aggressive and depressive functioning over time. With the relations to child adjustment established, our second goal was to examine the potential for family coercive processes to account for the relationship. Using combinations of questionnaire assessments of psychosocial functioning and family problem-solving interactional data from a community sample of 156 adolescents (male n=76; female n=80) residing in two-parent families, two studies were conducted toward these ends.

In Davis, Hops, Alpert, and Sheeber (1998), we examined two distinct forms of child aversive responses to parental aggressive behavior in conflict situations; aggressive and depressive. By distinguishing between these, we thought we could potentially find stronger relations between child responding and depressive functioning than had been noted in prior investigations (e.g., Cummings & Davies, 1994). If different child responses (i.e., depressive vs. aggressive behavior) are reinforced by parents, this pattern of responding could result in a sustainable and generalizable pattern of behavior in the child that could contribute to differential child outcomes (i.e., increases in depressive vs. aggressive symptomatology).

Observational data of family interactional behaviors were coded using the LIFE coding system and were collected during family problem-solving situations centered around salient parent-child disagreements. Interparent conflict behaviors in the study were defined as parent aggressive behavior directed toward the other parent (i.e., mom aggressive to dad; dad aggressive to mom). This interparental conflict behavior served as the antecedent condition for the child's response, defined as the display of aggressive or depressive behavior directed toward a parent as the very next response. Allison-Liker z-scores, reflecting the sequential connection between parent conflict behaviors and specific child responses served as the independent variables, with adolescents' reports of aggressive (assessed by the Youth Self Report; Achenbach & Edelbrock, 1983) and depressive (assessed by the Beck Depression Inventory; Beck, Ward, Mendelson, Mock, & Erbaugh, 1961) serving as the outcomes of interest collected over a two-year period.

Controlling for prior levels of child functioning in the first year (T1), we examined the extent to which the T1 child response patterns were related to increases in both T2 adolescent aggressive and depressive symptomatology. We found that adolescent aggression in response to parent conflict was predictive of *increases* in adolescent aggressive functioning over time; this was especially the case when the aggressive behavior was directed at mothers. The finding of consistent aggressive responding towards the mother supports prior research identifying the mother as the person most likely to receive aversive behavior from other family members (Patterson, 1979; Patterson, 1982). Mothers one down position, however, occurs in different ways depending upon the gender of the adolescent. After mothers attacked fathers, boys responded in kind to mothers, perhaps providing support for fathers. Girls, on the other hand, appeared to join father in attacking mothers, doing so immediately after mothers were attacked by fathers.

In viewing these results for evidence of a coercive process, the sequence for boys seems most consistent. If boys' aggression toward mothers ceases or reduces mothers' aggression towards fathers, then it's a win situation for both males, and reinforcement of the sons' aggressive responding. Further evidence for this process would be seen if there were lower levels of the specific antecedent conflictual response in families where this sequence was found. Post hoc analyses were conducted and indicated that, indeed, in families where the aggressive child responses were related to increases in aggressive functioning in boys (i.e., an attack on the mother in defense of dad), there was evidence of significantly lower levels of aversive behavior from the mother directed toward the fathers when compared to families in which the response pattern did not occur (t=2.10, p < .05).

Overall, our results with regard to depressive functioning were similar to those of other researchers (Cummings & Davies, 1994) in that child response patterns to aggressive parent interactions were more strongly related to future levels of adolescent aggressive than depressive functioning. Further, we did not find evidence for a negative reinforcement mechanism that would predict increased depressive symptomatology, but some evidence of a punishment paradigm. Girls whose sad or dysphoric behavior towards mothers was *suppressed* by mothers' aggressive behavior toward fathers experienced increased depressive symptomatology one year later. We speculated that the suppression of affective behavior may reflect the family's intolerance of adolescent emotional expression during stressful situations (Fainsilber-Katz & Gottman, 1997) and that such intolerance could potentially be associated with failure to assist the adolescent in development of skills for regulating affect which would then predict adolescent depressive symptomatology.

Given the weaker relations found in our first study as regards depressive symptomatology, in a second study (Davis, Sheeber, Hops, & Tildesley, in press), we operationalized parent conflict differently. We took note of Katz and Gottman's (1991) suggestion that available research has suffered from inadequate specification of the affective behaviors that comprise conflictual interactions. In particular, they highlighted the failure to distinguish between depressive and aggressive interactional behaviors, a flaw that has also characterized much of the work on family processes in depression (see Biglan, Rothlind, et al., 1989). This distinction between these two aversive behaviors has characterized our own programmatic efforts to examine family interaction processes related to both marital distress and depressive symptomatology. Hence, the current study utilized interparental depressive behavior in conflict situations (i.e., mom depressive to dad; dad depressive to mom) to define the interparental conflict antecedent to which children respond.

Within the same community sample and longitudinal design utilized in our first study, we found stronger predictive relations between the sequential responding of adolescents to depressive interparental conflict behavior and increases in adolescent depressive symptomatology, when compared to our results for aggressive interparental conflict behaviors. Specifically, the results showed that adolescents who display depressive behavior towards the father in response to the father directing depressive behavior toward the mother evidenced increases in depressive symptomatology across time. We noted as one possibility that within families where parents display depressive behavior in conflict situations, particularly fathers for whom the behavior is less typical, the parents may be more sensitive to their children's dysphoric behavior and react by ending the aversive interchange in which they were engaged, thus setting up a coercive pattern of family responding.

Support for a coercive process involving depressive behavior would be found if there was evidence of a decrease in fathers' depressive behavior directed towards their wives in families where this adolescent response pattern occurs, i.e., adolescents direct depressive behavior to fathers conditional upon father's directing the same behavior to wives compared to families where this did not occur. Post hoc analysis revealed that in families where the child response pattern was present and adolescent depressive symtomatology increased over time, the adolescent's depressive behavior suppressed father aversive behavior directed towards the mother (t=2.35, p < .05), thus thwarting the aversive parent conflict behavior. This suggests the presence of a negative reinforcement pattern for the adolescent's depressive behavior that may lead to sustainable patterns of depressive responding that may then generalize to other social environments in which negotiation and problem-solving skills are required.

Summary

From the results we have obtained thus far, it does appear that children respond to both aggressive and depressive interparental behavior in problem-solving situations and that these responses are directly related to increases in child aggressive and depressive symptomatology. Further, given that we controlled for current psychopathology in all analyses, these response patterns appear to be directly contributing to developmental outcomes rather than serving merely as marker variables of future problematic functioning. Moreover, our emerging evidence suggests that children's response behaviors decrease the level of aversive parent conflict behavior and that this type of coercive process may be responsible for maintaining child aggressive and depressive symptomatology as well as explaining future levels of child functioning.

Future Directions

Our directions toward the future revolve around two major areas of research. First, we are interested in continuing our examination of the family context surrounding adolescent depressive symptomatology and disorder by expanding on the results presented herein. Not only do we seek to validate the presence of coercive family processes identified in the current presentation as related to child functioning but also to continue in the line of Patterson's work (e.g., Snyder & Patterson, 1995) by examining the relative rate of reinforcement for depression as compared to how much parents' reinforce other behaviors displayed by the child. Further, we hope to strengthen the tests of our current hypotheses by designing specific strategies for testing the hypotheses that eliminate some of the limitations currently existing in our work. Second, we are interested in expanding our examination of microsocial processes associated with depressive behavior both across time and to other social contexts. Thus we consider it important to examine coercive processes in the interactions between depressed adolescents and their peers, confidants, and romantic partners. Relatedly, we are interested in examining whether processes that operate in the family of origin are replicated in the other social environments which the adolescents enter and create, thus potentially accounting for some of the continuity of depressive symptomatology across time.

Expanding Our Current Work

One major direction for our ongoing work is to develop more integrated models that would enable us to simultaneously examine multiple mechanisms associated with risk for depressive symptomatology and disorder. To date, we have examined the components of the coercive process in different samples and have pulled together the findings from across these studies to present a story of how coercive processes may be operational in the development and maintenance of depressive behavior. With this data as our starting point, we believe that we are in a good position to develop and conduct more comprehensive evaluations of our model as well as to investigate the coercive mechanism in conjunction other models.

We are currently conducting an investigation that will enable us to examine the three components of the coercive model using a longitudinal design, multimethod assessments that include microsocial observations, and in which we are targeting our recruitment to include fathers when they are in the home. We are also examining the coercive model in conjunction with other mechanisms by which family processes may influence risk for depressive behavior. For example, we are examining whether family interactional processes may contribute to the learning of depressogenic cognitive styles or impede the adolescents' ability to learn adequate skills for regulating emotional arousal. These mechanisms may account for initial displays of depressive behavior which may then be maintained by reinforcement processes. We will also have the opportunity to explicitly test our hypothesis that relevant family processes are analogous in clinical and subclinical populations.

Similarly, we would be hard-pressed to believe that any one mechanism could capture the complexity of the relations between child responses to marital conflict and their own subsequent adjustment. Thus, in future studies we are contemplating the development of more integrated models. For example, the risk posed by parental conflict, which heightens stress and arousal so that the child responds with crying or other forms of depressive behavior (stress model), should be increased if parents reinforce the resulting behavior by stopping their conflict (coercive model). Thus, the child may learn to use depressive behavior in other situations that are stressful. This sequence would be particularly detrimental if the child observed the mother being reinforced for similar behaviors during marital interactions (vicarious learning model) such that models of more effective conflict-resolution behaviors were not available to the child. With the incorporation of multiple mechanisms into examinations of child response to parent conflict, we may begin to more fully understand the impact of adverse family environments on the subsequent development and maintenance of depressive symptomatology and disorder.

In regards to our triadic examinations of family context and adolescent depression, we are also looking to create a hueristic framework for a more direct examination of the phenomena of child response in the presence of marital conflict. The studies presented herein were not designed to specifically examine child responses to conflict between parents. Rather, the focus when collecting the data was to view family members' behavior in an interaction task that was centered around parent-adolescent disagreements. Although we specified aversive parent interchanges as those aversive behaviors directed from one parent towards the other followed immediately by a child response to either parent, the extent to which our results are generalizable to marital conflict situations is unclear. We are working on developing an observational paradigm that will enhance our ability to examine child response to marital conflict so as to more directly examine our hypotheses and hence build on our results to date.

Other Areas to be Explored

We have not examined the mechanisms that account for the maintenance of depressive behavior in sufficient settings and populations to determine whether similar processes are operative outside of the family of origin. For example, in studying peer relations among adolescents, there is insufficient evidence that depressed teens exhibit the behaviors that we call depressive and that these are under the control of the social contingencies in the peer group. If these behaviors are learned in family settings, how effective are they in being transferred to extra-familial settings and exactly how will they be maintained there? This will require longitudinal studies in which we examine processes within the family and subsequent processes within the peer group of adolescents with high levels of depressive symptoms.

The intergenerational transfer of depressive symptoms has received considerable attention in the past few years (e.g., Hammen, 1991). However, more attention needs to be paid to observed depressive behavior as defined here in order to identify the mechanisms that may be involved in the transmission. Patterson (1998) has suggested that a focus on parenting practices may account for some of the cross-generational relations. Addressing this hypothesis will require observations of the ongoing social processes in each generation. For example, if we identify mechanisms in parent-adolescent interactions that serve to maintain depressive responding can we later show similar processes operating in social relations involving the adolescent—now young adult with their spouses and partners and subsequently with their offspring? Perhaps, maintenance of depressive behavior changes over time and with changing contexts. Only a detailed examination of the social interactions across generations within longitudinal studies will provide these answers.

Overall Summary

In this chapter, we have summarized our programmatic attempts to identify mechanisms operating within families that may be responsible for the development and maintenance of depressive behavior and depressive symptomatology over time and across generations. We adopted a theoretic framework that incorporates social interactional and systems theory and coercive processes within an interpersonal approach to depression. Across the course of our research, we have differentiated and provided evidence for the distinction between different forms of aversive behavior and their functional relations that operate within the family. While both depressive and aggressive behavior have different forms they both have the potential to suppress aggressive behavior in other family members. Evidence was provided in families of depressed mothers, depressed adolescents, and in community samples suggesting that the mechanisms of positive and negative reinforcement may be accounting for the maintenance of depressive behavior. We extended our efforts to examine similar processes that may be operating in more complex settings by observing triadic interactions within families and focusing on the impact of interparental conflict on children's responsiveness and their subsequent adjustment. In this context, the child's behavior is considered an active component of the social processes rather than simply a mediational variable. We presented some preliminary data suggesting that coercive processes are at work in these settings as well.

Clearly, there are many areas that remain to be explored relative to the interpersonal nature of depression and the mechanisms that may be contributing to the development and maintenance of depression. We hope that the current summary of our work serves as a basis upon which to build future studies.

Part III

Interventions for Antisocial Behavior

9

Interventions for
Antisocial Behavior: Overview

John B. Reid and J. Mark Eddy

The Target of Intervention: Microsocial Processes

In our life course model, the moment-by-moment interplay between the behaviors of the child and those of others is the lynchpin in the development of antisocial adjustment. A negative reinforcement paradigm appears at center stage in our model across childhood and adolescence: A demand is placed on the youngster, he or she reacts in a negative or coercive manner, the demand is withdrawn, and the aversive behavior is turned off. Such a pattern is difficult to break, not only because the interaction units happen so quickly, but also because negative reinforcement is an extraordinarily powerful mechanism for learning.

The interventions attempt to disrupt these microsocial patterns of interaction. Antisocial behavior cannot be weakened or changed without the consistent and long-term disruption of these patterns. It is our strong position that it is not sufficient to talk about these interactions after they occur because talking or even thinking about these *completed* sequences does not affect the strength of the patterns. Rather, changes in timing at the microsocial level are everything.

That being said, it is the perceived significance or meaning of youth antisocial behavior that causes the parent, teacher, counselor, or community to seek or not seek intervention. While talking about microsocial interactions may do little to change them, talking can result in adults initiating or abandoning their attempts to intervene. A variety of issues may arise during such talk. Some parents or teachers may be confused about the legitimacy of setting limits on their youngsters; others may be troubled by the sometimes apparent incompatibility between the child's compliance to adult standards and the child's need for self expression. Some adults may not have acknowledged their fear of confronting a coercive child, or more commonly, a coercive adolescent. Regardless of the issues at hand, attending properly to the cognitive "point of entry" of the involved adults is an important aspect of intervening. Interventions must be designed in such a way that they not only make sense to the adults involved, but that they also enhance and capitalize on their strengths and skills. To work, the interventions must be framed to empower, not to blame or demean the adults and family.

Since interventions require the adults who are immediately involved in the coercive interactions to make significant, and often very difficult, changes in their own behavior, their intense involvement and commitment to change are central to the success of the intervention. In this regard, the interventionist must act as a support and backup at every point in the process. Of great importance is that the interventionist is available to provide coaching and advice throughout the time it will take for the adults to disrupt and dismantle the over learned and powerful microsocial sequences. In our experience, this is not often a quick process, but one that unfolds over a period of months.

Addressing meaning is the first stage in penetrating and dealing with a host of "contextual" variables that form a cocoon protecting the development of antisocial behavior such as parental drug use, marital conflict, or living in a high-crime neighborhood. We view these factors as important only to the extent that they impact the ability of a parent to monitor, teach, and guide their child in a way that leads a child towards a prosocial form of adjustment. Thus, penetrating any of these aspects of the "cocoon" of a child with antisocial behavior problems is again only a means to get into the position to change microsocial processes; it is not an end in itself.

In summary, changing an adult's attitude about the role of parent *will not* reliably change microsocial processes, nor will getting the parents to deal with their own drug use or teaching the parent to better deal with domestic violence or situational stress. Even though it is often necessary to work in these areas, such work is not sufficient to change microsocial processes between parent and child that have become over learned. The child is not inert, but is an interactional force to be reckoned with in the intervention process. Unless the interactional process itself is changed, the child's development of antisocial behavior will not be deterred.

Using a Developmental Model to Inform the Design of Interventions

As is evident in previous chapters, it is our position that a developmental perspective is needed to understand the emergence of antisocial behavior. A general model that is consistent with the longitudinal research literature and summarizes our position is presented in Figure 9.1. The model traces the development of conduct problems from before birth through high school, and emphasizes those variables that either have been demonstrated or are assumed to be malleable. This model has informed the content and process of each of the interventions described in the chapters that follow. Here, we provide a narrative overview of the model and note where the interventions described in the remainder of this book fit within the context of the model.

Distal factors. At the top of the figure, a number of *distal factors* are listed that are related to the development of child antisocial behavior. We hypothesize that the relationship between each of these factors and child antisocial behavior is mediated by the microsocial processes that occur between the child and the adults (e.g., parent, daycare worker, teacher) in his or her social world. In terms of intervention, when one or more distal factor is present and such presence clearly disrupts the behaviors of a key adult, an intervention strategy must address the factor(s). However, it is definitely not true that a present distal factor must be directly attacked to remediate a disrupted adult-child relationship. For example, many of the parents

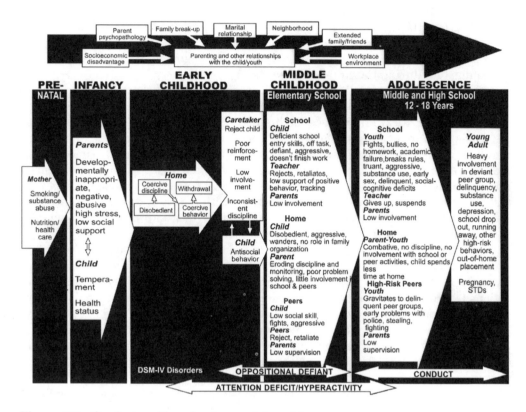

Figure 9.1. Conduct problem developmental model.

we have dealt with have presented with significant depression and have been under considerable economic and situational stress. Even in the ongoing presence of such powerful and disruptive distal factors, most parents have learned to modify their child's antisocial trajectory.

In our own research on distal factors, we have consistently shown relationships between family structural transitions (e.g., divorce and repartnering) and increases in the development of conduct problems and parent child coerciveness. Marion Forgatch and colleagues have developed well-articulated models of the relationships among such transitions, parent-child relations, and child outcomes. This research led her and her colleagues to develop an adaptation of our intervention strategy to help single and stepparents with oppositional or coercive children which is overviewed in chapter 12.

Pre-conception. In the late 1960s, when we began our research to develop an understanding of and interventions for conduct problems, we focused our efforts during the elementary school years, a period which we considered early in the development of such problems. The zeitgeist at the time was the pediatrician's rule: Ninety percent of the time child problems and sicknesses just go away. Thus, it was not until later in childhood that childhood aggression and oppositional defiance were considered serious problems. One outcome of this belief was that parents and teachers would not refer children to our clinic until they were at least 8 or 9 years old.

Over the years, we worked upwards from this age into the teenage years, and expanded our theoretical and intervention models along the way. While Beverly Fagot led us in our attempts to extend our developmental theory to younger children since the early 1980s, only recently have we begun to work on interventions for youngsters during the preschool years.

However, as illustrated in Figure 9.1, it can be argued that theory driven and direct interventions on the development of conduct problems can begin well before conception. Of critical importance at this point are two factors: exposure of biological parents to toxic substances and the social interactions of the members of the family of origin. Any substance that damages the material in the sperm or the egg may increase the likelihood that the resulting child is more irritable, inattentive, impulsive, and/or hyperactive, which in turn increases the likelihood that a child will enter into coercive microsocial interactions with adults and other children. Similarly, the more problematic the social interactions in a family of origin (whether that family be the natural family or an adoptive family), the more likely the parents are to respond in a negative manner to the troublesome behaviors of an infant. Thus, interventions that decrease the substance use or environmental toxin exposure of potential parents and interventions that improve the quality of family interactions (Stanley, Markman, St. Peters, & Leber, 1995) can set the stage for positive child development long before the conception of the child.

To date, we have developed several interventions that target these truly early factors. Marion Forgatch and colleagues' programs for single and stepparents are discussed in chapter 12 and target the negative microsocial interactions between parent(s) and child. Success in this regard cannot only have immediate positive consequences for the family, but also can decrease the chance of problems for future family members. Tom Dishion and colleagues' Adolescent Transitions Program, which is discussed in chapter 13, targets the alcohol, tobacco, and other drug use of early adolescents. The use of substances during this period not only increases the chance of chronic and serious drug use during adulthood but also increases the chance of the early initiation of sexual behavior.

Gestation and infancy. After conception and before birth, maternal substance use and general health take center stage along with family interactions. For example, maternal practices such as smoking and alcohol use during this critical period of neural development can lead to a heightened risk of temperamental difficulties and developmental delays in infancy and early childhood. In turn, these early problems make the child difficult to parent, increasing the risk of early coercive parent-child interaction and child abuse and neglect.

Problematic interactions between the mother, her partner, and the other people in her social world during this period heighten the risk of coercion, particularly if a child is temperamentally difficult. For example, an irritable baby cries, the parent responds, the baby keeps crying, the parent responds, the baby continues to cry. If the parent's reasonable responses continue to fail to turn off the crying, the parent might well try not so reasonable responses, which in turn may cause the distress of the baby to intensify. Alternatively, a baby may have a calm temperament, and respond well to skillful parenting when distressed. However, if a parent is under heavy stress, is in an abusive relationship, or is chemically dependent, he or she may not respond skillfully nor contingently, which initiates a cycle of escalating responses from the infant. As the distress of the baby increases, so does the distress of the parent. Either series of interactions may end with a severe response from the parent. Clearly, many combinations of child, parent, or contextual strengths, weaknesses, and liabilities can combine to produce negative reinforcement cycles in the interactions between parent and child. It is these cycles, we believe, that lead to coercive relationships that render the parent ineffective in socializing and preparing the child for the nearly endless series of challenges he or she will face over childhood and adolescence.

At this point, we are engaged only in basic research on this particular period of development. In several of our longitudinal studies, we are studying the parent-child interactions of study participants who we first studied when they themselves were children (Capaldi, 1998). Our current thinking on interventions here are greatly influenced by the benchmark studies of David Olds and colleagues. These researchers have demonstrated that interventions delivered by public health nurses beginning in the third trimester of pregnancy and extending through the second year of life can have substantial preventive effects on early antecedents of conduct problems (e.g., child abuse, coercive parenting, parental rejection) as well as long-term effects on the prevention of delinquency (Olds et al., 1998). The impressive and long-term success of his intervention strategy constitutes heavy support for the notion that decreasing parental substance use, increasing the skill and support of parents, reducing physical abuse and harsh discipline, and creating a stable, predictable, and safe early environment are key ingredients to any early prevention strategy for conduct and related problems.

Early childhood. Sometime during the second year of life, the young child comes to understand the wonders of "NO!", and the parent-child relationship is forever changed. When a toddler learns that following the "no" with a tantrum, or even just screaming the "no" word, will energize the mother's attempts at pacification, then the parents must learn to deal with a whole new set of issues, that we refer to as *noncompliance*. This is the age at which endless coercive sequences between parent and children can truly begin. If not managed skillfully, calmly, and consistently by the parent, the interlocking negative reinforcement properties inherent to these sequences can come to characterize and take over the parent-child relationship. Every attempt at socialization can become a battle; parental losses mount; and when the parent does prevail, victory feels hollow. Eventually the parent in such a situation avoids making demands and withdraws and becomes demoralized. Rather than taking the lead in interactions with the child, the parent who has lost control is reduced to ineffective and irritable responses when they cannot otherwise avoid confrontations. Occasionally, the parent may try to maintain a parity of sorts in the relationship by resorting to massive rejection or physical abuse.

Obviously, this situation can emerge because a child has a difficult temperament, because a parent is under high stress, has a low level of skills, or some combination of these. The key to the problem, however, is to be found in the coercive interactions between the parent and the child, and not within either individual alone. Thus, we do not believe that the root problem in such a situation is the anger and rejection that are consequences of this interaction, nor is the root problem the resulting low self-esteem of the parent and child. Professionals and parents alike often confuse these epiphenomena as causes, and clinical strategies designed on the basis of such causes are doomed to failure over the long run. Unfortunately, in the short run, such strategies may provide temporary comfort and a feeling of being understood to parents, which in turn may provide clinicians with enough positive feedback for them to conclude that their intervention attempts are successful.

The problems caused by a pervasive pattern of coercive interaction are not limited to disruptions in the parent's critical ability to use effective discipline or to their feelings of anger, rejection, and depression. Coerciveness during very early childhood can disrupt all aspects of the close, affectionate, mentoring, and educational parent-child relationship that are essential for preparing the child to meet the increasingly difficult demands of teachers, peers, neighbors, and others over childhood and adolescence. Thus, although preventive or clinical interventions for conduct problems during this period must focus on teaching the parent to set developmentally appropriate limits and to use effective, calm, and nonabusive discipline, it must also teach the parent to offer positive alternatives to the child's attempts at coercion and to gain or regain the ability to observe, promote, and systematically encourage these and other attempts by the child to master the art of positive and rewarding social interaction. If these skills can be taught, then the parent is in the position to use them to teach the youngster the skills that will be required in key social domains over development.

We have only recently begun to develop interventions for early childhood. Our first concerted effort has been the work of Phil Fisher to adapt and expand Patti Chamberlain's treatment foster care models for young children in foster care. Each year, more and younger children are placed out of their families of origin in foster homes. As a group, foster children are at extraordinary risk not only for externalizing problems, but also for internalizing problems and for school failure. Foster parents tend to receive scant training and little therapeutic support, even though the children in their care are enormously challenging and difficult. In chapter 10, Chamberlain, Fisher, and their colleague Kevin Moore describe interventions specifically designed to help foster parents and natural/adoptive parents deal with the behavioral, educational, and emotional needs of variously aged children of both genders who present with a variety of diagnoses and problems.

Middle childhood. Entry into structured school settings brings a number of challenges for children and parents alike. The social and work skills expected of the child increases dramatically with entry into the classroom and peer group settings (Kellam & Rebok, 1992). The child who has learned to be coercive in dealing with parents and siblings is likely to resist the demands for compliance that are endemic within these settings (Reid, 1993). Such a stance, in combination with associated deficits in emotion regulation and positive social skills, tends to quickly induct teachers and peers into the same coercive kinds of interchanges that are characteristic of interactions between oppositional children and their parents (Dodge, 1983; Walker & Buckley, 1973). The social rejection and academic failure that result from such exchanges place an additional burden on the parent. If the parent is already enmeshed in continuing conflict with the child in the home setting and is unable to help the child adjust to these new social arenas, the odds for maladaptation increase even further.

Even though the conduct problems of elementary school children have key, proximal antecedents in at least three social domains (family, classroom, peer group), we organize our *clinical* efforts around the family. Although this bias probably reflects our roots in the study of the family, it is also the locus of organization of normative social development at least through mid- to late adolescence. Whereas a child changes classes and teachers yearly, the family (or at least some aspect of the family) tends to be a stable source of ongoing influence for most children. Further, parents do have the potential to exert positive cross-situational influence in school and peer group domains (DeGarmo, Forgatch, & Martinez, 1999; Ladd and Golter, 1988). Our clinical and targeted preventive interventions are thus aimed not only at directly changing the way parents interact with their children at home, but also at the way that parents exert their influence in out of home settings, such as the school, the neighborhood, and the playground. Our universal preventive interventions use the same general strategy, but extend the work directly into the school setting (e.g., in the classroom and on the playground).

Many of the chapters that follow discuss interventions that are relevant to children in this particular age range. Most notably, in chapter 11, we discuss the LIFT (Linking the Interests of Families and Teachers) intervention, which includes parent training, classroom-based social skills training, and a *good behavior game* on the playground. In chapter 12, Forgatch and colleagues discuss their family interventions.

Adolescence. Obviously, a theory that emphasizes the importance of microsocial interactions must be responsive to the changing characteristics of such interactions across the lifespan. During adolescence, youth spend less time with any one adult (e.g., a parent, a day care provider, the same teacher for most of the day at school), and more time with one or more similarly aged youth. The level of social influence of peers thus increases, and without the guiding influences of the many adults that they now may (or may not) interact with, the more likely that peer influence becomes the dominant social force.

With children who have had difficult childhoods, the transfer of social influence over to peers is particularly likely. By adolescence, such children have undoubtedly alienated the potential prosocial peers in their lives, and their relationship with their parent(s) is probably shaky at best. As they leave their elementary school and enter into a larger high school, they now encounter youth from numerous other schools who, like them, have few friends and are disliked by adults. These youth cluster together, become friends, and within a year or two, are quite likely to begin to smoke and drink, to have sex, and to get arrested for one of any number of status or non-status offenses. By the time they reach high school, they are well on their way to having extensive police records and to dropping out of academics all together.

Despite this type of trajectory, most of such children continue to live at home and to see their parents on a daily basis. Their parents continue to be the adults who at least have the potential to know the most about them, and in turn, to influence them the most. Thus, even during adolescence, we continue to employ a family-based treatment model. In chapter 10, Patti Chamberlain and colleagues discuss their foster care based treatment models. In chapter 11, we discuss the fifth grade version of our LIFT program, which attempts to prepare youth to enter and deal better with the middle school world. Tom Dishion and Kate Kavanagh discuss their various interventions for working with teens and their parents in chapter 13.

10

Multidimensional Treatment Foster Care: Applications of the OSLC Intervention Model to High-Risk Youth and Their Families

Patricia Chamberlain,
Philip A. Fisher, and
Kevin Moore

Foster care is a model of service delivery with roots in the social welfare movement. It was first developed as a means of helping neglected children and children in poverty and was based on the notion that a loving home and access to resources would set needy youth on the path to success. In the past two decades, a variation of foster care has been developed that targets treating youth with severe behavioral and emotional problems. Multidimensional treatment foster care (MTFC, also called therapeutic or specialized foster care) is now being used throughout the United States as an alternative to more restrictive residential and group care placements for troubled youth (Chamberlain & Reid, 1998; Chamberlain, 1994; Fisher, Ellis, & Chamberlain, 1999; Hudson, Nutter, & Galaway, 1994a, 1994b). In fact, MTFC is now one of the most widely used forms of out-of-home placement for children and adolescents in the United States. and is considered the least restrictive form of residential care (Kutash & Rivera, 1996). At any one time an estimated 1,200 U.S. youth are receiving MTFC for over 6 million client days at a cost of $.5 billion per year (Farmer, Burns, Chamberlain, & Dubs, 2001). The MTFC model extends the traditional foster care model in two important ways. First, it engages foster parents as active members of the treatment team. Second, it makes a number of additional resources available to both foster parent and child.

In this chapter, we discuss how OSLC has implemented the MTFC model for a variety of populations of youngsters and their families who were at the extreme end of the continuum of antisocial behavior and risk for such behavior. In addition, we describe using an adaptation of the MTFC approach as a preventive intervention for maltreated preschoolers placed in state foster care. We will concentrate this review on the studies that have been conducted by OSLC on the efficacy of MTFC and on key components of the model that relate to positive outcomes for children and families in follow-up. Prior to describing study results, we will briefly describe the MTFC approach in general, and the OSLC MTFC model specifically.

Definition of MTFC

MTFC is a family-based intervention for children and adolescents with significant behavioral, emotional, and mental health problems. The MTFC model has been broadly defined as a service that provides treatment for troubled children within the private homes of trained families (Rivera & Kutash, 1994). MTFC differs from most residential and group care settings in several important ways: community families are recruited, trained, and supported to provide placements, children generally attend public schools, usually one and no more than two youngsters are placed in a home, and most MTFC programs include a family therapy component with the biological parent(s) (or relatives or other after care resource). MTFC is significantly less costly than group care. In comparison to institutional settings, MTFC has a relatively high degree of ecological similarity to youths' home environments—especially in terms of children's day-to-day activities and the systems of authority. It therefore allows for ease of transition from the treatment setting back to the biological family. Because MTFC often involves working with youths' biological families during placement in foster care, it is possible to set up behavior management programs with biological families that are similar to those being used by the foster families. This appears to of reduce recidivism, especially in comparison to group care (Chamberlain 1990; Chamberlain & Friman, 1997; Eddy & Chamberlain, 2000). Moreover, MTFC maximizes continuity of care and facilitates a sense of universality of the treatment structure from the youth's perspective. Indeed, MTFC has been shown to be useful in treating a number of antisocial and problem behaviors (reviewed in Meadowcroft, Thomlison, & Chamberlain, 1994).Typically, mental health professionals closely supervise the placement and treatment of children in treatment foster care systems (Galaway, Nutter, & Hudson, 1995). The intensity of professional involvement is typically aided by the low child to staff ratio (Meadowcroft & Trout, 1990); most treatment foster care programs assign fewer than 10 cases per social worker (Galaway et al., 1995). In addition to providing individual contact with the child, mental health professionals oversee training and support of the treatment foster parents. Most programs provide both pre-service and in-service training, and most also provide ongoing foster parent support groups (Galaway et al., 1995). The amount of training and support provided by mental health professionals, rather than theoretical orientation, provides the binding similarity between treatment foster care programs: a wide variety of theories are used to guide treatment foster care programs, and some report that they do not follow any specific orientation (Galaway et al., 1995). Because the program's theoretical orientation determines the type of training treatment foster parents receive and also influences the child's treatment plan, empirical work examining success rates of different treatment orientations is critical to understanding how treatment foster care can be most effective (Webb, 1988).

The OSLC Multidimensional Treatment Foster Care Model

Since 1983 the Oregon Social Learning Center (OSLC) has operated MTFC programs for troubled youth who are in need of out-of-home placement. We began with a focus on chronic juvenile offenders and today continue to serve that group as well as several others including children and adolescents with severe emotional disturbance, adolescents with developmental delays and problems with sexual acting out, females referred from juvenile justice, and preschoolers placed in state foster care.

Program components are multifaceted and interventions occur in multiple settings, including MTFC homes, biological parent/relative homes, schools, and in community settings (e.g., sports activities, church groups, clubs, camps.) Interventions also target peer relations. Modalities include intensive training and support in behavior management techniques for MTFC parents, behavioral parent training for biological parents, skill training and supportive therapy for youths, school-based behavioral interventions and other academic support, and psychiatric consultation and medication management, as needed. Components of the model are described in full in Chamberlain (1994; in press), Chamberlain and Mihalic, 1998, and Fisher and Chamberlain (2000) and are reviewed briefly here.

Recruitment, training, and supervision of MTFC homes. Community families are recruited based on their experience with children and adolescents, willingness to act as treatment agents, and nurturing family environment. Recruitment and selection of MTFC parents occurs during a 4-step process including a telephone screening interview, filling out an application, participating in a home visit, and completing a 20-hour preservice training. Project case managers and a former MTFC parent, who serves as the foster parent trainer, conduct preservice training. Training emphasizes using behavior management methods in a structured daily living environment, including emphasizing frequent reinforcement of appropriate child behavior, providing close supervision, and having clear rules and limits. MTFC parents are taught how to implement an individualized plan for each youth that takes into account his/her needs and the MTFC family's schedule and values. A 3-level system is used for adolescents where privileges and level of supervision are based on his/her compliance with program rules, adjustment in school, and general progress. Ongoing supervision of MTFC parents takes place during weekly foster parent group meetings run by case managers and through daily telephone calls where data on the youngster's progress/problems during the past 24 hours are collected using the Parent Daily Report Checklist (PDR; Chamberlain & Reid, 1987). During those calls, MTFC parents identify problems they anticipate and discuss potential solutions.

The following sections on program components apply to the MTFC programs for adolescents and school-aged children. A description of the Early Intervention version of the MTFC model is described later in this chapter.

Individual and family treatment. Each youth participates in weekly individual therapy focused on skill building in such areas as problem solving, social perspective taking, and nonaggressive methods of self-expression. Individual therapists work for the program and have training and supervision in behaviorally oriented treatments. The youth's biological family or other aftercare resource participates in weekly family therapy focused on parent management training, including an emphasis on supervision, encouragement, discipline, and problem solving. When the youth is to return home after placement (85% of cases), there are frequent home visits beginning with 1- to 2-hour visits and increasing to overnight visits as the youth progresses through the program. Family therapists also work for the program and are experienced in using parent-training treatment.

School interventions. All children are enrolled in public schools, with 45% attending at least part of the day in special education classes. Prior to enrollment in school, a conference is set up with the school counselor and interested administrators. Youth carry a card to each class and have teachers sign off on attendance, homework completion, and attitude. Program back-up is provided to the school if youth become disruptive and need to be removed during the school day.

Emphasizing encouragement. We train and work intensively with MTFC parents to notice and reinforce youngsters for behaving appropriately. An emphasis is placed on shaping behavior in areas where the youth has low skills. Conceptualizing interventions in terms of shaping and reinforcement allows for a focus on strengthening skills and positive support for youth and their families.

Close supervision and consistent discipline. Consequences for rule infractions are tailored for each youth but include point and privilege loss, being demoted to a lower level, work chores for pre-specified amounts of time, and in extreme situations, short stays in detention. Consequences are consistently delivered for even minor rule violations (e.g., being 2 minutes late, not doing breakfast dishes). Youth are encouraged to accept consequences, to quickly complete any work assigned, and to start each day with a clean slate. MTFC parents are trained to deliver consequences in a nonangry, neutral way and to give youth credit for complying with the conditions of the consequence. For youth referred from juvenile justice, all parole violations are reported to parole/probation officers who follow through with appropriate sanctions such as privilege loss, short stays in detention, or in more serious cases, expulsion from the program. Youth are supervised closely, strict rules are established for being on time, their whereabouts in the community are known to MTFC parents and program staff, all free time is prearranged, and their whereabouts during out-of-home time is routinely checked. Youngster's peer associations are also closely monitored and contact with peers with known histories of delinquency is prohibited.

Case coordination and supervision. A case manager, along with the program director and clinical consultant, supervises the individual and family therapists in 2-hour weekly meetings and coordinates all treatment and supervision services. Case managers have low case loads (10 cases) to allow for intensive interaction with MTFC parents, therapists, biological/adoptive parents, child welfare case workers or parole/probation officers, teachers, and youth. Case managers are on call 24 hours per day, 7 days per week, and MTFC parents are encouraged to call them with questions, concerns, or problems. Biological parents also have on-call access to case managers and to program therapists.

Overview of the Implementation of the OSLC MTFC Model

The first OSLC MTFC program was designed in response to a state request for proposals for services to serious and violent juvenile offenders that would be an alternative to incarceration. During the ensuing years, over 300 juvenile offenders have been served using this model. Beginning in 1986, we adapted the MTFC model for youngsters with severe emotional and behavioral problems who had been hospitalized in the Oregon State Hospital. These children were 9 to 18 years old and had spent, on average, most of the past year in the state hospital. Based on that work, we began treating youngsters referred from the mental health and child welfare systems who were eligible for Medicaid services. These youngsters range in age from 4 to 18 and typically have experienced a number of previous out-of-home placements due to parental abuse or neglect. In 1996 we began an MTFC program for adolescents with developmental disabilities who also had histories of sexual acting out. These are youngsters who are in state custody, and for whom the typical residential settings do not provide adequate supervision, especially with respect to the youth's contacts with other children.

Because of the unique needs of the younger children, in 1996 we adapted the MTFC approach for 3- to 7-year-olds who were in state supported foster homes. These youngsters had experienced parental abuse/neglect and had been removed from their homes by the state child welfare agency. Children were referred to MTFC because of extreme and severe behavioral and emotional problems that made it impossible to maintain them in a regular state-supported foster home. The Early Intervention Foster Care model (EIFC) was subsequently developed to serve these children.

OSLC MTFC Outcome Studies

Overview. Each outcome study on MTFC reviewed in this section has been conducted as part of a program of research that aims at testing the feasibility, limits, and effectiveness of the model. We have used an outside-in strategy for this line of program development where we first establish the program in the community with local funding (rather than beginning research inside the center and then moving out to the community). Once details of the implementation are worked out, and the program is running, we conduct a pilot study to initially look at feasibility and effectiveness. Pilot data is then used to apply for funding to conduct a full-scale randomized trial. To this point we have used this approach (pilot then randomized trial) for three MTFC adaptations: for male juvenile offenders, for female juvenile offenders, and for an early intervention prevention foster care model, all of which are briefly reviewed in the next section.

The Allies Program, the MTFC model for developmentally delayed youngsters (Moore, 2001), is in the pre-pilot stage of development. The final stage of this strategy is to conduct effectiveness trials where the program is embedded in a larger system of care. Such a study is currently being initiated in San Diego County. Allies is designed to meet the needs of children and youth who have been placed in out-of-home care, have borderline (i.e., I.Q. 70-85) cognitive abilities, and severe behavioral and emotional modulation problems. Most of these children also have sexual acting-out and/or sexual offending as a referral problem. Allies was created in response to concerns of state-level social welfare administrators who wanted a specialized program that provided attention to the psychosocial needs of these children. More specifically, the cognitive limitations, unique interactional styles, and need for close supervision of this population were not adequately addressed within existing residential treatment models. In this adaptation of MTFC, individual therapy and skills training are tailored to match the child's cognitive and emotional level. Similar to the Monitor program, the Allies program has been designed to use parenting (foster and biological) practices as the primary mechanism for changing child problems. Early studies of behavioral parent training and recent studies involving the Monitor program demonstrate that systematically altering caregivers' day-to-day interactions with, and reactions to, the problematic behaviors of children can positively alter children's developmental trajectories. Consistent with this framework, the goal of Allies is to systematically change the child's social environment to control problematic or antisocial behavior and encourage developmentally appropriate pro-social behavior and development of academic/independent living skills.

Modifications made to the treatment approach that are specific to challenges experienced by a person who has low cognitive abilities include: (a) use of pictographs, (b) increased use of concrete and immediate reinforcers, (c) no group therapy, and (d) decreased amount and duration of verbal instruction and talking about problems, both in the foster home and when providing other treatment services. Some of the basic tenets of this approach include: (a) minimization of talk therapy that focuses on problem behavior and psychopathology, (b) re-framing pathological or mentalistic conceptualization of behaviors (e.g., laziness reframed as lack of stamina), (c) emphasis on the here and now with a focus on strengths and in-vivo skill development, (d) targeting antecedent behaviors.

Demographic and disruption rate data were evaluated for 24 consecutive referrals to the Allies program. Youth ranged in age from 6 to 20 years (M=13.8) with IQ scores ranging from 51 to 101 (M =76.3). They had a mean of 3.3 DSM-IV Axis I diagnoses and 6.3 previous out-of-home placements. In addition, 74 percent had no identified aftercare resource at entry in the program. Preliminary program evaluation data suggest that MTFC is a viable community-based alternative for this population of children in the social welfare and juvenile justice systems. For example, the total placement disruption rate during the first 6 months youths were in the program was 8.3% (n=2), and at 12 months this rate had increased to 36% (n =8). However, only 4.2% and 9%, respectfully, were terminated from the program. That is, we were able to contain most of the disruptions within the program, and over a 12-month period only 2 youths could not be contained in a community-based foster care setting.

Demographic and data on disruption rates for this population are presented in Tables 10.4 and 10.5. The data on disruptions include those that were contained within the program (i.e., moving to another MTFC foster home) and disruptions that required termination from the program.

The Monitor Study. This pilot study was the first in a series of studies to test the feasibility and effectiveness of the OSLC MTFC model. The Monitor program was funded by the state child protection service as a community-based diversion program for youth committed to the state training schools because of severe and chronic delinquency. All youth were in detention at the time of referral to the program. A juvenile court judge had mandated that the youngsters were to participate in a residential treatment program. Adolescents who have been removed from their homes because of chronic delinquent behavior have traditionally had one of two placement options: group homes or residential treatment centers. Our MTFC model provided an alternative to congregate care.

We used a matched comparison design to examine the rates of incarceration for boys and girls who participated in MTFC compared to those who had received treatment in other community-based diversion programs. MTFC youths were matched from a pool of 435 youths (who all had been diverted to placement in community-based programs) on three variables: age, sex, and date of commitment to the state training school.

Outcomes examined were the number of days spent incarcerated during the first 2 years post treatment, and program completion (vs. expulsion or run away) rates. Results showed that youngsters in MTFC spent significantly fewer days in lock-up during follow-up—a difference in cost (estimating incarceration costs at $100/day) of $122,000 over a 2-year period. In addition, significantly fewer MTFC youth were incarcerated following treatment. Although, on average, youth in both groups spent the same amount of time in treatment, more MTFC participants completed their treatment programs, and there was a significant relationship between the number of days in treatment and the number of days of subsequent incarceration for youth in the MTFC but not in the comparison group. This study provided the preliminary data and feasibility information to set the stage for the larger randomized trial, Mediators of Male Delinquency (1991 Chamberlain P.I.; funded by the National Institute of Mental Health, Violence and Traumatic Stress Branch, James Breiling, Project Officer).

Mediators Study (Chamberlain & Reid, 1998). Seventy-nine boys between the ages of 12 and 17 were referred by the juvenile justice system over a 4-year period. All boys were screened for eligibility by a committee of juvenile court personnel who decided whether youngsters would be placed in the state training school or some other out-of-home care setting. Prior to referral, study boys averaged 14 previous criminal referrals, and 4.6 previous felonies. All 79 subjects had been detained in the year before entering the study; the average number of days spent in detention was 76. The mean age at entry into the study was 14.9 years (SD = 1.3), and the mean age at first arrest was 12.6 years (*SD* = 1.82). Boys were randomly assigned to placement in MTFC or group care (GC).

In GC, boys went to one of 11 group care programs located throughout the state. Group Care programs had from 6 to 15 youths in residence. Although programs differed somewhat in terms of their theoretical orientations, variations of the positive peer culture approach (Vorrath & Brendtro, 1985) were most often used. Youths participated in individual and group therapy as part of their programs. They most often attended in-house schools (83% of cases). Family contact was encouraged, and when families could commute to program sites (55% of cases), family therapy was typically provided.

Prior to placing boys in program settings, we interviewed senior line staff (in GC) or foster parents (in MTFC) to examine assumptions about change mechanisms and to look at daily program practices, including discipline strategies, supervision rules and restrictions, and the roles of peers and adults in the treatment process. Based on the theoretical and intervention models, we expected to find differences in daily treatment methods with the MTFC foster parents relying primarily on direct adult interventions in dealing with the youngsters and GC staff using peer mediated interventions. To examine treatment fidelity for the two approaches, an interview examining program practices was conducted at each placement site after boys had been there for 3 months. We found significant differences between programs in the two treatment conditions in several areas (Chamberlain, Ray, & Moore, 1996). For example, group therapy was conducted at least weekly in 90% of the GC placements, and it was not offered at all in MTFC. Adults in GC and MTFC differed in terms of who they thought had the most influence on boys' success (e.g., significantly more adult vs. peer influence in MTFC than in GC). In GC, adults spent less one-on-one time with boys than they did in MTFC. In GC, peers had more influence on deciding house rules and discipline than in MTFC. Finally, GC boys spent more time with peers than did their counterparts in MTFC.

Immediate and 1-year follow-up outcomes. A central question was whether or not it would be feasible and safe to place such chronic and serious offenders in alternative nuclear families in the community. For the first 6 months after referral, youngsters in MTFC spent significantly more days actually in their placements than did boys in GC (M = 129.8; SD = 54.2 and M = 76.6; SD = 62.9, respectively; F [1, 68] = 14.2, p =. 001). During the second 6 months, MTFC boys spent an average of 67.9 days (SD = 65.3) in placement and GC boys spent an average of 84.3 days (SD = 75.9, n.s.). Fewer boys in MTFC than in GC ran away from their placements (30.5% vs. 57.8%, respectively), chi square = 5.59, df = 1, p = .02. A greater proportion of MTFC boys than GC boys ultimately completed their programs (73% vs. 36%, respectively) chi square = 10.96, p = .001. During the year after referral, boys in MTFC spent significantly fewer days in lock-up than did GC boys (p = .001). This included fewer days in local detention facilities (MTFC, M = 32; GC, M = 70) and fewer days in the state training schools (M = 21 and 59 days, respectively). Overall, compared to GC boys, boys in MTFC spent 60% fewer days incarcerated during the year following referral.

The second major question addressed by this study was whether or not MTFC would be effective, compared to GC, in reducing subsequent crime and delinquent activity. For this question, we analyzed arrests for criminal activity that were documented in official juvenile court records for the period examined from 1 year prior to enrollment through 1 year post-discharge or expulsion from treatment. We also examined delinquent and criminal activities self-reported by participants for the year after baseline.

A two-by-two mixed ANOVA (group by time) was conducted to examine potential differences between MTFC and GC arrest rates from baseline to 12 months post termination from GC or MTFC. The group-by-time interaction was significant (F[1, 77] = 3.93, p = .003), with MTFC boys showing larger drops in official arrest rates. Mean rates for arrests are shown in Figure 10.1.

To examine the clinical significance of the differences in changes in arrests, we analyzed the percentage of boys in each condition who completely desisted from being arrested after enrollment into the study. In the MTFC group, 41% (15) of the boys had no further arrests during the 12-month post-treatment period examined. The comparable figure for GC boys was 7% (3 boys). In MTFC, 13.5% (5) of the boys had one additional arrest after study enrollment. The comparable figure for GC was 7% (3) of the boys.

To assess the rates of self-reported delinquency, three subscales of the Elliott Behavior Checklist (EBC; Elliott, Huizinga, & Ageton, 1985) were examined: General Delinquency, Index Offenses, and Felony Assaults. On all three subscales, EBC scores for 1 year post-baseline showed significant differences between the groups with boys in MTFC reporting significantly fewer criminal activities. The means, standard deviations, and significance levels for the EBC subscales are shown in Table 10.1.

Longer-term outcomes. We have continued to gather arrest data on this sample, which is shown in Table 10.2. As can be seen there, boys in MTFC continue to have significantly fewer arrests through 4-year follow-up (probabilities for all years < .05).

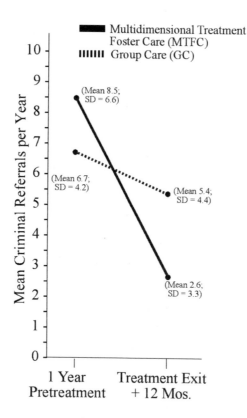

Figure 10.1. Total number of driminal referrals at baseline and from placement in either multidimensional treatment foster care or group care (from Chamberlain & Reid, 1998).

A full-scale follow-up study is currently being conducted on this sample (Eddy, 1999). The aim of that study, in addition to investigating long-term outcomes for study boys, is to examine the influence of contextual and social factors on antisocial

Table 10.1. Elliott Behavior Checklist Self-Report Scales.

Variable	M	SD	F(1,77)	p
General Delinquency				
Group home	28.9	32.4		
MTFC	12.8	20.5	6.5	.01
Index Offenses				
Group home	8.6	11.9	5.3	.03
MTFC	3.2	7.2		
Felony Assaults				
Group home	2.7	3.8	4.1	.05
MTFC	1.2	2.7		

Note. There were 42 boys in GC and 37 in MTFC. GC = group care; MTFC = multidimensional treatment foster care.

Table 10.2. Cumulative Arrest Rates for MTFC and GC boys 2–4 Years Post Placement.

	MTFC		GC	
Placement + 2 years	3.2	(3.4)	6.7	(4.6)
Placement + 3 Years	5.4	(5.8)	8.5	(5.1)
Placement + 4 years	7.7	(7.8)	10.9	(7.1)

MTFC = multidimensional treatment foster care; GC = group care.

behavior and positive adjustment in young adulthood. Specifically, the initiation, maintenance, and desistance of antisocial behavior will be examined as a joint function of past behavior and outcomes and current influences, including social processes within peer, romantic and family relationships, employment, and other factors such as substance use and mental health problems

Program costs. At the time of the Mediators study, the MTFC program was funded by the Oregon Youth Authority (OYA) at the rate of $76 per boy per day, or $2,356 per month. This funding level, with 3% yearly cost of living adjustments, had been in effect since 1983, when the program started. Grant monies from NIMH were not used to augment treatment services but were dedicated to evaluation activities. Group Care programs varied in their amount of funding from $120 per day per youth to $160 per day, or from $3,720 to $4,960 per month. In a recent cost–benefit analysis conducted by the Washington State Institute for Public Policy (Aos, Phipps, Barnoski, & Lieb, 1999) it was calculated that the OSLC MTFC model saved taxpayers $43,661 per participant in criminal justice and avoided victim costs; for every dollar spent on MTFC, $22.58 of taxpayer benefits were estimated.

Gender differences in responsiveness to MTFC (Chamberlain & Reid, 1994). Although the original MTFC program was designed for male adolescents in the juvenile justice system, shortly after having that program up and referred all of the girls, we began to receive referrals from court counselors for females. The local juvenile department referred all of the girls for placement in MTFC because of a history of severe and chronic criminal activity. In an initial pilot study, we examined data on initial risk factors, in-program behavior, and outcomes for girls vs. boys in MTFC. We found that while MTFC was equally effective for boys and girls in terms of reducing criminal behavior in follow-up, girls presented some unique problems in treatment. We wanted to understand why, after having provided placements for both girls and boys, foster parents were less willing to have girls placed with them even though, on many levels, boys presented a greater threat to their personal property and family safety. In terms of initial risk factors, we found that, compared to boys, girls had more disrupted childhoods (e.g. they had been placed out of their homes significantly more often; $M = 4.26$ previous placements vs. 2.5 for boys), they were more likely to run away from placement (86% vs. 56% for boys), and they had more frequent histories of attempted suicide (29% vs. 6%). PDR data collected over the course of treatment shed light on the negative experiences MTFC parents reported for girls. In Figure 10.2, mean rates of problem behaviors per day for the first and last months of treatment are shown for girls and boys. As can be seen there, we found a gender by time interaction. The boys' rate of problem behaviors improved over time. Girls, on the other hand, had low rates of problem behaviors at first which then increased. Even though they got along well with MTFC parents initially, this

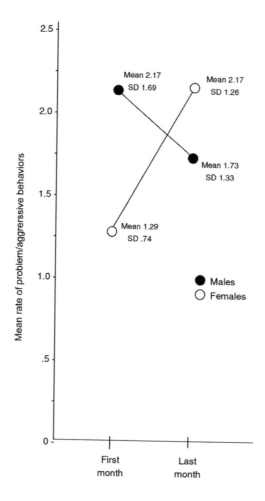

Figure 10.2. Parent daily reports of aggression/problem behaviors (from Chamberlain & Reid, 1994).

relationship tended to deteriorate over the course of the placement. Boys and girls had equal program completion rates and there were no significant differences in rates of arrest at 1 year post–placement.

The Relationship Study (Chamberlain, 1997a). Currently, we are conducting a randomized trial for females referred from juvenile justice that includes many of the same design features as the Mediators study, including during-treatment measures hypothesized to predict follow-up adjustment. In addition to the variables that were measured in the Mediators study, we are assessing relational aggression, trauma and abuse, mental health diagnoses, health-related factors, and girls relationships' with friends and intimate partners. A complete description of preliminary findings can be found in Chamberlain and Moore (in press). An overview is provided here.

Family factors: We assessed girls' histories of family transitions and stability by interviewing girls and mothers about the number of parent figures girls have lived with since birth. A parental transition was counted any time a parent figure came in or out of the girl's home, or when they were placed in the custody of another

Table 10.3. Percent of Juvenile Justice Boys and Girls Meeting Clinical Cutoffs on BSI (from Chamberlain & Moore, 2000).

Diagnosis	Boys	Girls
Depression	8%	40%
Anxiety	11%	80%
Paranoid	10%	67%
Somatic	5%	87%
Hostility	4%	47%

adult or in residential care. At baseline, study girls had an average of 16 parental transitions, a little over one for each year of their lives, on average. On a number of family variables, we are able to compare rates of risk factors for boys and girls referred from juvenile justice. In general, families of girls tend to be more chaotic than those of boys. For example, on parental criminality, 43% of girls' mothers had been convicted of a crime, compared to 9.5% of boys' mothers. Seventy percent of girls' fathers had been convicted of a crime vs. 22% of boys' fathers. Both of these differences were significant at the $p = .05$ level. Seventy-two percent of the girls had at least one parent convicted as compared to 22% of the boys. Rates of out-of-home placements for girls and boys were examined and again a significant difference ($p < .01$) was found with girls averaging 3.9 previous out-of-home placements and boys averaging 1.33.

We also assessed the occurrence of mental health problems for girls and boys using the Brief Symptom Inventory (BSI; Derogatis & Spencer, 1982). Percentages of girls and boys in the two juvenile justice-referred samples who met clinical cut off criteria on each of five BSI scales are shown in Table 10.3. On every scale, girls report higher levels of symptoms than boys. DISC-2 data confirm a high rate of psychiatric symptoms for girls; of the 36 girls interviewed so far, 53% of them have met criteria for three or more DSM-IV Axis 1 disorders. This is clearly a highly distressed group of youngsters who have substantial mental health problems.

It is well documented in the literature that girls tend to commit fewer and less serious crimes than boys. In our samples, males referred to a parallel study had 14 offenses prior to entering the study. The first 25 girls who entered the study have an average of 9.9 prior offenses ($p < .05$). Interestingly, before entering the study, boys had spent an average of 73 days in detention during the past year, whereas girls (with fewer offenses) spent an average of 131 days in detention during the past year.

Preliminary outcomes for this sample show that at 1-year follow-up girls in the MTFC condition are spending significantly fewer days in lock-up than those in group care (M=45.4 days vs. 111.7 days for girls in GC) and more time in MTFC treatment than girls in GC (232 vs. 99, $p < .05$). During the coming year we will examine outcomes relative to criminal behavior for the first half of this sample.

Preliminary conclusions and directions. The Oregon MTFC model attempts to provide girls with the basic MTFC program components, plus individualized services and supports that address their specific needs. Basic program components are organized around the notion of providing girls with a safe and supportive family living environment. Because the girls we are working with have such severe histories of chaos and disruption in their living situations, a primary goal is to stabilize them and to stop the pattern of moving from one placement to the next, especially when placement changes are unplanned and are a reaction to a negative set of circumstances. Like their male counterparts referred from juvenile justice, girls enrolled in our MTFC program have histories of chronic and severe delinquency and need to be well supervised by adults and separated from delinquent peers, particularly in situations where they are unsupervised. They also seem to benefit from being given clear and teaching-oriented direction and mentorship by a positive female adult (e.g., the female MTFC·parent). The role of the female MTFC parent is well defined in this regard.

Another important consideration is the orientation of girls toward planning for their futures. Findings from the work of Rutter (1989) and others (Walsh, 1999) suggest that, for female adolescents, a planning orientation is protective against future antisocial behavior. In the MTFC model, each girl works weekly with an individual therapist who is available to address issues of her choosing. The therapist introduces the notion of future planning and assists the girl to identify a plan and to take steps toward its actualization. In addition, the girl's individual therapist helps her problem solve around difficulties she may be encountering in the MTFC home, in school, with peer relations, or in other situations. The individual therapist follows the girl's agenda with regard to working on issues related to sexual and physical abuse. Clinically, we think it is unwise to direct girls to deal with these issues, given that doing so typically increases their levels of anxiety and stress. Girls are encouraged to identify themes and topics to work on in the context of the individual therapy.

The Early Intervention Foster Care Pilot Study (Fisher, Ellis, & Chamberlain, 1999; Fisher, Gunnar, Chamberlain, & Reid, 2000). Given that the original OSLC MTFC model was designed for delinquent adolescents, there was a clear need for adaptation of the policies and procedures in order to meet the developmental needs of this preschool age population. In particular, the literature on risk factors among preschool-aged foster children suggests that three problems commonly co-occur that are crucial for understanding and redirecting the life-course trajectories of these high-risk youngsters (Halfon, Mendonca, & Berkowitz, 1995; Landsverk, & Garland, 1999; Landsverk, Litrownik, Newton, Granger, & Remmer, 1996). These are (a) behavior and conduct problems (especially externalizing problems) and (b) emotion regulation difficulties. Moreover, there is extensive evidence that parenting practices in biological and foster families, including engaging and monitoring the child, consistent discipline, and use of positive reinforcement, mediate the course of these and other risk factors (Chamberlain & Reid, 1998; Patterson, Reid, & Dishion, 1992). Further rationale for the focus on parenting strategies is that prior to entry into school, parental figures are the child's primary agents of socialization. Consequently, at this developmental stage, interventions that strengthen the parenting by foster and biological families have been found to exert a powerful preventative effect on long-term outcomes (see Reid & Eddy, 1997, for a review). We hope to alter the life course trajectory of these children away from antisocial behavior and towards a more positive psychosocial adjustment.

A pilot study of the EIFC program was funded in January of 1997 by the NIMH Prevention Branch and ran through January of 1998. The study examined the effects of MTFC on children's behavior, neuroendocrine (specifically salivary cortisol) activity, and foster parent behavior and stress levels during the initial adjustment to a new foster home. To accomplish these objectives, data were collected from three groups of 10 children each, including children referred for services to the EIFC program by the state child welfare system after one or more placement disruptions and/or because of highly disruptive and aggressive behavior; non-referred children receiving regular foster care services through the state system (RFC group); and a community comparison group (CC) of same-aged children living with their natural families. The pilot study did not include random assignment to the EIFC and RFC conditions. As a result of non-random assignment in the pilot study, the children in the EIFC condition were generally more troubled and had more severe maltreatment histories than those in the RFC group.

Parenting strategies and foster parent stress. ANOVAs were conducted on three parenting scales. For monitoring, there was a statistically significant effect for group (F[2, 18] = 18.01, $p < .001$). Post-hoc analyses revealed that at both time points the RFC group was significantly different from both the EIFC and CC groups, which were not different from each other. For discipline, there was an effect for time (F[1, 18] = 5.058, $p < .05$), with the mean number of discipline items dropping from initial to final assessment. There was also a significant effect for group (F[2, 18] = 21.69, $p < .001$), again with the RFC group significantly different from both the EIFC and CC groups, which were not different from each other at both time points. A similar statistically significant pattern for the group factor was observed for the positive reinforcement scale (F[2, 15] = 4.96, $p < .05$), with the RFC foster parents scoring significantly lower than either EIFC or CC caregivers at both time points. There was a marginally significant time by treatment group interaction (F[2, 12] = 3.24, $p = .08$) in the amount of stress reported by foster parents as a result of child problem behaviors. Post-hoc analysis indicated EIFC decreased stress, while the RFC group showed an increase in reported stress.

Child behavior. A mixed model ANOVA examining number of child symptoms reported by caregivers showed a significant effect for group (F[2, 26] = 21.27, $p < .001$) and a significant group X time interaction (F(2,26)=4.33, $p < .05$). Post hoc analyses indicated that this interaction was driven by the EIFC group, which decreased in the number of symptoms reported, and the RFC group, which increased in the number of symptoms reported.

Salivary Cortisol. In the EIFC group, following an initial elevation in basal cortisol over the first 5 weeks, levels decreased for the next 5 weeks. In weeks 11 and 12, they began to increase slightly, but the overall trend is a negative quadratic. In contrast, the RFC group showed a positive quadratic trend of a general decrease in cortisol over the first 6 weeks of the study, but then a sharp increase over the last 4 weeks. A group-by-time MANOVA revealed trends in the effect for time, F [4, 11[= 4.01, $p = .10$, and for the group-by-time interaction, F [10, 22] = 2.18, $p = .10$) As expected, a test of the within-subject group-by-time quadratic interaction effect was close to significant, $p = .06$, reflecting the reverse quadratic effects for the EIFC and RFC groups.

The circadian release patterns for cortisol at initial and final assessments are shown in Figure 10.3. A number of trends can be observed in these data. For instance, at initial assessment we found the RFC and CC groups to be fairly similar: Cortisol levels were highest at the a.m. collection and decreased throughout the day. In contrast, the EIFC group showed a decrease from a.m. to mid-morning but showed a slight increase between the mid-morning and p.m. collections. At the final assessment, the most notable change is in the release patterns of the EIFC group. Compared to the positive slope at initial assessment between mid-morning and p.m., the slope was negative—closer to the release pattern for typically developing children who have not been maltreated. Additionally, the RFC group showed increased elevations across all three time-points.

We examined the statistical significance of these trends via a mixed model, repeated measures MANOVA. In this analysis, assessment interval (initial vs. final assessment) and time of day (a.m., mid-morning, and p.m.) were within-subjects repeated measures, and group (EIFC, RFC, and CC) was the between-subjects factor. A significant effect was obtained for time of day, $F [2, 23] = 46.60, p < .001$, indicating decrease in cortisol from wakeup to bedtime across all groups and assessment intervals. No other main effects or interaction effects were found.

Given the multitude and magnitude of risks faced by maltreated preschoolers in the foster care system, and the growing numbers of youth in these circumstances, the need for empirically tested early intervention programs specifically designed for this population is evident. The research described here may be considered a first step in the development of such an intervention. What remains are several critical stages of research. First, it will be necessary to conduct a randomized efficacy trial in which the impact of the intervention under ideal circumstances can be evaluated (such a trial is currently underway). If changes similar to those obtained in the previous study are observed, this may provide justification for a larger scale effectiveness trial, in which the emphasis becomes demonstrating that the impact of the intervention is not lost in the dissemination of the approach to community settings. Only after these steps have been successfully undertaken will it be appropriate to begin emphasizing the incorporation of this approach into public policy discussions. And, only after public policy changes have been implemented based on empirically tested intervention methods can we hope to see a reduction in the risks faced by very young children in foster care.

Future directions. Empirical work to evaluate the effectiveness of MTFC programs at OSLC will continue. As new populations are identified can potentially benefit from this approach, the model will be adapted and randomized control trials will be conducted comparing MTFC to treatment as usual. It is only through this process that valid conclusions about the limits and effectiveness of this approach may be drawn. In addition, efforts are currently under way at OSLC to disseminate the MTFC model to community agencies. These efforts have two foci. First, agencies with the capability to implement their own treatment foster care programs and agencies that are already operating treatment foster care programs are being trained in the use of OSLC intervention components. Until recently, this particular approach to dissemination happened when OSLC was approached by outside agencies. However, in 1997, the University of Colorado Center for the Study and Prevention of Violence in collaboration with the Office of Juvenile Justice and Delinquency Prevention selected OSLC MTFC program as one of 10 model programs. Selection as one of the Blueprints for Violence Prevention has created an external process for dissemination in which we are now engaged. Another approach to dissemination involves incorporating aspects of the MTFC model into existing child welfare systems responsible for providing conventional foster care.

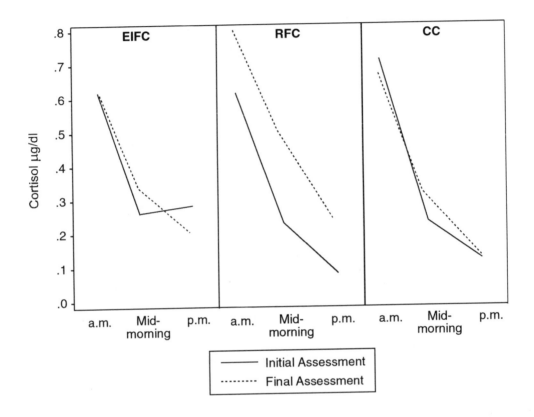

Figure 10.3. Circadian cortisol release patterns: Initial and final assessments.

As with the in-house programs at OSLC, the ultimate goal of these dissemination efforts is to demonstrate their efficacy through empirical study. Implementing MTFC program components in community settings and conducting high-quality research in these settings is a process that has been termed going to scale. Going to scale presents an entirely new set of challenges that we expect will keep us occupied for the next two decades at OSLC.

11

Preventive Efforts During the Elementary School Years: The Linking the Interests of Families and Teachers (LIFT) Project

John B. Reid and J. Mark Eddy

By the early 1980s, it was clear to us that our outpatient parent-training programs could help many families decrease and manage the antisocial behaviors of their children. However, we had concluded that continuing to focus our professional efforts on the development of such services was not going to result in a significant change in the prevalence of child antisocial behavior, even within our own community. While a few high-rate offenders commit most crimes, treating these youth required an investment of professional time and effort that was quite exhausting and expensive. Even when we were able to make an impact on the behaviors of these youth, we often felt that a more intensive intervention was needed if such an impact was to generalize over time and across settings (Bank, Marlowe, Reid, Patterson, & Weinrott, 1991). While we had spent almost 20 years attacking the problem of antisocial behavior from a clinical front and gained much ground, new information and strategies were needed if we were going to make further headway.

It was at this point that the clinician researchers working at our center began to form interrelated working groups that specialized in the investigation of a particular facet of the problem of child antisocial behavior. Two OSLC working groups, one led by Jerry Patterson and one by Beverly Fagot, launched longitudinal studies designed to map out the life course development of antisocial behavior in the hopes that such knowledge would ultimately improve our therapeutic strategies. Another group, led by Patti Chamberlain, began to develop the intensive treatment environments that we felt our outpatient programs failed to provide, using an existing service system (e.g., foster care) as the primary mode of service delivery. Several other groups, led by Tom Dishion, by Marion Forgatch, and by John Reid, initiated the design of a variety of programs to help children, parents, and teachers create and maintain environments hypothesized to *prevent the initiation* of child antisocial behaviors. In this chapter, we discuss the work of the Reid group. We begin with an overview of the broader historical context within which our thinking about prevention began, and then describe our prevention research with elementary school children considered at risk for the development of severe child antisocial behaviors.

Historical Context

We certainly were not the first to recognize that clinical treatment was an unlikely candidate to decrease the prevalence of a societal problem like delinquency. In summarizing intervention work targeting physical health, Dubos (1959) wrote "No major disease in the history of mankind has been conquered by therapists and rehabilitative modes alone, but ultimately through prevention." For a variety of reasons, delinquency affirmed this statement: The shortage of therapists trained in effective clinical techniques, the difficulty in treating the problem even if a therapist is trained, and the relatively high population prevalence of youth displaying delinquent behaviors all mitigated against a clinical solution. Further, even if a large number of therapists could be adequately trained and their work supported, the absolute number of therapists in the field seemed insufficient to deal with the current numbers of existing delinquent youth, let alone the new youth who began to offend each year (see Albee, 1959; Albee, 1990; Albee & Gullota, 1997). Focusing our efforts on developing preventive strategies seemed like a logical next step.

While steps toward prevention had been taken many times during the previous centuries by a variety of groups, such work rarely had been guided by the scientific method. In the United States, the notion that delinquency needed to be *prevented* was popularized as far back as the early 1800s (see Eddy & Swanson-Gribskov, 1997), but not until the 1920s did prevention begin to mean something other than incarceration or clinical treatment. Preventive efforts over the next several decades were unimpressive, inconclusive, or simply failed to impact delinquency. It was not until the 1960s that the notion of prevention in terms of the specific problem of delinquency, as well as mental health in general, began to gain more widespread acceptance. During the Kennedy administration, federal funding was made available not only for large-scale delinquency prevention efforts but also for community mental health centers, whose mission was to include the prevention of mental health problems (Mrazek & Haggerty, 1994). This funding provided for the initiation of a variety of services, but it did not lead to gains in scientific knowledge about the problem or to sustained, effective preventive efforts. However, it did mark the beginning of the modern prevention movement in regards to mental health problems within the United States (Albee & Gullotta, 1997).

Prevention science began to coalesce during the 1970s with the establishment of field building experiences such as the annual Vermont Conference on the Primary Prevention of Psychopathology. Growth was accelerated through the work of President Carter's Commission on Mental Health, which recommended the establishment of a Center for Prevention within the National Institute of Mental Health (NIMH). Within a few years, a coordinator of Disease Prevention and Health Promotion was established at the National Institutes of Health, and research branches were created at the NIMH, the National Institute on Drug Abuse (NIDA), and the National Institute on Alcohol Abuse and Alcoholism. Early on in this same period, Congress also funded the Office of Juvenile Justice and Delinquency Prevention, a move that emphasized the importance of ongoing preventive efforts in the area of child antisocial behavior.

Since OSLC is a research institute that is supported solely by grants, the development of an institutionalized prevention presence within these scientific funding agencies presented us with a new set of opportunities to enter the field. Our first prevention grant was submitted to NIDA and targeted adolescents at high risk for substance use and abuse. The grant was funded in the late 1980s, with Dishion as principal investigator. Both parent and peer group interventions were employed in an attempt to prevent the onset of substance-related problems (see chapter 13). Our second prevention grant, proposing the establishment of a prevention intervention research center at OSLC, was submitted to NIMH. This grant was funded in 1990, with Reid as principal investigator. The major research activities of this first center grant were focused on one endeavor, the Linking the Interests of Families and Teachers (LIFT) project. The LIFT was a randomized clinical trial investigating the impact of parent training and peer social skills and problem-solving interventions on the development of Oppositional Defiant Disorder and Conduct Disorder in elementary school children and middle school youth. In the remainder of this chapter, we will discuss the rationale for our preventive approach, describe the LIFT intervention, and detail trial outcomes to date.

Rationale

As described in the early chapters in this book, we hypothesize that antisocial behaviors are initiated, maintained, and diversified through the social interactions of a child with his or her environment (Patterson, Reid, & Dishion, 1992; Reid, 1993). Once child antisocial behavior problems have begun (e.g., in the home), each new setting a child enters (e.g., daycare, school, peer group activities) provides new players with whom to engage in a coercive manner. If coercion becomes a regular part of the child's interactions within that setting, the child's behavior problems receive a high rate of reinforcement, which in turn increases the likelihood that the child will continue to employ such interactive strategies. The lengthier the time period over which a child displays antisocial behaviors, the more opportunities that child has to enter into coercive processes with diverse sets of individuals and the more complex the network of reinforcement for those behaviors becomes. The longer this process continues, the more difficult it is to create an effective remedy. Thus, the earlier an intervention occurs in the development of child antisocial behavior, the less complex the reinforcement system for those behaviors, and the more likely the behaviors can be changed.

From this standpoint, we aimed to create a preventive intervention program that targeted social interactional processes related to child antisocial behavior as early as possible in the life of a child and family. Not only are such processes at the core of our developmental model, but also numerous studies have shown that they are malleable antecedents to later conduct problems, and thus reasonable targets for intervention. However, we were committed to the idea that for our work to inform delinquency prevention efforts under *real world* conditions, we also had to construct an intervention that not only would be bounded by real world constraints but also would take advantage of the situations created by those constraints. Thus, we decided that our preventive intervention should (1) utilize an existing and widespread system of care that had maximal outreach within the child population at the earliest possible age, (2) have the potential to be conducted by staff with similar training to those already working within that system, and (3) operate on relatively small budget, since at that time, most systems of care had been cutting rather than expanding their budgets.

While we could conceive of a number of interventions that would meet the later two criteria when operated within a variety of different systems, there is only one existing system of care with widespread contact with young children in the United States: The public elementary school system. In our state, for example, 94% of all children between age 6 and 12 years attended a public school in each of the past 10 years. This proportion is high relative to some states, but regardless, there simply is no other system of care in any state that serves as large a proportion of children in the United States as the public schools. Besides being the only place that brings together the key players in the life of a child on a day-to-day basis, the public elementary school provides a variety of structured and relatively unstructured circumstances within which to intervene. Further, the school provides a familiar physical space for child, teacher, and parent meetings, putting each of these individuals on home turf rather than in our clinic. Finally, the school provides a context within which monitoring and assessment are standard procedures, and thus some of the fundamental activities of research are already a part of the existing system.

The earliest age that children are required to attend public elementary school in Oregon is 7 years, which roughly translates to the first or second grade. Interestingly, it is around this age in a child's life that the behavioral constellation underlying oppositional, conduct, and antisocial personality disorders are becoming more firmly established, probably in large part because of the increasing number of social situations in which the child engages in each day (see Patterson, Reid, & Dishion, 1992). Further, largely because of school attendance, it is also at this point when parent's direct involvement in the child's interaction with others tends to rather abruptly and significantly diminish. Transition points such as this appear to be times of serious risk and significant opportunity in the life course trajectory of a child (e.g., Patterson & Capaldi, 1991; Felner, Farber, & Primavera, 1983; Felner, Primavera, & Cauce, 1981), and as such, may be crucial times for preventive interventions. Clearly, the advantages of using the elementary school as the setting for a delinquency prevention program are many.

Once the elementary school was chosen as the setting of intervention and the first grade as the point of intervention, a key decision was whether to deliver a prevention program to an entire first grade population of children (e.g., a *universal* strategy; see Mrazek & Haggerty, 1994) or to only a subset of *at risk* or *clinical* children within that population (e.g., respectively, a *selected* or an *indicated* strategy). Certainly, the various prevention program strategies are not necessarily *either/or* propositions (see chapter 13 for an example of a combined universal/selected/ indicated strategy). However, we chose a universal strategy alone for three reasons.

On the theoretical side, we hypothesize that the driving force in a child's conduct problems are the reinforcement processes that occur in his or her day-to-day relationships. It is our position that antisocial behavior develops as an interaction between the child's antisocial behavior and the reactions of those with whom he or she interacts on a daily basis. Therefore, within our model, it is the *interaction* between the child and the social environments that is always the target of intervention. In a classroom or on the playground, every child and adult is involved in the development or non-development of each child's coercive behavior. The bystanders who tolerate or even encourage bullying or teasing are helping to further develop the bully's pattern. If in fact all children and adults are involved in the process, then universal interventions make sense as the foundation for attempts to prevent serious antisocial behavior. Since children spend most of their time with parents and siblings and teachers and peers, an intervention program based on our model must target the modification of these relationships. The most convenient way to access a child's universe of teacher and peer relationships is to work directly in the school and home settings with all children.

On the practical side, the present imprecision in the field of predicting exactly which children will commit antisocial behaviors as adolescents or adults is a powerful argument against the use of a selective screening strategy and a linked selective intervention as an initial step in prevention. This is particularly the case in the schools, given the reluctance of teachers to label young children as antisocial without powerful evidence and a good treatment alternative. We believe that a well-conceived universal intervention provides at least two valuable components. First it provides a mechanism for correcting theoretically important risk factors in developmental environments. Second, and just as important, it provides a universal assessment. Youngsters who don't respond to the universal intervention are automatically identified for selective or indicated interventions. Taking this approach forward leads to a fully integrated intervention strategy (Brown, 1997) in which universal, selected, and indicated interventions are interwoven. Importantly, all children in a given school or classroom would participate, with intervention activities an integral part of the curriculum.

The first step in the development of such an integrated approach to prevention is to design and evaluate the universal component. The universal component must be relatively non-invasive and affordable. In terms of effectiveness, it should result in the reductions of the proximal risk factors or antecedents that are targeted. In addition, and contrary to clinical interventions, a universal intervention is designed to have variation in impact. That is, the effect on individual children should be closely related to the pre-intervention status on the targeted risk or antecedent variables. For example, an intervention designed to reduce aggression on the playground should ideally have the greatest dampening effect on the most aggressive children, and no dampening effects (or maybe even a slight elevation effect) on the assertive behaviors of the shyest children.

On the scientific side, a universal strategy was highly appealing because it afforded the opportunity to examine several important questions. First, the body of work that was available on the *prevention* of antisocial behavior when we began to develop our preventive strategy provided little information on the relationship between pre-intervention levels of antisocial behavior and response to intervention. As noted above, variation in impact is a necessary feature of universal interventions. By conducting a universal intervention within an unselected population, we would be able to examine variations in impact across our primary constructs of interest, unfettered by the difficulties that restriction in range on key variables can introduce. Second, since we planned to examine whatever strategy we chose within the context of a randomized trial (e.g., participants randomly assigned to an intervention or control group), the control group in an unselected (e.g., universal) randomized design could serve as a replication and extension of the OSLC's Oregon Youth Study (OYS).

As discussed elsewhere, OYS participants (all boys) attended the fourth grade in public schools located in neighborhoods with higher than the local average delinquency rates in the early 1980s. In 1990, these same neighborhoods continued to have higher than average rates of youth arrest. By targeting schools in these same neighborhoods, by including boys and girls in the study, and by targeting fifth graders in addition to first graders, we not only could replicate and extend the OYS, but also target another group within the elementary school that was in the midst of a major transition (e.g., into middle school) and about which information on the impact of preventive interventions is sorely needed.

LIFT Preventive Intervention Components

Conducting simultaneous and integrated interventions in multiple settings, particularly within the school and the home, has been a principal feature of the clinical intervention work at OSLC since the early days (e.g., chapter 1 of this volume). The development of our own preventive intervention components was naturally informed by our own clinical work (e.g., Patterson, Reid, Jones, & Conger, 1975; Patterson, Chamberlain, & Reid, 1984; Reid & Kavanaugh; Forgatch & Toobert; Patterson & Dishion). It was also importantly influenced by the work of researchers such as Bob Wahler, Ed Seidman, LaRue Allen, Hill Walker, Bob Felner, Karen Bierman, John Coie, Carolyn Webster-Stratton, David Hawkins, Rico Catalano, John Lochman, Myrna Shure, and George Spivack. A huge debt is owed to Shep Kellam, who served as our mentor as we attempted to make the huge conceptual transition from treatment to prevention; from a narrow focus on a pre-post by group interaction to the articulation and measurement of variation in impacts. Reid also received an intensive post-doctoral training experience by serving on Initial Review Groups in the area of prevention since the mid 1980s. It was through discussions with experienced prevention scientists on these committees that our own prevention research program was developed and designed.

Our group at OSLC integrated all these sources of experience and expertise into our developmental models of coercive processes to develop low cost, brief preventive interventions that could be delivered by existing school personnel in three of the most significant settings in the life of an elementary school-aged child: the home, the classroom, and the playground. In the hopes of maximizing the overall impact of our intervention within a given domain, we designed the interventions to complement each other. Along these lines, collaboration within and between settings was strongly emphasized throughout the program. The name of the program itself, Linking the Interests of Families and Teachers (LIFT), was chosen to underscore the importance of such collaborative efforts.

Home Intervention

The home intervention targeted improvement in parental behaviors, specifically consistent and effective positive reinforcement, discipline, and monitoring skills. The curriculum was designed for delivery to a group of parents during 6 weekly 1.5 hour sessions. Groups were limited to 15 families, and all primary caregivers were invited to attend. To maximize participation, groups were offered on each weekday evening and one weekday afternoon, and free childcare was provided. To encourage the development of parent-to-parent friendships, parents were asked to attend the same time slot during each week. To increase parent familiarity with the school environment, meetings were held in neighborhood school classrooms. A variety of presentation and practice formats were used during each session, including brief lectures, video-taped illustrations, and role-plays. Readings and home practice activities were provided to reinforce and extend knowledge about the material presented in each session. If parents were unable to attend a group session, staff offered a home session during the same week. The content and general format of such sessions was the same as the group session. If such an in-person meeting was not possible, a packet of materials was delivered to the home that reviewed the content of the missed session. In addition, group leaders called parents each week to monitor progress on home practice assignments and to answer questions.

While the basic parenting skills presented in the LIFT first and fifth grade programs were the same, curriculum modifications were made to highlight the normative challenges faced by children during these transitional periods. Specifically, parents of first graders were taught coaching skills to assist children in the development of positive peer relationships, and parents of fifth graders were taught problem-solving skills helpful in dealing with the problems of adolescence. Throughout the 6-week program, the importance of parent-parent and parent-teacher communication and collaboration were emphasized. A group delivery format was used to encourage parent networking within a child's grade, and a phone and answering machine was installed in each intervention classroom to provide parents and teachers a non-threatening mode of communication. The phone/answering machine combination was dubbed the LIFT Line, and teachers were encouraged to put daily messages on the machine about homework and class activities. In addition, teachers sent home a weekly newsletter that summarized the content of the LIFT school program that week and offered suggestions for complementary parent-child activities.

Classroom Intervention

The classroom intervention targeted improvement in child prosocial behaviors with peers, including listening skills, emotion recognition and management skills, group cooperation skills, and problem-solving skills. Like the home curriculum, the classroom curriculum was designed for delivery within a group setting. Thirty-minute sessions were held as part of the regular school day twice a week for 10 weeks. Each session included a lecture by a LIFT instructor, group discussion time, and individual skill practice within a small and large group context. Session content was similar for first and fifth graders. However, content emphasis and group exercises were tailored to address normative issues faced by younger and older elementary school aged children. Further, fifth graders were taught study skills relevant to middle school level classes.

Playground Intervention

The playground intervention targeted child positive and aversive behaviors within the context of a regular school recess period. The intervention, a version of the Good Behavior Game (GBG, Barrish, Saunders, & Wolfe, 1969; Dolan et al., 1993), was conducted immediately following each of the 20 classroom sessions. Each classroom was broken down into several small groups of four to five students each. During the classroom intervention, each group was asked to sit and participate in activities together during the classroom sessions. During the regular recess period, group members could earn points toward a classroom and a group reward through the display of appropriate behavior (e.g., sharing, cooperating) and the inhibition of aversive behavior (e.g., hitting, pushing). LIFT instructors and teachers with regular school playground duties who actively roamed the playground throughout recess distributed points. Appropriate behaviors were acknowledged and rewarded by giving children an armband each time they were observed behaving positively. Aversive behaviors were tracked by giving children a check on a class chart each time they were observed behaving negatively. At the end of recess, armbands were collected in a class jar. When the jar was full, the entire class earned a reward. Group rewards were given on a daily basis and were based on the degree to which all the members of a group did not display negative behaviors during recess. At the end of recess, the total number of negative behaviors observed by group members were subtracted from good faith points granted at the beginning of recess, and the members of groups that retained a preset number of points were given stickers. Each day, the total points retained by each group were charted, and when the group met a predetermined goal, each individual in the group was allowed to select a prize.

Randomized Trial

The efficacy of the LIFT preventive intervention is being investigated in a randomized clinical trial that began in 1991. Details and immediate outcomes of the study are available in Reid, Eddy, Fetrow, and Stoolmiller (1999) and Stoolmiller, Eddy, & Reid (2000), and initial follow-up reports are provided in Eddy, Reid, and Fetrow (2000) and Eddy, Reid, Fetrow, and Stoolmiller (2002). The immediate outcomes of key interest were threefold: parent limit setting in the home, child behavior on the playground, and child social skills in the classroom. We hypothesized that the LIFT intervention package should produce immediate and observable impacts on these behaviors within families exhibiting moderate, but not severe, levels of problems in each of these areas. As discussed at the beginning of this chapter, in our clinical work, we have found that intensive long-term interventions are usually required when antisocial behavior problems are severe, and thus we did not expect a 10-week intervention package to have much of an impact with this segment of the population. The long-term outcome of key interest was a reduction in the prevalence of conduct disorder and related behavior problems (e.g., early substance use) in the targeted population. We reasoned that while we might not be able to decrease the levels of antisocial behavior for more severe problem children, decreasing the levels of the initial outcomes should be related to a delay in the onset of more severe problem behaviors, which in turn should decrease the probability that moderate problem level children would be involved in chronic and serious delinquency during adolescence.

Design

Following our previous comments, in order to map on the LIFT control group to the OYS, only public elementary schools located in high juvenile crime neighborhoods within Eugene-Springfield were eligible to participate. A high juvenile crime neighborhood was defined as an elementary school catchment area that had a higher than average number of households with at least one police contact due to juvenile misbehavior. During each of 3 years of the program phase of the study, two schools from the pool of schools in at risk catchment areas were randomly chosen as prevention program schools, two as control schools (e.g., no prevention program), and two as alternatives should one of the assigned schools decline to participate. A school was also randomly selected as either a first or a fifth grade school. All students and their families within the chosen grade at each of the 12 schools were invited to participate in the study. Eighty-five percent agreed to participate fully in the study, and the final sample comprised 671 students (51% female) and their families. Similar to the demographic composition of the neighborhoods within which these schools were located, participants tended to be White and to be in the lower-to middle-socioeconomic classes.

To measure the success or failure of the prevention program, participants were assessed in the fall of their first or fifth grade year, the intervention was conducted in assigned schools during the winter, and participants were assessed again in the spring. In subsequent years, assessments were conducted during the middle of the academic year. During each assessment period, children, parents, and teachers were interviewed and completed a variety of paper and pencil questionnaires, school and court records were collected, and children and families were directly observed in a variety of situations. At various times, observations were conducted within the classroom, on the playground, and during parent and child discussions of family problems.

Implementation of the LIFT Intervention Program

Intervention fidelity (e.g., was the program delivered as planned?), program utilization (e.g., did families participate?), and participant satisfaction (e.g., were participants pleased with the services received?) were high, and drop out from the study was very low. In terms of fidelity, independent observers on the actual content of prevention program sessions rated parent group leaders. In terms of fidelity, on average, 96% of the planned content was delivered within any given session. In terms of utilization, 93% of families received all parent training materials in some manner, either through the planned group sessions, or through home visits or receiving written materials and videotapes in the mail. In terms of satisfaction, 94% of families reported that they would recommend LIFT to other parents, and 79% reported that the program was either "quite helpful" or "very helpful". Complementing these figures, drop out from the prevention program was quite low (8%), due in part to the multiple modes of service delivery (e.g., individual sessions, phone call sessions, mailings of all materials) that were used to provide materials to parents who did not attend group meetings.

As indicated by the high degree of implementation, school personnel were highly involved in both the delivery and the evaluation of the program. We had no significant problem in getting cooperation from the participating schools in the randomized design. On the advice of Shep Kellam, we made the argument that the funds for the intervention were contingent on having a control group, and that the fairest way to decide which schools got the LIFT program was by chance. We assembled the school principals and had them draw numbers out of a hat. The drawing afforded an additional opportunity to discuss the advantages of a randomized design and to emphasize the importance of the project and the importance of careful evaluation. Giving the control schools $2,000 each in unrestricted funds was a powerful incentive, particularly since school funding was extremely tight in our community in the early 1990s.

Outcomes of the LIFT Trial to Date

The evaluation of a prevention trial differs in important ways from the evaluation of a clinical (or indicated) trial. In the latter, participants are selected who already demonstrate a serious or clinical level of problem or disorder. The analysis of outcome involves assessment of the main effect of the intervention on the disorder (e.g., some comparison of the pre-to post- intervention reductions in symptoms or arrest rates for the intervention and control groups). In a prevention study, the main focus is on individuals who may or may not be at risk, but who do not demonstrate the problem or disorder at the time of intervention. If one is evaluating a true population based, universal prevention trial aimed at conduct disorder, the intervention and control groups will include the whole range on risk or antecedent variables that we have identified in our developmental models. The sample will also demonstrate a distribution of conduct problems. At its simplest level, the analysis of impacts then will involve an assessment of the amount and variation of immediate impacts on the hypothesized antecedents that were targeted in the intervention. Given that beneficial immediate effects on key antecedents are demonstrated, one has grounds to move to the next step: To investigate if the intervention has an impact on the incidence of the problem or disorder over time. In our case, the ultimate question is thus: Do fewer individuals in the intervention group go on to develop serious patterns of delinquency?

Immediate Impacts

For children entering a classroom with antisocial behavior problems, there is substantial risk that coercive processes that were initially developed in interactions with parents and siblings in the home setting will continue to develop through coercive interactions with teachers and classmates in classrooms and playgrounds. These simultaneous processes are then hypothesized to underlie the development of more serious conduct problems and later delinquency. Thus, the development of coercive interactions with parents, peers, and teachers were the proximal targets of the LIFT intervention because they put youngsters at serious risk, not only for ever increasing levels of conduct problems within these critical developmental settings, but also for the outcomes of these problems, including rejection by peers and teachers, school failure, and further deterioration of the parent-child relationship. Given this theoretical frame, the universal intervention evaluated in this study intentionally targeted antecedents and social participants in three social domains: the family, the classroom, and the playground. Program components were designed to alter the behaviors and perceptions of all participating students, parents, and teachers. Thus, the most commonly used reporting agents in studies such as this (e.g., the child, the parents, the teachers, and the peers) were not only aware of the intervention status of a child, they were the targets of the intervention itself. To counter this problem, in designing the study, we intended to use unbiased observational strategies in each of the three social domains. We were successful in conducting pre- and post-intervention observational assessments on the playground to measure physically aggressive behavior among the children, and in the laboratory to measure mother aversive verbal behavior during mother-child interactions. However, due to the concerns of a few teachers that we might also be evaluating their behavior, we were unable to observe social interactions within the classroom.

Thus, although our assessments of immediate impacts were unbiased for peer interactions on the playground and for parent-child interactions, our assessments of social interactions in the classroom (e.g., teacher report) were probably confounded to some extent with intervention status. We attempted to reduce this problem by comparing pre-intervention ratings by the teachers with ratings by new teachers in the year following intervention, but it is likely that some of these teachers were aware of intervention status.

Statistical significance. Given these various caveats, the immediate impact of the intervention was encouraging (see Reid et al., 1999; Stoolmiller et al., 2000). First, the intervention had immediate and significant effects on physical aggression among the students on the playground, and the magnitude of the effect varied as a function of pre-intervention level. That is, the children most aggressive prior to the intervention showed the largest benefits. Given that children who aggress against their peers are at high risk for rejection and subsequent association with antisocial peers, this is an important immediate impact.

Second, a similar pattern of effects was found with mother aversive behavior, with those mothers in the LIFT program exhibiting the highest pre-intervention levels of aversive behaviors showing the largest immediate reductions. It is hypothesized that the immediate impacts in maternal discipline style will lead to longer term impacts on the mothers' ability to continue to socialize and influence their children.

Third, the teacher results were promising. Teacher rating data indicated a significant impact of the program on children's behavior in the classroom, which together with the gains at home and on the playground, should reduce the risk for future conduct problems for the youngsters participating in the LIFT intervention. In summary, the current analyses do indicate significant immediate impacts for each antecedent targeted in the intervention within most of the important subgroups in the study; importantly, the effects were observed for both first and fifth grade participants, indicating potential for the intervention strategy across the elementary school years.

Effect size. As detailed in Reid et al. (1999), effect sizes ranged from small to large in magnitude. The strongest effects were for the most distressed children and mothers as indexed by the pre-intervention score. For example, the effect size for child aversive physical behavior was 0.60 for children who were two standard deviations above the mean on this variable before the intervention. Since we did not take into account measurement error in our analyses, this value is a conservative estimate of the true effect (see Stoolmiller et al., 2000, for estimates of LIFT effect sizes that do take measurement error into account).

Clinical significance. The immediate or proximal goal of this universal intervention was to impact important hypothesized mediators of later conduct problems and delinquency for the relatively small percentage of the youngsters who would be expected to develop significant problems. As such, it is difficult to make judgments about the ultimate clinical or practical significance of the immediate impacts in the three settings at this time. However, it is possible to give a reasonably concrete picture of the immediate impact that was objectively observed on the playground.

Before intervention, playground observations revealed that youngsters in the control and intervention schools averaged approximately 0.2 aversive physical behaviors per minute, or about six per 30 minutes of daily recess (see Reid et al., 1999). Following intervention, children in the experimental and control conditions averaged 4.8 and 6.6 aversive behaviors per recess day, respectively. Given that approximately 21 children were in each recess group, children have 30 minutes of recess a day, and there are about 40 recesses per academic quarter, then in the quarter following intervention, compared to children in the experimental group, youngsters in an average control classroom were potentially exposed to about 1,700 more physically aversive transactions on the playground. It should be noted that physical aversive behavior included trivial as well as more serious acrimonious episodes. However, the observed difference suggests a genuine effect on the level of negative peer interactions on the playground.

Long-Term Outcomes

To date, fifth-grade participants in the LIFT study are in middle school or early high school, and first-grade participants are in mid to late elementary school. Because the more severe antisocial outcomes of interest generally do not manifest themselves until the adolescent years, our initial outcome analyses have focused on different variables for the two age groups.

For first graders, we have examined changes due to the intervention in teacher-reported acting out behaviors at school. This particular variable was chosen because relative to parent ratings, teacher impressions of problem behavior in elementary school are highly related to later serious antisocial behavior (Patterson et al., 1992). Early attention deficit disordered behaviors (e.g., hyperactivity, inattention, impulsivity) seem to be particularly salient in accelerating the onset of serious conduct problems (see Loeber & Lahey, 1997), probably because of the challenges that such children present to the adults trying to manage their behaviors. Using Longitudinal Growth Modeling, we found positive outcomes for LIFT participants in terms of teacher perceptions of child behavior: children assigned to the LIFT group were less likely than control group participants to show an increase in the severity of attention deficit symptoms following the intervention (see Figure 11.1).

For fifth graders, we have examined the effect of the intervention on delaying police arrest, on delaying extensive substance use, and on delaying association with deviant peers (see Eddy et al., 2000, and Eddy et al., 2002). As discussed throughout this book, early arrest (before age 14 years) is highly predictive of chronic and serious delinquency just as engaging in other high risk behaviors early in life is related to chronic problems later on. For example, it is clear that although many

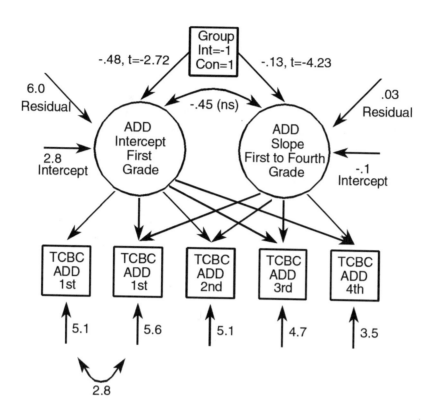

Figure 11.1. Comparative post-intervention growth rates of attention deficit symptoms.

youth in at risk neighborhoods will engage in patterned drinking at some point in adolescence, it is early onset that is predictive of serious alcohol abuse during adulthood. The most powerful and proximal factor related to both arrests and patterned drinking during early adolescence is associating with peers who also engage in such activities.

Thus, using event history analysis, we examined differences in LIFT and control participants in terms of the time to (1) first report by police of an arrest, (2) first report by teachers of spending time with various kinds of deviant peers, and (3) first report by the youth of using a variety of substances (see Eddy et al., 2000; Eddy et al., 2002). Participants who had experienced these events prior to the beginning of the study were excluded from the analyses. We did find differences between the two groups, favoring the LIFT intervention group, in terms of patterned alcohol use and affiliating with misbehaving peers. Youth in the LIFT group also appeared to be less likely to have tried marijuana, although this trend was not statistically significant. Finally, youth in LIFT were significantly less likely than youth in the control group to be arrested in the 30 months period following the completion of the program. Interestingly, these effects were found for children regardless of how problematic their behavior was prior to the start of the intervention: Even children who were behaving in more antisocial ways in the fall prior to the program benefited.

Strength of the effect. Effect sizes for the first and the fifth grade findings are quite strong. For first graders, the effect size for change in teacher rated attention deficit behaviors was 1.5 within group standard deviations, considered very large by conventional social science standards (Cohen, 1991). For fifth graders, the largest effect size was for initiating affiliation with misbehaving peers: children in the control group were 2.2 times more likely to initiate this behavior than children in the prevention program group (see Eddy et al., 2002). The likelihood for boys in the control group initiating affiliation with smoking and with stealing/vandalizing peers was 1.9 and 1.8 times higher than for boys in the prevention program group. The probability for children in the control group initiating patterned alcohol, marijuana, and tobacco use were respectively 1.8, 1.5, and 1.1 times higher than children in the prevention program group. Finally, the probability of a first arrest in the control group was 2.4 times higher than in the LIFT group. Thus, to date there are several important distal impacts of the LIFT prevention program for both first and the fifth grade participants.

Conclusion

To date, the results of our randomized trial of the LIFT universal intervention have been encouraging and stimulating. Most of our intervention work, prior to the Adolescent Transitions Study (see chapter 13) and this LIFT study, was characterized by intensive, clinical level, time-unlimited interventions, with parents of extremely aggressive and oppositional children and delinquent adolescents. The main thrust of these earlier interventions was to build up the skills of badly demoralized parents who had lost the ability to socialize and mentor their youngsters. We tried not only to help parents in face-to-face socialization at home, but to help them monitor, mentor, and structure up the youngsters' learning environments at school and in the peer group. We did whatever it took to transform the parent child relationship—and it often took a great deal of energy and the coordinated efforts of highly trained clinicians (see Bank et al., 1990, for a good example).

The LIFT intervention was a radical departure from this intense approach, and we felt it was quite risky. Rather than interrupting serious antisocial behaviors that were well developed, we thought we had learned enough from our developmental studies, reviewed in the first half of this volume, to identify the early antecedents and to target them with precise interventions in multiple settings. Rather than rely totally on the parent to exert influence on the reinforcing contingencies in multiple social domains, we tried to change them directly by working with peers and teachers. If one really believes, as we do, that aggressive behavior develops through the coercive transactions that occur across social settings, then a universal multi-setting intervention is essential. The task of intervention is to change the way people respond to coercive behavior. For example, if one wants to change a bully, one must stop bystanders from egging him/her on. The LIFT intervention, then, was an attempt to change the early trajectory of antisocial behavior by brief interventions in several settings, rather than by a huge, and late, intervention in one setting.

The magnitude of the proximal effects on targeted antecedents was quite surprising to us. In fact, we hypothesized that the universal intervention would have significant impact only on the children at moderate risk. We felt that the children who demonstrated the highest levels of conflict with parents, teachers, and peers would not respond to anything but an intense clinical intervention. The fact that the children most at risk showed the greatest response to intervention was truly surprising at first. However, as demonstrated by the large effects on aggressive behavior on the playground, it may be that a modest intervention, focused carefully on the social reinforcement and exchange system of a social learning environment, can have major effects on selected risk factors. The fact that we were able to get consistent and positive participation by nearly every child, parent, and teacher in target classrooms may have been an important key to changing normative behavior in the three key social domains.

From our own experience in this trial, and from the feedback of teachers and parents who participated, in future studies, we would expand the LIFT intervention in a variety of ways. First, we would offer the intervention to all grades and classrooms in elementary schools, so that parents, teachers, and children got a refresher course each year in the parent and social skills training. Second, we would study the mobility patterns of families in the target schools and offer the intervention to clusters of schools, through which children tend to migrate. Although lower-income families in many areas tend to move frequently, they often don't move far. For example, in this trial, we started with students in 12 schools. Within 3 years, these same students were in over 100 different schools, but most were local, and almost all were in Oregon. In order to have any chance of providing a consistent and programmatic preventive intervention over the elementary school years, it would have to be implemented within a geographic region that encompassed the highest density migration routes. Third, we would conduct the playground intervention all year long, and develop similar interventions for other unstructured settings that provide high risks for engaging in, and being exposed to, child aggressive behavior. Some initial ideas in this regard include increased monitoring and point incentive programs for children who arrive early for school, as well as for behavior in the school cafeterias, hallways, and on school buses. Lines of students, which occur at multiple points before, during, and after the school day, are also prime spots for problems. For example, at school bus stops, parents could rotate responsibilities for monitoring and limiting aggressive interactions.

There is still a great deal of work to be done in evaluating the long-term impacts of the LIFT trial on the development of conduct problems and delinquency. We have presented evidence to indicate that the intervention program offered at fifth grade delays the onset of serious mileposts such as first arrest, initiation of substance use, affiliation with high-risk peers. The intervention offered at first grade reduced the incidence of attention deficit problems, a factor hypothesized to increase the risk for early conduct disorder. Although it is tempting to conclude that LIFT initiated reductions in problem interactions with peers, teachers, and parents were the causal ingredients involved in delaying onset of the various outcome behaviors, we cannot make that leap until we use the longitudinal data to test true mediational models. Thus, we are continuing to collect data on LIFT participants to find out if the immediate impacts of the program reduce the incidence of chronic and serious problems later in life.

12

Extending and Testing the Social Interaction Learning Model with Divorce Samples

Marion S. Forgatch and David S. DeGarmo

This chapter describes an extension of the social interaction learning (SIL) model to divorce. The basic SIL hypothesis is that disrupted parenting practices mediate relationships between child adjustment and such family background contexts as divorce. The Oregon Divorce Study (ODS) tested the SIL model with two independent samples. In phase I (ODS-I), we specified divorce models using a passive longitudinal design with a sample of 197 recently separated single mothers with sons ages 5 through 12. The goal was to identify processes within divorcing families that facilitated and impeded parent functioning and child adjustment. In the second phase of the study (ODS-II), an intervention based on the ODS-I models was designed and tested. We used random assignment to experimental or no-intervention control conditions to test the theoretical model with a new sample of 238 single mothers and their sons ages 6 through 10. The findings, which are summarized in this chapter, supported the SIL model.

Divorce and repartnering are common events in the United States, with at least 50% of modern marriages projected to terminate in separation and/or divorce (Bumpass, 1984). Divorced families repartner about 75% of the time, and the risk of another schism is greater than for first-time marriages (Bumpass, 1984; Bumpass & Sweet, 1989; Bumpass, Sweet, & Martin, 1990). Thus, divorce samples are characterized by multiple family structure changes. These transitions are associated with many background factors that are predictors of disrupted parenting practices and adjustment problems for parents and youngsters. The SIL model specifies parenting practices to be more proximal than background contexts for children's adjustment. The variability in parenting effectiveness and parent and child adjustment outcomes makes divorce samples ideal for studying processes and mechanisms of adjustment.

Maternal parenting practices tend to become disrupted with family structure transitions. Compared to mothers in two-biological parent (nuclear) families, mothers rearing their children on their own or in repartnered families initiate more conflict bouts with their children, attain less effective interpersonal problem-solving outcomes, and provide children with less monitoring, control, warmth, and positive involvement (Anderson, Lindner, & Bennion, 1992; Bray & Berger, 1993; Brody,

Neubaum & Forehand, 1988; Capaldi & Patterson, 1991; DeGarmo & Forgatch, 1999; Hetherington, 1993; Hetherington & Clingempeel, 1992; Peterson & Zill, 1986; Vuchinich, Vuchinich, & Wood, 1993). Thus, divorce and its sequelae are associated with disturbances in the putative mediators for child adjustment.

Youngsters in divorced and repartnered families display more problems than their counterparts in nuclear families. The problems include academic problems, disrupted peer relations, emotional distress, and antisocial behavior (Bray & Berger, 1993; Cherlin et al., 1991; Furstenberg & Teitler, 1994; Hetherington & Clingempeel, 1992; Simmons, Burgeson, Carlton-Ford & Blyth, 1987; Zill, Morrison, & Coiro, 1993). Divorce and repartnering per se, however, do not appear to cause the children's problems because there is considerable variability in adjustment. Most children from divorced families develop normally (Amato & Keith, 1991; Anderson, Greene, Nelson, & Wolchik, in press-b; Chase-Lansdale, Cherlin, & Kiernan, 1995; Hetherington, Cox, & Cox, 1985). Of those who display difficulty after divorce, a portion developed problems before their parents separated (Block, Block, & Gjerde, 1986; Cherlin et al., 1991). For other children, however, the difficulties appear to emerge after the separation (Amato, 1993; Shaw, Emery, & Tuer, 1993). This variability suggests that the mechanisms accounting for adjustment may lie in something more than divorce.

The Oregon Divorce Model

Our process model for understanding adjustment in divorced families is based on findings from the literature and from studies at OSLC. We conceptualize divorce as a comprehensive context that influences a dynamic interconnecting set of systems within the family. One subsystem shapes another, affecting future iterations within the larger system. Feedback processes operating between mother and child contribute to the long-term adjustment of both. The Oregon Divorce Model is displayed in Figure 12.1. On the left side of the figure, family process between mother and child is depicted shortly after separation. Moving toward the right side of the figure, changes over time are incorporated into the model.

We have differentiated the mother's function into domains as person and as parent. The person subsystem describes interconnections among maternal resources, stress, support, and adjustment. This aspect of the model reflects an expansion of the SIL model, emphasizing ways in which family and parental background factors promote and disrupt parental adjustment and parenting practices.

Mother as person. Divorce and its sequelae present many challenges to mothers, including significant reductions in resources, increases in stress, and disruptions in social support. Resources include the assets and deficits people bring with them through life transitions. For example, resources such as a good education and a well-established career can reduce the number and types of stressors mothers have to manage. Too much stress, absence of quality support, and/or the combination of the two can promote maternal adjustment problems, such as depression, irritability, and antisocial behavior. Adjustment problems tend to interfere with healthy adult relationships and further disrupt support. The bi-directional path between stress and support, which has been documented in the literature, delineates processes through which stress may activate support, which then can function to reduce stress and benefit adjustment. However, stress can amplify adjustment problems, such as irri-

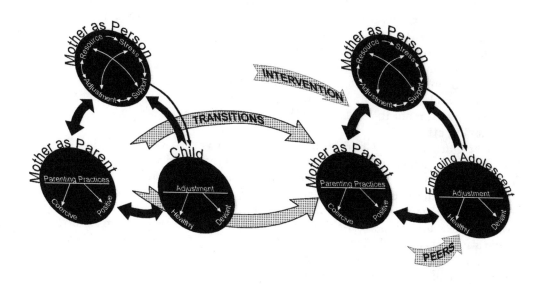

Figure 12.1.   Divorce Model.

tability and depression, and interfere with support processes. Thus, within the domain of mother as person, the interconnection among limited resources, extensive stress, and disrupted support can contribute to maternal adjustment problems and interfere with effective parenting.

Mother as parent. The SIL model specifies two main dimensions of parenting, coercive discipline and effective parenting practices. Coercive discipline is presumed to contribute to the development and maintenance of deviant child behavior. Effective parenting presumably contributes to healthy adjustment.

Coercive discipline functions at a microsocial level, often starting with innocuous but negative actions that escalate into conflict. When coercive interchanges are standard fare in a family, they become overlearned and generalize to other social settings. Families provide training in social interaction with practice at multiple levels (e.g., with siblings, parents, and parent-child). Three coercive patterns are particularly relevant to the SIL model: negative reciprocity, escalation, and negative reinforcement. Reciprocity takes place when one person responds in kind to another. Escalation develops from reciprocal aversive exchanges that increase in intensity (e.g., from shouting to humiliation, hitting, or another intense behavior). Negative reinforcement reflects the use of certain behaviors to escape or avoid aversive situations. An important example of negative reinforcement occurs in the course of conflict bouts that begin with a parental demand and are terminated with a child's aversive behavior. This negatively reinforces the child's use of coercion.

Five effective parenting practices have been specified in the SIL model as contributing to healthy child adjustment. Skill encouragement incorporates ways in which adults promote competencies using positive reinforcement contingent on prosocial behavior. Discipline involves the establishment of appropriate rules with

the application of mild sanctions for violating the rules with short, relatively immediate sanctions (e.g., time out, short work chores, privilege removal). Monitoring (also
called supervision) requires parents to keep track of their children in terms of the
following: where they are, whom they are with, what they are doing, the adults in
charge, and the transportation arrangements. Problem solving involves skills that
facilitate resolution of disagreements, negotiation of rules, and establishment of
agreements about positive consequences for following the rules (e.g., allowance, extra
privileges) and sanctions for violating the rules (e.g., work chores, privilege removal).
Positive involvement includes the many ways that parents provide their youngsters
with loving attention.

Child adjustment. Children are exposed to a variety of difficult family situations before, during, and after their parents separate. Our model specifies that the
effect of such background contexts on child adjustment is mediated by the quality
of parenting the youngsters receive. Child adjustment, in turn, has an impact on
mothers in their role as person and as parent. For example, our longitudinal data
from single mothers in ODS-I showed that child adjustment problems shortly after
separation contributed to increasing stress in the next 4 years for mothers. Higher
stress, in turn, contributed to reduced parenting effectiveness. Other data sets have
shown that the relationship between parenting and child behavior is bi-directional.
For example, coercive parenting has been shown to contribute to levels of child
coercive behavior, which in turn increased the likelihood of coercive parent behavior (Patterson, 1984).

A developmental model. With the passage of time comes change, and change
creates system-wide disturbances. In all families, there will be normative transitions (e.g., children's maturation into adolescence) as well as changes that are less
predictable (e.g., more family structure transitions). In the Divorce Model, we specify three influences in the developmental trajectory of the family: family structure
change, maturation into adolescence, and intervention. Family structure change
influences the entire system, although it is assumed to operate primarily within the
mother's world as person. Maturation into adolescence brings new social forces into
play (e.g., peer influences) and new demands on parenting, both of which affect the
adolescent's adjustment. Intervention can operate on any subsystem in the family
depending on the theoretical framework guiding the program. A preventive
intervention designed for divorced samples should be able to ameliorate existing
problems, reduce risk factors for future problems, and promote healthy development.

Family structure transitions influence the mothers' world as an adult. The gain
or loss of an intimate partner affects the quality and amount of support the mother
receives at home, with improvement or deterioration in her personal adjustment
and her parenting ability. For example, repartnering can benefit parenting practices
if the couple relationship is stable, healthy, and supportive of parenting (Anderson,
Greene, Hetherington, & Clingempeel, in press-a; Hetherington & Stanley-Hagan,
1999). However, multiple transitions are associated with diminished parenting
effectiveness, and this is presumed to account for increased problems in child adjustment at home and at school. If children have adjustment problems, the parenting
demands are more difficult, and this can prove stressful to the couple's relationship.
Problems between the couple tend to interfere with effective parenting, and the cycle
generating dysfunction continues. In the literature, findings are mixed concerning
the effect of couple discord on children; some studies report direct effects, others

mediated effects. Our model specifies that the path from marital discord to child adjustment problems be mediated by ineffective parenting. Currently, we are conducting an experimental test of that model with stepfamilies using a program that intervenes with both the marital relationship and parenting practices. In the coming years, the data from that study will be employed to shed light on that complex issue.

Normative transitions are introduced into the model as children grow into adolescents. Parents must adapt their child-rearing techniques to accommodate their youngster's changing needs. Parents of emerging adolescents must address many new questions. For example, in our society, we consider it reasonable to allow adolescents more independence. How much freedom is appropriate and under what conditions? How do we negotiate the rules that define adolescents' rights and responsibilities along with consequences for respecting or violating the rules? These issues should be influenced by how well the adolescent functions with independence. To complicate matters even more, adolescents spend increasing time with their peers, making peers commensurately more influential as socializing agents. Consequently parents must learn to evaluate peers and adapt accordingly their supervision of youngsters during their time with friends.

Intervention can influence the entire family system. If new skills are introduced within one subsystem, the larger system can benefit. An intervention can function as an experimental test of theory providing several conditions are met: (a) random assignment to experimental and control groups, (b) effective delivery of the intervention, (c) benefits to the experimental group relative to the control, and (d) demonstration that the putative mechanisms contributed to these benefits. The theoretical framework specifies where intervention should have the greatest impact. In our model, the putative mechanisms are parenting practices. Thus, we taught mothers effective parenting strategies and did not intervene with children. If the intervention produced benefits to parenting practices and these parenting effects produced commensurate positive effects for the children, then the theoretical model would be supported.

Correlational Support for the Model

The model shown in Figure 12.1 has considerable support in the literature. For example, we know that divorce leads to dramatic reductions in income, particularly for female-headed families (Gongla & Thompson, 1987; Weitzman, 1985, 1996). In national populations, per capita income declines average between 13% and 35% (Arendell, 1986; Cherlin, 1992; Peterson, 1996). Reduced income contributes to other stressful circumstances, such as changes in family living arrangements, education, and employment (DeGarmo & Forgatch, 1999; Forgatch, Patterson, & Ray, 1996; Lorenz et. al., 1997; Patterson & Forgatch, 1990.) Most divorcing families tend to return to pre-divorce levels of stress over time (Forgatch et. al., 1996; DeGarmo & Forgatch, 1997; Lorenz et al., 1997). However, families with lower incomes tend to experience more disruptive events, and if income remains low, stress remains high (Lorenz et. al., 1997).

Maternal stress contributes to emotional disturbances such as depression and irritability (Coyne & Downey, 1991; Coyne, Kessler, Tal, Turnbull, & Wortman, 1987;

Forgatch, et al., 1996; Patterson & Forgatch, 1990). If these affective disruptions become chronic, the quality of the mothers' support is likely to suffer (Belle, 1982; Downey & Feldman, 1996; Patterson & Forgatch, 1990; Simons & Johnson, 1996). In a series of studies with the data from ODS-I, we developed process models to describe ways in which stress and distressed affect interfered with the quality of relationships between divorced mothers and their support confidants. The data were based on observations of problem-solving discussions between the mothers and their confidants about the mothers' personal and parenting problems. Confidant and maternal characteristics predicted both the quality of support that confidants provided mothers and the quality of the problem-solving outcomes the dyads achieved (DeGarmo & Forgatch, 1997b; Forgatch & DeGarmo, 1997; Patterson & Forgatch, 1990). The ability to solve personal and parenting problems predicted better parenting practices, which in turn were associated with healthy child adjustment (Forgatch & DeGarmo, 1997).

The positive or disruptive processes that lead to levels of functioning in the mother's person domain can likewise operate in her relationships with her children (Forgatch & DeGarmo, 1997; Patterson & Forgatch, 1990; Simons & Johnson, 1996). In the parent domain, we have identified several facets of effective parenting: positive involvement, skill encouragement, problem solving, discipline, and monitoring (Forgatch et al., 1996; Patterson, 1982). Cross-sectional, longitudinal, and experimental studies have shown that these parenting practices contribute to children's adjustment outcomes (Dishion, Patterson, & Kavanagh, 1992; Forgatch, 1991; Forgatch et al., 1996; Kazdin, 1987; Patterson & Forgatch, 1995; Wolchik et al., 1993).

As described earlier, family structure transitions tend to co-occur with several background factors associated with disrupted parenting practices (Bank, Forgatch, Patterson & Fetrow, 1993; Capaldi & Patterson, 1991; Conger, Patterson, & Ge, 1995; Forgatch et al., 1996; Hetherington, Stanley-Hagan, & Anderson, 1989; Patterson & Forgatch, 1990; Simons, Beaman, Conger, & Chao, 1993). These background factors include stress, maternal depression, socioeconomic disadvantage, and antisocial parents. Data from several studies support mediation models in which disturbances in these contexts contribute to inept parenting practices, which in turn interfere with healthy adjustment for her children (Bank, Forgatch, Patterson, & Fetrow, 1993; Forgatch & DeGarmo, 1997; Forgatch & DeGarmo, 1997; Forgatch, Patterson, & Ray, 1996; Forgatch, Patterson, & Skinner, 1988; Simons & Johnson, 1996; Wolchik et al., 1993). Children's adjustment problems feed back into the mother's stress and parenting processes and the cycle proceeds (Forgatch et al., 1996). Thus, the family is embedded in a context of interlocking systems in which each subsystem can impede or promote healthy development.

Preventive Intervention as an Experimental Test

Correlational studies from passive longitudinal studies provide the basic research that guides the design of intervention programs by suggesting the mechanisms of adjustment (Forgatch & Knutson, in press). In ODS-I, coercive discipline and inept monitoring were associated with children's antisocial behavior (Bank, et al., 1993; Forgatch, 1991; Forgatch et. al., 1996; Forgatch & DeGarmo, 1997). Without an experimental manipulation, however, discipline and monitoring cannot be specified as causal mechanisms of the antisocial behavior. Tests of causal status can be achieved through randomized experimental designs in which one group receives an intervention that targets the putative mechanisms, while another group does not receive it. In this way the intervention, which is an experimental manipulation, provides a test of the theoretical model. In the example with discipline and monitoring as hypothesized mechanisms of antisocial behavior, parents in the experimental condition would be taught to reduce coercive discipline and increase monitoring, while the control parents continued without intervention. If differential changes were to emerge for the parenting practices (e.g., the experimental group improved or maintained levels while the control group worsened) and those benefits were to be associated with commensurate change in antisocial behavior, the theoretical model would be supported.

In selective prevention programs that target risk groups, the type of risk is a critical factor that directs the focus, sequence, and format of the intervention. Divorce is a risk factor for many aspects of adjustment for youngsters (e.g., academic failure, peer relationship problems, externalizing behavior, and internalizing problems). Presumably, in samples of divorcing families, there are arrays of children with varying levels of different problems. Some have one problem, some have several, some are problem free and about to develop one or more problems, and some are problem free and will remain so. This contrasts with clinical trials in which each child in the sample is screened to have substantial levels of a specific problem and individuals vary only in degree. Because of the homogeneity of clinical samples and the intensity of the treatment, greater effects can be achieved with smaller samples. Preventive interventions often target risk samples with heterogeneity in the topography and level of problems, and the interventions tend to be less intensive than in treatment programs. Thus, prevention trials often require substantially more power to achieve their effects, effect sizes for the distal variables are likely to be smaller than in clinical trials, and the intervention must operate on mechanisms that affect multiple outcomes.

Some prevention programs take a direct route to promote change; other programs target mediators of the more distal outcomes using an indirect approach to the intervention. For example in the prevention program conducted by Kellam and his associates (Dolan et al., 1993; Kellam, Rebok, Ialongo, & Mayer, 1994), children were trained directly in mastery learning and results were observed in their reading achievement. Other programs have been provided to multiple agents (parents, teachers, children) in multiple settings (classrooms, playgrounds) and the results observed through measures of child behavior in multiple domains (Reid & Eddy, 1997; Reid, Eddy, Fetrow, & Stoolmiller, 1999). The ODS-II program used an indirect approach in the intervention with a more explicit focus on testing the theoretical model. The program took place with the mothers, with no intervention with the children. Thus, changes in child adjustment could be more directly attributed to benefits to the mothers' parenting practices.

Testing the SIL Model in ODS-II

Based on correlational studies conducted in ODS-I and by other investigators, we designed an intervention program for recently separated mothers in ODS-II. The program was designed to teach parenting practices and other skills to promote healthy adjustment following marital separation. The primary hypotheses were: a) that the intervention would benefit parenting practices for mothers in the experimental group relative to those in the control group, b) that benefits to parenting practices would benefit child adjustment, c) that maternal adjustment would also benefit from the intervention program.

Participants

Two hundred thirty-eight recently separated single mothers and their sons were recruited through media advertisements, flyers distributed throughout the community, and divorce court records. In eligible families, mothers had been separated from their partner within the prior 3 to 24 months, resided with a biological son in grades one through three, and did not cohabit with a new partner. The sample was restricted to boys because they are more likely than girls to exhibit adverse effects of divorce as preadolescents (Guidubaldi & Perry, 1985; Hetherington, 1991; Shaw et al., 1993).

At baseline, mothers had been separated for an average of 9.2 months. Mothers' mean age was 34.8 years (*SD*=5.4; range 21.4 to 49.6); boys' mean age was 7.8 years (*SD*=.93; range 6.1 to 10.4). The racial/ethnic composition of the boys in the sample was 86% White, 1% African American, 2% Latino, 2% Native American, and 9% from other minority groups. This approximated the racial distribution in the community. The mean annual family income was $14,900, which was similar to that reported for other female-headed households with children in the county (i.e., $15,300; U. S. Department of Commerce, Bureau of Census, 1993). Seventy-six percent of the families were receiving public assistance. Families tended to be small, with 2.1 children on the average. Mothers were fairly well educated and working, although their jobs were within the lower ranges of occupational status.

Design and Intervention Procedures

Families were assigned randomly with approximately 2/3 to the experimental group (n =153) and 1/3 to the control group (n = 85). Mothers in the experimental group were invited to participate in the intervention; families in the control condition received no intervention.

The intervention consisted of a series of 14 parent group meetings held weekly in the early evening hours at OSLC. There were 13 parent groups, which ranged in size from 6 to 16 (M = 9.5). In addition to the group meetings, interventionists made mid-week telephone calls to encourage use and tailor procedures and to trouble-shoot problems with the weekly home practice assignments. Childcare and meals were provided during meetings for mothers and their youngsters, and transportation was available if needed.

The intervention program is fully described in the manual *Parenting through Change* (Forgatch, 1994). The manual contains information for group leaders and materials for mothers. For leaders, each session is detailed with agenda, objectives, rationales, procedures, exercises, role-plays, and group process suggestions. Parent materials include summaries of principles, home practice assignments, charts, and other necessary materials. The program includes a 30-minute videotape, *The Divorce*

Workout (Forgatch & Marquez, 1993), which shows three families using effective parenting practices to help their children adjust to the divorce transition. Sessions provided training in parenting practices (e.g., discipline, skill encouragement, monitoring, problem solving) and other issues relevant to divorcing women (e.g., regulating negative emotions, managing interpersonal conflict).

The intervention was cost efficient. Approximate weekly time for interventionists included the following: preparation (60 minutes), session (90 minutes), post-session details (30 minutes), midweek calls (60 minutes), and supervision (120 minutes). With two interventionists per group, 13 groups, 14 sessions per group, and 153 participants, the average professional time per family would be 14.27 hours. Assuming $50/hour for interventionist, a very rough cost estimate would be about $713 per family.

Participation

The mean participation rate for four follow-up assessments was 86.5. Participation rates were not significantly different between families in the experimental and control conditions. Table 12.1 displays participation by group at each assessment.

Experimental mothers attended an average of 8.5 intervention sessions ($SD=5.7$, range 0–15). From practical experience with the intervention, we decided that the essential components of the curriculum could not be covered with fewer than four sessions. Sixty one percent of the experimental group attended at least four sessions. Two groups made up the bulk of the experimental group, those who never participated in intervention (19%) and those who participated in most of the intervention (42% attended at least 10 sessions).

Assessment Procedures

Multiple-informant, multiple-method assessments were conducted five times: at baseline, 6 months, 12 months, 18 months, and 30 months. These assessments included structured interviews with mothers and children, achievement testing with the children, observations of mother-child interactions in the laboratory, questionnaires, repeated telephone interviews, and collection of records data (i.e., school, motor vehicle, and criminal). At 24 months, parents completed telephone interviews and questionnaires in a minor assessment. Teacher report data were collected annu-

Table 12.1. Assessment Participation Rates Shown as Percentages.

	Full Sample		Control		Experiment	
	N	%	N	%	N	%
BL	238	100	85	100	153	100
6 mos.	222	93.3	70	92.9	143	93.4
12 mos.	195	81.9	70	82.3	125	81.6
18 mos.	197	82.8	68	80.0	129	84.3
30 mos.	209	87.8	76	89.4	133	86.9
Mean		85.6		86.2		86.6

ally at baseline, 12, 24, and 36 months. Maternal parenting practices were based on direct observations of mother-child interactions in the laboratory. Teachers, children, and coders evaluated child outcomes variables. Coders and teachers were never the same from one assessment to another. Coders did not know which families were in experimental or control conditions, and teachers did not know that children were participating in an intervention trial. Mothers and children signed informed consents. Each participant was paid approximately $10 per hour for time spent in assessment.

Parenting outcomes. The parenting measures were based on observations of mother-child interactions obtained in the laboratory during a set of structured interaction tasks (SIT). SIT activities lasted 45 minutes and involved four mother-son problem-solving discussions about current hot conflicts (5 minutes each), a teaching task (10 minutes), an unstructured activity (5 minutes), a situation during which the ked the child not to play with a set of attractive toys present in the room (5 minutes), and a time for refreshments (5 minutes).

The SIT tasks were videotaped and scored using the Interpersonal Process Code (IPC; Rusby, Estes, & Dishion, 1991) and a global rating system (Forgatch, Knutson, & Mayne, 1992). Randomly selected pairs of coders scored approximately 15% of the interactions to assess inter-coder agreement. The mean Cohen's Kappa across five waves for content was .78 (range = .77 to .80); affect was .70 (range = .67 to .76)

Analytic Strategy

There were clear expectations for the direction of effects specified in the experimental design. The hypotheses were based on findings from ODS-I, which specified certain parenting practices as predictors of child adjustment. The ODS-II intervention was designed to improve these parenting skills and thereby prevent and ameliorate adjustment problems for children of divorce. Improvements in parenting due to the intervention were expected to benefit child adjustment. Therefore the tests for intervention effects were set at one-tailed alpha levels for the directional hypotheses concerning the impact of the intervention and two-tailed for relationships among control variables (see Aron & Aron, 1994, pp. 168-176 for a discussion).

Effects on Parenting Practices

Our first objective was to demonstrate that the intervention benefited the hypothesized parenting mechanisms. Because the model specifies several specific dimensions of parenting, we assessed each one and evaluated change over time. Table 12.2 displays the mean scores and standard deviations for the individual parenting practices at baseline, and 6, 12, 18, and 30 months for the experimental and control groups. We evaluated the impact of the intervention on parenting practices with multivariate repeated measures analysis of variance (MANOVA) using polynomial contrasts adjusted for time spacing. In these analyses, T-tests compare linear coefficients between groups for time effects. These are equivalent to F-tests with equal time spacing. Differences between groups are displayed at each assessment point when statistically significant. The critical dimension of the analysis was the linear group-by-time interaction term, which indicates whether or not differences

Table 12.2. Intervention Effects on Individual Parenting Practices Over Time.

	Experimental		Control		Sig. Contrast	Linear Time Effect	Linear Group x Time Effect
	M	SD	M	SD			
Negative Reinforcement						T = 4.64***	T = 2.80**
BL	1.74	(1.87)	1.39	(1.45)			
6 mo.	2.29	(2.26)	1.61	(1.39)	E > C*		
12 mo.	1.55	(1.54)	1.89	(1.62)			
18 mo.	2.02	(2.06)	2.20	(1.94)			
30 mo.	2.23	(1.89)	2.70	(2.63)			
Negative Reciprocity						T = 0.67	T = 1.64t
BL	1.62	(2.31)	0.81	(1.84)	E > C*		
6 mo.	2.09	(2.31)	2.02	(2.26)			
12 mo.	0.75	(1.76)	1.36	(1.86)	C > E*		
18 mo.	1.38	(1.90)	1.79	(2.06)			
30 mo.	1.62	(2.07)	1.60	(2.18)			
Inept Discipline						T = 6.32***	T = 2.32*
BL	1.83	(0.64)	1.91	(0.61)			
6 mo.	2.00	(0.73)	1.93	(0.68)			
12 mo.	1.95	(0.77)	2.06	(0.74)			
18 mo.	1.97	(0.77)	2.14	(0.68)	C > Et		
30 mo.	2.09	(0.71)	2.34	(0.70)	C > E*		
Positive Involvement						T = -3.60***	T = -2.35**
BL	4.13	(0.59)	4.12	(0.43)			
6 mo.	3.93	(0.68)	3.92	(0.58)			
12 mo.	3.98	(0.74)	3.82	(0.60)	E > Ct		
18 mo.	4.01	(0.63)	3.91	(0.55)			
30 mo.	4.01	(0.62)	3.81	(0.64)	E > C*		
Skill Encouragement						T = -1.55*	T = -1.25
BL	7.98	(1.63)	8.08	(1.26)			
6 mo.	7.52	(1.78)	7.40	(1.60)			
12 mo.	7.42	(1.91)	7.01	(1.86)			
18 mo.	8.07	(1.19)	7.72	(1.40)	E > Ct		
30 mo.	7.67	(1.26)	7.36	(1.52)	E > Ct		
Monitoring						T = -4.86***	T = -1.44t
BL	4.53	(0.54)	4.48	(0.47)			
6 mo.	4.35	(0.56)	4.26	(0.61)			
12 mo.	4.46	(0.59)	4.21	(0.64)	E > C**		
18 mo.	4.32	(0.57)	4.21	(0.64)			
30 mo.	4.33	(0.48)	4.12	(0.56)	E > C**		
Problem Solving						T = 6.54***	T = 0.96
BL	2.67	(0.58)	2.59	(0.58)			
6 mo.	2.69	(0.60)	2.57	(0.60)			
12 mo.	2.85	(0.55)	2.75	(0.56)			
18 mo.	2.80	(0.61)	2.85	(0.56)			
30 mo.	2.94	(0.59)	2.90	(0.56)			

Group X Time Omnibus F(28,2258) (Hotelling's Trace) =   1.45*

***$p \leq .001$; **$p \leq .01$; *$p \leq .05$; t$p \leq .10$

All p values are 1-tailed except BL contrasts, which are 2-tailed.

E = Experimental; C = Control

in linear trajectories for the two groups over the 30-month interval were statistically significant.

The first three measures in the table reflected different dimensions of coercive discipline. Negative reinforcement and negative reciprocity were both microsocial scores based on the full 45 minutes of sequentially scored observational data from the SIT. Negative reinforcement was defined as frequency of conflict bouts initiated by the mother that were terminated by the child. Negative reciprocity was based on the Haberman binomial Z-score, which describes the conditional likelihood of a mother's reciprocal use of negativity with her child (Gottman & Roy, 1990). Inept discipline was a scale score based on coder global ratings of discipline following their coding of the full 45 minutes of the laboratory SIT. Items describing discipline included overly strict, authoritarian, oppressive, erratic, inconsistent, haphazard, used nagging or nattering to get compliance.

The T-tests for the group-by-time interactions indicate that the intervention benefited experimental mothers relative to control mothers for each of the coercive discipline practices (i.e., negative reinforcement, negative reciprocity, and aversive discipline). For control mothers, there was a fairly steady increase in negative reinforcement and inept discipline from BL to 30 months. In fact, there was a main effect for time, indicating that both groups showed an increase over the 30 months. For the experimental mothers, all three measures of coercive discipline showed reduction from BL to 12 months. For negative reciprocity, the difference between the two groups was statistically significant. For negative reinforcement, the reduction was not linear. By 6 months, E-group mothers showed an unexpected significant increase relative to C-group mothers. However, by 12 months, there was a precipitous drop in negative reinforcement, whereas there was a continuing increase in negative reinforcement for C group mothers. For the global measure, inept discipline, the two groups began to differ in level at 18 months with a marginal effect favoring experimental mothers that became significant at 30 months.

For the four positive parenting practices, there were main effects for time for all four measures. Three measures displayed deteriorating levels: positive involvement, skill encouragement, and monitoring. Problem-solving outcome, however, improved overall. The group by time interaction was significant for positive involvement and marginal for monitoring.

Positive involvement was a scale score obtained from coder ratings made following each of the 8 tasks in the structured interaction task. Items included: warm, empathetic, encouraging, affectionate, and treated child with respect. The group by time interaction term for the linear effect was significant, favoring E-group mothers. The mean difference between the two groups was marginal at 12 months and statistically significant at 30 months.

Skill encouragement was based on coder ratings of mothers' ability to promote her child's healthy development through contingent encouragement and scaffolding strategies observed during the 10-minute teaching task. Items in the scale score included: breaks task into manageable steps, reinforces success, prompts appropriate behavior, and corrects in a nonaversive way. At 18 and 30 months, there was a marginal difference in mean scores favoring experimental mothers.

Monitoring was a scale score from parent interviewer impressions and coder ratings from the SIT. Items evaluated maternal supervision during the assessment and outside the laboratory. At 12 and 30 months, the experimental mothers monitored their sons more closely than did control mothers.

Problem-solving outcome (PSO) scores were based on coder ratings of the outcome of the three mother-identified topics for the problem-solving discussions. PSO is a scale comprising nine items (e.g., solution quality, extent of resolution, likelihood of follow through, apparent satisfaction). There were no significant differences for group trajectories for PSO.

Our theoretical model specifies individual parenting practices as contributing to child outcomes. However, effective parenting reflects the ability to integrate the different dimensions. Thus, we combined the individual parenting scores into three factor scores to carry out modeling procedures. Each parenting score was subjected to principal components factor analysis and yielded a single factor solution at each of the five assessments. Coercive discipline comprised three indicators: negative reinforcement, negative reciprocity, and inept discipline. Positive parenting comprised four indicators: positive involvement, skill encouragement, problem solving, and monitoring. Effective parenting comprised two positive parenting measures (positive involvement and skill encouragement) and two coercive discipline measures (negative reinforcement and negative reciprocity). The findings for the three factor scores are presented in Table 12.3.

Table 12.3. Intervention Effects on Parenting Factor Scores Over Time.

	Experimental		Control		Sig. Contrast	Linear Time Effect	Linear Group x Time Effect
	M	SD	M	SD			
Coercive Discipline						$T = 2.40^{**}$	$T = 3.18^{***}$
BL	-0.06	(1.04)	-0.26	(0.80)			
6 mo.	0.08	(1.14)	-0.13	(0.78)			
12 mo.	-0.18	(0.92)	0.09	(0.89)	C > E*		
18 mo.	-0.10	(0.99)	0.12	(0.93)			
30 mo.	-0.06	(0.95)	0.17	(1.12)	C > Et		
Positive Parenting						$T = -1.81^{*}$	$T = -1.85^{*}$
BL	0.18	(1.06)	0.13	(0.79)			
6 mo.	0.13	(1.04)	0.01	(1.02)			
12 mo.	0.21	(0.95)	-0.12	(0.97)	E > C*		
18 mo.	0.17	(0.99)	0.01	(0.95)			
30 mo.	0.17	(0.92)	-0.19	(1.01)	E > C*		
Effective Parenting						$T = -2.53^{**}$	$T = -3.42^{***}$
BL	0.08	(1.09)	0.28	(0.74)			
6 mo.	0.00	(1.12)	0.09	(0.84)			
12 mo.	0.19	(0.95)	-0.15	(0.88)	E > C*		
18 mo.	0.13	(0.98)	-0.11	(0.97)	E > Ct		
30 mo.	0.11	(0.90)	-0.19	(1.11)	E > C*		

Group X Time Omnibus F(8,1140) (Hotelling's Trace) =   1.93*

***$p \leq .001$; **$p \leq .01$; *$p \leq .05$; t$p \leq .10$

All p values are 1-tailed except BL contrasts, which are 2-tailed.

Omnibus F based on Coercive Discipline and Positive Parenting only. E = Experimental; C = Control

The main effect for time showed deterioration in all three factors. However, the group by time interactions showed that the intervention benefited mothers in the experimental group relative to those in the control. The cross-sectional contrasts showed that the times of greatest impact were at 12 and 30 months. Benefits to parenting practices showed classic prevention trajectories for this risk sample. Mothers in the experimental group tended to maintain stable trajectories, whereas those in the control group deteriorated.

Intervention Effects on Boys' Adjustment

In the models described in the coming sections, we conducted analyses with multivariate path models using structural equation modeling (SEM) for change in boy outcomes from baseline to 12 months. The basic strategy was to test for intervention effects on parenting practices, which would then produce commensurate change in the boys' outcomes. We controlled for initial status levels. In the figures, paths are displayed in the form of standardized coefficients. Measures represented multiple methods of assessment, tapped a variety of settings, and were selected to minimize response bias. We assumed that effect sizes comparing experimental and control groups would be larger for the proximal parenting practices than for the more distal child outcomes.

Overall, we found significant benefits to boys in the E-group relative to boys in the C-group in several areas of functioning. Benefits were found for teacher ratings of aggression, externalizing, adaptive functioning, and prosocial behavior at school, laboratory tests for reading achievement, boys' self report of depression, peer relations, association with deviant peers, and noncompliant behavior observed in the laboratory. The next section outlines how benefits to the parenting mechanisms were related to boy outcomes.

Intervention effects on noncompliance and aggression. Noncompliance has been identified as a basic building block of antisocial behavior because noncompliance can progress to more serious problems such as physical aggression (Chamberlain & Patterson, 1995; Patterson, Reid, & Dishion, 1992). The model in Figure 12.2 tested the hypothesis that intervention benefits to effective parenting would reduce noncompliance and aggression from BL to 12 months. Effective parenting was the score described with Table 12.3. Noncompliance was a factor combining observations of noncompliance from the family SIT and the child interviewer's ratings of the boy's compliance (Martinez & Forgatch, submitted). Aggression was from the Aggression scale of the Teacher Rating Form (TRF) (Achenbach & Edelbrock, 1986).

The model showed good fit to the data with adequate measurement factor loadings [$X^2_5 = 7.01$, p = .22, n = 134]. Baseline (BL) associations on the left side of the model showed that effective parenting predicted lower levels of noncompliance by the boy, and noncompliance was associated with teacher-rated aggression. The intervention effect was shown on the right-hand side controlling for BL levels. The intervention predicted improvements in effective parenting ($\beta = .20$). Improved parenting was associated with reductions in noncompliance ($\beta = -.54$), which was associated with decreased levels of aggression ($\beta = .22$). Thus, the hypothesis was supported. Note that higher baseline levels of effective parenting predicted greater reduction in noncompliance over time, and higher levels of baseline noncompliance predicted more increase in aggression over time.

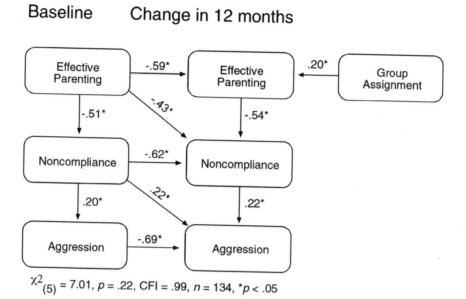

Figure 12.2. Intervention effects on noncompliance and aggression.

Intervention effects on achievement. In the prior model, ineffective parenting lead to increases in problem behavior. Coercive parenting can also interfere with the development of prosocial behavior, such as academic achievement. Patterson and colleagues (DeBaryshe, Patterson, & Capaldi, 1993; Patterson et al., 1992; Ramsey, Patterson, & Walker, 1990) specified and tested pathways through which school failure would develop from a parenting failure. The hypothesis was that parental negative reinforcement would lead to noncompliance, so that when children were directed to do homework, they would refuse. Failure to engage in relevant academic behavior at home would generalize to the school setting, and that would interfere with achievement. We tested the model supported with correlational data from the earlier studies with the experimental data in ODS-II. The results are shown in Figure 12.3.

Negative reinforcement was described with Table 12.2; noncompliance was described in the prior analysis. Homework was a three-agent factor (mother, teacher, child) with items describing homework quality, completion, and turning homework in on time. Adaptive functioning was a TRF t-score, with four items in which teachers compared youngsters to same-aged pupils on work effort, learning, happiness, and appropriate behavior. Reading achievement was evaluated in the laboratory using the Woodcock Johnson psycho-educational battery (Woodcock & Mather, 1990).

The model showed good fit to the data with adequate measurement factor loadings [$X^2_{17} = 27.04$, p = .06, CFI=.97, n = 126]. The hypothesis was supported both as a static model and as an experimental test. The baseline static model appears on the left-hand side of the model. Maternal negative reinforcement predicted noncompliance ($\beta = .40$), which in turn was associated with poor homework ($\beta = -.23$). Quality homework was associated with adaptive functioning ($\beta = .53$), and adaptive

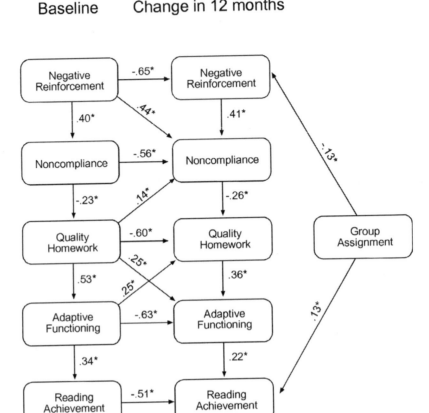

Figure 12.3. Intervention effects on achievement.

functioning predicted reading achievement (β = .34). The experimental manipulation appears on the right side of the model, showing the effect of the intervention on change from BL to 12 months, controlling for BL levels. As hypothesized, the intervention group produced a reduction in negative reinforcement (β = -.13), which predicted decreases in noncompliance (β = .41). Decreases in noncompliance were associated with improved homework quality (β = -.26), which predicted improved adaptive functioning at school (β = .36), which predicted better reading achievement (β = .22). Note the direct path from group to improved reading achievement. This path is only significant with a listwise deletion sample with these constructs. The path from group to negative reinforcement, however, is significant regardless of sample size.

   Benefits to teacher-rated school adjustment. The next model tested the intervention effects of change in effective parenting on change in general school adjustment as rated by teachers (Forgatch & DeGarmo, 1999). This model controlled for socioeconomic status (SES) and employed latent variables for parenting and child outcome. Effective parenting had two indicators, prosocial parenting (i.e., positive involvement, skill encouragement, and problem solving outcome) and coercive parenting (i.e., negative reinforcement and negative reciprocity). The latent variable factor for teacher report of school adjustment comprised t-scores from the TRF for externalizing behavior and adaptive functioning, and a measure of prosocial behavior from the Chedoke-McMaster Teacher Questionnaire (Boyle, Offord, Racine, & Fleming, 1993).

The model showed good fit to the data with adequate measurement factor loadings [X^2 = 38.96, df = 38, p = .43, n = 155]. The findings supported the parenting hypothesis. Group assignment predicted change in parenting, which in turn predicted change in school adjustment. Results are shown in Figure 12.4.

The intervention predicted increases in effective parenting (β= .18) controlling for SES, baseline levels of effective parenting, and baseline school adjustment. Supporting the parenting model, increases in effective parenting predicted increases in school adjustment (β= .37). Higher levels of SES predicted increases in observed parenting practices from baseline to follow-up (β= .34). The cross-lag paths indicated that baseline levels of effective parenting predicted increases in school adjustment (β= .32), but the boys' baseline level of school adjustment did not predict change in parenting.

Intervention effects on boys' report of maladjustment. The next model assessed the effect of the intervention boys' self-ratings of depressed mood and peer adjustment (Forgatch & DeGarmo, 1999). Again we used latent constructs and controlled for SES. The parenting measure was the same as in the previous model. Boy maladjustment was assessed using the Child Depression Inventory (CDI; Kovacs, 1985) for depression and the Loneliness in Children measure (Asher, Hymel, & Renshaw, 1984) for dissatisfaction with peer relations. The results are shown in Figure 12.5.

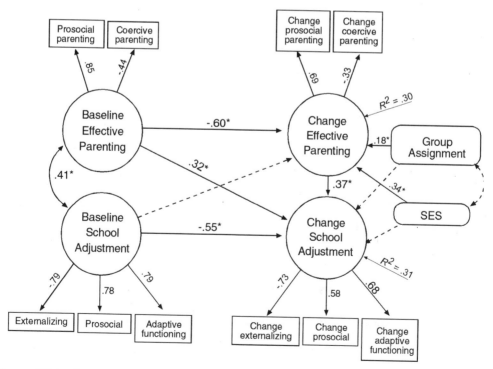

Figure 12.4. Intervention effects on teacher-rated school adjustment.

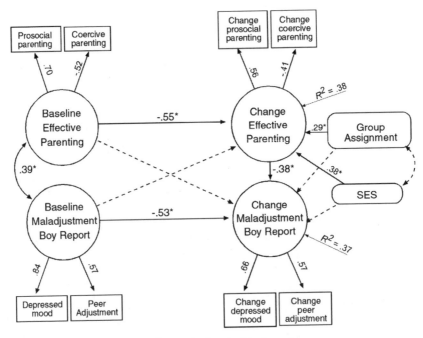

Figure 12.5. Intervention effects on boy-rated maladjustment.

The model fit the data and the hypothesis was supported [$X^2_{(20, N=187)}$ = 19.88, p = .47, comparative fit index = 1.00]. Controlling for SES, and baseline measures, group assignment predicted increases in effective parenting (β= .29), which in turn predicted decreases in boys' maladjustment (β= -.38). There were no significant cross-lag relationships for baseline parenting or boy maladjustment.

Intervention effects on deviant peer association. The next model shows intervention effects on effective parenting, which in turn was associated with reductions in deviant peer association (DPA). The measure of effective parenting was the measure described with Table 12.3; the measure of deviant peer association was based on boy report using the Describing Friends questionnaire developed at OSLC.

The model showed good fit to the data with adequate measurement factor loadings [$X^2_{(2)}$ = 1.64, p = .44, CFI=1.0, n = 193]. Note that the effective parenting variable was not associated with DPA at baseline when children were in grades one to three and there was minimal variance in DPA. However, the change analysis indicated that the intervention benefited effective parenting (β = .19), which predicted decreased likelihood to grow in child-reported deviant peer association over the course of one year (β = -.16). The results are displayed in Figure 12.6.

Intervention Effects on Maternal Adjustment

We expected the intervention to benefit maternal adjustment in terms of depression, standard of living, stress, and distress. In addition to the parenting dimensions of the intervention, the intervention contained components to help mothers manage contextual disruptions that accompany divorce and to promote the mothers' healthy adjustment. Specific intervention components relevant to maternal adjustment included recognition and regulation of negative emotions, communication and problem-solving skills, stress reduction techniques, and adult relationship skills (Forgatch, 1994).

Standard of living and distress. The stress literature shows that disruptive life events and changes in social position following divorce lead to acute stressors and subsequent depression (DeGarmo & Kitson, 1996; Lorenz et al., 1997). Along with reductions in depression, we hypothesized that maternal stress and changes in standard of living for the experimental group would show differential adjustment patterns compared to the control group. The data partially supported our hypotheses.

We assessed three types of stressors: 1) daily hassles in the family (Family Events Checklist: Patterson, 1982); 2) negative life events (Sarason, Johnson, & Siegel, 1978); 3) and financial stress. Table 12.4 displays the mean scores and standard deviations for maternal depression using the CES-D and the three stress measures at baseline, and 6, 12, 18, and 30 months for the experimental and control groups. We evaluated the impact of the intervention on these measures of maternal distress using repeated measures analysis of variance (MANOVA). Differences between groups are displayed at each assessment point when statistically significant. The critical dimension of the analysis was the linear group-by-time interaction term, which indicates whether or not differences in linear trajectories for the two groups over the 30-month interval were statistically significant.

The main effect for time revealed an overall decrease in negative life events and financial distress. The intervention benefited experimental mothers in terms of depression and financial stress as indicated by the significant group by time T-scores. The cross sectional data showed that for depression, a marginal difference in level emerged at 30 months. For financial stress, experimental mothers appeared to benefit by 6 months, with benefits improving and continuing in the ensuing assessments. No differences were found between the groups for negative life events, although a marginal benefit to experimental mothers emerged at 30 months on the measure of family stressors.

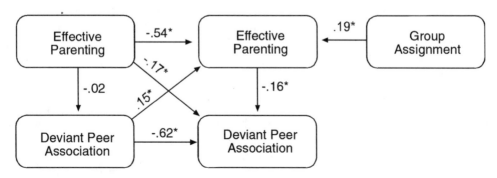

Figure 12.6. Intervention effects on deviant peer association.

Table 12.4. Intervention Effects on Maternal Outcomes.

	Experimental		Control		Sig. Contrast	Linear Time Effect	Linear Group x Time Effect
	M	SD	M	SD			
	CES-D					T = -0.82	T = 1.98*
BL	14.72	(10.61)	16.40	(9.41)			
6 mo.	14.16	(12.13)	14.46	(10.04)			
12 mo.	15.59	(10.32)	14.14	(9.45)			
18 mo.	14.17	(10.43)	14.60	(8.83)			
30 mo.	15.82	(10.82)	13.20	(9.94)	C > Et		
	Negative Life Events					T = -5.30	***T = -0.03
BL	2.39	(1.60)	2.16	(1.87)			
6 mo.	1.29	(1.39)	1.17	(1.32)			
12 mo.	1.10	(1.27)	1.16	(1.40)			
18 mo.	1.12	(1.41)	1.24	(1.60)			
30 mo.	1.27	(1.43)	1.02	(1.39)			
	Family Events Stress					T = -0.77	T = 0.66
BL	7.86	(3.54)	7.22	(3.44)			
6 mo.	7.35	(3.81)	7.05	(3.80)			
12 mo.	7.08	(3.95)	7.15	(4.07)			
18 mo.	7.41	(3.67)	7.07	(3.91)			
30 mo.	7.67	(4.19)	6.70	(3.47)	C > E^t		
	Financial Stress					T = -2.19*	T = 2.07*
BL	2.85	(0.60)	2.75	(0.69)			
6 mo.	2.92	(0.76)	2.76	(0.64)	C > E^t		
12 mo.	2.83	(0.80)	2.56	(0.67)	C > E*		
18 mo.	2.94	(0.80)	2.63	(0.75)	C > E*		
30 mo.	2.84	(0.80)	2.51	(0.71)	C > E**		

Group X Time Omnibus $F_{(16,1950)}$ (Hotelling's Trace) =   1.03

***$p \leq .001$; **$p \leq .01$; *$p \leq .05$; $^t p \leq .10$
All p values are 1-tailed except BL contrasts, which are 2-tailed.
E = Experimental; C = Control

Depression. Although the divorce literature supports a 2-year adjustment slope of depression after divorce (Kitson, 1992; Lorenz et al., 1997), we hypothesized that the intervention would accelerate depression recovery and prevent future clinical depression. The hypothesis was partially supported. The data showed that experimental mothers were marginally less clinically depressed by 2.5 years after separation. Odds ratios for clinical depression are shown in Table 12.5 with a stepwise logistic regression. The measure of depression was the CES-D self-report questionnaire, in which a cutting score of 16 or higher represents clinical levels (Radloff, 1977).

Mothers in the experimental group were roughly .25 less likely to be clinically depressed at 30 months following baseline. Mothers of older children were about 1.4 times more likely to be clinically depressed than were mothers of younger children. Antisocial mothers, measured by scales 4 (Psychopathic Deviate) and 9 (Hypomania) of the MMPI (Hathaway & McKinley, 1943), were almost twice as likely to be depressed. In ODS-I, mothers of younger children were more likely to repartner, and repartnering was associated with less maternal stress and depression. In ODS-II, controlling for repartnering in the first year in step three, the effect for experimental mothers to be less clinically depressed decreased slightly to marginal significance.

Intervention Effects on Girls' Adjustment

As described earlier, we recruited 36 sibling sisters of the focal boys as participants. Because of the small listwise sample size (7 control and 21 experimental listwise), we had limited power to detect intervention effects for girls. Two changes were associated with the mothers' participation in the intervention, each of which paralleled changes found for boys.

Experimental-group boys compared to control-group boys showed a marginal reduction in self-reported depressed mood from baseline to 6 months [$F_{(1,205)}$ = 1.62, p = .10, one-tailed]. Experimental-group girls compared to controls showed a marginally significant group by time linear effect from BL to 12 months [$F_{(1,26)}$ = 2.78, p = .05, 1-tailed] and from BL to 18 months [$F_{(1,24)}$ = 2.37, p<.06, 1-tailed]. These trajectories indicated that girls in the control group increased in depressed mood, while girls in the experimental group decreased. There were no significant mean differences in self-reported depressed mood for the experimental group girls compared to control group girls, however.

Reductions in maternal negative reciprocity directed toward girls were similar to reductions mothers displayed with boys, as shown earlier in Table 12.1. There was a significant linear group by time effect from BL to 18 months [$F_{(1,25)}$ = 3.48, p < .05]. In addition, the mean negative reciprocity score was marginally significant for the control group (z = 1.92) but was not significant for the experimental (z = .73) at 12 months. At 18 months, the contingency scores were significantly different (z = 3.82 and 1.01, respectively, t = 2.67, p < .01).

We view these findings as weak but promising signs that (a) mothers were able to generalize some parenting skill to their daughters, and (b) the girls may have benefited from the intervention. Because of the limited power to detect effects with such small samples, these findings are likely to be underestimations.

Table 12.5. Odds Ratio for Predictors of Material Clinical Depression at 30 Month Follow Up.

	Step 1	Step 2	Step 3
Group	.73*	0.74[t]	0.74[t]
Boy's age		1.36[t]	1.37[t]
Mom's age		1.19	1.14
Antisocial Mom		1.87**	1.84**
SES		0.84	0.84
Repartnering			0.53

**p ≤ .01.; *p ≤ .05.; [t]p ≤ .10

Conclusion

With more than half of modern marriages predicted to end in divorce (Bumpass, 1984; Martin & Bumpass, 1989), and divorce a risk factor for the adjustment of parents and children (Amato & Keith, 1991), we need programs that can prevent and ameliorate the problems of families who enter this process. The ODS-II preventive intervention program proved beneficial for both recently separated single mothers and their early-school-aged sons. The randomized experimental design contrasted families in the experimental group with those in the no-intervention control group. Trajectories over the 30-month assessment were stable for experimental mothers and deteriorating for control families for the factor scores of parenting practices. Effective parenting benefits translated to reductions in non-compliance (observed) and aggressive behavior (teacher ratings), and improvements in adaptive functioning at school (teacher ratings), reading achievement (test scores), peer relations (child self-report), and deviant peer association (child self-report). Sons and daughters both reported trends for reductions in depressed mood. Mothers directly benefited in terms of reduced financial stress and depression. Thus, our initial data provide evidence that the ODS-II intervention, which is cost effective, can promote positive outcomes in a family system embedded in the context of the divorce process. What effect will change in the parenting mediators have on the adjustment of the youngsters as they become adolescents and their families move through new transitions? These questions will be addressed in the follow-up of the study, which is beginning in the year 2000.

13

The Adolescent Transitions Program: A Family-Centered Prevention Strategy for Schools

*Thomas J. Dishion and
Kathryn Kavanagh*

An ecological framework is essential for designing interventions that address mental health problems as a public health issue (Biglan, 1995; Dishion, & Stormshak in press; Kelly, 1988). A critical problem in child clinical psychology is that interventions designed in university settings: (a) are inaccessible to the vast majority of families; (b) do not produce effects reliably when implemented in community settings; or (c) are based on interventions derived from narrowly defined clinical groups that do not reflect the reality of the psychosocial profiles of families in need.

Hoagwood and Koretz (1996) suggested that intervention and prevention research would benefit policy if interventions were designed to fit in or alter existing service-delivery systems. This perspective is consistent with the public health perspective: Effective interventions are needed that reach a large number of individuals, even if the associated effect size is relatively small (Biglan, 1995).

Within the United States, the vast majority of children attend school up to the age of 13-14. Many of the behavior problems that define the risk trajectory for serious delinquency and early onset substance use are apparent within a public school setting (Dishion & Patterson, 1993; Loeber & Dishion, 1983). In addition, schools are the key setting where youth aggregate into peer groups, some of which exacerbate risk for problem behavior (Dishion, Duncan, Eddy, Fagot, & Fetrow, 1994; Kellam, 1990; Rutter, 1985). For these reasons, we "consider schools as potential sites for service delivery, as well as potential objects of intervention activity" (Trickett & Birman, 1989, p. 361).

We know from previous research that intervention effects can span home and school if we coordinate parenting and school interventions (Dishion, Patterson, & Kavanagh, 1992; Patterson, 1974b). With this body of research in mind, we designed the Adolescent Transitions Program (ATP)[1] to focus exclusively on parents, to address the family dynamics of adolescent problem behavior, to link with school procedures, to be delivered cost effectively, and to comprehensively address the wide range of risk typical to school settings.

257

Enhancing communication and cooperation between parents and school staff can drastically impact parents' potential for monitoring, limit setting, and supporting academic progress (Gottfredson, Gottfredson, & Hybl, 1993; Reid, 1993). Simply increasing specific information to parents regarding their child's attendance, homework, and class behavior results in improved monitoring and support for at-risk children's academic and social success (Blechman, Taylor, & Schrader, 1981; Heller & Fantuzzo, 1993).

Interventions directed at engaging parents in changing their practices should be comprehensive and responsive to the developmental history of the child and family. Two key issues toward this end are: (a) titrating the level of need (the risk status of the child) to the level of support provided to parents and (b) integrating diverse intervention levels to maximize and support protective parenting practices in a community setting (Dishion & Kavanagh, in press).

Adolescent Transitions Program

The Multilevel Approach

In 1988, we combined our 10 years of family treatment experience with research on problem behavior to design a program of research aimed at reducing problem behavior among high-risk adolescents.

In the beginning, we conducted a randomized control study comparing the effectiveness of four treatment conditions: parent only, teen only, parent and teen, and self-directed. We examined the impact of these four intervention strategies on drug use, reducing adolescent problem behaviors, and improving parent–child interactions (Dishion & Andrews, 1995; Dishion, Andrews, Kavanagh, & Soberman, 1996; Dishion, et al. 1992).

Systematic analyses of process and outcome variables were conducted on data from 220 youth and their families. This work lead to our current, more comprehensive model of preventive interventions for families of early adolescents, which is designed to effect service delivery in schools. Project Alliance, the current ongoing, longitudinal, school-based study of two cohorts, includes 999 multi-ethnic urban youth and their parents, randomly assigned to intervention or control conditions.

The intervention model is best described as a "tiered" strategy, with each level of intervention building on the previous level. Using prevention nomenclature, the three levels represent *universal, selected,* and *indicated* family interventions. Universal interventions reach all parents within a school setting, selected addresses the needs of at-risk families, and the indicated level is best described as family treatment (model displayed in Figure 13.1).

For the remainder of the chapter, we will provide an overview of each intervention level, the ingredients of which address pragmatic, as well as research issues of implementing family-centered interventions within a school setting.

Universal Intervention

A Parenting Resource Center. We have found several useful strategies for engaging parents at the universal level. In our experience, the first step in establishing

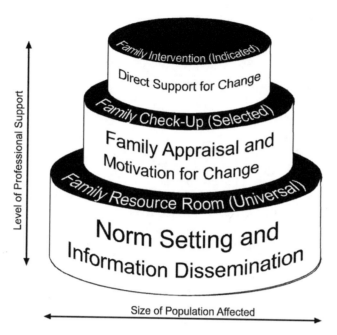

Figure 13.1. A multilevel model for parenting interventions within a school ecology.

family-based services in a school setting is creating a Parenting Resource Center (PRC). The goals of the PRC are to: (a) establish an infrastructure for collaboration between school staff and parents; (b) support norms for protective parenting practices; and (c) disseminate information encouraging family management practices that promote school success in order to prevent the development of early-onset alcohol and other drug use. The PRC also provides the vehicle through which a program of multilevel interventions can be offered during the school year.

The PRC has been a resource to school staff wanting to develop effective strategies for positive collaborative relationships with parents. Additional physical resources include written and video information on parenting and important community resources for families of early adolescents. In addition, the PRC serves as a nexus of home–school communication by having both written and recorded information available to parents about homework, problem situations, and resources within the school. We found that this daily communication from school enhances parents' awareness of homework assignments and classroom activities relevant to their child and also facilitates follow-up parent involvement.

Home visits. Along with others concerned with family engagement (e.g., Szapocznik & Kurtines, 1989), we found home visiting to be a key strategy for increasing participation in family-centered interventions and we were able to demonstrate the effectiveness of home visiting between our two cohorts.

The home visit was used on the second cohort only (Dishion & Kavanagh, in press). Approximately 60% of intervention parents agreed to a summer visit to set goals for the coming school year and to assess their child's past year in the areas of grades, peers, attendance, problem behaviors, and drug use.

One of the main goals of a universal intervention is to direct those families in need to the appropriate intervention. In comparing the two cohorts, we found that 41% of the identified risk population agreed to participate in a Family Check-Up (FCU), our selected level of intervention, without any prior contact with the PRC consultant. However, given the summer visit in cohort two, 62% agreed to participate in the FCU. It appears, then, that proactive contact with families in a universal intervention promotes engagement in family-centered resources.

Videotapes and rating forms. Another promising tool involving parent self-assessment at the universal level uses videotape examples and a simple pencil-and-paper rating form. The video, "Parenting in the Teenage Years" (Dishion & Kavanagh, 1995), was developed to help parents identify observable risk factors in the context of parent-child interaction. Designed to be viewed by parents during the first week of school, the video presents examples of teen risk behavior. It also focuses on the use of effective family management skills (positive reinforcement, monitoring, limit setting, and relationship skills) to facilitate parents' evaluation of their own level of risk, as well as their child's level of risk.

Health curriculum. A fourth intervention at the universal level, which should occur during the fall term, includes a six-week health curriculum for students referred to as SHAPe (*S*uccess, *H*ealth, *a*nd *P*eace). This curriculum has student lessons on promoting school success, reducing substance use, and reducing conflict (see Figure 13.2). Delivered by the PRC consultant, it is accompanied by weekly parent–child homework activities, which result in information about parent norms and practices that promote positive youth behaviors.

Community awareness. In our experience, grading students for completion of these parent–child activities promotes maximal parent engagement. We have also experimented with the use of public access television to extend the impact of the program and find it a promising media for increasing parent participation in these activities. In addition, parent information is summarized by topic and put into a newsletter, along with information from the student classes, to promote dissemination to all families in the school community (see Dishion & Kavanagh, in press).

Selected Intervention

The Family Check-Up. The Family Check-Up is a selected intervention offering family assessment, professional support, and motivation to change. As described by Dishion and Kavanagh (in press), it is an in-depth method that supports parents' accurate appraisal of their child's risk status and provides parenting resources for reducing risk factors and promoting adjustment.

The FCU, based on motivational interviewing by Miller and Rollnick (1991), is a three-session intervention: (a) the initial interview, (b) a comprehensive multi-agent, multimethod assessment, and (c) a family feedback session, using motivational skills to encourage maintenance of current positive practices and change of disruptive practices.

We have incorporated the Miller and Rollnick FRAMES (1991) model of motivational interviewing, which follows five behavior-change principles:

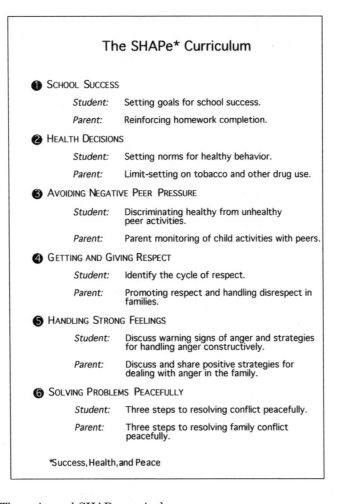

Figure 13.2. The universal SHAPe curriculum.

F = Provide data-based *feedback* about behavior and its implications for the future.

R = Communicate the client's *responsibility* for the behavior change process.

A = Receive sound *advice* from an expert in developmental and behavior change issues.

M = Offer a *menu* of options for behavioral change and include the clients in menu development.

E = Show *empathy* for the clients and their situation.

S = Help the clients leave the feedback meeting with a sense of *self-efficacy* by assisting them in a selection of behavior-change goals that is realistic, measurable, and under their control.

Feedback. Focusing on the process of family intervention is an ongoing research problem. Over the years, innovative family intervention researchers have suggested

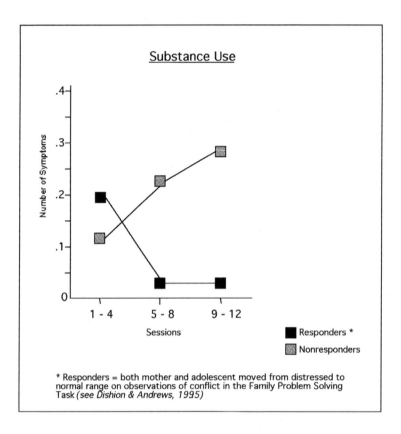

Figure 13.3.   Reductions in substance use during parent group treatment.

that providing feedback to parents from the findings of psychological assessments is conducive to change (Sanders & Lawton, 1993). The critical feature of such feedback is that it be presented in a supportive and motivating manner.

The chances that something as simple as providing supportive feedback to families can actually change behavior is certainly an optimistic sign for prevention and behavior change theory. Other child and family researchers have used information feedback as part of the behavior change process and reported positive effects, with respect to building a collaborative set with the family (Sanders & Lawton, 1993).

We have used the feedback process as the initial step to building collaboration with parents in our parenting groups. In fact, it is interesting to note that for the families that made clinically significant change in the parent groups, they did so quite suddenly by the fifth session. We show in Figure 13.3 that parents reported reductions in child substance use by session five, when the family was found to make clinically significant changes in observed parent-child conflict. Perhaps the rapid change is a function of providing feedback to parents prior to the groups, based on their participation in our initial assessment.

Change. During the 1980s, the Oregon Social Learning Center (OSLC) began to study client resistance in behavior family therapy. In a series of studies, Patterson and colleagues (Chamberlain, Patterson, Reid, Forgatch, & Kavanagh, 1984; Patterson & Chamberlain, 1994; Patterson & Forgatch, 1985) found that teaching and confrontation actually elicited *resistance* to change, whereas support, reframing, and questioning were more *conducive* to change. This body of work forms the basis for the motivational interviewing component of the FCU, which focuses on connecting with parents at their current stage in the change process and supporting their decision making regarding future parenting.

Motivation. The FCU uses motivational interviewing and assessment information to assist parents in identifying appropriate services and change strategies. Typically, this occurs when parents come to the PRC because of concerns about their adolescents' adjustment at home or at school. Another motivation-enhancing opportunity occurs when parents are notified of discipline problems in the school. PRC staff should be part of school staffing committees, in order to catch problems early and make recommendations for family intervention, as opposed to child intervention, which is typical of schools.

Referrals. Lastly, when PRC personnel become part of a school system, the staff, teachers, counselors, or administrators proactively start to refer a child when they first identify concerns about behavior, peer associations, or emotional adjustment. When this happens, in order to promote parent engagement, we find the best procedure is to have school personnel recommend the FCU as a way to gather more information about the school's concerns. This also presents an opportunity to address any concerns the parents may have about their adolescents' well-being.

Related studies. Rao (1998) examined the impact of the FCU in a study involving 40 high-risk families that were randomly assigned to an FCU intervention or a wait-list control. The analysis revealed that following the FCU, parents reported substantial reductions in their child's behavior problems, which was correlated with changes in their own parenting practices. Similar trends were noted for teacher and youth report of behavior problems. The wait-list control group parents, in contrast, did not perceive changes in their children's behavior or their own parenting practices.

More recently, O'Leary (2001) randomly assigned 40 high-risk parents of preschool children to control on the FCU intervention, finding statistically reliable increases in the parents' *proactive structure*, based on direct observations. These initial findings fit within a body of literature that supports research-based interventions for families (Dishion, & Stormshak in press; Dishion & Patterson, 1992; Patterson, Dishion, & Chamberlain, 1993).

In addition to finding a main effect for the FCU on parent reports of parenting and young adolescent problem behavior, Rao (1998) documented the process of change. She found therapist adherence to the FRAMES model for therapist–client interaction during the feedback session to be associated with parental reports of improvement, which in turn, correlated with changes in the adolescents' problem behaviors (data summarized in Figure 13.4).

Project Alliance. In our multi tiered intervention trial, a preliminary study of factors related to which family, peer, or school factors were predictive of which parents volunteered for the FCU. We found that for high-risk families, the students drifted into a deviant peer group in middle school, which precipitated the parent engagement in the FCU (Kavanagh, Dishion, Medici Skaggs, & Schneiger, 1998). At the moderate risk level, lower levels of risk and higher academic achievement best

Therapy Process as an Impetus
for Family Change*

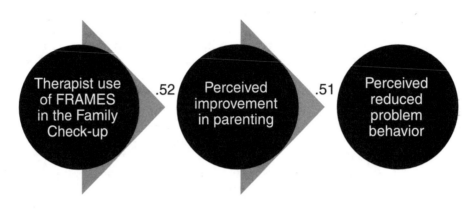

*Rao, 1998.

Figure 13.4.   Therapy process as an impetus for family change.

predicted engagement in the FCU functions as a selected intervention. In that context, they are optimally delivered when parents find their young adolescent falling under the control of problematic peers.

Indicated Intervention

A menu of services. The indicated level of intervention provides direct professional support to parents. An extensive literature exists on the effectiveness of motivational interviewing as a brief intervention with individual adults, couples, and families (Dishion, Stormshak, in press). However, it is helpful to embed the FCU in a menu of intervention services that directly or indirectly promote the caregivers' potential to guide, support, and manage the day-to-day presentations of positive and problem behavior.

The presumption underlying the menu of family intervention services is that a variety of family-centered interventions can be equally effective in reducing problem behavior. Perhaps Webster-Stratton most convincingly demonstrated this for families with problematic preschoolers (Webster-Stratton, 1984; Webster-Stratton, Kolpacoff, & Hollingsworth, 1988).

The indicated intervention menu includes a brief family intervention, school monitoring system, parent groups, behavioral family therapy, and case-management services, which is grounded in OSLC family management practices. However, as discussed in other areas of counseling and clinical psychology (Miller & Rollnick, 1991), it is motivating to the change process to have a variety of intervention options.

The Family Management Curriculum. The Family Management Curriculum (FMC; Dishion, et al. in press; see Figure 13.5) provides a framework for working with fam-

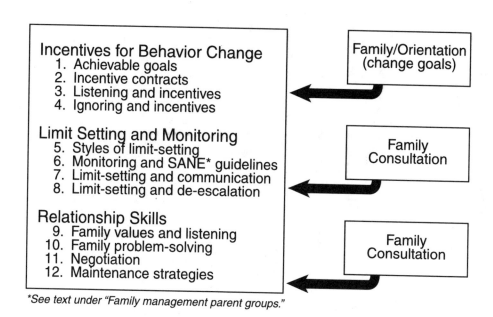

Figure 13.5. Outline of the Family Management Curriculum.

ilies individually or in groups at the indicated level. This curriculum, derived from over 30 years of research at OSLC, was originally designed to work with individual families (Patterson, Reid, Jones, & Conger, 1975) to support parents' efforts to reduce problem behavior (Forehand & McMahon, 1981; Patterson, 1974b). As stated earlier, we have adapted this content to a curriculum format for group work with parents.

Our outcome analyses of the multilevel, family-based interventions in middle school are preliminary. We examined the relation between PRC contacts and growth in deviant peer involvement and problem behavior in middle school. Consistent with Figure 13.6, we expected that the FCU and follow-up contact would be associated with reductions in growth in deviant peer involvement during middle school. Figure 13.6 reveals that the number of PRC contacts over the middle school period was, indeed, significant and related to the child's report of decreased deviant peer involvement. As of this writing, these findings reflect less than two-thirds of the current sample (n = 558), and in fact, as indicated above, we had much higher rates of engagement in our second cohort.

Family management parent groups. The FMC provides detailed suggestions on how to conduct a 12-session parent group with a family management focus, including exercises, rationales, role-plays, and forms for each session (Dishion et al., in press). It also serves as a template for individual work with families, including brief, focused intervention and more extended individual work, such as social interactional family therapy (see Forgatch & Patterson, 1998).

There are three broad foci in the FMC: (a) using incentives to promote positive behavior change; (b) limit-setting and monitoring; and (c) family communication and problem-solving. The first phase utilizes positive reinforcement programs to increase specific behaviors, such as cooperating with parent requests or doing homework.

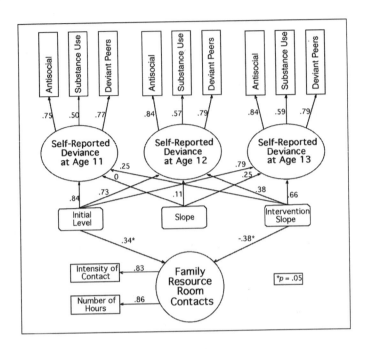

Figure 13.6. Family contacts and growth in deviant peers.

Well-used incentives can have a dramatic effect on reducing problem behavior and result in a more positive family atmosphere. This is also the first step in supporting the parents as leaders in the behavior change process.

In the second phase, we work with parents on limit-setting and monitoring regarding articulation of rules (e.g., come home directly after school, avoid unsupervised homes). Limits are useless unless parents are willing to follow through with consequences. We offer parents the SANE guidelines (Dishion & Kavanagh, in press; see also Dishion & Patterson, 1996), a simple schema to help them self-assess limit-setting practices. We discuss those guidelines as:

S = Consequences need to be *small*, so they can be used frequently, if necessary.
A = Parents need to think of consequences that *avoid* punishing the parent, such as month-long groundings.
N = Consequences need to be *nonabusive*, for obvious reasons, but also so that parents will feel comfortable using them frequently.
E = Consequences need to be *effective* because consistent consequences are effective.

The final but most important component of the FMC is relationship skills, which include basic communication skills (e.g., listening), problem-solving, and negotiation. We turn to relationship skills last, to avoid regressing into more conflict in families struggling with family management issues. Relationship skills

Table 13.1. Observed Mother and Child Negative Engagement in Family Problem-Solving by Intervention Condition and Phase.

Intervention Condition	n	Baseline		n	Termination	
		M (and SD)			M (and SD)	
Mother						
Parent only	25	0.63	(0.63)	23	0.39	(0.44)[a]
Teen only	31	0.67	(0.85)	31	0.52	(0.59)[a]
Parent and teen	31	0.56	(0.81)	29	0.46	(0.47)[a]
Self-directed	27	0.49	(0.51)	25	0.56	(0.84)
Control	39	0.62	(0.54)	35	0.90	(0.89)
Child						
Parent only	26	1.27	(1.33)	24	0.81	(0.88)[a]
Teen only	32	1.09	(1.28)	32	0.80	(0.89)[b]
Parent and teen	31	1.33	(1.58)	31	0.93	(1.09)[a]
Self-directed	27	0.78	(0.82)	25	1.06	(1.32)
Control	39	1.22	(1.14)	35	1.36	(1.53)

Note. Scores refer to the rate-per-minute of observed behavior.
[a]Statistically reliable positive intervention effect at termination, in contrast to controls.
[b]Statistically marginal ($p < .10$) intervention effect, in contrast to controls.

are not as useful when the source of conflict (cooperating with parents, school failure, and so forth) is ongoing.

There is a body of literature that supports a focus on parenting in interventions to reduce risk factors for early-onset substance use (see Dishion, 1996). In our original components analysis of ATP (Dishion & Andrews, 1995), there were immediate effects for parent groups guided by the FMC:

1. We found reductions in observations of parent–child conflict in videotaped problem-solving tasks (see Table 13.1).
2. Teachers rated the high-risk boys and girls, who received only family-centered services, as less antisocial at school.
3. Dishion et al. (1996) reported reduced substance use within the year following ATP involvement, in particular, early-onset tobacco use (see Figure 13.7).

Most importantly, the process of change was what we expected. Table 13.2 shows the correlations among changes in observed parent–child negative engagement and reductions in teacher-reported antisocial behavior at school. Note that change in mothers' and adolescents' negative engagement correlated with change in externalizing behavior at school ($r = .24$ and $.33$, respectively).

These findings have recently been replicated by another group of intervention researchers, who also document reduced levels of antisocial behavior and improved parenting practices among parents of high-risk young adolescents living in rural settings (Irvine, Biglan, Smolkowski, Metzler, & Ary, 1999). The pattern of results are consistent with a body of literature on family-centered intervention approaches

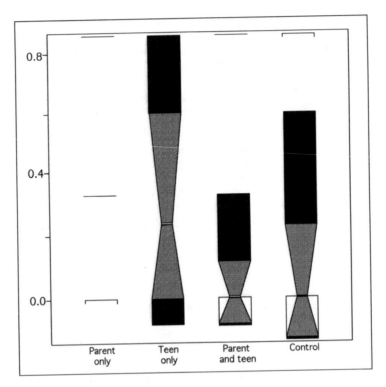

Figure 13.7. Monthly tobacco use by intervention conditions.

Table 13.2. Correlated Change in Observations of Parent-Child Interaction and Teacher Ratings of Externalizing Behavior at School.

Reliable Change Scores	1	2	3
1. Child negative engagement	1.00		
2. Mother negative engagement	.61*	1.00	
3. Teacher ratings of externalizing	.33*	.24*	1.00

Note. *$p < .05$

to preventing or reducing adolescent substance use (for reviews, Dishion, 1996; Henggeler, et al., 1986; Patterson, et al. 1993).

Process issues. To be effective in leading a family management group with parents of young adolescents, it is critical to attend to both the curriculum and the interpersonal group dynamics. We studied the process of change by videotaping all two-hour group sessions for the 109 families that received the parent curriculum in our original study (Dishion et al., 1996). We coded both the client and therapist interactions using the Interpersonal Process Code (IPC; Rusby, Estes, & Dishion, 1990) and created construct scores (see Table 13.3) based on attendance, parent ratings, therapist ratings, and direct observations (parent engagement, client on-task, therapist on-task, and parent-oriented process).

Table 13.3. Convergent Validities for Indicators on Intervention Quality Constructs.

		1	2	3	4
Parent Engagement					
1.	Attendance	1.00			
2.	Homework completion	.79*	1.00		
3.	Skill acquisition	.38*	.36*	1.00	
Client On-Task					
1.	Group directives	1.00			
2.	Group converse	.30*	1.00		
3.	Social learning task	.45*	.55*	1.00	
4.	Client engagement	.39*	.16[a]	.36*	1.00
Therapist On-Task					
1.	Advise	1.00			
2.	Converse	.47*	1.00		
3.	Directives	.51*	.44*	1.00	
4.	Social learning	.47*	.61*	.61*	1.00
5.	Effectiveness	.26*	.48*	.29*	.49*
Group Process					
1.	Client off topic	1.00			
2.	Client positive	.43*	1.00		

Note: *$p < .05$. [a]$p < .10$

Inspection of Table 13.3 suggests excellent convergence on these four constructs. Of particular interest is the parent engagement construct, indicated by the parents' attendance, homework completion, and scores on a post-test measure of family management (see Andrews, Soberman, & Dishion, 1995). Homework completion and attendance were highly intercorrelated ($r = .79$). The remaining three constructs were derived from direct observations of client and therapist behaviors, and therefore, high convergence was not particularly surprising.

To understand whether group process was associated with change in the parent groups, two approaches were taken. First, the four construct scores were correlated with simple change scores (pre-post differences) in observed parent-child negative engagement. These analyses were somewhat unusual, with respect to the lack of predictive validity. Basically, therapist on-task was correlated, but in a direction opposite than expected. Families that deteriorated in their negative engagement experienced more on-task therapist interactions. Our clinical sense is that rigid adherence to the FCM, without attending to group process issues, may be iatrogenic to the change process. However, it could also be that families in distress may elicit more on-task therapist behavior.

The process variables were examined to predict clinically significant change, using the Jacobsen and Truax (1991) index, with three groups determined to be empirically based on norms for both clinical and normal samples: (a) deteriorated (normal at entry, distressed at termination); (b) unchanged distressed; and (c) unchanged normal and clinically improved (distressed at entry, normal range at termination). Two process construct scores differentiated these four groups: therapist on-task ($F = 2.59$, $p < .06$, $df = 3,96$) and parent-oriented process ($F = 4.35$, $p < .01$, $df = 3,96$).

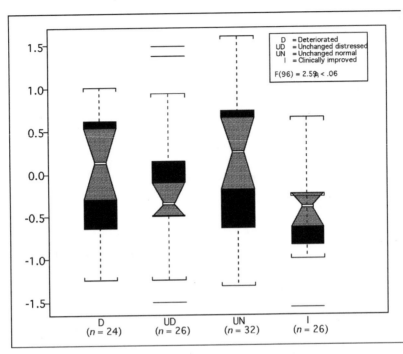

Figure 13.8. Observed therapist on-task behavior and clinically significant change.

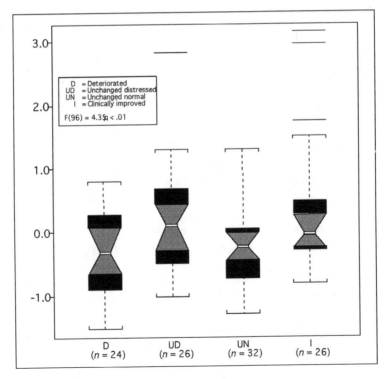

Figure 13.9. Observed parent-oriented group process and clinically significant change.

As in the correlational analyses, therapist on-task was highest for the deteriorated and unchanged normal group (see Figure 13.8). In contrast, parent-oriented process was highest for the unchanged distress and clinically improved group (see Figure 13.9). These analyses suggest that therapist behavior, in some sense, is partially reactive to client circumstances. However, the parent-oriented process finding is consistent with Webster-Stratton and Herbert's (1993) ideas about the importance of a collaborative, supportive group process to foster change.

Perhaps most surprising, from a cognitive behavior perspective, is the lack of covariation between the parent engagement construct and change using both correlational and group comparison techniques. To better understand the nature of parent engagement in these groups, we compared the level of parent engagement across families with different levels of education (less than high school, high school, some college, and college graduation).

We found that the level of parent engagement increased linearly, in accordance with the educational level of the parents, $F(3, 121) = 4.3$, $p < .01$. Parents with a college education were the most likely to attend groups, complete homework, and score well on the social learning post-test. However, contrary to expectation, parent education and parent engagement were uncorrelated with change.

Summary

This chapter describes the ATP multilevel strategy for delivering family-centered interventions to young adolescents in a public school setting. Revisions in ATP are empirically based and pragmatically focused. For example, our original formulation of ATP contained cognitive–behavioral groups for high-risk adolescents. These were found to improve family interactions on the one hand, but unfortunately, also led to iatrogenic effects on smoking and teacher-reported problem behavior (Dishion, McCord, & Poulin, 1999).

Revising ATP to focus primarily on supporting parenting practices, we integrated the family-centered perspective within a school environment to increase the potential of ATP to make a difference in the public health of families of adolescents, which increases the ability to reach high-risk parents (and maximize effectiveness).

Until recently, family-based interventions have been difficult to integrate within a prevention model, primarily because of the expense of the service, but also due to the issue of reaching families in need. Implementation of family intervention within a school setting, however, also addresses these cost issues. For the future, we hope school counselor programs will include intensive training on how to work with parents in academic settings.

Integrating the three intervention levels helps address the related problem of identification and motivation to participate. The multilevel strategy can also address the full range of needs of parents, from preventing adolescent drug use and problem behavior to reducing problem behavior among early starters.

In our experience, integration of parent interventions into typical parent-school communications, such as homework assignments, parent-teacher conferences, and discipline contacts is possible and well received by both parents and teachers. Our findings suggest that the overall strategy is effective: Proactive engagement of families can increase engagement of high-risk families in interventions shown to improve parenting and improve problem behavior in young adolescents.

---

[1] This research was initiated at Oregon Social Learning Center and transferred to the University of Oregon in 1999.

14

Future Extensions of the Models

Gerald R. Patterson

According to the dictionary, a theory is a "plausible body of principles offered as an explanation of a phenomena" while a model is "a system of inferences presented as a mathematical description of a state of affairs" (Dishion & Patterson 1999). While in our writings we have perhaps mistakenly used the terms interchangeably, there is no question but that our general strategy has been to focus on the more mundane modeling rather than theory building.

At the level of theory building, our focus has shifted a great deal in emphasizing intra-individual levels of analyses. We now understand that predictions about rates of deviant behaviors require simultaneous information about contingencies available for both social competencies and for deviant behavior (e.g., it is the relative rate of reinforcement for antisocial behavior that is the key). We hope that the findings summarized in the present volume will stimulate renewed interest in extending the experimental studies began back in the 1970s (Woo, 1978; Devine 1971; & Atkinson 1971). Hopefully others will also engage in the onerous task of analyzing contingencies that are embedded in longitudinal data sets.

While traversing the circumplex that defines Figure 14.1, we find ourselves emerging with yet another change in focus. This one is subtle and relates to an increasing emphasis upon concepts such as selectivity (Donahoe & Palmer, 1994). At the intra-individual level, we have come to believe that the developing individual is essentially a self-maximizing organism that actively selects among responses, settings, and individuals. This is in stark contrast to the metaphor of the inert tabula rasa that could well have characterized our studies back in the 1960s and 1970s. Active selection is at the core of the process by which deviant peers are selected; it is also at the core of what forms of deviancy are the outcomes.

But within that broad theoretical framework, most of the development in the last few decades has been in learning how to define and measure our concepts more cleanly. Given the longitudinal nature of these data, our model tinkering has increasingly focused on developmental issues such as early, and late, onset delinquency, growth, or the lack of it, during some time intervals, the process by which young couples select each other. Always, it has been the case that what we studied was limited primarily by what it is that we knew how to measure. There have been some recent developments in assessment that lead us to believe that we may now be able to expand the models.

In the sections that follow, we briefly describe explorations that should produce three significant changes in the Oregon Models.

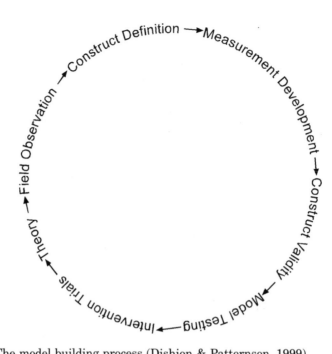

Figure 14.1. The model building process (Dishion & Patternson, 1999).

Toward More Complete Models of Child Behavior

Most of us are trained to view human behavior from a single perspective. In the 1960s one might think all of human behavior can be understood if one studies operants, by a single-minded focus upon attachment process, by the study of cognitions, by studying genes, by studying emotion, or social information processing. Most of us continue on this trajectory by sampling only a small number of journals and even being highly selective as to which articles are read.

We plan to expand the current narrow focus of the coercion model on contingencies to measures of negative emotion and social cognition. We also plan to expand the range of mechanisms invoked to explain both deviant and socially competent child behaviors. Data are now being collected in Wichita that should result in fundamental changes in our understanding of the causal mechanisms for children's aggression and social competencies as well.

As shown in Figure 14.1, the Wichita data will be used first to test the direct contribution hypotheses implied in most of the writing about attributions, negative reinforcement, and negative emotions. The theorists, in their single-minded jousting with the null hypothesis, demonstrates that their favorite variable does indeed correlate with antisocial outcomes. In demonstrating that their favored variable is better than no theory at all, they move swiftly to the implicit assumption that they have also identified *the* cause for children's aggression. We believe that a simple multivariate test, such as the one shown in Figure 14.2, will do a great deal to insert a little humility into such discussions.

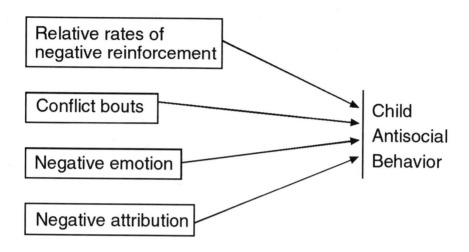

Figure 14.2. Multivariate models of antisocial behavior.

It seems odd, on the face of it, that one could study cognitions about aggression without examining them in the context of either negative emotions or contingencies being supplied for these behaviors. Alternatively why should the study of contingencies for aggression necessarily occur in a social vacuum? What contributions do negative attributions made about siblings and parents make to contingencies? Do negative attributions increase (or decrease) the functional value of successful outcomes (e.g., make them more or less reinforcing)? What contributions do negative attributions made about siblings and parents make to the process? For example, does it increase the risk for more frequent conflict bouts?

Figure 14.3 shows one hypothetical model that tests some of these hypotheses. As shown, our first best guess is that the relative rates of negative reinforcement during family conflict bouts will account for the bulk of the variance in latent constructs assessing future antisocial child behavior. In the original formulation, Snyder and Patterson (1995) hypothesized that in addition to relative rate of reinforcement, the frequency of conflict bouts should make a unique contribution analogous to the frequency of training trials. As shown in the hypothetical model, we also assume that coding facial affect for negative emotion will enhance the power of the negative reinforcement variable. Furthermore, negative attributions are thought to contribute indirectly to antisocial outcomes by enhancing the risk for increasing frequency of conflict bouts and social exchanges characterized by intense negative emotion. We should test for the possibility of a significant interaction effect for these paths (e.g., negative, reinforcement by negative emotion.

The expanded coercion models must also address the fact that almost all of the micro-social analyses have focused on exchanges with a single agent. Based on the Snyder and Patterson (1995) study, we now know that with children the relative rates of reinforcement from conflict bouts with parents account for from 40% to 60% of the variance in the outcome measures of aggression used thus far. However, we

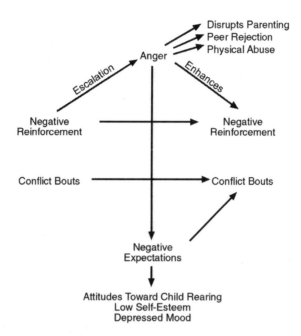

Figure 14.3. Adding thinking and feelings.

also know from Banks programmatic studies that sibling interactions contribute uniquely to the variance in addition to parent contribution. But what we need are multi-variable designs that tell us what the combined contribution would be and how much is unique to mother, to father, and to siblings. Do these contributions change as function of age/gender of child?

In that same context, it is clear from Dishion's programmatic work that deviant peers make yet further contributions. Again in a multivariate design, is the contribution of relative rates of positive and negative reinforcement for deviancy significant above and beyond what the family contributes? The models would suggest that this must indeed by true for the young adolescent, but at what age does this contribution first become significant?

We remain deeply committed to the idea that knowing the relative rates of reinforcement provided by parents, siblings, and peers will not give us a complete picture. The best prediction about future outcomes should require an equivalent amount of information describing contingencies (and cognitions) as they relate to socially competent behavior. This will require that we invent new assessment procedures that give us reliable estimates. As noted in chapter 4, this is an area that we are only beginning to explore.

Non-Partitioned Genes

One of the great ironies in social science is that we finally have hundreds of studies examining the contributions of habitability to myriad social behaviors in children, including aggression. The sad fact is that these studies have not furthered out knowledge of aggression by. The generation of twin and adoption designs are narrowly focused on the question of how much (variance) can be portioned into heritability (G) or environment (E). Because of the well-known myriad methodological problems (truncated distributions of E, failure to satisfy EEA, etc.) the estimates of variance accounted for by E or by G are shaky at best. However, even if the estimates where accurate, we would remain uninformed about how G and E variables contribute to our understanding of children's aggression or social competency.

Currently, OSLC staff, such as Leve, Stoolmiller, and Reid, have submitted several different proposals designed to address the question of genetic contributions to children's aggression and social competency. The genetically informed design would start at birth with information about pregnancy complications, birth weight, birth difficulties, as well as the antisocial status of the biological parents. The contribution of the biological variables to each of the mechanisms driving the progressions that move from distressed infant, to coercive toddler, to hyperactive, and finally antisocial 6-year-old were detailed in chapter 2. The distinctive feature characterizing these studies will be the focus on relating the biological contributions to the specific mechanisms that drive aggressive behavior, rather than to fruitless efforts to estimate the percentage of variance ascribable to E or to G, to shared vs. unshared environments.

We need yet another longitudinal study that employs an at-risk sample, this time of twins. Given an initial assessment at 12 months, we would plan to replicate and extend the assessment procedures used by Shaw and earlier still by Martin and Maccoby (chapter 2). This key study would include observation data collected every 6 months so that we can plot the growth of new forms of deviant behavior. Presumably the interval from 12 to 36 months is critical do the developmental of an early-onset trajectory

Explain Changes in Societal Rates of Crime

As briefly noted in the discussion of delinquency models in chapter 7, it was to have been sociology's task to explain differences among communities in crime rates. It is sad to say that the structural variables proposed by the leaders in that field generate a mixed set of outcomes.

Divorce, unemployment and poverty do not reliability account for changes in societal rates of crime. This is a complex problem characterized by its own set of methodological issues. For example, it is clear that the FBI data sets reflect biases of one kind, while victim surveys have their own unique distortions. Nevertheless, models such as the Oregon delinquency models should be tested against the societal rates task. As things now stand, each politician and newscaster generates their own spin on why it is that current delinquency rates are decreasing. As noted in chapter 7, the Oregon models are relatively clear about which variables should be directly related to changes in rates. Rates of juvenile crime should increase when the prevalence of 9 to 10 year-old antisocial boys increases and this in turn would be predicted by increases in prevalence of households characterized by ineffective parenting practices. Currently there is no one at OSLC competently trained to address these problems.

Modern Questions about Treatment Process

By the mid-1980s, the Center had moved beyond the study of parent resistance and its impact upon therapist behaviors. In a relatively brief span of time, we initiated three major longitudinal studies and began planning a major investment in the newly developing prevention science. Now, in the year 2000, we find ourselves engaged in a new activity that will inevitably lead to further changes in the underlying models.

Several of the Oregon prevention groups are now committed to training substantial numbers of new therapists that will man small community clinics (in Norway) or treatment foster care centers in their own areas. This has led to the development of manuals for therapists to use in training families and manuals for the training of therapists. The new training regimes emphasize repeated role-playing activities as a means for carefully shaping the behavior of family members and simultaneously shaping the behavior of the therapist who is to bring this about.

In a half century of clinical trials, we had simply never specified in detail what the procedures were to be, and why they had to be this way. The mandate becomes that of evaluating the efficacy of this kind of training. The prediction must be that individuals who are given this level of micro training would be more effective than would trainees who simply read the manual and work out the details for themselves. We expect some such analyses to be coming out of the Norway project by 2004.

Family as a System: Just for Fun

I have always envied the facility that systems analysts such as Arny Sameroff (1989) have in presenting their worldviews. However, like Belsky et al. (1989), I am not really impressed with the actual outputs from studies attempting to empirically apply systems ideas to family processes. It is the occasional publication by developmental writers such as Oyama (1989) and Thelen (1989) keep me convinced that I need to continue reading this literature, but at best, I find myself a casual consumer of work in this area. In that context, my latest reading of Sameroff's (1989) chapter leads me to believe that over the years, the Oregon group has drifted a long way from its early operant beginnings. In fact, it is my sense that what we are doing fit at least four of Sameroff's five core requirements for a systems perspective. I thought it might be a useful exercise to list the sense in which there might be such a fit.

1. *Wholeness and Order (Continuity in Development)*. Within the coercion models, we repeatedly stress the key role played by changes in the form of coercive and antisocial behavior (e.g., from overt to covert forms). Within the model, these changes are thought to define a second order deviancy factor that itself is quite stable over time (Patterson, 1993). In this sense, the whole is greater than the sum of the parts. Our long fascination with progressions, sequences, and current preoccupation with trajectories provide a nice fit to Sameroff's discussion of wholeness and continuities requirements (Sameroff, 1989). There is also continuity to the coercion model in the sense

that while temper tantrums at age 4 differ in form from temper tantrums at age 24 years, they constitute part of the core definition of coerciveness at both ages. Continuity is about the stability in the relations among the parts. The structural relations continue while the specific forms change over time.

2. *Self-Stabilization.* "Dynamic systems respond to contextual perturbations, either by homeostatic of homeorhetic processes. . . ." Sameroff (1989, p. 222). As detailed in chapter 6, much of the recent study of family processes is centered on the question of how it is that contexts (e.g., depression, poverty, divorce, stress, neighborhood) have an impact on family microsocial exchange). For example, we know that stress and depression increase maternal irritable exchanges, and this in turn disrupts various parenting practices.

Context alters process; in some sense, process probably also alters context. We view the family as engaged with a never-ending process of accommodating contextual changes that include the maturation of the child, the aging of parents and friends, and changes in occupation. One of the particular values of the coercion models that examine context is to have the search contain information about the central role of contingencies within this process. For example, as the child grows from what he is at age 3 to what he is at age 6, the context shifts from home to public school and enlarges to include peers. What is the impact of these changes in microsocial processes; in particular, how do the contingencies supplied by family members and peers shift during these changes in context?

3. *Self-Reorganization and Adaptation.* "Adaptive, self-organization occurs when the system encounters new constants in the environment that cannot be balanced by existing system mechanisms. Adaptation is defined locally as change that permits the system to maintain its setpoints best in new circumstances." Sameroff (1989, p. 223). Given that the environment changes, for example when the child begins grade one he will find that his existing repertoire does not always function perfectly in each of his interactions with teachers and peers. The encounter requires some adaptive response on the part of the child.

According to the coercion models, the reorganization of existing systems to meet the new challenge will involve selective shopping. Given the new social environment the child will strive to maximize his payoffs given the constraints imposed by his prior history of learning. Presumably, he will select settings, peers, and activities that maximize his payoffs given what he brings to any particular setting.

It follows that given changes in the social environment, children will apply their selective shopping procedures with differential success. This, in turn, would imply that for some, the adaptation will include adjusting to lower overall rates of support and this, in turn, could lead to long-term depression that leads to yet more extreme methods for adapting.

As Sameroff (1989) points out, one can view coercion itself as an adaptation to a change in state provided by another family member. Here the family members' reaction determine the utility of this particular adaptation.

4. *Hierarchical Interactions.* Sameroff (1989), in an earlier critique of the systems qualities found in our studies, quite properly pointed out that we have overlooked the hierarchical relation between child and his family. At that time we had studied parents separately from siblings, and in some instances, the impact of male vs. female siblings on the identified problem child. Bank's elegant work on sibling contributions (see chapter 4) shows that the family is not just an aggregate of reinforcing agents. He demonstrates that the contributions made by siblings to negative outcome are quite unique. His work would be an important prelude to studies of the unique contributions of some dyads. The assumption here would be that an analysis at the level of dyads or triads as done by Belsky et al. (1989) would provide information above and beyond what is inherent in information about individual family members.

Our recent obsession with the growth phenomena leads, via serendipity, back to the hierarchy metaphor. As we view it in Figure 14.4, there are four major junctures that lead to an adult career as a repeated offender. The sequence of junctions defines a hierarchical structure where at each point there are two possible outcomes. In each case, the path to the left leads to yet more extreme deviancy, while the one to the right leads to normal or at least marginal adjustment. As shown, the first critical juncture rests on the resolution of the compliance problem.

Two-year-olds who achieve at least 70% compliance are likely to become normally socialized children and adults, while those who fail move toward increasing risk. At the second juncture, the coercive child will progress to the hyperactivity label (arrested socialization) or move to future extreme as an antisocial child. Those

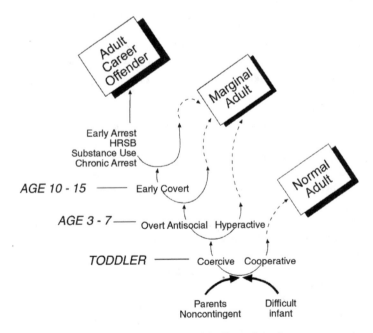

Figure 14.4. Deviancy development may be hierarchically ordered.

overtly antisocial children (55%) who move on to receive advanced covert training are at grave risk to become multiple offending adults p = .48. Conversely, those overtly antisocial boys who do not move on to covert antisocial training are at very low risk for career adult offending p = .06. The developmental sequence itself is hierarchically nested.

5. *Dialectical Contradiction.* Individuals come to know their world through their own activity. The contradiction lies in the fact that as one acts on the environment, they are constantly changing it; in effect, they are changing the thing that they strive to know. As Sameroff (1989) points out in his critique of our work, the coercion models provide rich examples of such contradictions. For example, the parent intends their scolding as punishment for teasing ones

There are other aspects of the Oregon models that are beginning to take on dynamic characteristics. Before we entered our growth modeling phase, we spent some time examining phenomena that seemed to fit bidirectional relationships, or the more complex positive or negative feedback loops. We studied possibilities found in both treatment process (Patterson & Chamberlain, (1988) and in family process itself (Patterson & Bank, 1989). For example the Patterson, Bank, Stoolmiller (1990) report presents a dramatic instance of bidirectional effects by first showing that both parental monitoring and discipline were highly stable when assesses at grade four and then re assessed at grade six. The stability path coefficients for the latent constructs were .66 and .77, respectively. On the other hand, as shown in Figure 14.5, part of the long-term stability in parenting practices reflects the contributions of trying to parent a problem child. The difficult child is constantly disrupting parental efforts to discipline or monitor. It may be, of course, as claimed by Rowe (1994) that the difficulty can be completely explained as a heritable trait. What is shown in Figure 14.5 is that when the latent construct for the antisocial child is introduced at T1, it accounts for a surprising amount of variance in determining how the parental monitoring and discipline unfold in the next 2 years. Having an extremely difficult child to deal with increases the likelihood that parental monitoring will be disrupted 2 years later. Notice that taking the child into account reduces our estimate of parental stability from .77 for monitoring to .42. Stability is not in the child per se. Nor is stability in the parent. It is in the dyad.

You can turn this around and ask the question "How much of the stability of child behavior is in the child, and how much of it is in the parent?" In the Patterson and Bank (1989) study, the change score for parental discipline was significantly related (-.32 p<.05) to the change score for child antisocial behavior.

It is also apparent that what happens within the family has an impact upon what happens on the playground at school. For example, Patterson and Bank (1989) explored the well-known relationship between being antisocial and being rejected by normal peers (see chapter 5). They found the expected (path -.42) relationship, but then went on to demonstrate that this relationship probably has some dynamic characteristics to it. Over a 2-year interval, the stability for the antisocial child latent construct was .65. Notice, however, in Figure 14.6 that when peer rejection at T1 is put into the model, it is shown to be massively significant

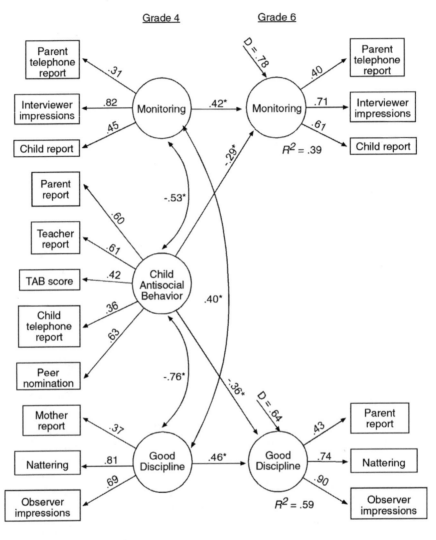

$N = 206$, $X^2_{(96)}$=118.97; $p = .074$; BBN = .897; BBNN = .971; $^*p < .05$

Figure 14.5. Bidirectional relations (Patterson, Bank, & Stoolmiller, 1990).

(-.46; p = .05) in predicting future antisocial behavior. Future parent discipline practices are significantly related to future antisocial behavior, but so is prior knowledge of rejection by peers.

One might imagine several reasons why it is that rejection by peers could function as a positive feedback loop that contributes to future maintenance or growth in antisocial behavior. In keeping with the perspective in the current volume, we assume that the mechanism will be shown to be increased risk for interaction with

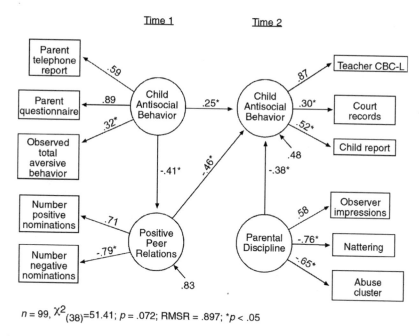

Figure 14.6. Rejecting peers as a feedback loop (Patterson & Bank, 1989).

other problem children who reinforce them for antisocial behavior. The new Wichita studies will permit precise tests of this assumption.

The new generation of studies will permit us to examine contributions of more than just parenting mechanisms to long-term outcomes. Obviously the picture will eventually be complicated with the contribution of multiple mechanisms from within and outside the home.

References

Achenbach, T. M. (1985). *The Child Behavior Checklist for 2- to 3-year-old children.* Burlington; University of Vermont.

Achenbach, T. M. (1991a). *Manual for the Teacher's Report Form and 1991 profile.* Burlington, VT: University of Vermont, Department of Psychiatry.

Achenbach, T. M. (1991b). *Manual for the Child Behavior Checklist/4–18 and 1991 profile.* Burlington, VT: University of Vermont, Department of Psychiatry.

Achenbach, T. M., & Edelbrock, C. S. (1979). *Child behavior checklist.* Bethesda, MD: National Institute of Mental Health.

Achenbach, T. M., & Edelbrock, C. S. (1983). *Manual for the Child Behavior Checklist and Revised Child Behavior Profile.* Burlington,VT: University of Vermont, Psychiatry Department.

Achenbach, T. M., Howell, C. T., Quay, H. C., & Conners, C. K. (1991). *National survey of problems and competencies among four- to sixteen-year-olds: Parents' reports for normative and clinical samples* (Vol. 56(3)(225)): Monographs of the Society for Research in Child Development.

Aiken, L. S., & West, S. G. (1991). *Multiple regression: Testing and interpreting interactions.* Newbury Park, CA: Sage Publications.

Ainsworth, M. D. S., & Wittig, B. A. (1969). Attachment and exploratory behavior of one-year-olds in a strange situation. In B. M. Foss (Ed.), *Determinants of Infant Behavior* (Vol. 4, pp. 111–136). London: Methuen.

Ainsworth, M. S., Blehar, M. C., Waters, E., & Wall, S. (1978). *Patterns of attachment: A psychological study of the strange situation.* Potomac, MD: Lawrence Erlbaum.

Albee, G. W. (1959). *Implications for the future.* New York, Basic Books, Inc.

Albee, G. W. (1990). The futility of psychotherapy. *Journal of Mind & Behavior, 11*(3–4), 369–384.

Albee, G. W., & Gullotta, T. P. (1997). Primary prevention's evolution. In G. W. Albee, & T. P. Gullotta, (Eds.), *Primary prevention works* (pp. 3–22). Thousand Oaks, CA: Sage Publications, Inc.

Albee, G. W., & Gullotta, T. P. (Eds.), *Primary prevention works, Vol. 6: Issues in children's and families' lives.* CA: Thousand Oaks: Sage.

Allison, P. D., & Hauser, R. M. (1991). Reducing bias in estimates of linear models by remeasurement of a random subsample. *Sociological Methods and Research, 19*(4), 466–492.

Allison, P. D., & Liker, J. K. (1982). Analyzing sequential categorical data on dyadic interaction: A comment on Gottman. *Psychological Bulletin, 91*(2), 393–403.

Altmann, S. (1965). Sociobiology of the rhesus monkey. II. Stochastics of social communication. *Journal of Theoretical Biology, 8,* 490–522.

Amato, P. R. (1993). Children's adjustment to divorce: Theories, hypotheses, and empirical support. *Journal of Marriage and the Family, 55*(February), 23–38.

Amato, P. R., & Keith, B. (1991). Parental divorce and the well-being of children: A meta-analysis. *Psychological Bulletin, 110*(1), 26–46.

American Psychiatric Association (1994). *Diagnostic and statistical manual of mental disorders (4th ed.).* APA: Washington, DC.

Anderson, D. (1964). *Applications of a behavior modification technique to the control of a hyperactive child* Unpublished Masters Thesis, University of Oregon.

Anderson, E. R., Greene, S. M., Hetherington, E. M., & Clingempeel, W. G. (in press). The dynamics of parental remarriage: Adolescent, parent, and sibling influence. In E. M. Hetherington & J. D. Aresteh (Eds.), *Coping with divorce, single-parenting, and remarriage: A risk and resiliency perspective*. Hillsdale, NJ: Erlbaum.

Anderson, E. R., Greene, S. M., Nelson, K. A., & Wolchik, S. A. (in press). Children's well-being in stepfamilies: A meta-analysis.

Anderson, E. R., Lindner, M. S., & Bennion, L. D. (1992). The effect of family relationships on adolescent development during family reorganization. In E. M. Hetherington & W. G. Clingempeel (Eds.), *Coping with marital transitions: Monographs of the Society for Research in Child Development* (Vol. 57, pp. 178–200). Chicago: University of Chicago Press.

Anderson, J. A. (1998). *An introduction to neural networks*. Cambridge, MA: The MIT Press.

Andrews, D. W., Soberman, L. H., & Dishion, T. J. (1995). The Adolescent Transitions Program: A school-based program for high-risk teens and their parents. *Education and Treatment of Children, 18*, 478–484.

Aos, S., Phipps, P., Barnoski, R., & Leib, R. (1999). *The comparative costs and benefits of programs to reduce crime: A review of national research findings with implications for Washington State*. Olympia: Washington State Institute for Public Policy.

Arbuckle, J. L. (1996). Full information estimation in the presence of incomplete data. In G. A. Marcoulides & R. E. Schumaker (Eds.), *Advanced structural equation modeling: Issues and techniques* (pp. 243–277). Mahwah, NJ: Erlbaum.

Arbuckle, J. L. (1997). *Amos users' guide version 3.6*. Chicago: SmallWaters.

Arendell, T. (1986). *Mothers and divorce: Legal, economic and social dilemmas*. Berkeley: University of California Press.

Armsden, G. C., McCauley, E., Greenberg, M. T., Burke, P. M., & Mitchell, J. R. (1990). Parent and peer attachment in early adolescent depression. *Journal of Abnormal Child Psychology, 18*, 683–697.

Arnold, J., Levine, A., & Patterson, G. R. (1975). Changes in sibling behavior following family intervention. *Journal of Consulting and Clinical Psychology, 43*, 683–688.

Aron, A., & Aron, E. (1994). *Statistics for psychology*. Englewood Cliffs, NJ: Prentice Hall.

Asarnow, J. R., Goldstein, M. J., Thompson, M., & Guthrie, D. (1993). One-year outcomes of depressive disorders in child psychiatric in-patients: Evaluation of the prognostic power of a brief measure of expressed emotion. *Journal of Child Psychology and Psychiatry, 34*(2), 129–137.

Asher, S. R., & Coie, J. D. (1990). *Peer rejection in childhood*. New York: Cambridge University Press.

Asher, S. R., Hymel, S., & Renshaw, P. D. (1984). Loneliness in children. *Child Development, 55*, 1456–1464.

Atkeson, B. M., & Forehand, R. (1978). Parent behavioral training for problem children: An examination of studies using multiple outcome measures. *Journal of Abnormal Child Psychology, 6*, 449–460.

Avison, W. R., & McAlpine, D. D. (1992). Gender differences in symptoms of depression among adolescents. *Journal of Health and Social Behavior, 33*(June), 77–96.

Azar, S. T., Robinson, D. R., Hekimian, E., & Twentyman, C. T. (1984). Unrealistic expectations and problem-solving ability in maltreating and comparison mothers. *Journal of Consulting and Clinical Psychology, 52*, 687–691.

Baldwin, D. V., & Skinner, M. L. (1989). A structural model for antisocial behavior: Generalization to single-mother families. *Developmental Psychology, 25*, 45–50.

Bandura, A. (1973). *Aggression: A social learning analysis*. Englewood Cliffs, NJ: Prentice Hall, Inc.

Bank, L., Burraston, B., & Snyder, J. (2001). Sibling conflict and ineffective parenting as predictors of adolescent antisocial behavior and peer relations: Additive and interactional effects. *Manuscript submitted for publication*.

Bank, L., Dishion, T. J., Skinner, M. L., & Patterson, G. R. (1990). Method variance in structural equation modeling: Living with "glop." In G. R. Patterson (Ed.), *Depression and aggression in family interaction* (pp. 247–279). Hillsdale, NJ: Lawrence Erlbaum.

Bank, L., Duncan, T., Patterson, G. R., & Reid, J. B. (1993). Parent and teacher ratings in the assessment and prediction of antisocial and delinquent behaviors. *Journal of Personality, 61*(4), 693–709.

Bank, L., Forgatch, M. S., Patterson, G. R., & Fetrow, R. A. (1993). Parenting practices of single mothers: Mediators of negative contextual factors. *Journal of Marriage and the Family, 55,* 371–384.

Bank, L., Marlowe, J. H., Reid, J. B., Patterson, G. R., & Weinrott, M. R. (1991). A comparative evaluation of parent-training evaluations for families of chronic delinquents. *Journal of Abnormal Child Psychology, 19,* 15–33.

Bank, L., & Patterson, G. R. (1992). The use of structural equation modeling in combining data from different types of assessment. In J. C. Rosen & P. McReynolds (Eds.), *Advances in psychological assessment* (Vol. 8, pp. 41–74). New York: Plenum.

Bank, L., Patterson, G. R., & Reid, J. B. (1996). Negative sibling interaction patterns as predictors of later adjustment problems in adolescent and young adult males. In G. H. Brody (Ed.), *Sibling relationships: Their causes and consequences* (pp. 197–229). Norwood, NJ: Ablex Publishing Corporation.

Bank, L., Snyder, J., & Burraston, B. (2000). The consequences of antisocial behavior in older male siblings for younger brothers and sisters: Bad days at black rock. *Journal of Early Adolescence.*

Bardone, A. M., Moffitt, T. E., Caspi, A., Dickson, N., & Silva, P.A. (1996). Adult mental health and social outcomes of adolescent girls with depression and conduct disorder. *Development and Psychopathology, 8,* 811–829.

Barker, R. G. (1963). The stream of behavior as an empirical problem. In R. G. Barker (Ed.), *The stream of behavior: Explorations of its structure and content* (pp. 1–22). New York: Appleton-Century-Crofts.

Barker, R. G., & Wright, H. F. (1951). *One boy's day.* New York: Harper & Row.

Barkley, R. A. (ND). *Hyperactive children: A handbook for diagnosis and treatment.* New York: Guilford.

Barkley, R. A. (1990). *Attention deficit hyperactivity disorder: A handbook for diagnosis and treatment.* New York: Guilford.

Barkley, R. A., & Biederman, J. (1997). Toward a broader definition of the age-of-onset criterion for attention-deficit hyperactivity disorder. *Journal of American Academy of Child and Adolescent Psychiatry, 36,* 1204–1210.

Baron, R. M., & Kenny, D. A. (1986). The moderator-mediator variable distinction in social psychological research: Conceptual, strategies, and statistical considerations. *Journal of Personality and Social Psychology, 51,* 1173–1182.

Barrera, M., Jr., & Garrison-Jones, C. (1992). Family and peer social support as specific correlates of adolescent depressive symptoms. *Journal of Abnormal Child Psychology, 20,* 1–16.

Barrish, H. H., Saunders, M., & Wolfe, M. D. (1969). Good behavior game. Effects of individual contingencies for group consequences and disruptive behavior in a classroom. *Journal of Applied Behavioral Analysis, 2,* 119–124.

Barrow. (1991). *Theories about everything.* Columbia, NY: Fawcett.

Bates, J. E., Bayles, K., Bennett, D. S., Ridge, B., & Brown, M. M. (1991). Orgins of externalizing behavior problems at eight years of age. In D. J. Pepler & K. H. Rubin (Eds.), *The development and treatment of childhood aggression* (pp. 93–120). Hillsdale, NJ: Erlbaum.

Battle, E. S., & Lacey, B. (1972). A context for hyperactivity in children, over time. *Child Development, 43,* 747–773.

Baum, W. M. (1979). Matching, undermatching, and overmatching in studies of choice. *Journal of the Experimental Analysis of Behavior, 32*(2), 269–281.

Baumrind, D. (1971). Current patterns of parental authority. *Developmental Psychology, 4*(1, Pt. 2), 1–103.

Baumrind, D. (1993). The average expectable environment is not good enough: A response to Scarr. *Child Development, 64,* 1299–1317.

Beardslee, W. R., Keller, M. B., Lavori, P. W., Klerman, G. K., Dorer, D. J., & Samuelson, H. (1988a). Psychiatric disorder in adolescent offspring of parents with affective disorder in a non-referred sample. Special Issue: Childhood affective disorders. *Journal of Affective Disorders, 15,* 313–322.

Beauchaine, T. P. (1999, April). *Predicting maternal control strategies from responses to videotaped noncompliance vignettes.* Paper presented at the Paper presented at the biennial meeting of the Society for Research in Child Development, Albuquerque.

Beck, A. T., Ward, C. H., Mendelson, M., Mock, J. E., & Erbaugh, J. K. (1961). An inventory for measuring depression. *Archives of General Psychiatry, 4,* 561–571.

Bell, R. Q. (1968). A reinterpretation of the direction of effects in studies of socialization. *Psychological Review, 75*(2), 81–95.

Bell, S. M., & Ainsworth, M. D. S. (1972). Infant crying and maternal responsiveness. *Child Development, 43,* 1171–1190.

Belle, D. H. (1982). Social ties and social support. In D. Belle (Ed.), *Lives in stress: Women and depression* (pp. 133–144). Beverly Hills, CA: Sage.

Belsky, J. (1984). The determinants of parenting: A process model. *Child Development, 55,* 83–96.

Belsky, J., Rovine, M., & Fish, M. (1989). The developing family system. In M. R. Gunnar & E. Thelen (Eds.), *Systems and development.: The Minnesota Symposia on Child Psychology* (Vol. 22, pp. 119–166). Hillsdale, NJ: Erlbaum.

Belsky, J., & Vondra, J. (1989). Lessons from child abuse: The determinants of parenting. In D. Cicchetti & V. Carlson (Eds.), *Child maltreatment: Theory and research on the causes and consequences of child abuse and neglect* (pp. 153–202). New York: Cambridge University Press.

Biederman, J., Faraone, S. V., Milberger, S., Jetton, J. G., & et al. (1996). Is childhood oppositional defiant disorder a precursor to adolescent conduct disorder? Findings from a four-year follow-up study of children with ADHD. *Journal of American Academy of Child and Adolescent Psychiatry, 35,* 1193–1204.

Biglan, A. (1993). *Changing cultural practices: A contextualist framework for action research.* Reno, NV: Context Press.

Biglan, A. (1995). Translating what we know about the context of antisocial behavior into a lower prevalence of such behavior. *Journal of Applied Behavior Analysis, 28,* 479–492.

Biglan, A., Ary, D., Duncan, T., Duncan, S., Hops, H., & Metzler, C. (1996, May). *Peer and parental influences on the development of problem behavior.* Paper presented at the Poster presented at 5th National Conference on Prevention Research sponsored by the National Institute of Mental Health, Washington, DC.

Biglan, A., Hops, H., & Sherman, L. (1988). Coercive family processes and maternal depression. In R. D. Peters & R. J. McMahon (Eds.), *Social learning and systems approaches to marriage and the family.* (pp. 72–103). New York: Brunner/Mazel.

Biglan, A., Hops, H., Sherman, L., Friedman, L. S., Arthur, J., & Osteen, V. (1985). Problem-solving interactions of depressed women and their husbands. *Behavior Therapy, 16,* 431–451.

Biglan, A., Rothlind, J., Hops, H., & Sherman, L. (1989). Impact of distressed and aggressive behavior. *Journal of Abnormal Psychology, 98*(3), 218–228.

Billy, J. O., Rodgers, J. L., & Udry, J. R. (1984). Adolescent sexual behavior and friendship choice. *Social Forces, 62,* 653–678.

Blechman, E. A., Taylor, C. J., & Schrader, S. M. (1981). Family problem solving versus home notes as early intervention with high-risk children. *Journal of Consulting and Clinical Psychology, 49,* 919–926.

Black, M. M., Hutcheson, J. J., Dubowitz, H., Starr, R. H., Jr., & Berenson-Howard (1996). The roots of competence: Mother-child interaction among low income, urban, African American families. *Journal of Applied Developmental Psychology, 17*(3), 367–391.

Block J. H., & Block, J. (1980). The role of ego-control and ego-resiliency in the organization of behavior. In A. W. Collins (Ed.), *The Minnesota Symposia on Child Psychology: Vol. 13. Development of cognition, affect, and social relations* (pp. 39–101). Hillsdale, NJ: Lawrence Erlbaum.

Block, J. H., Block, J., & Gjerde, P. F., (1986). The personality of children prior to divorce: A prospective study. *Child Development, 57,* 827–840.

Block, J., & Gjerde, P. F. (1993, March). *Ego resiliency through time.* Paper presented at the meeting of the Society for Research in Child Development, New Orleans, LA.

Bowlby, J. (1969). *Attachment and loss. Volume 1: Attachment.* New York: Basic Books.

Branch, M. N., & Hackenberg, T. D. (1998). Humans are animals too: Connecting animal research to human behavior and cognition. In W. O'Donohue (Ed.), *Learning and behavior therapy* (pp. 15–35). Needham Heights, MA: Allyn & Bacon.

Boyle, M. H., Offord, D. R., Racine, Y. A., & Flemining, J. E. (1993). Evaluation of the revised Ontario Child Heath Study scales. *Journal of Child Psychology & Psychiatry & Allied Disciplines, 34,* 189–213.

Bray, J. H., & Berger, S. H. (1993). Developmental issues in Step Families

Brennan, P., Mednick, S., Kandel, E., Congenital determinants of violent and property offending. In D. J. Pepler, K. H. Rubin (Eds.) *The development and treatment of childhood aggression.* Hillsdale, NJ: Lawrence Erlbaum.

Brennan, P. A, & Mednick, S. A. (1997). Medical histories of antisocial individuals. In D. M. Stoff, J. Breiling, & J. D. Maser (Eds.) *Handbook of antisocial behavior* (pp. 269–279). New York: John Wiley & Sons.

Brestan, E. V., & Eyberg, S. M. (1998). Effective psychosocial treatments of conduct-disordered children and adolescents: 29 years, 82 studies, and 5,272 kids. *Journal of Clinical Child Psychology, 27,* 180–189.

Breznitz, Z., & Sherman, T. (1987). Speech patterning of natural discourse of well and depressed mothers and their young children. *Child Development, 58,* 395–400.

Brody, G. H., & Flor, D. L. (1998). Maternal resources, parenting practices, and child competence in rural, single-parent African American families. *Child Development, 69*(3), 803–816.

Brody, G. H., Neubaum, E., & Forehand, R. (1988). Serial marriage: A heuristic analysis of an emerging family form. *Psychological Bulletin, 103*(2), 211–222.

Brody, G. H., Stoneman, Z., & McCoy, J. K. (1994). Contributions of protective and risk factors to literacy and socioemotional competency in former Head Start children attending kindergarten. *Early Childhood Research Quarterly, 9*(3–4), 407–425.

Bronfenbrenner, U. (1988). Interacting systems in human development. Research paradigms: Present and future. In N. Bolger, A. Caspi, G. Downey, & M. Moorehouse (Eds.), *Persons in context: Developmental processes* (pp. 25–49). New York: Cambridge University Press.

Bronfenbrenner, U. (1989). Ecological systems theory. In P. Vasta (Ed.), *Annals of child development, Vol. 6. Six theories of child development: Revised formulations and current issues* (pp. 187–249). London: JaiPress.

Bronfenbrenner, U., & Ceci, S. J. (1994). Nature-nurture reconceptualized in developmental perspective: A bioecological model. *Psychological Review, 101,* 568–586.

Bronfenbrenner, U., McClelland, P., Wethington, E., Moen, P., & Ceci, S. J. (1996). *The state of Americans: This generation and the next.* New York: The Free Press.

Brown, H. C. (1997, August). *Randomized prevention trials as a basis for testing developmental theory: Discussion.* Paper presented at a meeting of the American Psychological Association, Chicago.

Brown, H. C., Indurkhya, A., & Kellam, S. G. (2000). Power calculations for data missing by design: Applications to a follow-up study of lead exposure and attention. *Journal of the American Statistical Association, 95,* 383–395.

Brown, R. T., Coles, C. D., Smith, I. E., Platzman, K. A., Silverstein, J., Erickson, S., & Falek, A.(1991). Effects of prenatal alcohol exposure at school age: II. Attention and behavior. *Neurotoxicology and Teratology. 13,* 369–376.

Bryk, A. S., & Raudenbush, S. W. (1992). Applications in the study of individual change. In A. S. Bryk & S. W. Raudenbush (Eds.), *Hierarchical linear models* (pp. 130–154). Newbury Park, CA: Sage.

Buehler, R. E., Patterson, G. R., & Furniss, J. M. (1966). The reinforcement of behavior in institutional settings. *Behaviour Research and Therapy, 4*, 157–167.

Bullock, B.M., & Dishion, T.J. (2000). Sibling collusion and problem behavior in early adolescence. *Journal of Abnormal Child Psychology*.

Bumpass, L. L. (1984). Children and marital disruption: A replication and update. *Demography, 21*(1), 71–82.

Bumpass, L. L., & Sweet, J. A. (1989). National estimates of cohabitation. *Demography, 26*(4), 615–625.

Bumpass, L. L., Sweet, J. A., & Martin, T. C. (1990). Changing patterns of remarriage. *Journal of Marriage and the Family, 52* (August), 747–756.

Burge, D., & Hammen, C. (1991). Maternal communication: Predictors of outcome at follow-up in a sample of children at high and low risk for depression. *Journal of Abnormal Psychology, 100,* 174–180.

Burgess, R. L. (1994). The family in a changing world: A prolegomenon to an evolutionary analysis. *Human Nature, 5,* 203–221.

Burgess, R. L., & Akers, R. L. (1966). A differential association-reinforcement theory of criminal behavior *Social Problems, 14,* 128–147.

Burgess, R. L., & Drais, A. A. (in press). Beyond the "Cinderella effect": Life history theory and child maltreatment. *Human Nature*.

Burton, L. M., Obeidallah, D. A., & Allison, K. (1996). Ethnographic insights on social context and adolescent development among inner-city African-American teens. In R. Jessor & A. Colby (Eds.), *Ethnography and human development: Context and meaning in social inquiry. The John D. And Catherine T. MacArthur Foundation series on mental health and development* (pp. 395–418). Chicago, IL: University of Chicago Press.

Buss, D. M. (1987). Selection, evocation, and manipulation. *Journal of Personality and Social Psychology, 53,* 1214–1221.

Cairns, R. B. (1979). *The analysis of social interaction: Methods, issues, and illustrations.* Hillsdale, NJ: Lawrence Erlbaum.

Cairns, R. B. (1996). Socialization and sociogenesis. In D. Magnusson (Ed.), *The lifespan development of individuals: Behavioral, neurobiological, and psychosocial perspectives: A synthesis* (pp. 277–295). New York: Cambridge University Press.

Cairns, R. B., & Cairns, B. D. (1991). Social cognition and social networks: A developmental perspective. In D. J. Pepler & K. H. Rubin (Eds.), *The development and treatment of childhood aggression* (pp. 249–278). Hillsdale, NJ: Lawrence Erlbaum.

Cairns, R. B., & Cairns, B. D. (1994). *Lifelines and risks: Pathways of youth in our time.* New York: Cambridge University Press.

Cairns, R. B., Cairns, B. D., Xie, H., Leung, M., & Hearne, S. (1998). Paths across generations: Academic competence and aggressive behaviors in young mothers and their children. *Developmental Psychology, 34*(6), 1162–1174.

Cairns, R. B., Hood, K. E., & Midlam, J. (1985). On fighting in mice: Is there a sensitive period for isolation effects? *Animal Behavior, 33,* 166–180.

Campbell, S. B., Breaux, A. M., Ewing, L. J., & Szumowski, E. K. (1986). Correlates and predictors of hyperactivity and aggression: A longitudinal study of parent-referred problem preschoolers. *Journal of Abnormal Child Psychology, 14,* 217–234.

Capaldi, D. M. (April, 1989). *The relation of family transitions and disruptions to boys' adjustment problems.* Paper presented at the meeting of the Society for Research in Child Development, Kansas City, MO.

Capaldi, D. M. (1991). Co-occurrence of conduct problems and depressive symptoms in early adolescent boys: I. Familial factors and general adjustment at 6th grade. *Development and Psychopathology, 3,* 277–300.

Capaldi, D. M. (1992). Co-occurrence of conduct problems and depressive symptoms in early adolescent boys: II. A 2-year follow-up at 8th grade. *Development and Psychopathology, 4,* 125–144.

Capaldi, D. M. (1994, November). *The impact of contextual variables on family process.* Paper presented at the a panel for American Society of Criminology, Miami, FL.

Capaldi, D. M. (1998). Intergenerational transmission of risk. *NICHD Grant HD 34511.* Available from the author, 160 E. 4th Avenue, Eugene, OR 97401, or at *www.oslc.org.*

Capaldi, D. M., & Clark, S. (1998). Prospective family predictors of aggression toward female partners for at-risk young men. *Developmental Psychology, 34,* 1175–1188.

Capaldi, D. M., & Crosby, L. (1997). Observed and reported psychological and physical aggression in young, at-risk couples. *Social Development, 6,* 184–206.

Capaldi, D., Crosby, L., & Stoolmiller, M. (1996). Predicting the time of first sexual intercourse for adolescent males. *Child Development, 67,* 344–369.

Capaldi, D. M., & Patterson, G. R. (1989*). Psychometic properties of fourteen latent constructs from the Oregon Youth Study.* New York: Springer-Verlag.

Capaldi, D. M., & Patterson, G. R. (1994). Interrelated influences of contextual factors on antisocial behavior in childhood and adolescence for males. In D. Fowles, P. Sutker, & S. Goodman (Eds.), *Progress in experimental personality and psychopathology research* (pp. 165–198). New York: Springer Publications.

Capaldi, D. M., & Stoolmiller, M. (1999). Co-occurrence of conduct problems and depressive symptoms in early adolescent boys: III. Prediction to young-adult adjustment. *Development and Psychopathology, 11,* 59–84.

Capaldi, D. M., Chamberlain, P., Fetrow, R. A., & Wilson, J. E. (1997). Conducting ecologically valid prevention research: Recruiting and retaining a "whole village" in multimethod, multiagent studies. *American Journal of Community Psychology, 25* (4), 471–492

Capaldi, D. M., Dishion, T. J., & Patterson, G. R. (1991). *Assessment of families for the Oregon Youth Study* (Technical report): Oregon Social Learning Center, 207 E. 5th Ave., #202, Eugene, OR 97401.

Capaldi, D. M., Forgatch, M. S., & Crosby, L. (1994). Affective expression in family problem-solving discussions with adolescent boys. *Journal of Adolescent Research, 9,* 28–49.

Capaldi, D. M., & Patterson, G. R. (1987). An approach to the problem of recruitment and retention rates for longitudinal research. *Behavioral Assessment, 9,* 169–177.

Capaldi, D. M., & Patterson, G. R. (1989*). Psychometric properties of fourteen latent constructs from the Oregon Youth Study.* New York: Springer-Verlag.

Capaldi, D. M., & Patterson, G. R. (1991). Relation of parental transitions to boys' adjustment problems: I. A linear hypothesis. II. Mothers at risk for transitions and unskilled parenting. *Developmental Psychology, 27,* 489–504.

Caplan, R. D., Vinokur, A. D., & Price, R. H. (1997). From job loss to reemployment: Field experiments in prevention-focused coping. In G. W. Albee & T. P. Gullotta (Eds.), *Primary prevention works Vol. 6. Issues in children's and families lives* (pp. 341–379). Thousand Oaks: Sage.

Carey, G. (1992). Twin imitation for antisocial behavior: Implications for genetic and family environment research. *Journal of Abnormal Psychology, 101*(1), 18–25.

Carlson, B. E. (1987). Dating violence: A research review and comparison with spouse abuse. *Social Casework: The Journal of Contemporary Social Work, 68*(1), 16–23.

Caspi, A., & Elder, G. H. (1988). Childhood precursors of the life course: Early personality and life disorganization. In E. M. Hetherington, R. M. Lerner, & M. Perlmutter (Eds.), *Child development in life-span perspective* (pp. 115–142). Hillsdale, NJ: Erlbaum.

Caspi, A., & Herbener, E. S. (1990). Continuity and change: Assorative marriage and the consistency of personality in adulthood. *Journal of Personality and Social Psychology, 58,* 250–258.

Caspi, A., Lyman, D., Moffitt, T. E., & Silva, P. A. (1993). Unraveling girls' delinquency: Biological, dispositional, and contextual contributions to adolescent misbehavior. *Developmental Psychology, 29,* 19–30.

Caspi, A., & Moffitt, T. E. (1995). The continuity of maladaptive behavior: From description to understanding in the study of antisocial behavior. In D. Cicchetti & D. J. Cohen (Eds.), *Developmental Psychopathology: (Vol. 2) Risk, disorder, and adaptation* (Vol. 2, pp. 472–511). New York: John Wiley & Sons, Inc.

Chaiken, J., & Rolph, J. E. (1985). *Identifying high-rate serious criminal offenders.* Santa Monica, CA: Rand Corporation.

Chamberlain, P. (1988). Description of the Client Resistance Coding System. In M. Hersen & A. S. Bellack (Eds.), *Dictionary of behavioral assessment techniques.* New York: Pergamon.

Chamberlain, P. (1990). Comparative evaluation of Specialized Foster Care for seriously delinquent youths: A first step. *Community Alternatives: International Journal of Family Care, 2*(2), 21–36.

Chamberlain, P. (1991). *Mediators of male delinquency: A clinical trial.* Grant NO. R01 MH 47458, Center for Studies of Violent Behavior and Traumatic Stress, NIMH, U.S. PHS.

Chamberlain, P. (1994). *Family connections: Treatment Foster Care for adolescents with delinquency.* Eugene, OR: Castalia.

Chamberlain, P. (1997a). Female delinquency: Treatment process and outcomes. *NIMH Grant No. MH 54257.* Available from the author, 160 E. 4th Ave., Eugene, OR 97401 or at *www.oslc.org.*

Chamberlain, P. (in press). *Treating chronic juvenile offenders.* Washington, DC: American Psychological Association.

Chamberlain, P., & Baldwin, D. V. (1988). Client resistance to parent training: Its therapeutic management. In T. R. Kratochwill (Ed.), *Advances, in school psychology* (Vol. VI, pp. 131–171). Hillsdale, NJ: Erlbaum.

Chamberlain, P., & Friman, P. C. (1997). Residential programs for antisocial children and adolescents. In D. M. Stoff, J. Breiling, & J. D. Maser (Eds.), *Handbook of antisocial behavior* (pp. 416–424). NY: John Wiley & Sons.

Chamberlain, P., & Mihalic, S. F. (1998). Multidimensional treatment foster care. In D. S. Elliott (Series Ed.), *Book eight: Blueprints for violence prevention.* Boulder, CO: Institute of Behavioral Science, University of Colorado.

Chamberlain, P., & Moore, K. (1998). A clinical model for parenting juvenile offenders: A comparison of group care versus family care. *Clinical Child Psychology and Psychiatry, 3,* 375–386.

Chamberlain, P., & Moore, K. J. (in press). Chaos and trauma in the lives of adolescent females with antisocial behavior and delinquency. In R. Geffner (Series Ed.) & Greenwald (Vol. Ed.) *Trauma and juvenile delinquency: Theory, research, and interventions.* Binghamton, NY: The Haworth Press.

Chamberlain, P., & Patterson, G. R. (1995). Discipline and child compliance in parenting. In M. H. Bornstein (Ed.), *Handbook of parenting* (Vol. IV, pp. 205–225). Hillsdale, NJ: Erlbaum.

Chamberlain, P., Patterson, G. R., Reid, J. B., Forgatch, M. S., & Kavanagh, K. (1984). Observation of client resistance. *Behavior Therapy, 15,* 144–155.

Chamberlain, P., & Ray, J. (1988). The therapy process code: A multidimensional system for observing therapist and client interactions in family treatment. In R. J. Prinz (Ed.), *Advances in behavioral assessment of children and families* (Vol. 4, pp. 189–217). Greenwich, CT: JAI Press.

Chamberlain, P., Ray, J., & Moore, K. J. (1996). Characteristics of residential care for adolescent offenders: A comparison of assumptions and practices in two models. *Journal of Child and Family Studies, 5,* 259–271.

Chamberlain, P., & Reid, J. B. (1987). Parent observation and report of child symptons. *Behavioral Assessment, 9,* 97–109.

Chamberlain, P., & Reid, J. B. (1994). Differences in risk factors and adjustment for male and female delinquents in Treatment Foster Care. *Journal of Child and Family Studies, 3*(1), 23–39.

Chamberlain, P. & Reid, J. B. (1998). Comparison of two community alternatives to incarceration for chronic juvenile offenders. *Journal of Consulting and Clinical Psychology, 6*, 624–633.

Chamberlain, P., & Reid, J. B. (in press). Comparison of two community alternatives to incarceration for chronic juvenile offenders. *Journal of Consulting and Clinical Psychology.*

Chamberlain, P. C. (1997b, April). *The effectiveness of group versus Family Treatment settings for adolescent juvenile offenders.* Paper presented at the Society for Research in Child Development, Washington, DC.

Chase-Lansdale, P., Cherlin, A.J., & Kiernan, K.E. (1995). The long-term effects of parental divorce on the mental health of young adults: A developmental perspective. *Child Development, 66,* 1614–1634

Chassin, L., Presson, C. C., & Sherman, S. J., (1990). Social psychological contributions to the understanding and prevention of adolescent cigarette smoking. *Personality & Social Psychology Bulletin, 16*, 133–151.

Cherlin, A. J. (1992). *Marriage, divorce, remarriage.* Cambridge, MA: Harvard University Press.

Cherlin, A. J., Furstenberg, F. F., Chase-Lansdale, P. L., Kiernan, K. E., Robins, P. K., Morrison, D. R., & Teitler, J. O. (1991). Longitudinal studies of effects of divorce on children in Great Britain and the United States. *Science, 252,* 1386–1389.

Chesney-Lind, M., & Shelden, R. G. (Eds.). (1992). *Girls: Delinquency and juvenile justice.* Pacific Grove, CA: Brooks/Cole.

Chilcoat, H. D., Dishion, T. J., & Anthony, J. C. (1995). Parent monitoring and the incidence of drug sampling in urban elementary school children. *American Journal of Epidemiology, 141*(1), 25–31.

Cicchetti, D. (1990). An historical perspective on the discipline of developmental psychopathology. In J. E. Rolf, A. Masten, D. Cicchetti, K. Nuechterlein, & B. S. Weintraub (Eds.), *Risk and protective factors in the development of psychopathology* (pp. 2–28). New York: Cambridge University Press.

Cicchetti, D., & Schneider-Rosen, K. (1986). An organizational approach to childhood depression. In M. Rutter, C. E. Izard, & P. B. Read (Eds.), *Depression in young people: Developmental and clinical perspectives* (pp. 71–134). New York: Guilford Press.

Cleveland, W. S. (1993). *Visualizing data.* New Jersey: AT&T Bell Laboratories.

Cloward, R., & Ohlin, L. I. (1960). *Delinquency and opportunity: A theory of delinquent gangs.* Glencoe, IL: Free Press.

Cohen, J., & Cohen, P. (1983). *Applied multiple regression/correlation analysis for the behavioral sciences* (2nd ed.). Hillsdale, NJ: Lawrence Erlbaum Associates.

Cohen, L. H., Burt, C. E., & Bjorck, J. P. (1987). Life stress and adjustment: Effects of life events experienced by young adolescents and their parents. *Developmental Psychology, 23,* 583–592

Cohen, P. (1991). A source of bias in longitudinal investigations of change. In L. M. Collins & J. L. Horn (Eds.), *Best methods for the analysis of change* (pp. 18–25). Washington, DC: American Psychological Association.

Cohn, D. A. (1990). Child-mother attachment of 6-year-olds and social competence at school. *Child Development, 61,* 152–162.

Coie, J. D., & Kupersmidt, J.B. (1983). A behavioral analysis of emerging social status in boys' groups. *Child development, 54,* 1400–1416.

Coie, J. D., Terry, R., Zakriski, A., & Lochman, J. (1995). Early adolescent social influences on delinquent behavior. In J. McCord (Ed.), *Coercion and punishment in long-term perspectives* (pp. 229–244). New York: Cambridge University Press.

Cole, D. A., & McPherson, A. E. (1993). Relation of family subsystems to adolescent depression: Implementing a new family assessment strategy. *Journal of Family Psychology, 7(1),* 119–133.

Collins, W. A., Maccoby, E. E., Steinberg, L., Hetherington, E. M., & Bornstein, M. (2000). Contemporary research on parenting: The case for nature *and* nurture. *American Psychologist,* 55, 218–232.

Condry, J., & Condry, S. (1976). Sex differences: A study of the eye of the beholder. *Child Development, 47*, 812–819.

Conduct Problems Prevention Research Group (1992). A developmental and clinical model for the prevention of conduct disorder: The FAST track program. *Development and Psychopathology, 4*, 509–527.

Conger, R. (1991, April). *Impact of life stressors on adult relationships and adolescent adjustment.* Paper presented at the meeting of the Society for Research in Child Development, Seattle, WA.

Conger, R. D., Conger, K. J., Elder, G. H., Jr., Lorenz, F. O., Simons, R. L., & Whitbeck, L. B. (1992). A family process model of economic hardship and adjustment of early adolescent boys. *Child Development, 63*, 526–541.

Conger, R.D., & Kileen, P. (1974). Use of concurrent operants in small group research: A demonstration. *Pacific Sociological Review, 17*, 399–416.

Conger, R. D., Patterson, G. R., & Ge, X. (1995). It takes two to replicate: A mediational model for the impact of parents' stress on adolescent adjustment. *Developmental Psychology, 66*, 80–97.

Conger, R. D., & Simons, R.L. (1995). Life course contingencies in the development of adolescent antisocial behavior: A matching law approach. In T.P. Thornberry (Ed.), *Developmental theories of crime and delinquency* (pp. 183–209). New Brunswick, NJ: Transaction Books.

Connolly, K., & Bruner, J. (Eds.). (1974). *The growth of competence.* New York: Academic Press.

Cox, A. D., Puckering, C., Pound, A., & Mills, M. (1987). The impact of maternal depression in young children. *Journal of Child Psychology and Psychiatry, 28,* 917–928.

Coyne, J. C. (1976). Depression and the response of others. *Journal of Abnormal Psychology, 85*, 186–193.

Coyne, J. C. (1999). Thinking interactionally about depression: A radical restatement. In T. C. J. C. Joiner (Ed.), *The interactional nature of depression.* (pp. 365–392). Washington, D.C.: American Psychological Association.

Coyne, J. C., Kessler, R. C., Tal, M., Turnbull, J., Wortman, C. B., & Greden, J. F. (1987). Living with a depressed person. *Journal of Consulting and Clinical Psychology, 55*, 347–352.

Crick, N. R., & Dodge, K. A. (1994). A review and reformulation of social information-procesing meachanisms in children's social adjustment. *Psychological Bulletin*, 115(1), 74–101.

Crittenden, P. (1995). *The Preschool Assessment of Attachment: Coding Manual.* Miami, FL: Family Relations Institute.

Cummings, E. M. (1987). Coping with background anger in early childhood. *Child Development, 58*, 976–984.

Cummings, E. M., Ballard, M., El-Sheikh, M., (1991). Responses of children and adolescents to interadult anger as a function of gender, age, and mode of expression. *Merrill-Palmer quarterly, 37*(4), 543–560.

Cummings, E. M., Ballard, M., El-Sheikh, M., & Lake, M. (1991). Resolution and children's responses to interadult anger. *Developmental Psychology, 27*, 462–470.

Cummings, E. M., & Davies, P. (1994). *Children and marital conflict: the impact of family dispute and resolution.* New York: Guilford Press.

Cummings, E. M., Iannotti, R. J., & Zahn-Waxler, C. (1985). The influence of conflict between adults on the emotions and aggression of young children. *Developmental Psychology, 21*, 495–507.

Cummings, E. M., Vogel, D., Cummings, J. S., & El-Sheikh, M. (1989). Children's responses to different forms of expression of anger between adults. *Child Development, 60*, 1392–1404.

Cummings, E. M., Zahn-Waxler, C., & Radke-Yarrow, M. (1981). Young children's responses to expressions of anger and affection by others in the family. *Child Development, 52*(1274), 1282

Cummings, J. S., Pellegrini, D. S., Notarius, C. I., & Cummings, E. M. (1989). Children's responses to angry adult behavior as a function of marital distress and history of interparent hostility. *Child Development, 60*, 1035–1043.

Cunningham, C. E., & Barkley, R. A. (1979). The interactions of hyperactive and normal children with their mothers during free play and structured task. *Child Development, 50*, 217–224.

Dadds, M. R., Sanders, M. R., Morrison, M., & Rebgetz, M. (1992). Childhood depression and conduct disorder: II. An analysis of family interaction patterns in the home. *Journal of Abnormal Psychology, 101*(3), 505–513.

Daniels-Bierness, T. (1989). Measuring peer status in boys and girls: A problem of apples and oranges. In B. H. Schneider, G. Attili, J. Nadel, & R. P. Weissberg (Eds.), *Social competence in developmental perspective* (pp. 107–120). Boston: Kluwer.

Darling, N., & Steinberg, L. (1993). Parenting styles as context: An integrative model. *Psychological Bulletin, 113,* 487–496.

Davies, P. T., & Cummings, E. M. (1994). Marital conflict and child adjustment: An emotional security hypothese. *Psychological Bulletin, 116*(3), 387–411.

Davis, B., Hops, H., Alpert, A., & Sheeber, L. (1998). Child responses to parent conflict and their effect on adjustment: A study of triadic relations. *Journal of Family Psychology, 12*(2), 163–177.

Davis, B., Sheeber, L., Hops, H. & Tildesley, E. (in press). Adolescent responses to depressive parental behaviors in problem-solving interactions: Implications for depressive symptoms. *Journal of Abnormal Child Psychology*.

Davison, M., & McCarthy, D. (1988). *The matching law: A research review*. Hillsdale, NJ: Lawrence Erlbaum.

Deater-Deckard, K. (2000). Parenting and child behavior adjustment in early childhood: A quantitative genetic approach to studying family processes. *Child Development, 71,* 468–484.

Deater-Deckard, K., & Dodge, K. A. (1997). Externalizing behavior problems and discipline revisited: Nonlinear effects and variation by culture, context, and gender. *Psychological Inquiry, 8,* 161–175.

DeBaryshe, B. D., Patterson, G. R., & Capaldi, D. M. (1993). A performance model for academic achievement in early adolescent boys. *Developmental Psychology, 29,* 795–804.

DeGarmo, D., & Forgatch, M. S. (1996a). Longitudinal determinants of observed confidant support for divorced mothers. *Manuscript submitted for publication.*

DeGarmo, D., & Forgatch, M. S. (1996b). *Lady Madonna delinquent at your feet: A longitudinal test of family management for single mothers* (Unpublished manuscript). Eugene, OR: Oregon Social Learning Center.

DeGarmo, D. S., & Forgatch, M. S. (1996c, June). *Visualizing continuity and change: Techniques with longitudinal data.* Paper presented at the Workshop presented at the annual Summer Institute of the Family Research Consortium. Continuity and change: Family structure and processes, San Diego, CA.

DeGarmo, D. S., & Forgatch, M. S. (1997a). Confidant support and maternal distress: Predictors of parenting practices for divorced mothers. *Personal Relationships, 4,* 305–317.

DeGarmo, D. S., & Forgatch, M. S. (1997b). Determinants of observed confidant support. *Journal of Personality and Social Psychology,* 336–345.

DeGarmo, D. S., & Forgatch, M. S. (1999). Contexts as predictors of changing maternal parenting practices in diverse family structures: A social interactional perspective to risk and resilience. In E. M. Hetherington (Ed.), *Coping with divorce, single parenting and remarriage: A risk and resiliency perspective* (pp. 227–252). Hillsdale, NJ: Erlbaum.

DeGarmo, D. S., Forgatch, M. S., & Martinez, C. R., Jr. (1999). Parenting of divorced mothers as a link between social status and boys' academic outcomes: Unpacking the effects of socioeconomic status. *Child Development, 70*(5), 1231–1245.

Derogatis, L. R., & Spencer, P. M. (1982). *The brief symptom inventory (BSI) administration, scoring, and procedures manual—I.* Baltimore: Clinical Psychometric Research.

Devine, V. T. (1971). *The coercion process: A laboratory analogue.* Unpublished doctoral dissertation, State University of New York at Stony Brook.

Diaz, R. M., Neal, C. J., & Vachio, A. (1991). Maternal teaching in the zone of proximal development: A comparison of low- and high-risk dyads. *Merrill-Palmer Quarterly, 37*(1), 83–107.

DiLalla, L. F., & Gottesman, I. (1991). Biological and genetic contributors to violence—Wisdom's untold tale. *Psychological Bulletin, 109,* 125 –129.

DiLalla, L. R., & Gottesman, I. I. (1989, April). *Early predictors of delinquency and adult criminality.* Paper presented at the Society for Research in Child Development, Kansas City, MO.

Dishion, T. J. (1990a). Family ecology of boys' peer relations in middle childhood. *Child Development, 61,* 874–892.

Dishion, T. J. (1990b). The peer context of troublesome child and adolescent behavior. In P. Leone (Ed.), *Understanding troubled and troubling youth: Multidisciplinary perspective* (pp. 128–153). Newbury Park, CA: Sage.

Dishion, T. J. (1996, September). *Advances in family-based interventions to prevent adolescent drug abuse.* Paper presented at the National Institute on Drug Abuse conference, Washington, DC.

Dishion, T. J., Stormshak, E. (in press). *An ecological approach to child clinical and counseling psychology.* Washington, DC: APA Books.

Dishion, T. J., & Andrews, D. W. (1995). Preventing escalation in problem behaviors with high-risk young adolescents: Immediate and 1-year outcomes. *Journal of Consulting and Clinical Psychology, 63,* 538–548.

Dishion, T. J., Andrews, D. W., & Crosby, L. (1995). Adolescent boys and their friends in early adolescence: I. Relationship characteristics, quality, and interactional processes. *Child Development, 66,* 139–151.

Dishion, T. J., Andrews, D. W., Kavanagh, K., & Soberman, L. (1996). Preventive interventions for high-risk youth: The Adolescent Transitions Program. In R. D. Peters & R. J. McMahon (Eds.), *Preventing childhood disorders, substance abuse, and delinquency* (pp. 184–214). Thousand Oaks: Sage.

Dishion, T. J., Biglan, A., Kavanagh, K., Metzler, C. W., & Soberman, L. H. (in press). Family Management Curriculum. In T. D. Dishion & K. Kavanagh (Eds.), *Adolescent problem behavior: Family Assessment and Interaction Sourcebook.*

Dishion, T. J., Capaldi, D., Spracklen, K. M., & Li, F. (1995). Peer ecology of male adolescent drug use. *Development and Psychopathology, 7,* 803–824.

Dishion, T. J., Capaldi, D., & Yoeger, K. (1999). Middle childhood antecedents to progression in male adolescent substance use: An ecological analysis of risk and protection. *Journal of Adolescent Research, 14,* 175–206.

Dishion, T. J., Crosby, L., Rusby, J., Shane, D., Patterson, G. R., & Baker, J. (1993). *Peer Process Code: A multidimensional system for observing family interaction.* Unpublished manuscript, Oregon Social Learning Center, Eugene, OR.

Dishion, T. J., Duncan, T. E., Eddy, J. M., Fagot, B. I., & Fetrow, R. (1994). The world of parents and peers: Coercive exchanges and children's social adaptation. *Social Development, 3,* 255–268.

Dishion, T. J., Gardner, K., Patterson, G. R., Reid, J. B., Spyrou, S., & Thibodeaux, S. (1983). *The Family Process Code: A multidimensional system for observing family interaction.* Unpublished manuscript, Oregon Social Learning Center, Eugene, OR.

Dishion, T. J., Eddy, J. M., Haas, E., Li, F., & Spracklen, K. (1997). Friendships and violent behavior during adolescence. *Social Development, 6,* 207–223.

Dishion, T. J., French, D. C., & Patterson, G. R. (1995). The development and ecology of antisocial behavior. In D. Cicchetti & D. J. Cohen (Eds.), *Developmental psychopathology. Volume 2: Risk, disorder, and adaptation* (pp. 421–471). New York: Wiley.

Dishion, T. J., & Kavanagh, K. (1995, July). *Cognitive behavioral intervention strategies for high-risk young adolescents: A comparative analysis of 1-year outcome effects.* Paper presented at the World Congress of Behavioural and Cognitive Therapies, Copenhagen, Denmark.

Dishion, T. J., & Kavanagh, K. (in press). *Adolescent problem behavior: An intervention and assessment sourcebook for working with families in schools.* New York: Guilford.

Dishion, T. J., & Kavanagh, K., & Kiesner, J. (in press). Prevention of early adolescent substance use among high-risk youth: A multiple gating approach to parent intervention. In R. S. Ashery (Ed.), *Research meeting on drug abuse prevention through family interventions:* NIDA Research Monograph.

Dishion, T. J,. Kavanagh, K., Veltman, M., McCartney, T., Soberman, L., & Stormshak, E. (in press). *The Family Management Curriculum.* New York: Guilford.

Dishion, T. J., Loeber, R., Stouthamer-Loeber, M., & Patterson, G. R. (1984). Skill deficits and male adolescent delinquency. *Journal of Abnormal Child Psychology, 12,* 37–54.

Dishion, T. J., McCord, J., & Poulin, F. (1999). When interventions harm: Peer groups and problem behavior. *American Psychologist, 54,* 755–764.

Dishion, T. J., & Medici Skaggs, N. (2000). An ecological analysis of monthly bursts in early adolescent substance use. *Applied Developmental Science, 4,* 89–97.

Dishion, T. J., & Patterson, G. R. (1992). Age effects in parent training outcome. *Behavior Therapy, 23,* 719–729.

Dishion, T. J., & Patterson, G. R. (1993). Childhood screening for early adolescent problem behavior: A multiple gating strategy. In M. Singer, L. Singer, & T. M. Anglin (Eds.), *Handbook for screening adolescents at psychosocial risk* (pp. 375–399). NY: Lexington.

Dishion, T. J., & Patterson, G. R. (1997a). Editorial: Relationship processes in social adaptation and maladaptation. *Social Development, 6,* 137–141.

Dishion, T. J., & Patterson, G. R. (1997b). The timing and severity of antisocial behavior: Three hypotheses within an ecological framework. In D. M. Stoff, J. Breiling, & J. D. Maser, *Handbook of antisocial behavior* (pp. 205–217). New York: Wiley & Sons.

Dishion, T. J., & Patterson, G. R. (1999). Model-building in developmental psychopathology: A pragmatic approach to understanding and intervention. *Journal of Clinical Child Psychology, 28,* 502–512.

Dishion, T. J., Patterson, G. R., & Griesler, P. C. (1994). Peer adaptation in the development of antisocial behavior: A confluence model. In L. R. Huesmann (Ed.), *Current perspectives on aggressive behavior* (pp. 61–95). New York: Plenum.

Dishion, T. J., Patterson, G. R., & Kavanagh, K. A. (1992). An experimental test of the coercion model: Linking theory, measurement, and intervention. In J. McCord & R. Tremblay (Eds.), *The interaction of theory and practice: Experimental studies of intervention* (pp. 253–282). New York: Guilford.

Dishion, T. J., Patterson, G. R., Stoolmiller, M., & Skinner, M. (1991). Family, school, and behavioral antecedents to early adolescent involvement with antisocial peers. *Developmental Psychology, 27,* 172–180.

Dishion, T. J., & Patterson, S. G. (1996). *Preventive parenting with love, encouragement, and limits: The preschool years.* Eugene, OR: Castalia.

Dishion, T. J., Poulin, F., & Medici Skaggs, N. (2000). The ecology of premature autonomy in adolescence: Biological and social influences. In K. A. Kerns & A. M. Neal-Barnett (Eds.), *Family and peers: Linking two social worlds.* Westport, CT: Praeger.

Dishion, T. J., Reid, J. B., & Patterson, G. R. (1988). Empirical guidelines for a family intervention for adolescent drug use. *Journal of Chemical Dependency Treatment, 1,* 189–224.

Dishion, T. J., Spracklen, K. M., Andrews, D. W., & Patterson, G. R. (1996). Deviancy training in male adolescent friendships. *Behavior Therapy, 27,* 373–390.

Dix, T. (1991). The affective organization of parenting: Adaptive and maladaptive processes. *Psychological Bulletin, 110,* 3–25.

Dodge, K. A. (1980). Social cognition and children's aggressive behavior. *Child Development, 51,* 162–170.

Dodge, K. A. (1983). Behavioral antecedents of peer social status. *Child Development, 54,* 1386–1399.

Dodge, K. A. (1983). Promoting social competence in school children. *Schools and Teaching, 1(2),* 67–76.

Dodge, K., Pettit, G. S., Bates, J. E., & Valente, E. (1995). Social-information-processing patterns partially mediate the effect of early physical abuse on later conduct problems. *Journal of Abnormal Psychology, 104,* 632–643.

Dodge, K. A., Schlundt, D., Shocken, J., & Delaguch, J. (1986). Social competence and children's social status: The role of peer group entry strategies. *Merrill-Palmer Quarterly, 29,* 309–336.

Dolan, L. J., Kellam, S. G., Brown, C. H., Werthamer-Larsson, L., Rebok, G. W., Mayer, L. S., Laudolff, J., Turkkan, J. S., Ford, C., & Wheeler, L. (1993). The short-term impact of two classroom-based preventive interventions on aggressive and shy behaviors and poor achievement. *Journal of Applied Developmental Psychology, 14,* 317–345.

Donahoe, J. W., & Palmer, D. C. (1994). *Learning and complex behavior.* Boston: Allyn & Bacon.

Downey, G., & Coyne, J.C. (1990). Children of depressed parents: An integrative review. *Psychological Bulletin, 108(1),* 50–76.

Downey, G., & Feldman, S. I. (1996). Implications of rejection sensitivity for intimate relationships. *Journal of Personality and Social Psychology, 70(6),* 1327–1343.

Dubos, R. J. (1959). *Miracle of health: Utopias, progress, and biological change.* New York: Doubleday.

Dumas, J. E., Gibson, J. A., & Albin, J. B. (1989). Behavioral correlates of maternal depressive symptomatology in conduct-disorder children. *Journal of Consulting and Clinical Psychology, 57,* 516–521.

Duncan, T. E., Duncan, S. C., & Stoolmiller, M. (1994). Modeling developmental processes using latent growth structural equation methodology. *Applied Psychological Measurement, 18,* 343–354.

Dunkel-Schetter, C., & Bennett, T. L. (1990). Differentiating the cognitive and behavioral aspects of social support. In B. R. Sarason, I. G. Sarason, & G. R. Pierce (Eds.), *Social support and interactional view* (pp. 267–296). New York: John Wiley and Sons.

Duran, E., & Duran, B. (1995). *Native American postcolonial psychology.* Albany, NY: State University of New York Press.

Eddy, J. M. (1999). Child and adolescent treatment and preventive intervention. *NIMH Grant. No. MH 59127.* Available from the author, 160 E. 4th Ave., Eugene, OR, 97401, or at *www.oslc.org.*

Eddy, J. M., & Chamberlain, P.C. (2000). Family management and deviant peer association as mediators of the impact of treatment condition on youth antisocial behavior. *Journal of Consulting and Clinical Psychology, 68,* 857–863.

Eddy, J. M., Dishion, T. J., & Stoolmiller, M. (1997). *The analysis of change in children and families: Methodological and conceptual issues.* Manuscript submitted for publication.

Eddy, J. M., Leve, L. D., & Fagot, B. I. (submitted). *Coercive family processes: A replication and extension of Patterson's Coercion Model.*

Eddy, M., & Fagot, B. I. (1991, April). *The coercion model of antisocial behavior: Generalization to 5-year-old children and their parents.* Paper presented at the Society for Research in Child Development, Seattle, WA.

Eddy, J. M., Reid, J. B., & Fetrow, R. A. (2000). An elementary school-based prevention program targeting modifiable antecedents of youth delinquency and violence: Linking the interests of families and teachers (LIFT). *Journal of Emotional and Behavioral Disorders, 8(3),* 165–176.

Eddy, J. M., Reid, J. B., Fetrow, R. A., & Stoolmiller, M. (2002). *Three year outcomes for a preventive intervention for conduct problems.* Manuscript submitted for publication.

Eddy, J. M., & Swanson-Gribskov, L. (1997). Juvenile justice and delinquency prevention in the United States: The influence of theories and traditions on policies and practices. In T. P. Gullota, G. R. Adams, & R. Montemayor (Eds.), *Delinquent violent youth* (pp. 12–52). Thousand Oaks, CA, Sage.

Elder, G. H., Jr., & Caspi, A. (1988). Economic stress in lives: Developmental perspectives. *Journal of Social Issues, 44,* 25–45.

Elder, G. H., Jr., Caspi, A., & van Nguyen, T. (1986). Resourceful and vulnerable children: Family influences in hard times. In R. K. Silbereisen, K. Eyferth, & G. Rudinger. (Eds.) *Development as action in context: Problem behavior and normal* (pp. 167–186) New York: Springer-Verlag.

Elder, G. H., Van Nguyen, T., & Caspi, A. (1985). Linking family hardship to children's lives. *Child Development,56,* 361–375.

Eley, T. C., Lichtenstein, P., & Stevenson, J. (1999). Sex differences in the etiology of aggressive and nonaggressive antisocial behavior: Results from two twin studies. *Child Development, 70,* 155–168.

Elliott, D. S., Huizinga, D., & Ageton, S.S. (1985). *Explaining delinquency and drug use.* Beverley Hills, CA: Sage.

Elliott, D. S., & Voss, H. L. (1974). *Delinquency and Dropout.* Lexington, MA: Lexington Books.

El-Sheikh, M., Cummings, E.M., & Goetsch, V. (1989). Coping with adults' angry behavior: Behavioral, physiological, and self-reported responding in preschoolers. *Developmental Psychology, 25,* 490–498.

Embry, D. D., Flannery, D. J., Vazsonyi, A. T., Powell, K. E., & Atha, H. (1996). PeaceBuilders: A theoretically driven, school–based model for early violence prevention. *American Journal of Preventive Medicine, 12*(5), 91–100.

Emde, R. N., Plomin, R., Robinson, J., Corley, R., DeFries, J., Fulker, D. W., Reznick, J. S., Campos, J., Kagan, J., & Zahn–Waxler, C. (1992). Temperament, emotion, and cognition at fourteen months: The MacArthur Longitudinal Twin Study. *Child Development, 63,* 1437–1455.

Emery, R. E. (1982). Interparental conflict and the children of discord and divorce. *Psychological Bulletin, 92*(2), 310–330.

Emery, R. E. (1988). *Marriage, divorce, and children's adjustment.* Newbury Park, CA: Sage.

Emery, R. E. (1992). Family conflicts and their developmental implications: A conceptual analysis of meanings for the structure of relationships. In C. Shantz & W. Hartup (Eds.), *Conflict in child and adolescent development.* (pp. 270–298). New York: Cambridge University Press.

Emery, R. E., Kitzmann, K., & Aaron, J. (1993, March). *Mothers' aggression before marriage and children's aggression after divorce.* Paper presented at the biennial meeting of the Society for Research in Child Development, New Orleans.

Emery, R. E., & O'Leary, K. D. (1982). Children's perceptions of marital discord and behavior problems of boys and girls. *Journal of Abnormal Child Psychology, 10*(1), 11–24.

Emery, R. E., & O'Leary, K. D. (1984). Marital discord and child behavior problems in a nonclinic sample. *Journal of Abnormal Child Psychology, 12*(3), 411–420.

Empey, L. T. (1978). *American delinquency: Its meaning and construction.* Homewood, IL: Dorsey Press.

Englund, M. M., Levy, A. K., Hyson, D. M., & Sroufe, L. A. (2000). Adolescent social competence: Effectiveness in a group setting. *Child Development, 71*(4), 1049–1060.

Erickson, M. L., & Empey, L. T. (1963). Court records, undetected delinquency, and decision-making. *Journal of Criminal Law, Criminology, and Police Science, 54,* 456–469.

Fagot, B. I. (1966). Conditioning effects on two apparatuses. *Psychonomic Science, 4,* 349–350.

Fagot, B. I. (1978). The influence of sex of the child on parental reactions to toddler children. *Child Development, 49,* 459–465.

Fagot, B. I. (1981). Male and female teachers: Do they treat boys and girls differently? *Sex Roles, 7,* 262–171.

Fagot, B. I. (1984). The consequences of problem behavior in toddler children. *Journal of Abnormal Child Psychology, 12,* 385–396.

Fagot, B. I. (1995a). Parenting boys and girls. In M. H. Bornstein (Ed.), *Handbook of parenting. Vol. 1. Children and parenting* (pp. 163–183). Hillsdale, NJ: Erlbaum.

Fagot, B. I. (1995b). Psychosocial and cognitive determinants of early gender-role development. In R. C. Rosen, C. M. Davis, & H. J. Ruppel (Eds.), *Annual review of sex research* (Vol. 6, pp. 1–31). Mount Vernon, IO: The Society for the Scientific Study of Sexuality.

Fagot, B. I. (1997). Attachment, parenting, and peer interactions of toddler children. *Developmental Psychology, 33*(3), 489–499.

Fagot, B. I. (1998). Social problem solving: Effect of content and parent sex. *International Journal of Behavioral Development, 22,* 389–401.

Fagot, B. (in press). The consequences of problem behavior in toddler children. *Journal of Abnormal Child Psychology.*

Fagot, B. I. & Gauvain, M. D. (1997). Mother-child problem solving: Continuity through the early years. *Developmental Psychology, 33*(3), 480–488.

Fagot, B. I., Gauvain, M. D., & Kavanaugh, K. (1996). Infant attachment and mother-child problem solving: A replication. *Journal of Social and Personal Relationships, 13,* 295–302.

Fagot, B. I., & Hagan, R. (1985). Aggression in toddlers: Responses to the assertive acts of boys and girls. *Sex Roles, 12,* 341–351.

Fagot, B. I., Hagan, R., Leinbach, M. D., & Kronsberg, S. (1985). Differential reactions to assertive and communicative acts of toddler boys and girls. *Child Development, 56,* 1499–1505.

Fagot, B. I., & Kavanagh, K. (1990). The prediction of antisocial behaviors from avoidant attachment classification. *Child Development, 61,* 864–873.

Fagot, B. I. & Leinbach, M. D. (1987a). Socialization of sex roles within the family. In B. Carter (Ed.), *Current conceptions of sex roles and sex typing* (pp. 89–100). New York: Pergamon Press.

Fagot, B. I., & Leinbach, M. D. (1987b). Unraveling the cat's cradle: The problem of gender. *Center Review, 1*(6), 8–9.

Fagot, B.I., Leinbach, M.D., & Hagan, R. (1986). Gender labeling and the adoption of sex-typed behaviors. *Developmental Psychology, 22,* 440–443.

Fagot, B. I. & Leve, L. (1998). Teacher ratings of externalizing behavior at school entry for boys and girls: Similar early predictors and different correlates. *Journal of Child Psychiatry and Psychology, 39,* 555–566.

Fagot, B. I., & Pears, K. C. (1996). Changes in attachment during the third year: Consequences and predictions. *Development and Psychopathology, 8,* 325–344.

Fagot, B. I., Pears, K. C., Capaldi, D. M., Crosby, L., & Leve, C. S. (1998). Becoming an adolescent father: Precursors and parenting. *Developmental Psychology, 34,* 1209–1219.

Fainsilber–Katz, L., & Gottman, J. M. (1993). Patterns of marital conflict predict children's internalizing and externalizing behaviors. *Developmental Psychology, 29*(6), 940–950.

Farmer, B., Burns, B., Chamberlain, P., & Dubs. (2001). *Assessing conformity to standards for TFC.* Manuscript in preparation.

Farrington, D. P. (1978). The family background of aggressive youths. In L. Hersov, M. Berger, & D. Shaffer (Eds.), *Aggression and antisocial behavior in childhood and adolescence* (pp. 73–93). Elmsford, NY: Pergamon.

Farrington, D. P. (1979). Environmental stress, delinquent behavior, and conviction. In I. G. Sarason & C. D. Spielberger (Eds.), *Stress and anxiety* (Vol. 6). Washington: Hemisphere.

Farrington, D. P. (1986). Age and crime. In M. Tonry & N. Morris (Eds.), *Crime and justice: An annual review of research* (Vol. 7, 189–250). Chicago: University of Chicago Press.

Farrington, D. P. (1991). Childhood aggression and adults' violence: Early precursors and later-life outcomes. In D. J. Pepler & K. H. Rubin (Eds.), *The development and treatment of childhood aggression* (pp. 5–29). Hillsdale, NJ: Lawrence Erlbaum Associates.

Farrington, D. P. (1992). The need for longitudinal-experimental research on offending and antisocial behavior. In J. McCord & R. E. Trembly (Eds.), *Preventing antisocial behavior: Interventions from birth through adolescence* (pp. 353–376). New York: Guilford.

Farrington, D. P., Gallagher, D., Morley, L., St. Ledger, R. J., & West, D. J. (1986). Unemployment, school leaving, and crime. *British Journal of Criminology, 26,* 335–356.

Farrington, D. P., & Hawkins, J. D. (1991). Predicting participation, early onset and later persistence in officially recorded offending. *Criminal Behaviour and Mental Health, 1,* 1–33.

Farrington, D. P., & West, D. J. (1990). The Cambridge Study in Delinquent Development: A long-term follow-up of 411 London males. In H. J. Kerner & G. Kaiser (Eds.), *Criminality: Personality, behavior, and life history* (pp. 115–138). Berlin: Springer-Verlag.

Farrington, D., & West, D. J. (1993). Criminal, penal and life histories of chronic offenders: Risk and protective factors and early identification. *Criminal Behaviour and Mental Health, 3,* 492–523.

Fauber, R. L., & Long, N. (1991). Children in context: the role of the family in child psychotherapy. *Journal of Consulting and Clinical Psychology, 59*(6), 813–820.

Feinman, S. (Ed.). (1992). *Social referencing and the social construction of reality in infancy.* New York: Plenum Press.

Felner, R. D., Farber, S. S., & Primavera, J. (1983). Transitions and stressful life events: A model for primary prevention. In R. D. Felner, L. A. Jason, J. N. Moritsuga, & S. S. Farber (Eds.), *Preventive psychology: Theory, research and action* (pp. 199–215). NY: Pergamon Press.

Felner, R. D., Primavera, J., & Cauce, A. M. (1981). The impact of school transitions: A focus for preventive efforts. *American Journal of Community Psychology, 9,* 449–459.

Fendrich, M., Warner, V., & Weissman, M. M. (1990). Family risk factors, parental depression, and psychopathology in offspring. *Developmental Psychology, 26,* 40–50.

Fergusson, D. M., & Horwood, L. J. (1987). The trait and method components of ratings of conduct disorder—Part I. Maternal and teacher evaluations of conduct disorder in young children. *Journal of Child Psychology and Psychiatry, 28,* 249–260.

Fergusson, D. M., Horwood, L. J., & Lynskey, M. (1994). The childhoods of multiple problem adolescents: A 15–year longitudinal study. *Journal of Child Psychology and Psychiatry, 35,* 1123–1140.

Fergusson, D. M., Lynsky, M. T., & Horwood, L. J. (1996) Origins of comorbidity between conduct and affective disorders. *Journal of the American Academic of Child and Adolescent Psychiatry, 35,* 451–460.

Ferster, C. B. (1973). A functional analysis of depression. *American Psychologist, 28*(857), 870.

Field, T. (1995). Infants of depressed mothers. *Infant Behavior and Development, 18,* 1–13.

Fisher, P. A., & Chamberlain, P. (2000). Multidimensional treatment foster care: A program for intensive parenting, family support, and skill building. *Journal of Emotional and Behavioral Disorders, 8,* 155–164.

Fisher, P. A., Ellis, B. H., & Chamberlain, P. (1999). Early intervention foster care: A model for preventing risk in young children who have been maltreated. *Children services: Social policy, research, and practice, 2*(3), 159–182.

Fisher, P. A., & Fagot, B. I. (1996). Development of consensus about child oppositional behavior: Increased convergence with entry into school. *Journal of Applied Developmental Psychology, 17,* 519–534.

Fisher, P. A., Gunnar, M. R., Chamberlain, P., & Reid, J. B. (2000). Preventive intervention for maltreated preschool children: Impact on children's behavior, neuroendocrine activity, and foster parent functioning. *Journal of the American Academy of Child and Adolescent Psychiatry, 39*(11), 1356–1364.

Fleischman, M. J. (1982). Social learning intervantions for aggressive children: From the laboratory to the real world. *The Behavior Therapist, 5,* 55–58.

Follette, W. C. (1995). Correcting methodological weaknesses in the knowledge base used to derive practice standards. In S. C. Hayes, V. M. Follette, R. M. Dawes, & K. E. Grady (Eds.), *Scientific standards of psychological practice: Issues and recommendations* (pp. 229–247). Reno, Nevada: Context Press.

Fontana, A. F. (1966). Familial etiology of schizophrenia. *Psychological Bulletin, 66,* 214–228.

Forehand, R. (1977). Child noncompliance to parent commands: Behavior analysis in treatment. In M. Hersen, R. M. Eisler & P. Muller (Eds.), *Progress in behavior modification* (Vol. 4). New York: Academic Press.

Forehand, R., Brody, G., Slotkin, J., Fauber, R., McCombs, A., & Long, N. (1988). Young adolescent and maternal depression: Assessment, interrelations, and family predictors. *Journal of Consulting and Clinical Psychology, 56(3)*, 422–426.

Forehand, R., McCombs, A., & Brody, G. H. (1987). the relationship of parental depressive mood states to child functioning: An analysis by type of sample and area of child functioning. *Advances in Behaviour Research and Therapy, 9*, 1–20.

Forehand, R., & McMahon, R. (1981). *Helping the noncompliant child: A clinician's guide to parent training*. New York: Guilford.

Forehand, R., King, H., Peed, S., & Yoder, D. (1975). Mother-child interaction: Comparison of a noncompliant clinic group and a non-clinic group. *Behavioral Research and Therapy, 13*, 79–84.

Forehand, R. L., & McMahon, R. J. (1981). *Helping the noncompliant child: A clinician's guide to parent training*. New York: Guilford.

Forgatch, M. S. (1987). The impact of maternal depression and parenting practices on boys in recently separated families. *Giornale Italiano do Psicologia e Pedagogia dell'Handicap e delle Disabilita di Apprendimento, 18–19*, 57–66.

Forgatch, M. S. (1989). Patterns and outcome in family problem solving: The disrupting effect of negative emotions. *Journal of Marriage and the Family, 5(1)*, 115–124.

Forgatch, M. S. (1991). The clinical science vortex: A developing theory of antisocial behavior. In D. J. Pepler & K. H. Rubin (Eds.), *The development and treatment of childhood aggression* (pp. 291–315). Hillsdale, NJ: Lawrence Erlbaum Associates.

Forgatch, M. S. (1996, April). *Evaluating the Oregon Divorce Prevention Study*. Paper presented at the Seminar presented at the Oregon Social Learning Center, Eugene.

Forgatch, M. S. (in press). *Parenting through change: Training manual*. Guilford Press.

Forgatch, M. S., & DeGarmo, D. S. (1997). Adult problem solving: contributor to parenting and child outcomes in divorced families. *Social Development, 6(2)*, 238–254.

Forgatch, M.S., & DeGarmo, D. S. (1999). Parenting through change: An effective prevention program for single mothers. *Journal of Consulting and Clinical Psychology, 67*, 711–724.

Forgatch, M. S., & DeGarmo, D. S. (in preparation). Dynamic social contexts and diverse family structures. In L. Burton & P. L. Chase-Lansdale (Eds.), *Diversity and families: Context and process*. Hillsdale, NJ: Erlbaum.

Forgatch, M. S., & DeGarmo, D. S. (in press). Confidant contributions to parenting and child outcomes in divorced families. *Social Development*.

Forgatch, M. S., Fetrow, B., & Lathrop, M. (1988). *Support and problem solving system*. Unpublished manual, Oregon Social Learning Center, Eugene.

Forgatch, M. S., & Knutson, N. M. (in press). Linking basic and applied research in a prevention science process. In H. Liddle, G. Diamond, R. Levant, & J. Bray (Eds.), *Family psychology intervention science*. Washington, DC: American Psychological Association.

Forgatch, M. S., Knutson, N., & Mayne, T. (1992). *Coder impressions of ODS lab tasks*. Eugene: Oregon Social Learning Center.

Forgatch, M. S., & Marquez, B. (1993). The divorce workout [videotape]. Eugene: Oregon Social Learning Center.

Forgatch, M. S., & Patterson, G. R. (1989). *Parents and adolescents living together: Part 2. Family problem solving*. Eugene, OR: Castalia.

Forgatch, M. S., & Patterson, G. R. (1998). Behavioral family therapy. In F. M. Dattilio (Ed.), *Case studies in couples and family therapy: Systematic and cognitive perspectives* (pp. 85–107). New York: Guilford.

Forgatch, M. S., Patterson, G. R., & Ray, J. A. (1996). Divorce and boys' adjustment problems: Two paths with a single model. In E. M. Hetherington & E. A. Blechman (Eds.), *Stress, coping, and resiliency in children and families* (pp. 67–105). Mahwah, NJ: Erlbaum.

Forgatch, M. S., Patterson, G. R., & Skinner, M. L. (1988). A mediational model for the effect of divorce on antisocial behavior in boys. In E. M. Hetherington & J. D. Arasteh (Eds.), *Impact of divorce, single parenting, and step-parenting on children.* Hillsdale, NJ: Erlbaum.

Forgatch, M. S., & Stoolmiller, M. (1994). Emotions as contexts for adolescent delinquency. *Journal of Research on Adolescence, 4,* 601–614.

Forgatch, M. S., & Stoolmiller, M. (1997, January). *Parenting through change: A selected intervention for recently separated single mothers.* Paper presented at the "Coping Theory and Intervention" Conference, Arizona State University, Tempe, AZ.

Frank, G. H. (1965). The role of the family in the development of psychopathology. *Psychological Bulletin, 64,* 191–205.

Frankel, K. A., & Bates, J. E. (1990). Mother-toddler problem-solving: Antecedents in attachment, home behavior, and temperament. *Child Development, 61,* 810–819.

Freeman, R. B. (1983). Crime and unemployment. In J. Q. Wilson (Ed.), *Crime and public policy* (pp. 89–106). San Francisco, CA: ICS Press.

Frijda, N. H. (1986). *The emotions.* Cambridge, England: Cambridge University Press.

Furstenberg, F. F., Jr. (1988). Child care after divorce and remarriage. In E. M. Hetherington, & J. D. Arasteh (Eds.) *Impact of divorce, single parenting, and stepparenting on children* (pp. 245–261). Hillsdale, NJ: Lawrence Erlbaum Associates.

Furstenberg, F. F., Jr., & Teitler, J. O. (1994). Reconsidering the effects of marital disruption: What happens to children of divorce in early adulthood? *Journal of Family Issues, 15*(2), 173–190.

Galaway, B., Nutter, R. W., & Hudson, J. (1995). Relationship between discharge outcomes for Treatment Foster-Care clients and program characteristics. *Journal of Emotional and Behavioral Disorders 3*(1), 46–54.

Gardner, F. E. M. (1989). Inconsistent parenting: is there evidence for a link with children's conduct problems? *Journal of Abnormal Child Psychology, 17,* 223–233.

Garrison, C. Z., Jackson, K. L., Marsteller, F., McKeown, R., & Addy, C. (1990). A longitudinal study of depressive symptomatology in young adolescents. *Journal of the American Academy of Child and Adolescent Psychiatry, 29*(4), 581–585.

Ge, X., Best, K. M., Conger, R. D., & Simons, R. L. (1996). Parenting behaviors and the occurrence and co-occurrence of adolescent depressive symptoms and conduct problems. *Developmental Psychology, 32*(4), 717–731.

Ge, X., Conger, R. D., Cadoret, R. J., Neiderhiser, J. M., Yates, W., Troughton, E., & Stewart, M. A. (1996). The developmental interface between nature and nurture: A mutual influence model of child antisocial behavior and parent behaviors. *Developmental Psychology, 32,* 574–589.

Ge, X., Conger, R. D., Lorenz, F. O., & Elder, G. H. (1992). Linking family economic hardship to adolescent distress. *Journal of Research on Adolescence, 2*(4), 351–378.

Gelfand, D. M., & Teti, D. M. (1990). The effects of maternal depression on children. *Clinical Psychology Review, 10*(3), 329–353.

Gendreau, P., Little, T., & Goggin, C. (1996). A meta-analysis of the predictors of adult offender recidivism: What works! *Criminology, 34,* 575–607.

Gersten, J. C., Langner, T. S., Eisenberg, J. G., & Simcha-Fagan, O. (1977). An evaluation of the etiological role of stressful life-change events in psychological disorders. *Journal of Health and Social Behavior, 18,* 228–244.

Gewirtz, J. L. (1954). Three determinants of attention seeking in young children. *Monograph of the Society for Research in Child Development, 19*(2, Serial No. 55).

Gewirtz, J. L. (1967). Deprivation and satiation of social stimuli as determinants of their efficacy. In J. P. Hill (Ed.), *Minnesota Symposia on Child Psychology,* (Vol. 1).

Gewirtz, J. L., & Boyd, E. F. (1977). Experiments on mother-infant interaction underlying mutual attachment acquisition: The infant conditions the mother. In T. Alloway, P. Pliner, & L. Krames (Eds.), *Attachment behavior* (pp. 109–143). New York: Plenum Press.

Gibbons, R. D., Hedeker, D., Waternaux, C., & Davis, J. M. (1988). Random regression models: A comprehensive approach to the analysis of longitudinal psychiatric data. *Psychopharmacology Bulletin, 24*, 438–443.

Glueck, S., & Glueck, E. (1959). *Predicting delinquency and crime.* Cambridge, MA: Harvard University Press.

Gold, J. (1966). Undetected delinquent behavior. *Journal of Research in Crime and Delinquency, 3*, 27–46.

Goldsmith, H. H., & Campos, J. J. (1986). Fundamental issues in the study of early temperament: The Denver Twin Temperament Study. In M. E. Lamb, A. L. Brown, & B. Rogoff (Eds.), *Advances in developmental psychology* (Vol. 4, pp. 231–283). Hillsdale, NJ: Erlbaum.

Gongla, P. A., & Thompson, E. H. (1987). Single-parent families. In M. B. Sussman & S. K. Steinmetz (Eds.), Handbook of marriage and the family (pp. 397–418). New York: Plenum Press.

Gore, S., Aseltine, R. H., Jr., & Colten, M. E. (1993). Gender, social-relational involvement, and depression. *Journal of Research on Adolescence, 3*, 101–125.

Gotlib, I., Lewinsohn, P., & Seeley, J. (1995). Symptoms versus a diagnosis of depression: Differences in psychosocial functioning. *Journal of Consulting and Clinical Psychology, 63*(1), 90–100.

Gotlib, I. H., & Hammen, C. L. (1992). *Psychological aspects of depression: Toward a cognitive-interpersonal integration.* New York: Wiley.

Gotlib, I. H., & Robinson, L. (1982). Responses to depressed individuals: Discrepancies between self- report and observer-rated behavior. *Journal of Abnormal Psychology, 91*, 231–240.

Gottfredson, D. C., Gottfredson, G. D., & Hybl, L. G. (1993). Managing adolescent behavior: A multiyear, multischool study. *American Educational Research Journal, 30*, 179–215.

Gottfredson, M. R., & Hirschi, T. (1990). *A general theory of crime.* Stanford, CA: Stanford University Press.

Gottman, J. M. (1979). *Marital interactions: Experimental investigations.* New York: Academic Press.

Gottman, J. M. (1989). *The specific affect coding system, version 2.0: Real time coding with affect wheel.* Unpublished manual, University of Washington, Seattle.

Gottman, J. M. (1991). Chaos and regulated change in families: A metaphor for the study of transitions. In P. Cowan E. M. Hetherington (Eds.), *Family transitions.* Hillsdale, NJ: Erlbaum.

Gottman, J. M., & Krokoff, L. J. (1989). Marital interaction and satisfaction: a longitudinal view. *Journal of Consulting and Clinical Psychology, 57*(1), 47–52.

Greenberg, M. T., Kusche, C. A., Cook, E. T., & Quamma, J. P. (1995). Promoting emotional competence in school–aged children: The effects of the PATHS curriculum. *Development and Psychopathology, 7*, 117–136.

Greenwood, P. W., Model, K. E., Rydell, C. P., & Chiesa, J. (1996). *Diverting children from a life of crime: Measuring costs and benefits* (0–8330–2383–7). Santa Monica: RAND prepared report for the University of California, Berkeley, James Irvine Foundation.

Griffin, W. A. (1993). Transitions from negative affect during marital interaction: Husband and wife differences. *Journal of Family Psychology, 6*, 230–244.

Grossman, D. C., Neckerman, H. J., Koepsell, T. D., Liu, P., Asher, K. N., Beland, K., Frey, K., & Rivara, F. P. (1997). Effectiveness of a violence prevention curriculum among children in elementary school. *Journal of the American Medical Association, 277*(20), 1605–1611.

Grych, J. H., & Fincham, F. D. (1990). Marital conflict and children's adjustment: A cognitive-contextual framework. *Psychological Bulletin, 108*(2), 267–290.

Grych, J. H., & Fincham, F. D. (1993). Children's appraisals of marital conflict: initial investigations of the cognitive-contextual framework. *Child Development, 64*, 215–230.

Guerin, D. W., Gottfried, A. W., & Thomas, C. W. (1997). Difficult temperament and behaviour problems: A longitudinal study from 1.5 to 12 years. *International Journal of Behavioral Development, 21*, 71–90.

Hack, M., Klein, N. K., & Taylor, H. G. (1995). Long-term developmental outcomes of low birth weight infants. *The Future of Children: Low birth weight, 5*(1), 176–196.

Halfon, N., Mendonea, A., & Berkowitz, G. (1995). Health status of children in foster care: The experience of the Center for the Vulnerable Child. *Archives of Pediatric and Adolescent Medicine, 149,* 386–392.

Halverson, C., & Waldrop, M. (1973). The relations of mechanically recorded activity level to varieties of preschool play behavior. *Child Development, 44,* 678–681.

Hammen, C. (1991). *Depression runs in families: The social context of risk and resilience in children of depressed mothers*. New York: Springer-Verlag.

Hammen, C. (1992). Life events and depression: The plot thickens. *American Journal of Community Psychology, 20,* 179–193.

Hammen, C., Burge, D., Burney, E., & Adrian, C. (1990). Longitudinal study of diagnoses in children of women with unipolar and bipolar affective disorder. *Archives of General Psychiatry, 47,* 1112–1117.

Hammen, C., Burge, D., & Stansbury, K. (1990). Relationship of mother and child variables to outcomes in a high-risk sample: A causal modeling analysis. *Developmental Psychology, 26,* 24–30.

Hammen, C. L., Adrian, C., Gordon, D., Jaenicke, C., & Hiroto, D. (1987a). Children of depressed mothers: Maternal strain and symptom predictors of dysfunction. *Journal of Abnormal Psychology, 96,* 190–198.

Hammen, C., Gordon, D., Burge, D., Adrian, C., Jaenicke, C., & Hiroto, D. (1987). Communication patterns of mothers with affective disorders and their relationship to children's status and social functioning. In K. Hahlweg & M. J. Goldstein (Eds.), *Understanding major mental disorder: The contribution of family interaction research*. New York: Family Process Press.

Harrington, R., & Vostanis, P. (1995). Longitudinal perspectives and affective disorder in children and adolescents. In I. M. Goodyer (Ed.), *The depressed child and adolescent: Developmental and clinical perspectives.* (pp. 311–341). Cambridge, UK: Cambridge University Press.

Harris, A., & Reid, J. B. (1981). The consistency of a class of coercive child behaviors across school settings for individual subjects. *Journal of Abnormal Psychology, 9,* 219–227.

Harris, J. R. (1995). Where is the child's environment? A group socialization theory of development. *Psychological Review, 102,* 458–489.

Harris, J. R. (1998). *The nurture assumption: Why children turn out the way they* do. New York: The Free Press.

Hart, B., & Risley, R. R. (1995). *Meaningful differences in the everyday experience of young American children*. Baltimore: Brookes.

Hartup, W. W. (1996). The company they keep: Friendships and their developmental significance. *Child Development, 67,* 1–13.

Hathaway, S., & Monachesi, E. D. (Eds.). (1953). *Analyzing and predicting juvenile delinquency with the MMPI*. Minneapolis: University of Minnesota Press.

Hathaway, S. R., & McKinley, J. C. (1943) *Minnesota multiphasic personality inventory.* (Vol. Rev. 1951) Minneapolis: University of Minnesota Press.

Hayes, S. N., & Wu, W. (1998), The applied implications of rule-governed behavior. In W. O'Donohue (Ed.), *Learning and behavior therapy* (pp. 374–391). Needham Heights, MA: Allyn & Bacon.

Haynes, S. N., & O'Brien, W. H. (1990). Functional analysis in behavior therapy. *Clinical Psychology Review, 10,* 649–668.

Heller, L. R., & Fantuzzo, J. W. (1993). Reciprocal peer tutoring and parent partnership: Does parent involvement make a difference? *School Psychology Review, 22,* 517–534.

Henggeler, S. W., Melton, G. B., & Smith, L. A. (1992). Family preservation using multisystemic treatment: An effective alternative to incarcerating serious juvenile offenders. *Journal of Consulting and Clinical Psychology, 60,* 953–961.

Henggeler, S. W., Rodnick, J. D., Borduin, C. M., Hanson, C. L., Watson, S. M., & Urey, J. R. (1986). Multisystemic treatment of juvenile offenders: Effects on adolescent behavior and family interaction. *Developmental Psychology, 22,* 132–141.

Herrnstein, R. J. (1961). Relative and absolute strength of response as a function of frequency or reinforcement. *Journal of Experimental Analysis of Behavior, 4,* 267–272.

Herrnstein, R. J. (1974). Formal properties of the matching law. *Journal of the Experimental Analysis of Behavior, 21,* 486–495.

Hetherington, E. M. (1991). The role of individual differences and family relationships in children's coping with divorce and remarriage. In P. A. Cowan & E. M. Hetherington (Eds.), *Family transitions* (pp. 165–194). Hillsdale, NJ: Lawrence Erlbaum Associates.

Hetherington, E. M. (1992). Coping with marital transitions: A family systems perspective. In E. M. Hetherington & W. G. Clingempeel (Eds.), *Coping with marital transitions: Monographs of the Society for Research in Child Development* (Vol. 57, pp. Serial No. 227, Vol. 57, Nos 2–3, pp 1–15). Chicago: University of Chicago Press.

Hetherington, E. M. (1993). An overview of the Virginia longitudinal study of divorce and remarriage with a focus on early adolescence. *Journal of Family Psychology,* 7(1), 39–56.

Hetherington, E. M., & Clingempeel, W. G. (1992). Coping with marital transitions: A family systems perspective. *Monographs of the Society for Research in Child Development, 57* (2–3, Serial No. 227).

Hetherington, E. M., Cox, M., & Cox, R. (1979). Family interaction and the social, emotional, and cognitive development of children following divorce. In V. Vaughn & T. Brazelton (Eds.), *The family: Setting priorities* (pp. 89–128). New York: Science and Medicine.

Hetherington, E. M., Cox, M., & Cox, R. (1981). Effects of divorce on parents and children. In M. Lamb (Ed.), *Nontraditional families* (pp. 233–287). Hillsdale, NJ: Erlbaum.

Hetherington, E. M., & Martin, B. (1979). Family interaction. In H. C. Quay & J. S. Werry (Eds.), *Psychopathological disorders of childhood* (2nd ed., pp. 30–82). New York: Wiley.

Hetherington, E. M., & Stanley-Hagan, M. (1999). The adjustment of children with divorced parents: A risk and resiliency perspective. *Journal of Child Psychology and Psychiatry, 40*(1), 129–140.

Hetherington, E. M., Stanley-Hagan, M., & Anderson, E. R. (1989). Marital transitions: A child's perspective. *American Psychologist, 44*(2), 303–312.

Hinde, R. A., Titmus, G., Easton, D., & Tamplin, A. (1985). Incidence of "friendship" and behavior toward strong associates versus nonassociates in preschoolers. *Child Development, 56,* 234–245.

Hinshaw, S. P. (1987). On the distinction between attentional deficits/hyperactivity and conduct problems/aggression in child psychopathology. *Psychological Bulletin, 101,* 443–463.

Hinshaw, S. P. (1992). Externalizing behavior problems and academic underachievement in childhood and adolescence: Causal relationships and underlying mechanisms. *Psychological Bulletin, 111,* 127–155.

Hoagwood, K., & Koretz, D. (1996). Embedding prevention services within systems of care: Strengthening the nexus for children. *Applied and Prevention Psychology, 5,* 225–234.

Hoffman, L. W. (1985). The changing genetics/socialization balance. *Journal of Social Issues, 41,* 127–148.

Hokanson, J. E., Loewenstein, D. A., Hedeen, C., & Howes, M. J. (1986). Dysphoric college students and roommates: A study of social behaviors over a three-month period. *Personality and Social Psychology Bulletin, 12*(3), 311–324.

Holden, G. W., & Ritchie, K. L. (1991). Linking extreme marital discord, child rearing, and child behavior problems: Evidence from battered women. *Child Development, 62*(2), 311–327.

Holleran, P. A. Littman, D. C., Freund, R., & Schmaling, K. B. (1982). A signal detection approach to social perception: Identification of negative and positive behaviors by parents of normal and problem children. *Journal of Abnormal Child Psychology, 10,* 547–557.

Hollingshead, A. B. (1975). *Four factor index of social status.* Unpublished manuscript. (Available from A. B. Hollingshead, Department of Sociology, Yale University, New Haven, CT).

Hops, H. (1971). *Covariation of social stimuli and interaction rates in the natural preschool environment.* Unpublished doctoral dissertation, University of Oregon, Eugene.

Hops, H. (1992). Parental depression and child behaviour problems: Implications for behavioural family intervention. *Behaviour Change, 9*(3), 126–138.

Hops, H. (1996). Intergenerational transmission of depressive symptoms: Gender and developmental considerations. In C. Mundt, M. J. Goldstein, K. Hahlweg, & P. Fiedler (Eds.), *Interpersonal factors in the origin and course of affective disorders.* (pp. 113–128). London: Gaskell/Royal College of Psychiatrists.

Hops, H., Alpert, A., & Davis, B. (1997). The development of same- and opposite-sex social relations among adolescents: An analogue study. *Social Development, 6.*

Hops, H., Biglan, A., Sherman, L., Arthur, J., Friedman, L., & Osteen, V. (1987). Home observations of family interactions of depressed women. *Journal of Consulting and Clinical Psychology, 55*(3), 341–346.

Hops, H., Davis, B., & Longoria, N. (1995). Methodological Issues in Direct Observation: Illustrations with the Living in Familiar Environments (LIFE) coding system. *Journal of Clinical Child Psychology, 24*(2), 193–203.

Hops, H., Lewinsohn, P., Andrews, J. A., & Roberts, R. E. (1990). Psychosocial correlates of depressive symptomatology among high school students. *Journal of Clinical Child Psychology, 19*(3), 211–220.

Hops, H., & Seeley, J. R. (1992). Parent participation in studies of family interaction: Methodological and substantive considerations. *Behavioral Assessment, 14*, 229–243.

Hops, H., Sherman, L., & Biglan, A. (1990). Maternal depression, marital discord, and children's behavior: A developmental perspective. In G. R. Patterson (Ed.), *Depression and aggression in family interaction.* (pp. 185–208). Hillsdale, NJ: Lawrence Erlbaum.

Hops, H., Walker, H. M., Fleischman, D. H., Nagoshi, J. T., Omura, R. T., Skindrud, K., & Taylor, J. (1978). CLASS: A standardized in-class program for acting-out children. II. Field Test Evaluations. *Journal of Educational Psychology, 79*, 636–644.

Hotaling, G. T., & Sugarman, D. B. (1986). An analysis of risk markers in husband to wife violence: The current state of knowledge. *Violence and Victims, 1*, 101–124.

Howell, J. C., Krisberg, B., & Jones, M. (1995). Trends in juvenile crime and youth violence. In J. C. Howell, B.K. Krisberg, J. D. Hawkins, & J.J. Wilson (Eds.), *Serious, violent, and chronic juvenile offenders* (pp. 1–35). Thousand Oaks, CA: Sage.

Hudson, J., Nutter, R. W. & Galway, B. (1994a). Treatment foster care programs: A review of evaluation research and suggested directions. *Social Work Research, 18*, 198–210.

Hudson, J., Nutter, R. W. & Galway, B. (1994b). Treatment foster care: Development and current status. *Community Alternatives: International Journal of Family Care, 6*, 1–24.

Huizinga, D., Loeber, R., & Thornberry, T.P. (1993). *Urban delinquency and substance use.* Washington, DC: OJJDP.

Irvine, A. B., Biglan, A., Smolkowski, K., Metzler, C. W., & Ary, D. V. (1999). The effectiveness of a parenting skills program for parents of middle school students in small communities. *Journal of Consulting & Clinical Psychology, 67*, 811–825.

Jacob, T. (1975). Family interaction in normal and disturbed families: A methodological and substantive review. *Psychological Bulletin, 82*, 33–65.

Jacob, T., & Tennenbaum, D. L. (1988). *Family assessment: Rationale, methods, and future dimensions.* New York: Plenum Press.

Jacobsen, N. S., & Truax, P. (1991). Clinical significance: A statistical approach to defining meaningful change in psychotherapy research. *Journal of Consulting and Clinical Psychology, 59*, 12–19.

Jacobson, J. L. and D. E. Wille (1986). The influence of attachment pattern on developmental changes in peer interaction from the toddler to the preschool period. *Child Development 57*: 338–347.

James, O. (1995). *Juvenile violence in a winner-loser culture: Socio-economic and familial origins of the rise in violence against the person.* New York: Free Association Books.

Jenkins, J. M., Smith, M. A., & Graham, P.J. (1989). Coping with parental quarrels. *Journal of the American Academy of Child and Adolescent Psychiatry, 28(2),* 182–189.

Jenkins, R. L., & Hewitt, L. (1944). Types of personality structure encountered in child guidance clinics. *American Journal of Orthopsychiatry, 14*(1), 84–94.

Jessor, R., & Jessor, S. L. (1977). *Problem behavior and psychological development: A longitudinal study of youth.* New York: Academic Press.

Johnson, P. L., & O'Leary, K. D. (1987). Parental behavior patterns and conduct disorders in girls. *Journal of Abnormal Child Psychology, 15,* 573–581.

Johnson, S. M., & Lobitz, G. K. (1974). Parental manipulation of child behavior in home observations: A methodological concern. *Journal of Applied Behavioral Analysis, 7,* 23–31.

Johnston, J. R., Gonzalez, R., & Campbell, L. E. (1987). Ongoing postdivorce conflict and child disturbance. *Journal of Abnormal Child Psychology, 15,* 493–509.

Jones, R. R. (1973). Behavioral observation frequency data: Problems in scoring, analysis, and interpretation. In L. A. Hamerlynck, L. C. Handy, & E. J. Mash (Eds.), *Behavior change; Methodology, concepts, and practice* (pp. 119–145). Champaign, IL: Research Press.

Jones, R. R., Reid, J. B., & Patterson, G. R. (1975). Naturalistic observation in clinical assessment. In P. McReynolds (Ed.), *Advances in psychological assessment* (Vol. 3, pp. 42–95). San Francisco, CA: Jossey–Bass.

Jouriles, E. N., Barling, J., & O'Leary, K. (1987). Predicting child behavior problems in maritally violent families. *Journal of Abnormal Child Psychology, 15,* 165–173.

Jouriles, E. N., Murphy, C. M., Farris, A. M., & Smith, D. A. (1991). Marital adjustment, parental disagreements about child rearing, and behavior problems in boys: Increasing the specificity of the marital assessment. *Child Development, 62*(6), 1424–1433.

Jouriles, E. N., Murphy, C. M., & O'Leary, K. D. (1989). Interspousal aggression, marital discord, and child problems. *Journal of Consulting and Clinical Psychology, 57*(3), 453–455.

Jouriles, E. N., Norwood, W. D., McDonald, R., Vincent, J. P., & Mahoney, A. (1996). Physical violence and other forms of marital aggression: Links with children's behavior problems. *Journal of Family Psychology, 10*(2), 223–234.

Jouriles, E. N., Pfiffner, L. J., & O'Leary, S. G. (1988). Marital conflict, parenting, and toddler conduct problems. *Journal of Abnormal Child Psychology, 16*(2), 197–206.

Kalmus, J. (1984). The intergenerational transmission of marital aggression. *Journal of Marriage and the Family, 52,* 11–19.

Kandel, D. B. (1978). Homophily, selection, and socialization in adolescent friendships. *American Journal of Sociology, 84,* 427–436.

Kandel, D. B. (1982) Epidemiological and psychosocial perspectives on adolescent drug use. *Journal of the American Academy of Child Psychiatry, 21,* 328–347.

Kandel, D. B. (1986). Processes of peer influence. In R.K. Silbereisen, K. Eyferth & G. Rudinger (Eds.), *Development as action in context: Problem behavior and normal youth development* (pp. 203–227). New York: Springer-Verlag.

Kandel, D. B., & Davies, M. (1982). Epidemiology of depressive mood in adolescents: An empirical study. *Archives of General Psychiatry, 39,* 1205–1212.

Kandel, B., Davies, M., & Baydar, N. (1990). The creation of interpersonal contexts: Homophily in dyadic relationships in adolescence and young adulthood. In L. Robins & M. Rutter (Eds.), *Straight and devious pathways from childhood to adulthood* (pp. 221–241). New York: Cambridge University Press.

Karpowitz, D. (1972). *Stimulus control in family interaction sequences as observed in the naturalistic setting of the home.* Unpublished doctoral dissertation, University of Oregon, Eugene.

Kaslow, N. J., Deering, C. G., & Racusin, G.R. (1994). Depressed children and their families. *Clinical Psychology Review, 14,* 39–59.

Kavanagh, K. (1986). *Tirotot: Telephone interview for parents of toddler children*. Unpublished instrument. (Available from the Oregon Social Learning Center, 160 East 4th Ave., Eugene, OR 97401–2426)

Kavanagh, K., Dishion, T. J., Medici Skaggs, N., & Schneiger, A. (1998). *Prediction of parent participation in a tiered model of assessment and intervention for early adolescent problem behavior*. Paper presented at Sixth Annual Meeting of the Society for Prevention Research, Park City, UT.

Kavanagh, K., & Hops, H. (1994). Good girls? Bad boys? Gender and development as contexts for diagnosis and treatment. In T. H. Ollendick & R. J. Prinz (Eds.), *Advances in clinical child psychology* (Vol. 16, pp. 45–79). New York: Plenum Press.

Kazdin, A. (1987). Treatment of antisocial behavior in children: Current status and future directions. *Psychological Bulletin, 102*, 187–203.

Kazdin, A. E. (1994). Interventions for aggressive and antisocial children. In L. D. Eron, J. H. Gentry, & P. Schlegel (Eds.), *Reason to hope: A psychosocial perspective on violence and youth* (pp. 341–382). Washington, DC: American Psychological Association.

Keenan, K., Loeber, R., & Green, S. (1999). conduct disorder in girls: A review of the Literature. *Clinical Child and Family Psychology Review, 2*, 3–17.

Kellam, S. G. (1990). Developmental epidemiological framework for family research on depression and aggression. In G. R. Patterson (Ed.), *Depression and aggression in family interaction* (pp. 11–48). Hillsdale, NJ: Erlbaum.

Kellam, S. G., Brown, C. H., Rubin, R. R., & Ensminger, M. E. (1983). Paths leading to teenage psychiatric symptoms and substance use: Developmental epidemilogical studies in Woodlawn. In S. B. Guze, F. J. Earls, & J. E. Barrett (Eds.), *Childhood psychopathology and development* (pp. 17–51). New York: Raven Press.

Kellam, S. G., & Rebok, G. W. (1992). Building developmental and etiological theory through epidemiologically based preventive intervention trials. In J. McCord & R. E. Tremblay (Eds.), *Preventing antisocial behavior: Interventions from birth through adolescence* (pp. 162–195). New York: Guildford Press.

Kellam, S. G., Rebok, G. W., Ialongo, N., & Mayer, L. S. (1994). The course and malleability of aggressive behavior from early first grade into middle school: Results of a developmental epidemiologically-based preventive trial. *Journal of Child Psychology and Psychiatry, 35*(2), 259–281.

Kellam, S. G., & Werthamer-Larsson, L. (1986). Developmental epidemiology: A basis for prevention. In M. Kessler & S. E. Goldston (Eds.), *A decade of progress in primary prevention* (pp. 154–180). Hanover, NH: University Press of New England.

Kelley, B. T., Loeber, R., Keenan, K., & DeLamatre, M. (1997). Developmental pathways in boys' disruptive and delinquent behavior. *U.S. Department of Justice, Office of Juvenile Justice and Delinquency Prevention, Juvenile Justice Bulletin*.

Kelly, J. G. (1988). *A guide to conducting preventive research in the community: First steps*. New York: Haworth.

Kendall, P. C., Ronan, K. E., & Epps, J. (1991). Aggression in children and adolescents: Cognitive behavioral treatment perspectives. In D. J. Pepler & K. H. Rubin (Eds.), *The development and treatment of childhood aggression* (pp. 341–360). Hillsdale, NJ: Lawrence Erlbaum Associates.

Keogh, B. K., Juvonen, J., & Bernheimer, L. P. (1989). Assessing children's competence: Mothers' and teachers' ratings of competent behavior. *Psychological Assessment, 1*(3), 224–229.

Kessler, R. C., McGonagle, K. A., Zhao, S., Nelson, C. B., Hughes, M., Eshleman, S., Wittchen, H. U., & Kendler, K. S. (1994). Lifetime and 12-month prevalence of DSM-III-R psychiatric disorders in the United States. *Archives of General Psychiatry, 51*, 8–19.

Kilgore, K., Snyder, J., & Lentz, C. (2000). The contribution of parental discipline, parental monitoring, and school risk to early-onset conduct problems in African-American boys and girls. *Developmental Psychology, 36*, 1–11.

Kindermann, T. A. (1993). Natural peer groups as contexts for individual development: The case of children's motivation at school. *Developmental Psychology, 29*, 970–977.

Kitson, G. C. (1992). *Portrait of divorce: Adjustment to marital breakdown*. New York: Guilford Press.

Klimes-Dougan, B., & Bolger, A.K. (1998). Coping with maternal depressed affect and depression: adolescent children of depressed and well mothers. *Journal of Youth and Adolescence, 27*(1), 1–15.

Knight, B. J., & West, D. J. (1975). Temporary and continuing delinquency. *British Journal of Criminology, 15*, 43–50.

Kochanska, G., & Kuczynski, L. (1989). *Patterns of mutual influence between well and depressed mothers*. Paper presented at the meeting of the Society for Research in Child Development, Kansas City, MO.

Kochanska, G., Kuczynski, L., Radke-Yarrow, M., & Welch, J. D. (1987). Resolutions of control episodes between well and affectively ill mothers and their young children. *Journal of Abnormal Child Psychology, 15*, 441–456.

Kornhauser, R. R. (1991). *Social sources of delinquency*. Chicago: University of Chicago Press.

Kovacs, M. (1985). The children's depression, inventory (CDI). *Psychopharmacology Bulletin, 21*(4), 995–998.

Kratzer, L., & Hodgins, S. (1997). Adult outcomes of child conduct problems: A cohort study. *Journal of Abnormal Child Psychology, 25*, 65–81.

Kupersmidt, J. B., & Patterson, C. J. (1991). Childhood peer rejection, aggression, withdrawal, and self-perceived competence as predictors of self-reported behavior problems in preadolescence. *Journal of Abnormal Child Psychology, 19*, 427–449.

Kutash, K., & Rivera, V. R. (1996). *What works in children's mental health services?* Baltimore: Paul H. Brookes Publishing Co.

Ladd, G. W. (1983). Social networks of popular, average, and rejected children in school settings. *Merrill-Palmer Quarterly, 29*, 283–307.

Ladd, G. W., & Golter, B. S. (1988). Parents' management of preschooler's peer relations: Is it related to children's social competence? *Developmental Psychology, 24*(1), 109–117.

Ladd, G. W., Price, J. M., & Hart, C. H. (1990). Preschoolers' behavioral orientations and patterns of peer contact: Predictive of peer status? In S.R. Asher & J. D. Coie (Eds.), *Peer Rejection in childhood* (pp. 90–118). Cambridge: Cambridge University Press.

Lahey, B. B., Hartdagen, S. E., Frick, P. J., McBurnett, K., Connor, R., & Hynd, G. W. (1988). Conduct disorder: Parsing the confounded relation to parental divorce and antisocial personality. *Journal of Abnormal Psychology, 97*, 334–337.

Lahey, B. B., & Loeber, R. (1997). Attention-deficit/hyperactivity disorder, oppositional defiant disorder, conduct disorder, and adult antisocial behavior: A life span perspective. In D. M. Stoff, J. Breiling, & J. D. Maser (Eds.), *Handbook of antisocial behavior* (pp. 51–59). New York: John Wiley & Sons.

Lamb, M. E., Easterbrooks, M. A., & Holden, G. W. (1980). Reinforcement and punishment among preschoolers: Characteristics, effects, and correlates. *Child Development, 51*(4), 1230–1236.

Lamb, M. E., Suomi, S., & Stephenson, G. (1979). *Social interaction analysis*. Madison, WI: University of Wisconsin Press.

Landsverk, J., & Garland, A. F. (1999). Foster care and pathways to mental health services. In P. Curtis & G. Dale, Jr. (Eds.), *The foster care crisis: Translating research into practice and policy* (pp. 193-210). Lincoln: University of Nebraska Press.

Landsverk, J., Litrownik, A., Newton, R., Granger, W., & Remmer, J. (1996). *Psychological impact of child maltreatment*. Final Report to National Center on Child Abuse and Neglect, Washington, DC.

Landy, S., & Peters, R. D. (1991). Toward an understanding of a developmental paradigm for aggressive conduct problems. In R. D. Peters & R. J. McMahon (Eds.), *Aggression and violence through the lifespan* (pp. 1–30). Newbury Park, CA: Sage.

Larson, R., & Richards, M. H. (1991). Daily companionship in late childhood and early adolescence: Changing developmental contexts. *Child Development, 62*, 284–300.

Larzelere, R. E., & Patterson, G. R. (1990). Parental management: Mediator of the effect of socioeconomic status on early delinquency. *Criminology, 28* (2), 301–324.

Laub, J. H., & Sampson, R. J. (1988). Unraveling families and delinquency: A reanalysis of the Gluecks' data. *Criminology, 26,* 355–380.

Laub, J. H., & Sampson, R. J. (1991). The Sutherland-Glueck debate: On the sociology of criminological knowledge. *American Journal of Sociology, 96,* 1402–1440.

Le Blanc, M., & Frechette, M. (1989). *Male criminal activity from childhood through youth.* New York: Springer-Verlag.

Leve, L. D., & Fagot, B. I. (1997). Prediction of positive peer relations from observed parent-child interactions. *Social Development, 6*(2), 254–269.

Leve, L. D., Winebarger, A. A., Fagot, B. I., Reid, J. B., & Goldsmith, H. H. (1998). Environmental and genetic variance in children's observed and reported maladaptive behavior. *Child Development, 69,* 1286–1298.

Levin G. R. & Simmons, J. J. (1962). Response to praise by emotionally disturbed boys. *Psych Report 1962,* 11, 10

Levitt, E. E. (1957). The results of psychotherapy with children: An evaluation. *Journal of Consulting and Clinical Psychology, 21,* 189–197.

Levitt, E. E. (1971). Research on psychotherapy with children. In A. E. Bergin & S. L. Garfield (Eds.), *Handbook of psychotherapy and behavior change,* (pp. 474–494). New York: John Wiley & Sons.

Lewinsohn, P. M., Hops, H., Roberts, R. E., Seeley, J. R., & Andrews, J. A. (1993). Adolescent psychopathology: I. Prevalence and incidence of depression and other DSM-III-R disorders in high school students. *Journal of Abnormal Psychology, 102*(1), 133–144.

Lewinsohn, P. M., Rohde, P., Seeley, J., & Fischer, S. (1993). Age-cohort changes in the lifetime occurrence of depression and other mental disorders. *Journal of Abnormal Psychology, 102*(1), 110–120.

Lewinsohn, P. M., Weinstein, M. S., & Shaw, D. A. (1969). Depression: A clinical-research approach. In R. D. F. C. M. Rubin (Ed.), *Advances in behavior therapy, 1968.* (pp. 231–240). New York: Academic Press.

Lindahl, K. M., & Markman, H. J. (1990). Communication and negative affect regulation in the family. In E. A. Blechman (Ed.), *Emotions and the family: For better or worse.* (pp. 99–115). Hillsdale, NJ: Lawrence Erlbaum Associates.

Loeber, R. (1980). *Child precursors of assaultive behavior.* Unpublished manuscript, Oregon Social Learning Center, Eugene, OR.

Loeber, R. (1982). The stability of antisocial and delinquent child behavior: A review. *Child Development, 53,* 1431–1446.

Loeber, R. (1991). Questions and advances in the study of developmental pathways. In D. Cicchetti & S. L. Toth (Eds.), *Rochester symposium on developmental psychopathology: 3. Models and integrations* (pp. 97–115). Rochester, NY: University of Rochester Press.

Loeber, R., & Dishion, T. (1983). Early predictors of male delinquency: A review. *Psychological Bulletin, 94,* 68–99.

Loeber, R., & Dishion, T. (1984). Boys who fight at home and school: Family conditions influencing cross-setting consistency. *Journal of Consulting and Clinical Psychology, 52*(5), 759–768.

Loeber, R., & Farrington, D. P. (Eds.). (1998). *Serious and violent juvenile offenders: Risk factors and successful interventions.* Thousand Oaks, CA: Sage.

Loeber, R., Weissman, W., & Reid, J. B. (1983). Family interaction of assaultive adolescents, stealers, and non-delinquents. *Journal of Abnormal Child Psychology, 11,* 1–14.

Loeber, R., Wung, P., Keenan, K., Giroux, B., Stouthamer-Loeber, M., Van Kammen, W. B., & Maughan, B. (1993). Developmental pathways in disruptive child behavior. *Development and Psychopathology, 5,* 103–133.

Loney, J., Langehorne, J. E., Jr., Paternite, C. E., Whaley-Klahn, M. A., Blair-Broeker, C. T., & Hacker, M. (1980). The Iowa HABIT: Hyperkinetic/Aggressive boys in treatment. In S. B. Sells, M. Roff, J. S. Strauss, & W. Pollin (Eds.), *Human functioning in longitudinal perspective: Studies of normal and psychopathological populations*. Baltimore: Williams & Wilkins.

Lorenz, F. O., Simons, R. L., Conger, R. D., Elder, G. H. J., Johnson, C., & Chao, W. (1997). Married and recently divorced mothers' stressful events and distress: Tracing change across time. *Journal of Marriage and the Family, 59*, 219–232.

Lovaas, O. I. (1987). Behavioral treatment and normal educational/intellectural functioning in young autistic children. *Journal of Consulting and Clinical Psychology, 55*, 3–9.

Lovaas, O. I. (1978). Parents as therapists. In M. Rutter & E. Schopler (Eds.) *Autism: A reappraisal of concepts and treatment*. (pp. 369–378). New York: Plenum Press.

Luthar, S. S., & McMahon, T. J. (1996). Peer reputation among inner-city adolescents: Structure and correlates. *Journal of Research on Adolescence, 6*(4), 581–603.

Lykken, D. J. (1957). The study of anxiety in the sociopathic personality. *Journal of Abnormal Psychology, 55*, 6–10.

Lykken, D. T. (1995). *The antisocial personalities*. Mahwah, NJ: Erlbaum.

Lykken, D. T., McGue, M., & Tellegen, A. (1987). Recruitment bias in twin research: The rule of two-thirds reconsidered. *Behavior Genetics, 17*, 343–362.

Lytton, H. (1977). Do parents create, or respond to, differences in twins? *Developmental Psychology, 13*, 456–459.

Lytton, H. (1980). *Parent-child interaction: The socialization process observed in twin and singleton families*. New York: Plenum.

Maccoby, E. E. (1980). Commentary. In G. R. Patterson (Ed.), *Mothers: The Unacknowledged Victim* (pp. 56–63). SRCD Monograph Vol 45 No 5.

Maccoby, E. E. (1992). The role of parents in the socialization of children: An historical overview. *Developmental Psychology, 28*, 1006–1017.

Maccoby, E. E. (1998). *The two sexes: Growing up apart, coming together*. Cambridge, MA: The Belknap Press of Harvard University Press.

Maccoby, E., & Martin, J. (1983). Socialization in the context of the family: Parent child interaction. In E. M. Hetherington (Ed.), *Socialization, personality and social development* (4th edition, Vol. IV, pp. 1–101). New York: John Wiley & Sons.

MacKinnen, C. E., Lamb, M. E., Belsky, J., & Baum, C. (1990). An affective-cognitive model of mother-child aggression. *Development and Psychopathology, 2*, 1–13.

MacKinnen-Lewis, C., Volling, B., Lamb, M. E., Dechman, K., Rabiner, K., & Curtner, M. E. (1994). A cross-contextual analysis of boy's social competence: From family to school. *Developmental psychology, 30*, 325–333.

Marcus, D. K., & Nardone, M. E. (1992). Depression and interpersonal rejection. *Clinical Psychology Review, 12*(4), 433–449.

Martin, J. A. (1981). A longitudinal study of the consequences of early mother infant interaction: A microanalytic approach. *Child Development, 46*(3 Serial No. 190).

Martin, J. A., Maccoby, E. E., Baran, K. W., & Jacklin, C. N. (1981). Sequential analysis of mother-child interaction at 18 months: A comparison of microanalytic methods. *Developmental Psychology, 17*, 146–157.

Martin, R. P. (1989). Activity level, distractibility, and persistence: Critical characteristics in early schooling. In G. A. Kohnstamm, J. E. Bates, & M. K. Rothbart (Eds.), *Temperament in Childhood*. New York: Wiley.

Martinez, C. R., Jr., & Forgatch, M. S. (submitted). Preventing problems with boys' noncompliance: Effects of a parent training intervention for divorcing mothers. *Journal of Consulting and Clinical Psychology*.

Masten, A. S., Morison, P., & Pellegrini, D. S. (1985). A revised class play method of peer assessment. *Developmental Psychology, 21*, 523–533.

Matas, L., Arend, R. A. & Sroute, L. A. (1978). Continuity in adaptation in the second year: The relationship between quality of attachment and later competence. *Child Development, 49*, 547–556.

McCartney, K., Harris, M. J., & Bernieri, F. (1990). Growing up and growing apart: A developmental meta-analysis of twin studies. *Psychological Bulletin, 107*, 226–237.

McCord, J. (1989). Theory, pseudotheory, and metatheory. In W. S. Laufer & F. Adler (Eds.), *Advances in criminological theory* (Vol. 1, pp. 127–145). New Brunswick: Transaction.

McCord, J. (1991). Competence in long-term perspective. *Psychiatry, 54*, 227–237.

McCord, J. (1996, December). *Prevention and the grounds for action.* Paper presented at the seminar on "Early Prevention," Stockholm, Sweden.

McCord, W., McCord, J., & Howard, A. (1960). Familial correlates of aggression in nondelinquent male children. *Journal of Abnormal & Social Psychology, 62*, 79–93.

McFarlane, A. H., Bellissimo, A., Norman, G. R., Lange, P., et al. (1994). Adolescent depression in a school-based community sample: Preliminary findings on contributing social factors. *Journal of Youth and Adolescence, 23*(6), 601–620.

McGee, R., Williams, S., & Silva, P. (1984). Background characteristics of aggressive, hyperactive, and aggressive-hyperactive boys. *Journal of American Academy of Child Psychiatry, 23*, 280–284.

McLloyd, V. (1990). The impact of economic hardship on black families and children: Psychological distress, parenting, and socio-emotional development. *Child Development, 61*, 311–346.

McNeil, C. B., Eyberg, S., Eisenstadt, T. H., Newcomb, K., & Funderburk, B. (1991). Parent-child interaction therapy with behavior problem children: Generalization of treatment effects to the school setting. *Journal of Clinical Child Psychology, 20*, 140–151.

Meadowcroft, P., Thomlison, B., & Chamberlain, P. (1994). Treatment Foster Care services: A research agenda for child welfare. *Child Welfare, 3*(1), 565–581.

Meadowcroft, P., & Trout, B. A. (Eds.), *Troubled youth in treatment homes: A handbook of therapeutic foster care*. Washington, DC: Child Welfare League of America.

Mednick, S. A., & Christiansen, K. O. (1977). *Biosocial bases of criminal behavior*. New York: Gardner.

Meehl, P. (1950). On the circularity of the laws of effect. *Psychological Bulletin, 47*, 52–75.

Metzler, C. E., & Dishion, T. J. (1992, November). *A model of the development of youthful problem behaviors.* Paper presented at the 18th Annual Convention for Association for Behavior Analysis, Boston.

Miklowitz, D. J., Goldstein, M. J., Nuechterlein, K. H., Snyder, K. S., & et al. (1988). Family factors and the course of bipolar affective disorder. *Archives of General Psychiatry, 45*, 225–231.

Miles, D. R., & Carey, G. (1997). Genetic and environmental architecture of human aggression. *Journal of Personality and Social Psychology, 72*, 207–217.

Miller, G. E., & Prinz, R. J. (1990). Enhancement of social learning family interventions for childhood conduct disorders. *Psychological Bulletin, 108*, 291–307.

Miller, W. R., & Rollnick, S. (1991). *Motivational interviewing: Preparing people to change addictive behavior*. New York: Guilford.

Mineka, S., Gunnar, M., & Champoux, M. (1986). Control in early socioemotional development: Infant rhesus monkeys reared in controllable vs. uncontrollable environments. *Child Development, 57*, 1240–1256.

Minuchin, S. (1974). *Families and family therapy*. Cambridge, MA: Harvard University Press.

Moffitt, T. E. (1993). Adolescence-limited and life-course-persistent antisocial behavior: A developmental taxonomy. *Psychological Review, 100*, 674–701.

Montemayor, R. (1982). The relationship between parent-adolescent conflict and the amount of time adolescents spend alone and with parents and peers. *Child Development, 53*, 1512–1519.

Montemayor, R., & Flannery, D. (1989). A naturalistic study of the involvement of children and adolescents with their mothers and friends: Developmental differences in expressive behavior. *Journal of Adolescent Research, 4,* 3–14.

Moore, K. J. (2001, August). Generalization of multidimensional treatment foster care to youth with borderline cognitive functioning. In P. Chamberlain & P. Sprengelmeyer (Chairs), *Applications of the Oregon Model to Populations of Difficult Youth.* Symposium conducted at the American Psychological Association's 109th annual Convention, San Francisco, California.

Mrazek, P. G. & Haggerty, R. J. (Eds) (1994). *Reducing risks for mental disorders: Frontiers for preventive intervention research.* Washington, D.C.: National Academy Press.

Mullins, L. L., Peterson, L., Wonderlich, S. A., & Reaven, N. M. (1986). The influence of depressive symptomatology in children on the social responses and perceptions of adults. *Journal of Clinical Child Psychology, 15*(3), 233–240.

Nagin, D., & Tremblay, R. E. (1999). Trajectories of boys' physical aggression, opposition, and hyperactivity on the path to physically violent and nonviolent juvenile delinquency. *Child Development, 70,* 1181–1196.

National Institute of Mental Health (1993). *The prevention of mental disorders: A national research agenda.* Bethesda, Maryland: NIMH.

Neiderhiser, J. M., Reiss, D., Hetherington, E. M., & Plomin, R. (in press). Relationships between parenting and adolescent adjustment over time: Genetic and environmental contributions. *Developmental Psychology.*

Newcomb, M. D. (1987). Consequences of teenage drug use: The transition from adolescence to young adulthood. *Drugs and Society, 1*(4), 25–60.

Nixon, S. B. (1965). *Increasing the frequency of attending resonses in hyperactive distractible youngsters by operant and modeling procedures.* Unpublished doctoral dissertation, Stanford University, Stanford, CA.

Nixon, S. (1968). Ways be which overly active students can be taught to concentrate on study activity Cooperative Research Project No. S 379. College of Education Stanford University.

O'Brien, M., Margolin, G., & John, R. S. (1995). Relation among marital conflict, child coping, and child adjustment. *Journal of Clinical Child Psychology, 24*(3), 346–361.

O'Brien, M., Margolin, G., John, R. S., & Krueger, L. (1991). Mothers' and sons' cognitive and emotional reactions to simulated marital and family conflict. *Journal of Consulting and Clinical Psychology, 59,* 692–703.

O'Connor, T. G., Rutter, M., Beckett, C., Keaveney, L., Kreppner, J. M., & the English and Romanian Adoptees Study Team (2000). The effects of global severe privation on cognitive competence: Extension and longitudinal follow up. *Child Development, 71*(2), 376–390.

O'Donnell, C. R., Manos, M. J., & Chesney-Lind, M. (1987). Diversion and neighborhood delinquency programs in open settings: A social network interpretation. In E. K. Morris & C. J. Braukermann (Eds.), *Behavioral approaches to crime and delinquency: A handbook of application, research, and concepts* (pp. 251–270). New York: Plenum Press.

Offord, D. R. (1996). The state of prevention and early intervention. In R. D. Peters & R. J. McMahon (Eds.), *Preventing childhood disorders, substance abuse and delinquency* (pp. 329–334). Thousand Oaks, CA: Sage.

Offord, D. R., Boyle, M. C., & Racine, Y. A. (1991). The Epidemiology of antisocial behavior in childhood and adolescence. In D. J. Pepler & K. H. Rubin (Eds.), *The development and treatment of childhood aggression* (pp. 31–54). Hillsdale, NJ: Lawrence Erlbaum Associates.

Olds, D. (1997). The prenatal/early infancy project: Fifteen years later. In G. W. Albee & T. P. Gullotta (Eds.), *Primary prevention works: Vol. 6. Issues in children's and families lives* (pp. 41–67). Thousand Oaks: Sage.

Olds, D. L., Eckenrode, J., Henderson, C. R., Jr., Kitzman, H., Powers, J., Cole, R., Sidora, K., Morris, P., Pettitt, L. M., & Luckey, D. (1997). Long-Term effects of home visitation on maternal life course and child abuse and neglect: Fifteen-Year follow-up of a randomized trial. *Journal of the American Medical Association, 278,* 637–643.

Olds, D. L., Henderson, C. R., Chamberlin, R., & Tatelbaum, R. (1986). Preventing child abuse and neglect: A randomized trial of nurse home visitation. *Pediatrics, 78,* 65–78.

Olds, D., Henderson, C. R., Jr., Cole, R., Eckenrode, J., Kitzman, H., Luckey, D., Pettitt, L., Sidora, K., Morris, P., & Powers, J. (1998) Long-Term effects of nurse home visitation on children's criminal and antisocial behavior. *Journal of the American Medical Association, 280*(14), 1238–1244.

Olds, D. L., Henderson, C. R., Jr. & Kitzman, H. (1994). Does prenatal and infancy nurse home visitation have enduring effects on qualities of parental care giving and child health at 25 to 50 months of life? *Pediatrics, 93,* 89–98.

O'Leary, C. (2001). *The Family Check-Up in high-risk families: Examining the impact in early childhood.* Unpublished doctoral dissertation, University of Oregon, Eugene.

Olson, S. L., Bates, J. E., & Bayles, K. (1984). Mother-infant interaction and the development of individual differences in children's cognitive competence. *Developmental Psychology, 20*(1), 166–179.

Olweus, D. (1979). Stability of aggressive reaction patterns in males: A review. *Psychological Bulletin, 86,* 852–875.

Olweus, D. (1994). *Bullying at school.* Cambridge, UK: Blackwell Publishers.

Osgood, D. W., Wilson, J. K., Bachman, J. G., O'Malley, P. M., & Johnston, L. D. (1996). Routine activities and individual deviant behavior. *American Sociological Review, 61,* 635–655.

Otnow-Lewis, D., Yeager, C. A., Cobham-Portorreal, C. S., Klein, N., Showalter, B. A., & Anthony, A. (1990). A follow-up of female delinquents: Maternal contributions to the prepetuation of deviance. *Journal of the American Academy of Child and Adolescent Psychiatry, 30,* 197–201.

Owens, E., Shaw, D. S., & McGuire, M. (1993, March). *Infant temperament and maternal responsiveness in a low SES sample: Reciprocal influences during the second year of life.* Paper presented at the convention of the Society for Research in Child Development, New Orleans.

Oyama, S. (1989). Ontogeny and the central dogma: Do we need the concept of genetic programming in order to have an evolutionary perspective? In M. E. Gunnar & E. Thelen (Eds.), *Systems and development: The Minnesota Symposia on Child Psychology* (Vol. 22, pp. 1–34). Hillsdale, NJ: Erlbaum.

Paikoff, R. L., & Brooks-Gunn, J. (1990). Physiological processes: What role do they play during the transition to adolescence? In R. Montemayor, G. R. Adams, & T. P. Gullotta (Eds.), *From childhood to adolescence: A transitional period?* (pp. 310–348). Newbury Park, CA: Sage.

Pajer, K. A. (1998). What happens to "bad" girls? A review of the adult outcomes of antisocial adolescent girls. *American Journal of Psychiatry, 155,* 862–870.

Park, K. A., & Waters, E. (1989). Security of attachment and preschool friendships. *Child Development, 60,* 1076–1081.

Parkhurst, J. T., & Hopmeyer, A. (1998). Sociometric popularity and peer-perceived popularity: Two distinct dimensions of peer status. *Journal of Early Adolescence, 18*(2), 125–144.

Parton, D. A., & Ross, A. O. (1965). Social reinforcement of children's motor behavior: A review. *Psychological Bulletin, 64,* 65–73.

Pasamanick, B., Rogers, M. E., & Lilienfeld, A. M. (1956). Pregnancy experience and the development of behavior disorders in children. *American Journal of Psychiatry, 112,* 613–618.

Patterson, G. R. (1960) A nonverbal technique for the assessment of aggression children. *Child Development, 31,* 643–653.

Patterson, G. R. (1965). Responsiveness to social stimuli. In L. Krasner & L. P. Ullmann (Eds.), *Research in behavior modification* (pp. 157–178). New York: Holt, Rinehart and Winston, Inc.

Patterson, G. R. (1971). Behavioral intervention procedures in the classroom and in the home. (pp 751–775). In A. E. Bergin & S. L. Garfield (Eds.) *Handbook of Psychotherapy and Behavior Change: an empirical analysis* (pp 751–775). NY: John Wiley.

Patterson, G. R. (1973). Changes in status of family members as controlling stimuli: A basis for describing treatment process. In L. A. Hamerlynck, L. C. Handy, & E. J. Mash (Eds.), *Behavior change: Methodology, concepts, and practice* (pp. 169–191). Champaign, IL: Research Press.

Patterson, G.R. (1974a). A basis for identifying stimuli which control behavior in natural settings. *Child Development, 45,* 900–911.

Patterson, G. R. (1974b). Interventions for boys with conduct problems: Multiple settings, treatments, and criteria. *Journal of Consulting and Clinical Psychology, 42,* 471–481.

Patterson, G. R. (1976). The aggressive child: Victim and architect of a coercive system. In E. J. Mash, L. A. Hamerlynck, & L. C. Handy (Eds.), *Behavior modification and families. I. Theory and research. II. Applications and developments* (pp. 267–316). New York: Brunner/Mazel.

Patterson, G. R. (1977a). A three-stage functional analysis for children's coercive behaviors: A tactic for developing a performance theory. In D. Baer, B. C. Etzel, & J. M. L. Blanc (Eds.), *New developments in behavioral research: Theories, methods, and application, in honor of Sidney W. Bijou* (pp. 59–79). Hillsdale, NJ: Lawrence Erlbaum Associates.

Patterson, G. R. (1977b). Accelerating stimuli for two classes of coercive behaviors. *Journal of Abnormal Child Psychology, 5,* 335–350.

Patterson, G. R. (1979a). A performance model for coercive family interaction. In R. B. Cairns (Ed.), *Social interaction: Methods, analysis, and illustrations* (pp. 119–162). Hillsdale, NJ: Erlbaum.

Patterson, G. R. (1979b). Treatment for children with conduct problems: A review of outcome studies. In S. Feshbach and A. Fraczek (Eds.), *Aggression and behavior change: Biological and social process* (pp. 83–132). New York: Praeger.

Patterson, G. R. (1980). Mothers: The unacknowledged victims. *Monographs of the Society for Research in Child Development, 45*(5, Serial No. 186).

Patterson, G. R. (1982). *A social learning approach: Vol. 3: Coercive family process.* Eugene, OR: Castalia.

Patterson, G. R. (1983). Stress: A change agent for family process. In N. Garmezy & M. Rutter (Eds.), *Stress, coping, and development in children* (pp. 235–264). New York: McGraw-Hill.

Patterson, G. R. (1984a) Microsocial process: A view from the boundary. In J. Masters (Ed.), *Boundary areas in social and developmental psychology* (pp. 43–66). New York: Academic Press.

Patterson, G. R. (1984b). A performance theory for coercive family interaction. In R. B. Cairns (Ed.), *The analysis of social interactions: Methods, issues, and illustrations* (pp. 117–162). Hillsdale, NJ: Erlbaum.

Patterson, G. R. (1984c). Siblings: Fellow travelers in coercive family process. In R. J. Blanchard & D. C. Blanchard (Eds.), *Advances in the study of aggression* (pp. 173–214). Orlando, FL: Academic Press.

Patterson, G. R. (1985). Beyond technology: The next stage in developing an empirical base for parent training. In L. L'Abate (Ed.), *Handbook of family psychology and therapy (Vol. 2)* (pp. 1344–1379). Homewood, IL: Dorsey.

Patterson, G. R. (1986a). Performance models for antisocial boys. *American Psychologist, 41,*(4) 432–444.

Patterson, G. R. (1986b). The contribution of siblings to training for fighting: A microsocial analysis. In D. Olweus, J. Block, & M. Radke-Yarrow (Eds.), *Development of antisocial and prosocial behavior: Research, theories, and issues* (pp. 235–261). Orlando, FL: Academic Press.

Patterson, G. R. (1988). Family process: Loops, levels, and linkages. In N. Bolger, A. Caspi, G. Downey, & M. Moorehouse (Eds.), *Persons in context: Developmental processes* (pp. 114–151). New York: Cambridge University Press.

Patterson, G. R. (1990). Some comments about cognitions as causal variables. *American Psychologist, 45,* 984–985.

Patterson, G. R. (1991, April). *Interaction of stress and family structure and their relation to child adjustment: An example of across site collaboration.* Paper presented at the meeting of the Society for Research in Child Development, Seattle, WA.

Patterson, G. R. (1992). Developmental changes in antisocial behavior. In R. D. Peters, R. J. McMahon, & V. L. Quinsey (Eds.), *Aggression and violence throughout the life span* (pp. 52–82). Newbury Park, CA: Sage.

Patterson, G. R. (1993). Orderly change in a stable world: The antisocial trait as a chimera. *Journal of Consulting and Clinical Psychology, 61*, 911–919.

Patterson, G. R. (1994). Some alternatives to seven myths about treating families of antisocial children. In C. Henricson (Ed.), *Crime and the family: Conference report: Proceedings of an international conference* (Occasional Paper 20, pp. 26–49). London: Family Policy Studies Centre.

Patterson, G. R. (1995). Coercion as a basis for early age of onset for arrest. In J. McCord (Ed.), *Coercion and punishment in long-term perspective* (pp. 81–105). New york: Cambridge University Press.

Patterson, G. R. (1996a, December 2–3, 1996). *The bidirectional relation between prevention trials and coercion theory.* Paper presented at the at a conference H. Stattin (Chair) on "Current Knowledge on Early Prevention", Stockholm Sweden.

Patterson, G. R. (1996b). Some characteristics of a developmental theory for early onset delinquency. In M. F. Lenzenweger & J. J. Haugaard (Eds.), *Frontiers of developmental psychopathology* (pp. 81–124). New York: Oxford University Press.

Patterson, G. R. (1997a). Performance models for parenting: A social interactional perspective. In J. E. Grusec & L. Kuczynski (Eds.), *Parenting and children's internalization of values: A handbook of contemporary theory* (pp. 193–235). New York: John Wiley & Sons.

Patterson, G. R. (1997b, August). *Randomized prevention trials as a basis for testing developmental theory.* Paper presented at the Panel for the annual American Psychological Association, Chicago.

Patterson, G.R. (1998a). Continuities—a search for causal mechanisms: comment on the special section. *Developmental Psychology, 34*(6), 1263–1268.

Patterson, G. R. (1998b, February). Some contributions of a family transitions model to early arrest. Paper presented at Festschrift for Mavis Hetherington San Diego.

Patterson, G. R. (1999a, September). *Early- and late-onset juvenile offending as it relates to new forms of deviancy.* Paper presented at the symposium, R. Sampson (Chair), "Understanding trajectories of criminal or antisocial behavior: Multiple pathways or general explanations?" Presented at the Life History Conference, Kauai, HI.

Patterson, G. R. (1999b). A proposal relating a theory of delinquency to societal rates of juvenile crime: Putting Humpty Dumpty together again. In M. J. Cox & J. Brooks-Gunn (Eds.), *Conflict and cohesion in families: Causes and consequences* (pp. 11–35). Mahwah, NJ: Lawrence Erlbaum.

Patterson, G. R. (in press-a). Performance models for parenting: A social interactional perspective. In J. Grusec & L. Kuczynski (Eds.), *Parenting and the socialization of values: A handbook of contemporary theory.* New York: Wiley & Sons.

Patterson, G. R., & Anderson, D. (1964). Peers as social reinforcers. *Child Development, 35*, 951–960.

Patterson, G. R., & Bank, L. (1986). Bootstrapping your way in the nomological thicket. *Behavioral Assessment, 8*, 49–73.

Patterson, G. R., & Bank, L. (1987). When is nomological network a construct? In D. R. Peterson & D. B. Fishman (Eds.), *Assessment for decision* (pp. 249–279). New Brunswick, NJ: Rutgers University Press.

Patterson, G. R., & Bank, L. I. (1989). Some amplifying mechanisms for pathologic processes in families. In M. R. Gunnar & E. Thelen (Eds.), *Systems and development: The Minnesota symposia on child psychology* (pp. 167–209). Hillsdale, NJ: Erlbaum.

Patterson, G. R., Bank, L., & Stoolmiller, M. (1990). The preadolescent's contributions to disrupted family process. In R. Montemayor, G. R. Adams, & T. P. Gullotta (Eds.), *From childhood to adolescence: A transitional period?* (pp. 107–133). Newbury Park, CA: Sage.

Patterson, G. R., & Bechtel, G. G. (1977). Formulating the situational environment in relation to states and traits. In R. B. Cattell & R. M. Dreger (Eds.), *Handbook of modern personality study* (pp. 254–268). New York: John Wiley & Sons.

Patterson, G. R., & Brodsky, G. (1966). A behaviour modification programme for a child with multiple problem behaviours. *Journal of Child Psychology and Psychiatry, 7,* 277–295.

Patterson, G. R., & Capaldi, D. M. (1990). A mediational model for boys' depressed mood. In J. E. Rolf, A. Masten, D. Cicchetti, K. Nuechterlein, & S. Weintraub (Eds.), *Risk and protective factors in the development of psychopathology* (pp. 141–163). Boston, MA: Syndicate of the Press, University of Cambridge.

Patterson, G. R., & Capaldi, D. M. (1991). Antisocial parents: Unskilled and vulnerable. In P. A. Cowan & E. M. Hetherington (Eds.), *Family transitions* (pp. 195–218). Hillsdale, NJ: Lawrence Erlbaum.

Patterson, G. R., Capaldi, D. M., & Bank, L. (1991). An early starter model for predicting delinquency. In D. J. Pepler & K. H. Rubin (Eds.), *The development and treatment of childhood aggression* (pp. 139–168). Hillsdale, NJ: Lawrence Erlbaum Associates.

Patterson, G. R., & Chamberlain, P. (1988). Treatment process: A problem at three levels. In L. C. Wynne (Ed.), *State of the art in family therapy research: Controversies and recommendations* (pp. 189–223). New York: Family Process Press.

Patterson, G. R., & Chamberlain, P. (1994). A functional analysis of resistance during parent training therapy. *Clinical Psychology: Science and Practice, 1,* 53–70.

Patterson, G. R., Chamberlain, P., & Reid, J. B. (1982). A comparative evaluation of parent training procedures. *Behavior Therapy, 13,* 638–650.

Patterson, G. R., & Cobb, J. A. (1971). A dyadic analysis of "aggressive" behaviors. In J. P. Hill (Ed.), *Minnesota symposia on child psychology* (Vol. 5, pp. 72–129). Minneapolis, MN: University of Minnesota.

Patterson, G. R., & Cobb, J. A., & Ray, R. S. (1972). Direct intervention in the classroom: A set of procedures for the aggressive child. In F. W. Clark, D. R. Evans, & L. A. Hamerlynck (Eds.), *The Proceedings of the Third Banff International Conference on Behavior Modification, April, 1971. Implementing behavioral programs for schools and clinics* (pp. 151–201). Champaign, IL: Research Press.

Patterson, G. R. Cobb, J., Ray, R. (1973). A social engineering technology for re-training the families of antisocial boys pp. In H. Adams & I. P. Unikel (Eds.), *Issues and Trends in behavior therapy* (pp. 139–225). Springfield, IL: C. G. Thomas Publishers

Patterson, G. R., & Cobb, J. A. (1973). Stimulus control for classes of noxious behaviors. In J. F. Knutson (Ed.), *The control of aggression: Implications from basic research* (pp. 144–199). Chicago: Aldine.

Patterson, G. R., Crosby, L., & Vuchinich, S. (1992). Predicting risk for early police arrest. *Journal of Quantitative Criminology, 8,* 333–355.

Patterson, G. R., DeBaryshe, B. D., & Ramsey, E. (1989). A developmental perspective on antisocial behavior. *American Psychologist, 44,* 329–335.

Patterson, G. R., & DeGarmo, D. S. (1997a, March). *Growth in antisocial behavior: Who, when, and why.* Paper presented at the Eleanor Maccoby Festschrift, Wye River Conference Center, Queenstown, MD.

Patterson, G. R., & DeGarmo, D. S. (1997b, November). *In search of growth in antisocial behavior: Prelude to early-onset delinquency.* Paper presented at the American Society of Criminology, San Diego, CA.

Patterson, G. R., DeGarmo, D., & Knutson, N. (in press). Hyperactive and antisocial behaviors: Comorbid or two points on same process? *Development and Psychopathology.*

Patterson, G. R., & Dishion, T. J. (1985). Contributions of families and peers to delinquency. *Criminology, 23,* 63–79.

Patterson, G. R., & Dishion, T. J. (1988). Multilevel family process models: Traits, interactions, and relationships. In R. A. Hinde & J. Stevenson-Hinde (Eds.), *Relationships within families: Mutual influences* (pp. 283–310). Oxford: Clarendon.

Patterson, G. R., Dishion, T. J., & Bank, L. (1984). Family interaction: A process model of deviancy training. *Aggressive Behavior, 10,* 253–267.

Patterson, G. R., Dishion, T. J., & Chamberlain, P. (1993). Outcomes and methodological issues relating to treatment of antisocial children. In T. R. Giles (Ed.), *Handbook of effective psychotherapy* (pp. 43–88). New York: Plenum.

Patterson, G. R., Dishion, T. J., & Chamberlain, P. (993). Adolescent growth in new forms of problem behavior: Macro- and micro-peer dynamics. *Prevention Science*.

Patterson, G. R., Dishion, T. J., & Yoerger, K. (2000). Outcomes and methodological issues relating to treatment of antisocial children. In T. R. Giles (Ed.),. *Handbook of effective psychotherapy,* (pp. 43–88). New York: Plenum

Patterson, G. R., & Fagot, B. I. (1967). Selective responsiveness to social reinforcers and deviant behavior in children. *The Psychological Record, 17,* 369–368.

Patterson, G. R., & Fleischman, M. J. (1979). Maintenance of treatment effects: Some considerations concerning family systems and follow-up data. *Behavior Therapy, 10,* 168–185.

Patterson, G. R., & Forgatch, M. S. (1985). Therapist behavior as a determinant for client resistance: A paradox for the behavior modifier. *Journal of Consulting and Clinical Psychology, 53,* 846–851.

Patterson, G. R., & Forgatch, M. S. (1987). *Parents and adolescents living together: Part 1: The basics.* Eugene, OR: Castalia.

Patterson, G. R., & Forgatch, M. S. (1990). Initiation and maintenance of process disrupting single-mother families. In G. R. Patterson (Ed.), *Depression and aggression in family interaction* (pp. 209–245). Hillsdale, NJ: Erlbaum.

Patterson, G. R., & Forgatch, M. S. (1995). Predicting future clinical adjustment from treatment outcome and process variables. *Psychological Assessment, 7*(3), 275–285.

Patterson, G. R., Forgatch, M. S., Yoerger, K., & Stoolmiller, M. (1998). Variables that initiate and maintain an early-onset trajectory for juvenile offending. *Development and Psychopathology, 10,* 541–547.

Patterson, G. R., & Granic, I. (2001). *Coercive processes from a dynamic systems perspective.* Manuscript in preparation, Oregon Social Learning Center, Eugene.

Patterson, G. R., & Hinsey, W. C. (1964). Investigations of some assumptions and characteristics of a procedure for instrumental conditioning in children. *Journal of Experimental Child Psychology, 1,* 111–122.

Patterson, G. R., Jones, R., Whittier, J., & Wright, M. A. (1965). A behavior modification technique for the hyperactive child. *Behaviour Research and Therapy, 2,* 217–226.

Patterson, G. R., Littman, R. A., & Bricker, W. (1967a). Assertive behavior in children: A step towards a theory of aggression. *Monographs of the Society for Research in Child Development, 32*(5), 1–43.

Patterson, G. R., McNeal, S., Hawkins, N., & Phelps, R. (1967b). Reprogramming the social environment. *Child Psychology and Psychiatry, 8,* 181–195.

Patterson, G. R., & Moore, D. (1979). Interactive patterns as units of behavior. In S. Suomi, M. Lamb, & G. Stephenson (Eds.), *Social interaction analysis: Methodological issues* (pp. 77–96). Madison, WI: University of Wisconsin Press.

Patterson, G. R., & Narrett, C.M. (1990). The development of a reliable and vailid treatment program for aggressive young children. *International Journal of Mental Health, 19,* 19–26.

Patterson, G. R., & Reid, J. B. (1970). Reciprocity and coercion: Two facets of social systems. In C. Neuringer & J. L. Michael (Eds.), *Behavior modification in clinical psychology* (pp. 133–177). New York: Appleton-Century-Crofts.

Patterson, G. R., & Reid, J. B. (1984). Social interactional processes within the family: The study of moment-by-moment family transactions in which human social development is embedded. *Journal of Applied Developmental Psychology, 5,* 237–262.

Patterson, G. R., Reid, J. B., Jones, R. R., & Conger, R. E. (1975). *A social learning approach to family intervention. I. Families with aggressive children.* Eugene, OR: Castalia.

Patterson, G. R., Reid, J. B., & Dishion, T. J. (1992). *A social interactional approach: Vol. 4: Antisocial boys*. Eugene, OR: Castalia.

Patterson, G. R., Shaw, D. S., Snyder, J. J., & Yoerger, K. (2001). *In search of growth in antisocial behavior*. Manuscript submitted for publication.

Patterson, G. R., & Stoolmiller, M. (1991). Replications of a dual failure model for boys' depressed mood. *Journal of Consulting and Clinical Psychology, 59,* 491–498.

Patterson, G. R., & Stoolmiller, M. (1999, November). *Comparison of different mechanisms for children's antisocial behavior*. Paper presented at the a symposium, Paul S. Strand (Chair), "Applications of matching theory and behavioral momentum to child behavior therapy" at the 33rd annual convention of the Association for the Advancement of Behavior Therapy, Toronto, Canada.

Patterson, G. R., & Stouthamer-Loeber, M. (1984). The correlation of family management practices and delinquency. *Child Development, 55,* 1299–1307.

Patterson, G. R., & Yoerger, K. (1993). Development models for delinquent behavior. In S. Hodgins (Ed.), *Mental disorder and crime* (pp. 140–172). Newbury Park, CA: Sage.

Patterson, G. R., & Yoerger, K. (1997a). A developmental model for late-onset delinquency. In D. W. Osgood (Ed.), *Motivation and delinquency: Nebraska Symposium on Motivation* (Vol. 44, pp. 119–177). Lincoln: University of Nebraska Press.

Patterson, G. R., & Yoerger, K. (1997b, September). *Intraindividual growth in covert antisocial behavior: A key precursor to police arrest*. Paper presented at the VIIIth International Conference of Developmental Psychology, Rennes, France.

Patterson, G. R., & Yoerger, K. (1998, August). *Growth in deviancy: Initiation into systems theory*. Paper presented as the invited address for the G. Stanley Hall Award at the convention of the American Psychological Association, San Francisco.

Patterson, G. R., & Yoerger, K. (1999). Intraindividual growth in covert antisocial behavior: A necessary precursor to chronic and adult arrests? *Criminal Behaviour and Mental Health, 9,* 86–100.

Patterson, G. R., & Yoerger, K. (in press). A developmental model for late-onset delinquency. In D. W. Osgood (Ed.), *Motivation and Delinquency*. Lincoln, NE: University of Nebraska Press.

Pears, K. C. (1997). *Social referencing, attachment and risk status*. Unpublished manuscript.

Pears, K. C. (1999). *Perspective-Taking and Adjustment in* Preschoolers. Unpublished dissertation, University of Oregon, Eugene, OR.

Pears, K. C., & Capaldi, D. M. (in press). Intergenerational transmission of abuse: A two-generation, prospective study of an at-risk sample. *Child Abuse and Neglect: The International Journal*.

Pears, K. C. and Fagot, B., I. (1995, March). *Maternal behavior and the quality of preschool attachment*. Paper presented at the biennial meeting of the Society for Research in Child Development, Indianapolis, IN.

Peterson, J. L., & Zill, N. (1986). Marital disruption, parent-child relationships, and behavior problems in children. *Journal of Marriage and the Family, 48,* 295–307.

Peterson, R. R. (1996). A re-evaluation of the economic consequences of divorce. *American Sociological Review, 61,* 528–536.

Phares, V. (1992). Where's Poppa?: The relative lack of attention to the role of fathers in child and adolescent psychopathology. *American Psychologist, 47,* 656–664.

Phares, V., & Compas, B. E. (1992). The role of fathers in child and adolescent psychopathology: Make room for daddy. *Psychological Bulletin, 111,* 387–412.

Pike, A., McGuire, S., Reiss, D., Heterington, E. M., & Plomin, R. (1996). Family environment and adolescent depressive symptoms and antisocial behavior: A multivariate genetic analysis. *Developmental Psychology, 32,* 590–603.

Plomin, R. (1990). *Nature and nurture: An introduction to human behavioral genetics*. Pacific Grove, CA: Brooks/Cole Publishing Company.

Plomin, R., & D. Daniels (1987). Why are children in the same family so different from one another? *Behavioral and Brain Sciences, 10,* 1–16.

Plomin, R., Fulker, D. W., Corley, R., & DeFries, J. C. (1997). Nature, nurture, and cognitive development from 1 to 16 years: A parent–offspring adoption study. *Psychological Science, 8,* 442–447.

Porter, B., & O'Leary, K. D. (1980). Marital discord and childhood behavior problems. *Journal of Abnormal Child Psychology, 8(3),* 287–295.

Poulin, F., Cillisen, A. H., Hubbard, J. A., Coie, J. D., Dodge, K. A., & Schwartz, D. (1997). Children's friends and behavioral similarity in two social contexts. *Social Development, 6,* 224–236.

Poulin, F., & Dishion, T. J. (1997, April). *Iatrogenic effects among high-risk adolescents aggregated within interventions: An analysis of durability and process.* Paper presented at the Society for Research in Child Development, Washington, DC.

Poulin, F., Dishion, T. J., & Burraston, B. (in press). Three-Year iatrogenic effects associated with aggregating high-risk adolescents in cognitive-behavioral preventive interventions. *Applied Developmental Science.*

Poulin, F., Dishion, T. J., & Haas, E. (1999). The peer influence paradox: Friendship quality and deviancy training within male adolescent friendships. *Merrill-Palmer Quarterly, 45,* 42–61)

Poznanski, E. O., & Mokros, H. B. (1994). Phenomenology and epidemiology of mood disorders in children and adolescents. In W. M. Reynolds & H. F. Johnston (Eds.), *Handbook of depression in children and adolescents.* (pp. 19–40). New York: Plenum.

Price, J. M., & Dodge, K. A. (1989), Peers contribution to children's social maladjustment: Description and intervention. In T.J. Berndt & G.W. Ladd (Eds.), *Peer relations in child development* (pp. 341–370). New York: Wiley.

Prange, M. E., Greenbaum, P. E., Silver, S. E., Friedman, R. M., Kutash, K., & Duchnowski, A. J. (1992). Family functioning and psychopathology among adolescents with severe emotional disturbances. *Journal of Abnormal Child Psychology, 20(1),* 83–102.

Premack, D. (1959). Toward empirical behavioral laws: Instrumental positive reinforcement. *Psychological Science, 66,* 219–233.

Puig-Antich, J., Kaufman, J., Ryan, N. D., Williamson, D. E., Dahl, R. E., Lukens, E., Todak, G., Ambrosini, P., Rabinovich, H., & Nelson, B. (1993). The psychosocial functioning and family environment of depressed adolescents. *J.Am.Acad.Child Adolesc.Psychiatry, 32(2),* 244–253.

Pulkkinen, L. (1986). Offensive and defensive aggression in humans: A longitudinal perspective. *Aggressive Behavior, 13,* 197–212.

Putallaz, M. (1987). Maternal behavior and children's sociometric status. *Child development, 58,* 324–340.

Quay, H. C. (1987). Patterns of delinquent behavior. In H. C. Quay (Ed.), *Handbook of juvenile delinquency* (pp. 118–138). New York: John Wiley and Sons.

Rachlin, H. (1995). Behavioral economics without anomalies. Special issue: Behavioral economics. *Journal of the Experimental Analysis of Behavior, 64,* 397–404.

Radke-Yarrow, M. (1998). *Children of depressed mothers*. New York: Cambridge University Press.

Radloff, L. S. (1977). The CES-D Scale: A self report depression scale for research in the general population. *Applied Psychological Measurement, 1(3),* 385–401.

Ramsey, E., Patterson, G.R., & Walker, H.M. (1990). Generalization of the antisocial trait from home to school settings. *Journal of Applied Developmental Psychology, 11,* 209–223.

Rao, S. A. (1998). *The short-term impact of the Family Check-Up: A brief motivational intervention for at-risk families*. Unpublished doctoral dissertation, University of Oregon.

Raudenbush, S. W. (1995). Hierarchical linear models to study the effects of social context on development. In J. M. Gottman (Ed.), *The analysis of change* (pp. 165–201). Mahwah, NJ: Erlbaum.

Raush, H. L. (1965). Interaction sequences. *Journal of Personality and Social Psychology, 2,* 487–499.

Raush, H.L., Barry, W.A., Hertel, R.K., & Swain, M.A. (1974). *Communication, conflict, and marriage.* San Francisco: Jossey-Bass.

Recorla, R. A. (1988). Pavlovian conditioning: It's not what you think it is. *American Psychologist, 43,* 151–160.

Redl, F., & Wineman, D. (1957). *The aggressive child.* New York: The Free Press.

Reid, J. B. (1967). *Reciprocity in family interaction.* Unpublished doctoral dissertation, University of Oregon, Eugene.

Reid, J. B. (1970). Reliability assessment of observation data: A possible methodological problem. *Child Development,* 41, 1143–1150.

Reid, J. B. (1985). Behavioral approaches to intervention and assessment with child-abusive families. In P. Bornstein & A. Kazdin (Eds.), *Handbook of clinical behavior therapy with children* (pp. 772–802). Homewood, IL: Dorsey Press.

Reid, J. B. (1986). Social interactional patterns in families of abused and non-abused children. In C. Zahn-Waxler, E. M. Cummings, & R. Iannotti (Eds.), *Altruism and aggression: Biological and social origins* (pp. 238–255). New York: Cambridge University Press.

Reid, J. B. (1993). Prevention of conduct disorder before and after school entry: Relating interventions to development findings. *Journal of Development and Psychopathology, 5,* 243–262.

Reid, J. B. (Ed.). (1978). *A social learning approach to family intervention: II. Observation in home settings.* Eugene, OR: Castalia.

Reid, J. B. Baldwin, D. V., Patterson, G. R., & Dishion, T. J. (1988). Observations in the assessment of childhood disorders. In M. Rutter, A. H. Tuma, & I. S. Lann (Eds.), *Assessment and diagnosis in child psychopathology* (pp. 156–195). New York: Gilford Press.

Reid, J. B., & Eddy, J. M. (1997). The prevention of antisocial behavior: Some considerations in the search for effective interventions. In D. M. Stoff, J. Breiling, & J. D. Maser, (Eds.). *The handbook of antisocial behavior* (pp. 343–356). NY: John Wiley & Sons.

Reid, J. B., Eddy, J. M., Fetrow, R. A., & Stoolmiller, M. (1999). Description and immediate impacts of a preventive intervention for conduct problems. *American Journal of Community Psychology, 24*(4), 483–517.

Reid, J. B., Kavanagh, K. (1985). A social interactional approach to child abuse: Risk, prevention and treatment. In M. Chesney & R. Rosenman (Eds.), *Anger and hostility in behavioral and cardiovascular disorders* (pp. 241–257). New York: Hemisphere/McGraw-Hill.

Reid, J. B., Kavanagh, K. A., & Baldwin, D. V. (1987). Abusive parents' perceptions of child problem behaviors: An example of parental bias. *Journal of Abnormal Child Psychology, 15,* 457–466.

Reid, J. B., Patterson, G. R., & Loeber, R. (1982). The abused child: Victim, instigator, or innocent bystander? In D. Bernstein (Ed.), *Response structure and organization* (pp. 47–68). Lincoln: University of Nebraska Press.

Reid, J. B., Taplin, P. S., & Lorber, R. (1981). A social interactional approach to the treatment of abusive families. In R. B. Stuart (Ed.), *Violent behavior: Social learning approaches to prediction, management, and treatment* (pp. 83–101). New York: Brunner/Mazel.

Reiss, A. J., Jr. (1986). Why are communities important in understanding crime? In A. J. Reiss, Jr. & M. Tony (Eds.), *Communities and crime* (pp. 1–33).

Reiss, D., Hetherington, E. M., Plomin, R., Howe, G. W., Simmens, S. J., Henderson, S. H., O'Connor, T. J., Bussell, D. A., Anderson, E. R., & Law, T. (1995). Genetic questions for environmental studies: Differential parenting and psychopathology in adolescence. *Archives of General Psychiatry, 52,* 925–936.

Repetti, R. L. (1996). The effects of perceived daily social and academic failure experiences on school-age children's subsequent interactions with parents. *Child Development, 67,* 1467–1482.

Research Project: Family relationships and parent-child interactions. *Journal of Family Psychology, 7*(1), 76–90.

Ricciuti, H. N., & Dorman, R. (1983). Interaction of multiple factors contributing to high-risk parenting. In R. A. Hoekelman (Ed.), *Pediatric round table No. 7. Minimizing high-risk parenting* . Media, PA: Harwell.

Rivera, V. R., & Kutash, K. (1994). Therapeutic foster care services, In V. R. Rivera & K. Jutash, *Literature series on the components of a system of care.* Tampa, FL: Research and Training Center for Children's Mental health, University of South Florida, Florida Mental Health Institute.

Roberts, W. L. (1986). Nonlinear models of development: An example from the socialization of competence. *Child Development, 57*(5), 1166–1178.

Roberts, W. L., & Strayer, J. (1987). Parents' responses to the emotional distress of their children: Relations with children's competence. *Developmental Psychology, 23*(3), 415–422.

Robins, L. N. (1966). *Deviant children grown up*. Baltimore: Williams Watkins.

Robins, L. N. (1981). Epidemiological approaches to natural history research: Antisocial disorders in children. *Journal of the American Academy of Child Psychiatry, 20,* 566–580.

Robins, L. N. (1986). The consequences of antisocial behavior in girls. In D. Always, J. Block, & M. Radke-Yarrow. *Development of antisocial and prosocial behavior: Research, theories, and issues* (pp. 385–414). Orlando, FL: Academic Press.

Robins, L. N. (1992). The role of prevention experiments in discovering causes of children's antisocial behavior. In J. McCord & R. E. Tremblay (Eds.), *Preventing antisocial behavior: Interventions from birth through adolescence* (pp. 3–20). New York: Guilford.

Robinson, E. A. (1985). Coercion theory revisited: Toward a new theoretical perspective on the etiology of conduct disorders. *Clinical Psychology Review, 5,* 1–29.

Robinson, E. A., & Eyberg, S. M. (1981). The dyadic parent-child interaction coding system: Standardization and validation. *Journal of Consulting and Clinical Psychology, 49,* 245–250.

Rodkin, P. C., Farmer, T. W., Pearl, R., & Van Acker, R. (2000). Heterogeneity of popular boys: Antisocial and prosocial configurations. *Developmental Psychology, 36*(1), 14–24.

Rogers, C. R. (1957). The necessary and sufficient conditions of therapeutic personality change. *Journal of Consulting Psychology, 21,* 95–103.

Rose, R. J., & Kaprio, J. (1987). Shared experience and similarity of personality: Positive data from Finnish and American twins. *Behavioral and Brain Sciences, 10,* 35–36.

Rosenbaum, A., & O'Leary, K. D. (1981). Marital violence: Characteristics of abusive couples. *Journal of Consulting and Clinical Psychology, 49,* 63–71.

Rowe, D. C. (1994). *The limits of family influence: Genes, experience and behavior*. New York, Guilford.

Rowe, D. C. (1997). Are parents to blame? A look at *The Antisocial Personalities. Psychological Inquiry, 8,* 251–260.

Rowe, D.C., & Gulley, B.L. (1992). Sibling effects on substance use and delinquency. *Criminology, 30,* 217–233.

Rueter, M. A., & Conger, R. D. (1995). Interaction style, problem-solving behavior, and family problem-solving effectiveness. *Child Development, 66,* 98–115.

Rusby, J., Estes, A., & Dishion, T. (1990). School observations and Family Interaction Task: Interpersonal Process Code (IPC). Unpublished coding system. (Available at Oregon Social Learning Center, 160 East 4th Avenue, Eugene, OR 97401-2426.)

Rusby J., Estes, A., & Dishion, T. J. (1991). *Interpersonal process code* (unpublished technical manual). Eugene, OR: Oregon Social Learning Center.

Rutter, M. (1985). Family and school influences on behavioural development. *Journal of Child Psychology & Psychiatry & Allied Disciplines, 26,* 349–368.

Rutter, M. (1989). Pathways from childhood to adult life. *Journal of Child Psychology and Psychiatry and Allied Disciplines, 30*(1), 23-51.

Rutter, M. (1990). Commentary: Some factors and process considerations regarding effects of parental depression on children. *Developmental Psychology, 26,* 60–67.

Rutter, M., & Giller, H. (1983). *Juvenile delinquency: Trends and perspectives.* Middlesex, England: Penguin.

Sameroff, A. J. (1989). Commentary: General systems and the regulation of development. In M. R. Gunnar & E. Thelen (Eds.), *Systems and development: The Minnesota Symposia on Child Psychology* (Vol. 22, pp. 219–235). Hillsdale, NJ: Erlbaum.

Sameroff, A. J., Bartko, W. T., Baldwin, A., Baldwin, C., & Seifer, R. (1998). Family and social influences on the development of child competence. In M. Lewis & X. Feiring (Eds.), *Families, risk, and competence* (pp. 161–185). Mahwah, NJ: Lawrence Erlbaum Associates.

Sameroff, A. J., & Seifer, R. (1983). Familial risk and child competence. *Child Development, 54*(5), 1254–1268.

Sampson, R. J., & Groves, W. B. (1989). Community structure and crime: Testing social-disorganization theory. *American Journal of Sociology, 94,* 774–802.

Sampson, R., J. & Laub, J. H. (1990). Crime and deviance over the life course: The salience of adult social bonds. *American Sociological Review, 55,* 609–627.

Sampson, R. J., & Laub, J. H. (1993). *Crime in the making: Pathways and turning points through life.* Cambridge, MA: Harvard University Press.

Sampson, R. J., & Laub, J. H. (1994). Urban poverty and the family context of delinquency: A new look at structure and process in a classic study. *Child Development, 65,* 523–540.

Sanders, M. R., & Dadds, M. R. (1993) *Behavioral family intervention.* Neidem Heights, MA: Allyn and Bacon.

Sanders, M.R., Dadds, M.R., Johnston, B.M., & Cash, R. (1992). Childhood depression and conduct disorder: I. Behavioral, affective, and cognitive aspects of family problem-solving interactions. *Journal of Abnormal Psychology, 101,* 495–504.

Sanders, N. R., & Lawton, J. M. (1993). Discussing assessment findings with families: A guided participation model of information transfer. *Child and Family Behavior Therapy, 15,* 5–33.

Sanford, M., Szatmari, P., Spinner, M., Munroe-Blum, H., Jamieson, E., Walsh, C., & Jones, D. (1995). Predicting the one-year course of adolescent major depression. *Journal of the American Academy of Child and Adolescent Psychiatry, 34*(12), 1618–1628.

Sanson-Fisher, B., & Jenkins, H. J. (1978). Interaction patterns between inmates and staff in a maximum security institution for delinquents. *Behavior Therapy, 9,* 703–716.

Santrock, J. W. (1972). Relation of type and onset of father absence to cognitive development. *Child Development, 43,* 455–469.

Sarason, I. G., Johnson, J. H., & Siegel, J. M. (1978). Assessing the impact of life changes: Development of the life experiences survey. Journal of Consulting and Clinical Psychology, 46(5), 932–946.

Scarr, S. (1985). Constructing psychology: Making facts and fables for our times. *American Psychologist, 40,* 499–512.

Scarr, S. (1992). Developmental theories for the 1990s: Development and individual differences. *Child Development, 63,* 1–19.

Schafer, J. L. (1997). *Analysis of incomplete multivariate data.* London: Chapman & Hall.

Schlegel, A., & Barry, H. (1989). *Adolescence: An anthropological inquiry.* New York: The Free Press, Macmillan Inc.

Schuck, J. R. (1974). The use of causal nonexperimental models in aggression research. In J. DeWit & W. W. Hartup (Eds.), *Determinants and origins of aggressive behavior* (pp. 381–389). The Hague: Mouton.

Serbin, L. A., Cooperman, J. M., Peters, P. L., Lehoux, P. M., Stack, D. M., & Schwartzman, A. E. (1998). Intergenerational transfer of psychosocial risk in women with childhood histories of aggression, withdrawal, or aggression and withdrawal. *Developmental Psychology, 34,* 1246–1262.

Shantz, C. U., & Hobart, C. J. (ND). Social conflict and development. In C. U. Shantz (Ed.), *Conflict in child and adolescent development* (pp. 71–94). New York: Cambridge University Press.

Shaw, C., & McKay, H. (1942). *Juvenile delinquency and urban areas.* Chicago: University of Chicago Press.

Shaw, D.S., & Emery, R.E. (1988). Chronic family adversity and school-age children's adjustment. *J.Am.Acad.Child Adolesc.Psychiatry, 27(2),* 200–206.

Shaw, D. S., Emery, R. E., & Tuer, M. D. (1993). Parental functioning and children's adjustment in families of divorce: A prospective study. Journal of Abnormal Child Psychology, 21(1), 119–134.

Shaw, D. S, Keenan, K., & Vondra, J. I. (1994). Developmental precursors of externalizing behavior: Ages 1 to 3. *Developmental Psychology, 30,* 355–364

Shaw, D. S., Owens, E. B., Vondra, J. I., Keenan, K., & Winslow, E. B. (1996). Early risk factors and pathways in the development of early disruptive behavior problems. *Development and Psychopathology, 8,* 679–699.

Shaw, D. S., & Winslow, E. B. (1997). Precursors and correlates of antisocial behavior from infancy to preschool. In D. M. Stoff, J. Breiling, & J. D. Maser (Eds.), *Handbook of antisocial behavior* (pp. 148–158). New York: Wiley.

Sheeber, L., Hops, H., Alpert, A., Davis, B., & Andrews, J. (1997). Family support and conflict: prospective relations to adolescent depression. *Journal of Abnormal Child Psychology, 25(4),* 333–344.

Sheeber, L., Hops, H., Andrews, J.A., Alpert, A., & Davis, B. (1998). Interactional processes in families with depressed and nondepressed adolescents: reinforcement of depressive behavior. *Behaviour Research and Therapy, 36,* 417–427.

Sheeber, L., & Sorensen, E. (1998). Family relationships of depressed adolescents: a multimethod assessment. *Journal of Clinical Child Psychology, 27(3),* 268–277.

Shinn, M. R., Ramsey, E., Walker, H., Stieber, S., & O'Neill, R. (1987). Antisocial behavior in school settings: Initial differences in at-risk and normal populations. *The Journal of Special Education, 21,* 69–84.

Shure, M. B. Spivack, G. (1972). Means-end thinking, adjustment, and social class among elementary school aged children. *Journal of Consulting and Clinical Psychology, 38,* 348–353.

Silverthorn, P., & Frick, P.J. (1999). Developmental pathways to antisocial behavior: The delayed-onset pathway in girls. *Development and Psychopathology, 11,* 101–126.

Simmons, R. G., Burgeson, R., Carlton-Ford, S., & Blyth, D. A. (1987). The impact of cumulative change in early adolescence. *Child Development, 58(5),* 1220–34.

Simons, R. (1994). *Proposal III. Rural communities, family processes, and child outcomes.* In R. D. Conger's Grant Application: Research on mental disorders in rural populations. (Grant Application to Department of Health and Human Services, Public Health Service): Iowa State University.

Simons, R. L., & Johnson, C. (1996). The impact of marital and social network support on quality of parenting. In G. R. Pierce, B. R. Sarason, & I. G. Sarason (Eds.), *Handbook of Social Support and the Family* (pp. 269–287). New York: Plenum Press.

Simons, R. L., Beaman, J., Conger, R. D., & Chao, W. (1993). Stress, support, and antisocial behavior trait as determinants of emotional well-being and parenting practices among single mothers. *Journal of Marriage and the Family, 55,* 385–398.

Simons, R. L., Wu, C.-I., Conger, R. D., & Lorenz, F. O. (1994). Two routes to delinquency: Differences between early and late starters in the impact of parenting and deviant peers. *Criminology, 32,* 247–276.

Simons, R. L., Wu, C., Johnson, C., & Conger, R. D. (1995). A test of various perspectives on the intergenerational transmission of domestic violence. *Criminology, 33,* 141–172.

Simons, R. L., Wu, C.-I., Conger, R. D., & Lorenz, F. O. (1994). Two routes to delinquency: Differences between early and late starters in the impact of parenting and deviant peers. *Criminology, 32,* 247–276.

Slavin, L. A., & Rainer, K. L. (1990). Gender differences in emotional support and depressive symptoms among adolescents: A prospective analysis. *American Journal of Community Psychology, 18*(3), 407–421.

Slesnick, N., & Waldron, H.B. (1997). Interpersonal problem-solving interactions of depressed adolescents and their parents. *Journal of Family Psychology, 11*(2), 234–245.

Smith, M. A., & Jenkins, J. M. (1991). The effects of marital disharmony on prepubertal children. *Journal of Abnormal Child Psychology, 19*(6), 625–644.

Snow, J. (1855). *The mode of communication of cholera.* London: Churchill.

Snyder, D. K., Klein, M., Gdowski, C. L., Faulstich, C., & LaCombe, J. (1988). Generalized dysfunction in clinic and nonclinic families: A comparative analysis. *Journal of Abnormal Child Psychology, 16,* 97–109.

Snyder, J. J. (1977). Reinforcement analysis of interaction in problem and nonproblem families. *Journal of Abnormal Psychology, 86,* 528–535.

Snyder, J. J. (1990, July). *Negative reinforcement and treatment outcome.* Paper presented at the Oregon Social Learning Center, Eugene.

Snyder, J. J. (1991). Discipline as a mediator of the impact of maternal stress and mood on child conduct problems. *Development and Psychopathology, 3,* 263–276.

Snyder, J. (1995). Coercion: A two-level theory of antisocial behavior. In W. O'Donohue & L. Krasner (Eds.), *Theories of behavior therapy: Exploring behavior change* (pp. 313–348). Washington, D.C.: APA Press.

Snyder, J. (2000). *Playground behavior in kindergarten: Aggression and victimization.* Unpublished technical report, Wichita State University, Wichita, KS.

Snyder, J., & Brown, K. (1983). Oppositional behavior and noncompliance in preschool children: Environmental correlates and skills deficits. *Behavioral Assessment, 5,* 333–348.

Snyder, J., Dishion, T.J., & Patterson, G.R. (1986). Determinants and consequences of associating with deviant peers during preadolescence and early adolescence. *Journal of Early Adolescence, 6,* 29–43.

Snyder, J. J., Edwards, P., McGraw, K., Kilgore, K., & Holton, A. (1994). Escalation and reinforcement in mother-child conflict: Social processes associated with the development of physical aggression. *Development and Psychopathology, 6,* 305–321.

Snyder, J., Horsch, E., & Childs, J. (1997). Peer relationships of young children: Affiliative choices and the shaping of aggressive behavior. *Journal of Clinical Child Psychology, 26,* 145–156.

Snyder, J. J., & Huntley, D. (1990). Troubled families and troubled youth: The development of antisocial behavior and depression in children. In P. E. Leone (Ed.), *Understanding troubled and troubling youth* (pp. 194–225). Newbury Park, CA: Sage.

Snyder, J. J., & Patterson, G. R. (1986). The effects of consequences on patterns of social interaction: A quasi-experimental approach to reinforcement in the natural environment. *Child Development, 57,* 1257–1268.

Snyder, J. J., & Patterson, G. R. (1995). Individual differences in social aggression: A test of a reinforcement model of socialization in the natural environment. *Behavior Therapy, 26,* 371–391.

Snyder, J. J., & Schrepferman, L. (2000, November). *Self-reported discipline tactics: What parents can and cannot tell us.* Paper presented at the annual conference of the Association for the Advancement of Behavior Therapy, New Orleans, LA.

Snyder, J., Schrepferman, L., & St. Peter, C. (1997). Origins of antisocial behavior: Negative reinforcement and affect dysregulation of behavior as socialization mechanisms in family interaction. *Behavior Modification, 21,* 187–215.

Snyder, J., West, L., Stockemer, V., Gibbons, S., & Almquist-Parks, L. (1996). A social learning model of peer choice in the natural environment. *Journal of Applied Developmental Psychology, 17,* 215–237.

Sroufe, L. A. (1989). Pathways to adaptation and maladaptation: Psychopathology as developmental deviation. In D. Cicchetti (Ed.), *The emergence of a discipline: Rochester Symposium on Developmental Psychopathology* (pp. 13–40). Hillsdale, NJ: Lawrence Erlbaum Associates.

Sroufe, L. A. (1990). Considering normal and abnormal together: The essence of developmental psychopathology. *Development and Psychopathology, 2,* 335–348.

Sroufe, L. A., Schort, E., Motti, F., Lawroski, N., & LaFreniere, P. (1985). The role of affect in social competence, In. C.E. Izard & J. Kagan (Eds.), *Emotions, dognition, and behavior* (pp. 289–319). New York: Cambridge University Press.

Stanley, S. M., Markman, H. J., St. Peters, M., & Leber, B. D. (1995). Strengthening marriages and preventing divorce: New directions in prevention research. *Family Relations: Journal of Applied Family & Child Studies, 44*(4), 392–401.

Stark, K. D., Humphrey, L. L., Crook, K., & Lewis, K. (1990). Perceived family environments of depressed and anxious children: Child's and maternal figure's perspectives. *Journal of Abnormal Child Psychology, 18*(5), 527–547.

Stattin, H., & Magnusson, D. (1991). Stability and change in criminal behaviour up to age 30. *The British Journal of Criminology, 31,* 327–346.

Stattin, H., & Magnusson, D. (1996). Antisocial behavior: A holistic approach. *Development and Psychopathology, 8,* 617–645.

Steinberg, L., & Silverberg, S.B. (1986). The vicissitudes of autonomy in early adolescence. *Child Development, 57,* 841–851.

Stets, J. E. (1991). Psychological aggression in dating relationships: The role of interpersonal control. *Journal of Family Violence, 6,* 97–114.

Stewart, M. A., Cummings, C., Singer, S., & DeBlois, C. S. (1981). The overlap between hyperactive and unsocialized aggressive children. *Journal of Child Psychology and Psychiatry, 22,* 35–45.

Stoff, D. M., Breiling, J., & Masters, J. D. (Eds.). *The handbook of antisocial behavior.* NY: John Wiley & Sons.

Stokes, T. F., & Osnes, P.G. (1977). An operant pursuit of generalization. *Behavior Therapy, 20,* 337–355.

Stolberg, A. L., & Anker, J. M. (1983). Cognitive and behavioral changes in children resulting from parental divorce and consequent environmental changes. *Journal of Divorce, 7,* 23–41.

Stoolmiller, M. (in press). Synergistic interaction of child manageability problems and parent-discipline tactics in predicting future growth in externalizing behavior for boys. *Developmental Psychology.*

Stoolmiller, M. (1990). *Parent supervision, child unsupervised wandering, and child antisocial behavior: A latent growth curve analysis.* Unpublished doctoral dissertation, University of Oregon, Eugene.

Stoolmiller, M. (1992). *Differences between families in extended chains of coercive behaviors.* Unpublished manuscript, Oregon Social Learning Center, Eugene.

Stoolmiller, M. (1994). Antisocial behavior, delinquent peer association, and unsupervised wandering for boys: Growth and change from childhood to early adolescence. *Multivariate Behavioral Research, 29,* 263–288.

Stoolmiller, M. (March, 1996). *Visual-graphical techniques for the analysis of growth curves: Correlated change and predictors of growth in substance use for male adolescents.* Paper presented at the annual meeting of the Society for Research in Adolescence, Boston, MA.

Stoolmiller, M. (1998a). Correcting estimates of shared environmental variance for range restriction in adoption studies using a truncated multivariate normal model. *Behavior Genetics, 28,* 429–441.

Stoolmiller, M. (1998b). *Implications of the restricted range of family environments for estimates of heritability and nonshared environment in behavior genetic adoption studies.* Manuscript in preparation.

Stoolmiller, M., Duncan, T., Bank, L. & Patterson, G. R. (1993). Some problems and solutions in the study of change; Significant patterns in client resistance. *Journal of Consulting and Clinical Psycology, 61,* 920–928.

Stoolmiller, M., Eddy, J. M., & Reid, J. B. (2000). Detecting and describing preventative intervention effects in a universal school-based randomized trail targeting delinquent and violent behavior. *Journal of Consulting and Clinical Psychology, 68,* 296–306.

Stouthamer-Loeber, M., Loeber, R., Farrington, D. P., Zhang, Q., Van Kammen, W., Maguin, E. (1993). The double edge of protective and risk factors for delinquency: Interrelations and developmental patterns. *Development & Psychopathology, 5*(4), 683–701.

Straus, M. A., Gelles, R. J., & Steinmetz, S. K. (1980). *Behind closed doors: Violence in the American family.* Garden City, NY: Anchor/Doubleday.

Strober, M. (1995). Family-genetic aspects of juvenile affective disorders. In I. M. Goodyer (Ed.), *The depressed child and adolescent: developmental and clinical perspective.* (pp. 149–170). Cambridge, UK: Cambridge University Press.

Sugarman, D. B., & Hotaling, G. I. (1989). Dating violence: Prevalence, context, and risk markers. In M. A. Pirog-Good & J. E. Stets (Eds.), *Violence in dating relationships: Emerging social issues* (pp. 3–32). New York: Praeger.

Suomi, S. (1995, December). *Gender differences in Rhesus monkeys: Biobehavioral development and implications for prevention research.* Seminar presented at the Oregon Social Learning Center, Eugene.

Szapocznik, J., & Kurtines, W. M. (1989). *Breakthroughs in family therapy with drug-abusing and problem youth.* New York: Springer.

Tambs, K., Harris, J. R., & Magnus, P. (1995). Sex-specific causal factors and effects of common environment for symptoms of anxiety and depression in twins. *Behavior Genetics, 25,* 33–44.

Taplin, P. (1974). *Changes in parental consequation as a function of intervention.* Unpublished doctoral dissertation, University of Wisconsin.

Taplin, P., & Reid, J. B. (1977). Changes in parent consequences as a function of family intervention. *Journal of Consulting and Clinical Psychology, 45,* 973–981.

Taylor, T., & Biglan, A. (in press). Behavioral family interventions for improving childrearing: A review of the literature for clinicians and policymakers. *Clinical Child and Family Psychology Review.*

Thelen, E. (1989). Self-organization in developmental processes: Can system approaches work? In M. E. Gunnar & E. Thelen (Eds.), *Systems and development: The Minnesota Symposia on Child Psychology* (Vol. 22, pp. 77–118). Hillsdale, NJ: Erlbaum.

Thornberry, T. P. (1990). *Empirical support for interactional theory: A review of the literature* (Working Paper No. 5): Rochester Youth Development Study, Hindelang Criminal Justice Research Center, The University at Albany.

Thornberry, T. P., & Krohn, M. D. (1997). Peers, drug use, and delinquency. In D. M. Stoff, J. Breiling, & J. D. Maser (Eds.), *Handbook of antisocial behavior* (pp. 218–233). New York: John Wiley and Sons, Inc.

Timberlake, W. (1995). Reconceptualizing reinforcement: A causal-system approach to reinforcement and behavior change. In W. O'Donohue & L. Krasner (Eds.), *Theories of behavior therapy: Exploring behavior change* (pp. 59–96). Washington, DC: American Psychological Association.

Tooliatos, J., & Lindholm, B. W. (1980). Teachers' perceptions of behavior problems in children from intact, single parent, and stepparent families. *Psychology in the Schools, 17,* 264–269.

Tremblay, R. E., Kurtz, L., Mâsse, L. C., Vitaro, F., & Pihl, R. O. (1995). A bimodal preventive intervention for disruptive kindergarten boys: Its impact through mid-adolescence. *Journal of Consulting and Clinical Psychology, 63,* 560–568.

Tremblay, R. E., Masse, B., Perron, D., & Leblanc, M. (1992). Early disruptive behavior, school achievement, delinquent behavior, and delinquent personality: Longitudinal analyses. *Journal of Consulting and Clinical Psychology, 60,* 64–72.

Trickett, E. J, & Birman, D. (1989). Taking ecology seriously: A community development approach to individually based preventive interventions in schools. In L. A. Bond & B. E. Compas (Eds.) et al., *Primary prevention and promotion in the schools. Primary prevention of psychopathology, Vol. 12* (pp. 361–390). Newbury Park, CA: Sage.

Troy, M., & Sroufe, L. A. (1987). Victimization among preschoolers: Role of attachment relationship history. *Journal of the American Academy of Child & Adolescent Psychiatry, 26*(2), 166–172.

Tryon, W. W. (1993). The role of motor excess and instrumented activity measurement in attention deficit hyperactivity disorder. *Behavior Modification, 17*, 371–406.

Tryon, W. W. (1995a). Neural networks for behavior therapists: What they are and why they are important. *Behavior Therapy, 26*, 295–318.

Tryon, W. W. (1995b). Resolving the cognitive behavioral controversy. *The Behavior Analyst, 18*, 83–86.

Tryon, W. W. (1995c). Synthesizing animal and human behavior research via neural network learning theory. *Journal of Behavior Therapy and Experimental Psychiatry, 26*, 303–312.

Tryon, W. W. (1996a). Nocturnal activity and sleep assessment. *Clinical Psychology Review, 16*, 197–213.

Tryon, W. W. (1996b). Yes—Neural network learning theory can resolve the behavioral cognitive controversy. *The Behavior Therapist*(May), 70,72–73.

Tryon, W. W., Pinto, L. P., & Morrison, D. F. (1991). Reliability assessment of pedometer activity measurements. *Journal of Psychopathology and Behavioral Assessment, 13*, 27–44.

Tryon, W. W., & Williams, R. (1996). Fully proportional actigraphy: A new instrument. *Behavior Research Methods, Instruments, and Computers, 28*, 392–403.

Turkheimer, E. (1991). Individual and group differences in adoption studies of IQ. *Psychological Bulletin, 110*, 392–405.

Turnbull, C. M. (1972). *The mountain people*. New York: Simon & Schuster.

Turner, P. J. (1991). Relations between attachment, gender, and behavior with peers in preschool. *Child Development, 62*, 1475–1488.

Utting, D., Bright, J., & Henricson, C. (1993). *Crime in the family: Improving child rearing and preventing delinquency* (Vol. 16). London: Family Policy Studies Centre.

van den Boom, D. C. (1994). The influence of temperament and mothering on attachment and exploration: An experimental manipulation of sensitive responsiveness among lower-class mothers with irritable infants. *Child Development, 65*, 1457–1477.

van den Boom, D. C. (1995). Do first-year intervention effects endure? Follow-up during toddlerhood of a sample of Dutch irritable infants. *Child Development, 66*, 1798–1816.

Van den Oord, E. J. C. G., & Rowe, D. C. (1997). Effects of censored variables on family studies. *Behavior Genetics, 27*, 99–112.

Verschueren, K., & Marcoen, A. (1999). Representation of self and socioemotional competence in kindergartners: Differential and combined effects of attachment to mother and to father. *Child Development, 70*(1), 183–201.

Vitaro, F., Tremblay, R.E., Gagnon, C., & Boivin, M. (1992). Peer rejection from kindergarten to grade 2: Outcomes, correlates, and prediction. *Merrill-Palmer Quarterly, 38*, 382–400.

Vitaro, F., Tremblay, R.E., Kerr, M., Pagani, L., & Bukowski, W.M. (1997). Disruptiveness, friends' characteristics, and delinquency in early adolescence: A test of two competing models of development. *Child Development, 68*, 676–689.

Vorrath, H., & Bredtro, L. K. (1985). *Positive Peer Culture*. Chicago: Aldene.

Vuchinich, S., Crosby, L., & Patterson, G. R. (ND). Influences on the duration of parent-adolescent conflicts. *Child Development*.

Vuchinich, S., Emery, R.E., & Cassidy, J. (1988). Family members as third parties in dyadic family conflict: strategies, alliances, and outcomes. *Child Development, 59*, 1293–1302.

Vuchinich, S., Vuchinich, R., & Wood, B. (1993). The interparental relationship and family problem solving with preadolescent males. Child Development, 64, 1389–1400.

Vygotsky, L. S. (1978). *The mind in society: The development of higher psychological processes*. Cambridge, MA: Harvard University Press.

Wahler, R. G., & Dumas, J. E. (1983, June). *Stimulus class determinants of mother-child coercive exchanges in multidistressed families: Assessment and intervention*. Paper presented at the Vermont Conference on Primary Prevention of Psychopathology, Bolton Valley Winter/Summer Resort, VT.

Wahler, R. G., & Dumas, J. (1986). Maintenance factors in coercive mother-child interactions: The compliance and predictability hypotheses. *Journal of Applied Behavior Analysis, 19,* 207–219.

Walker, H. M., & Buckley, N. K. (1973). Teacher attention to appropriate and inappropriate classroom behavior: An individual case study. *Focus on Exceptional Children, 5,* 5–11.

Walker, H. M. & McConnell, S. R. (1988*). The Walker-McConnell Scale of Social Competence and School Adjustment*. Austin, TX, Pro-Ed.

Walker, H. M. (1995*). The acting out child: Coping with classroom disruption*. Longmont, CO: Sopris West.

Wallerstein, J., & Kelly, J. B. (1980). *Surviving the breakup*. New York: Basic Books.

Walsh, S. (1999). *Gender differences in the protective effects of planning orientation on the sexual activity and deviant peer influence of at-risk adolescents*. Unpublished doctoral dissertation, University of Oregon, Eugene.

Walter, H., & Gilmore, S.K. (1973). Placebo versus social learning effects in parent training procedures designed to alter the behaviors of aggressive boys. *Behavior Therapy, 4,* 361–371.

Walters, E. C. (1965). Prediction of post-natal development from fetal activity. *Child Development, 36,* 801–808.

Watson, J. S. (1979). Perception of contingency as a determinant of social responsiveness. In E. B. Thoman (Ed.), *Origins of the infant's social responsiveness* (pp. 33–64). Hillsdale, NJ: Erlbaum.

Wearden, J. H., & Burgess, I. S. (1982). Matching since Baum (1979). *Journal of the Experimental Analysis of Behavior, 38,* 339–348.

Webb, D. B. (1988) Specialized foster care as an alternative therapeutic out-of-home placement model. *Journal of Clinical Child Psychology*, 17(1), 34–43.

Weber, F. D. (1998). *The dose-effect relationship in family therapy for conduct disordered youth*. Unpublished doctoral dissertation, University of Oregon.

Webster-Stratton, C. (1984). Randomized trial of two parent-training programs for families with conduct-disordered children. *Journal of Consulting and Clinical Psychology, 52,* 666–678.

Webster-Stratton, C. (1985). Mother perceptions and mother-child interactions: Comparison of a clinic-referred and non-clinic group. *Journal of Clinical Child Psychology, 14,* 334–339.

Webster-Stratton, C. (1989). Systematic comparison of consumer satisfaction of three cost-effective parent-training programs for conduct problem children. *Behavior Therapy, 20* (1), 103-116.

Webster-Stratton, C. (1990). Long-term follow-up of families with young conduct problem children: From preschool to grade school. *Journal of Clinical Child Psychology, 19,* 144–149.

Webster-Stratton, C., & Herbert, M. (1993). What really happens in parent training? *Behavior Modification, 17,* 407–456.

Webster-Stratton, C., Kolpacoff, M., & Hollingsworth, T. (1988). Self-administered videotape therapy for families with conduct-problem children: Comparison with two cost-effective treatments and a control group. *Journal of Consulting and Clinical Psychology, 56,* 558–566.

Wechsler, D. (1967). *Manual for the Wechsler Preschool and Primary Scale of Intelligence*. New York: Psychological Corporation.

Weinrott, M. R., Reid, J. B., Bauske, B. W., & Brummett, B. (1981). Supplementing naturalistic observations with observer impressions. *Behavioral Assessment, 3,* 151–195.

Weissman, M. M., Fendrich, M., Warner, V., & Wickramaratne, P. (1992). Incidence of psychiatric disorder in offspring at high and low risk for depression. *J.Am.Acad.Child Adolesc.Psychiatry, 31*(4), 640–648.

Weissman, M. M., Prusoff, B. A., Gammon, G. D., Merikangas, K. R., Leckman, J. F., & Kidd, K. K. (1984). Psychopathology in the children (ages 6–18) of depressed and normal parents. *Journal of American Academy of Child Psychiatry, 13,* 78–84.

Weitzman, L. J. (1985). *The divorce revolution: The unexpected social and economic consequences for women and children in America.* New York: The Free Press.

Weitzman, L. J. (1996). The economic consequences of divorce are still unequal: Comments on Peterson. *American Sociological Review, 55,* 209–223.

Wells, K. D. (1995, August). *Discussion of "Time out for timeout? Its place in today's behavior therapy".* Paper presented at the Annual Meeting of the American Psychological Association, New York.

Wells, L. E., & Rankin, J. H. (1991). Families and delinquency: A meta-analysis of the impact of broken homes. *Social Problems, 38*(1), 71–89.

Werner, E. E., & Smith, R. S. (1977). *Kauai's children come of age.* Honolulu: University of Hawaii Press.

West, D. J. (1982). *Delinquency: Its roots, careers, and prospects.* Cambridge, MA: Harvard University Press.

Whalen, C. K., Henker, B., Castro, J., & Granger, D. (1987). Peer perceptions of hyperactivity in medication effects. *Child Development, 58,* 816–828.

Wiggins, J. S. (1973). *Personality and prediction principles of personality assessment.* Reading, MA: Addison Wesley.

Wiggins, J. S. (1988). *Personality and prediction: Principles of personality assessment.* Malabar, FL: Krieger Publishing.

Williams, B. (1986). Reinforcement, choice, and response strength. In R. A. Atkinson, R. Herrnstein, & G. Lindzey (Eds.), *Steven's handbook of experimental psychology* (pp. 167–244). San Diego, CA: Academic Press.

Wilson, H. (1974). Parenting in poverty. *British Journal of Social Work, 4,* 241–254.

Wilson, H. (1980). Parental supervision: A neglected aspect of delinquency. *British Journal of Criminology, 1980,* 203–235.

Wilson, H. (1987). Parental supervision re-examined. *British Journal of Criminology, 27,* 275–301.

Wilson, J. Q. (Ed.). (1983). *Crime and public policy.* San Francisco, CA: ICS Press.

Wilson, J. Q., & Herrnstein, R. J. (1985). *Crime and human nature.* New York: Simon & Schuster.

Windle, M. (1992). A longitudinal study of stress buffering for adolescent problem behaviors. *Developmental Psychology, 28*(3), 522–530.

Wiltz, N. A., Jr., & Patterson, G. R. (1974). An evaluation of parent training procedures designed to alter inappropriate aggressive behavior of boys. *Behavior Therapy, 5,* 215–221.

Wolchik, S. A., West, S. G., Westover, S., Sandler, I. N., Martin, A., Lustig, J., Tein, J. Y., & Fisher, J. (1993). The children of divorce parenting intervention: Outcome evaluation of an empirically based program. *American Journal of Community Psychology, 21*(3), 293–331.

Wolfgang, M. E., Figlio, R. M., & Sellin, T. (1972). *Delinquency in a birth cohort.* Chicago, IL: University of Chicago Press.

Woo, D. (1978). *Experimental studies of the reinforcement trap.* Unpublished masters thesis, University of Oregon, Eugene.

World Health Organization (1992). *Annual report on homicide.* Geneva, Switzerland: WHO.

Wright, J. C., Giammarino, M., & Parad, H.W. (1986). Social status in small groups: Individual-group similarity and the social Amisfit. *Journal of Personality and Social Psychology, 50,* 523–536.

Youngblade, L. M. & Belsky, J. (1992). Parent-child antecedents of 5-year-olds' close friendships: A longitudinal analysis. *Developmental Psychology, 28*(4), 700–713.

Zahn-Waxler, C., Cummings, E. M., McKnew, D. H., Jr., & Radke-Yarrow, M. (1984). Altruism, aggression, and social interactions in young children with a manic-depressive parent. *Child Development, 55*, 112–122.

Zill, N. (1978). *Divorce, marital happiness, and mental health of children: Findings from FCD national survey of children.* Paper presented at the Workshop on Divorce and Children, National Institute of Mental Health, Bethesda, MD.

Zill, N. (1988). Behavior, achievement, and health problems among children in stepfamilies: Findings from a national survey of child health. In E. M. Hetherington, & J. D. Arasteh (Eds.) *Impact of divorce, single parenting, and stepparenting on children* (pp. 325–368). Hillsdale, NJ: Lawrence Erlbaum Associates.

Zill, N., Morrison, D. R., & Coiro, M. J. (1993). Long-term effects of parental divorce on parent-child relationships, adjustment, and achievement in young adulthood. *Journal of Family Psychology, 7*(1), 91–103.

Zimring, F. E. (1984). Kids, groups and crime: Some implications of a well-known secret. In G. Hawkins & F. E. Zimring (Eds.), *The pursuit of criminal justice* (pp. 299–317). Chicago: University of Chicago Press.

Zoccolillo, M. (1993). Gender and the development of conduct disorder. *Development and Psychopathology, 5*, 65–78.

Zuckerman, M., & Lubin, B. (1985). *Manual for the MAACL-R: The Multiple Affective Adjective Check List, Revised.* San Diego: Educational and Industrial Testing Service.

Index

About the Editors

Gerald R. Patterson is currently a Senior Research Scientist at the Oregon Social Learning Center. He is also the author of *Coercive Family Process* (1982) and coauthor of *Antisocial Boys* (1992).

John Reid has worked as a scientist at the Oregon Social Learning Center since its inception almost 30 years ago. His focus is presently on investigating the development and early prevention of conduct problems and substance abuse.

James Snyder is currently a Professor of Psychology at Wichita State University. His research publications focus on identifying social processes in family and peer relationships that increase risk for antisocial behavior and depression. Dr. Snyder also provides clinical services to families and children, and is actively involved in the development and implementation of preventive interventions targeting behavior problems during the preschool and early elementary school years.

DATE DUE

11/18/03			
5/7/04			
8/10/04			
11/19/04			
MAY 0 9			
MAY 0 9			
DE 13 '05			
3/3/08			

Demco, Inc. 38-293